P9-CJI-960

The
ESSENTIAL WINE BOOK
Oz Clarke

REVISED AND UPDATED

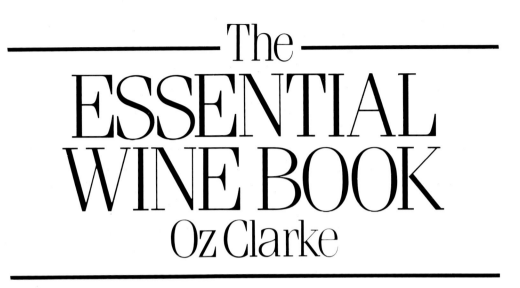

The
ESSENTIAL
WINE BOOK
Oz Clarke

REVISED AND UPDATED

A Fireside Book
Published by Simon & Schuster Inc.
New York London Toronto Sydney Tokyo

CONTENTS

The Essential Wine Book
Revised and updated edition
Copyright © Webster's Wine Price Guide &
Mitchell Beazley Publishers 1985, 1988
Text copyright © Oz Clarke 1985, 1988
All rights reserved
including the right of reproduction
in whole or in part in any form

Fireside
Simon & Schuster Building, Rockefeller Center
1230 Avenue of the Americas
New York, New York 10020

FIRESIDE and colophon are registered trademarks of
Simon & Schuster Inc.
Originally published in Great Britain by
Mitchell Beazley Publishers
as *Oz Clarke's Wine Factfinder and Taste Guide*
Created and designed by Webster's Wine Price Guide
Limited, in association with Mitchell Beazley
International Limited, Artists House,
14-51 Manette Street, London W1V 5LB
Printed and bound in Spain by Sirven Grafic
L. D. B-37-1989
10 9 8 7 6 5 4
Library of Congress Catalog Card Number: 88-38270

ISBN 0-671-67049-2

Typesetting and Colour Reproduction by
Modern Reprographics Ltd, Hull, England.

Without limiting the rights under copyright
reserved above no part of this publication
may be reproduced, stored in or introduced
into a retrieval system, or transmitted, in any
form or by any means (electronic,
mechanical, photocopying, recording or
otherwise), without the prior written
permission of both the copyright owner and
the above publisher of this book.

Editor Miren Lopategui
Art Editor Ruth Prentice
Assistant Editors Jean Gordon and Naomi Good
Picture Researcher Anne-Marie Ehrlich
Maps David Mallott
Managing Editor Carole McGlynn

AUTHOR'S INTRODUCTION

Before I say anything else, let me state categorically that the only way to approach wine is to want to enjoy it. Every other wish is subordinate to that, and some are indeed anathema.

To want to master the black and white facts without occasionally letting the red and white perfumes and scents swim across your mind and make you feel ever so slightly giddy with pleasure is to miss the whole heart of the thing. To want to impress your friends and colleagues yet be unable to feel your eyes pop with excitement at the blast of fresh fruit on a new Beaujolais is to miss the whole heart of the thing. To pontificate, to let opinions rule your appreciation of wine and to be unable to feel, as the candles gutter and the moon rises on a warm summer night, that the wine on the table, however unsung and lacking in renown, is, for that short moment, perfection itself, is to miss the whole heart of wine – and of life too.

That said, there is no doubt that once you allow yourself to be swept along on the tide of different flavours and styles, countries and traditions, you'll get far more fun by understanding more about wine: what really does make one wine different from another, one better, one worse, one more enjoyable young, one more enjoyable old, one more enjoyable warm, one more enjoyable cold. Hence this book.

First and foremost, I want you to share my enthusiasm. Wine has given me more fun, made me more friends, furnished me with more laughs than anything else in life. If I felt that it was necessary to abandon all those experiences to write a book about the factual side of wine, I wouldn't have bothered. I haven't attempted to put all the minutiae of production into this book. If I did it would be 1,000 pages long, bloodless and cold. What I *have* attempted is to take the whole world of wine, and, by using the most relevant facts and figures for each area and each type of wine, build up a colourful picture for the consumer of what makes each wine tick. What it tastes like, why it's different from its neighbours, why it's special – whether or not we should spend our time and money seeking it out and buying it, and what we should expect if we do: facts of taste, quality, style and volume.

To this end, the chapters of the book are set out in such a way that if you want to use it for dipping into and for reference you should be able to find immediately the section on every wine relevant to your inquiry, and if you just want a good read, you can go straight through from introduction to conclusion without a break.

Each country and each major wine style has its own introduction. This may be an exposition of what makes Bordeaux such a great wine area, how the champagne method really works, or it may be an impassioned plea to drink more of the sweet wines of the Loire before the producers give up and plant turnips. It is followed by a section called 'Grape Varieties and Wine Styles', which gets down to the fundamentals – what grapes are used, how soil or wine-making methods affect taste, and what kind of flavours and styles finally emerge from the bottle when you pull the cork.

'Classification' and 'Organization/s' are discussed next. Sometimes classification systems are quite complex and sometimes they are almost non-existent; in some areas the co-operative movement is vital and of a high quality, while in others it may only be single growers who will give you decent wine and so on. All information that points you towards the wines you want to drink.

'Reading The Label' logically follows. Increasingly, labels are easy to understand. Where they are not, I have tried to make the subject a bit clearer. Which leads me to a description of sensations and flavours in 'What Does It Taste Like?'.

'The Good Years' sets out to show how you can best judge at what age and from what vintage a wine will give you most pleasure. Sometimes an area's vintages are all very similar but the wines are at their best at a certain age – usually younger rather than older!! – and sometimes, as with Bordeaux, burgundy, port and some German wines, vintages are so important that I have gone back in detail over 10 to 20 years to pick out the best and warn you off the mediocre.

'Enjoying The Wines' gives you some ideas on when to drink them; either by themselves, or with food, and if so, what kind of foods. My publisher is worried about my relentless enthusiasm for sausages, smoked meats and stews to go with the lesser wines but I tell him, every time I visit those regions that's all I'm ever offered to eat. So you can take the sausages with a pinch of salt and maybe choose some of my other recommendations instead!

Finally, I have summarized my opinions on value and price in 'What Do I Get For My Money?' and indicated how widely available wines are outside their region of origin, in 'Availability'. But that's not quite all. There's a consumer checklist for each group of wines, listing good years with value assessments on the basis of quality and price, there are little essays on matters of extra importance squeezed into boxes and crammed into corners of the pages – there are loads of colour pictures and maps, and a vast array of labels to show how the world's wines parade themselves – there's a glossary of unfamiliar and technical wine terms, articles on how wine is made, storing wine, choosing . . . I can't go on like this, I'm running out of ink. Why don't you read on and see for yourself. And, once more, enjoy it!

Cheers!

CHOOSING THE WINE YOU WANT

The world of wine used to be a pretty simple place. There weren't that many areas making exciting, individual wine, and they were pretty easy to pinpoint, since they each had tastes no-one else had tried to imitate, largely because, in most areas of the world, wine-making was a very parochial affair. One winemaker would be unlikely to know much about the wine styles over the next range of hills, let alone over the infinite barrier of country and continent. Most wine was simply at the mercy of the climate, causing unripe grapes and sour wine in the cool areas and, much more significantly, heavy, unripe grapes and over-strong, or, frequently, unstable wine in the warmer areas. The few originals – the Rheingau in Germany, Bordeaux, burgundy, Champagne and Hermitage in France, Rioja and sherry in Spain, Barolo and Chianti in Italy, the Napa in California, port in Portugal – all created recognizable styles without opposition or rivalry.

How things have changed! Nowadays, if I say I like burgundy, Bordeaux or hock, I can find a dozen different areas of the world which are producing wines of a similar style. Not only that, but as each region gets more confident, it adds its own stamp to what started out as merely an attempt to imitate.

The world has turned full circle. In times when technology was much less advanced than now, the classic wines spawned imitations which were laughably inadequate. With

REDS

Style	'Claret': (a) light, blackcurranty Cabernet-style The Cabernet Sauvignon and Merlot grapes are the favourite material for red winemakers throughout the world. Red Bordeaux provides the model for most of these, but the lightest, freshest styles are from the Loire valley.	**GOOD ALTERNATIVES**	
		France	Côtes de Duras
			Buzet
			Bergerac
		Italy	Cabernet or Merlot from Alto Adige, Trentino, Friuli
		USA	Cabernet or Merlot from Pacific North-West and Long Island
Model	Bourgueil or Chinon	Australia	Cabernet from Tasmania
Grape	Cabernet Franc	New Zealand	Cabernet

Style	'Claret': (b) Full, rich, blackcurranty, often with oak aging	**GOOD ALTERNATIVES**	
		France	Cahors (Tannat and Auxerrois grapes)
Model	Cru Classé Médoc		Cabernet from Aix-en-Provence
Grape	Cabernet Sauvignon and Merlot		Cabernet from Coteaux des Baux en Provence
			Cabernet from Mas de Daumas Gassac
		Italy	Cabernet and Cabernet-Sangiovese blends from Tuscany (Sassicaia, Tignanello, Carmignano)
		Spain	Cabernet from Raimat and Penedès
		USA	Cabernet Sauvignon or Merlot from California
		Australia	Cabernet Sauvignon, Cabernet-Shiraz, Cabernet-Merlot wines
		South Africa	Cabernet Sauvignon from single estates
		Chile	Cabernet Sauvignon wines

the revolution in wine-making technology during the last 15 years, these erstwhile imitations are by no means second best any more. Led by the Californian wine school at Davis, and the Australian Roseworthy College, scientists' research has brought about a vital understanding of what makes wine so endlessly varied, and has evolved techniques to deal with the climate problems of vineyards anywhere in the world, by dissecting every stage in wine-making, from the propagation of the vines to the eventual consumption of the finished product. With that understanding came the power to begin duplicating the methods and style of the Old Masters in France and Germany. California, Australia, South Africa and, most recently, New

Zealand, New York State, and enterprising winemakers in Italy, Spain and the South of France have thrown up a string of classic wines owing their conception to a desire to equal and surpass traditional models, but now full of styles and flavours that their originals would do well to imitate.

It makes for an incredibly exciting world of wines, but also a confusing one. So let's pick some of the main styles we might know we like, and check out some of the alternative 'sources of supply'.

The chart below is meant to provoke experimentation. Some of the great wines don't have real alternatives, but I have picked a few 'models' and alternatives that you may have fun trying.

Style	*'Claret': (c) Big, plummy reds* From Bordeaux these are largely Merlot-based in Pomerol and St-Emilion, but there are also good models in warmer areas like Tuscany	**GOOD ALTERNATIVES**	
		France	Merlot and Cabernet Sauvignon Vins de Pays
		Italy	Nebbiolo d'Alba, Rosso di Montalcino
		Spain	Penedès (non-Cabernet).
Model	Pomerol (Bordeaux) or Brunello di Montalcino (Tuscany)	USA	Zinfandel, some Cabernet, California
		Australia	Shiraz
Grape	Merlot and Cabernet Sauvignon (Pomerol) Sangiovese Grosso (Brunello)	South Africa	Mature Pinotage

Style	*Light and fruity Beaujolais-type* Beaujolais is the best known of the light fresh reds to be drunk almost immediately, but other areas also produce their own version.	**GOOD ALTERNATIVES**	
		France	Gamay de Touraine Modern Côtes du Rhône, Ventoux, Luberon and southern Vins de Pays Anjou
		Italy	Casteller from Trentino Santa Maddalena from Alto Adige Kalterersee from Alto Adige Dolcetto from Piedmont
Model	Beaujolais	USA	Young Zinfandel from California
		Australia	Modern style Shiraz
Grape	Gamay	South Africa	Young Pinotage

CHOOSING THE WINE YOU WANT

Style	**Burgundy-type** Attempts to re-create burgundy are generally most successful in a light sim-ple style rather than a heavy rich style.	GOOD ALTERNATIVES	
		Italy	Pinot Noir from Alto Adige
		Spain	Rioja Reserva (from Tem-pranillo grape)
		USA	Some Pinot Noir from Napa, North Coast, California
Model	Côte d'Or		Pinot Noir from Pacific North-West
Grape	Pinot Noir	Australia	Pinot Noir from Western Australia and Victoria
		New Zealand	Pinot Noir from South Island

WHITES

Style	**Light Chablis-type whites** The majority of these wines are made from the Chardonnay grape in the lighter, cool-climate style of true Chablis.	GOOD ALTERNATIVES	
		France	Chardonnay from Haut Poitou
			Auvernat from Orleans
			Auvernat from Cheverny
			Côte Chalonnaise
Model	Chablis	Italy	Pinot Bianco
Grape	Chardonnay		Chardonnay from Alto Adige
			Cortese from Piedmont
		USA	Chardonnay from Pacific North-West
		Australia	Chardonnay from Tasmania
		South Africa	Chenin from KWV

Style	**Fuller, 'oaky' white burgundy-types** These are wines which have gained some richness and vanilla softness from matura-tion in oak barrels.	GOOD ALTERNATIVES	
		France	Cru Classé Graves
		Italy	Chardonnay from Trentino (top estates only)
		Spain	Viura from Rioja (old-style)
			Chardonnay from Catalonia
Model	Meursault	USA	Chardonnay from Napa, Sonoma, Monterey
Grape	Chardonnay		Chardonnay from Long Island
		Australia	Chardonnay from Western Australia, South Australia, Vic-toria, New South Wales
		New Zealand	Chardonnay, especially from South Island

Style	**Germanic or 'fruity'** Based on grapes which, to a greater or lesser extent, are aromatic and perfumed.	GOOD ALTERNATIVES	
		Italy	Rhein Riesling or Müller-Thurgau from Alto Adige, Friuli and Trentino
		USA	Johannisberg Riesling from Pacific North-West and New York State
Model (a) Light, dry	Kabinett Riesling or Alsace Riesling		
Grape	Riesling	Australia	Rhine Riesling from Tasmania, Victoria, South Australia and Western Australia
		New Zealand	Rhine Riesling
		Luxembourg	Most dry whites
		England	Most dry whites

		GOOD ALTERNATIVES	
Model (b) Perfumed, dry Grape	Alsace Gewürztraminer Gewürztraminer	Italy	Gewürztraminer from Alto Adige Tocai from Friuli
		Spain	Gewürztraminer and Muscat from Catalonia
		USA	Gewürztraminer from Pacific North-West
		Australia	Gewürztraminer
		New Zealand	Gewürztraminer
		Austria	Gewürztraminer Kabinett

		GOOD ALTERNATIVES	
Model (c) Perfumed, medium Grape	Niersteiner Gutes Domtal Mostly Müller-Thurgau	Spain	Alella
		New Zealand	Müller-Thurgau
		South Africa	Steen
		Austria	Welsch Riesling
		Bulgaria	Riesling

		GOOD ALTERNATIVES	
Style	*Light 'green' whites* These are tangy, sharp whites, primarily to be drunk young.	France	Sauvignon Vins de Pays from Loire Ugni Blanc from Charente Colombard from Gascogne Sauvignon from Côtes de Duras Bergerac Sauvignon from St-Bris Sauvignon from single estates Graves, Entre-Deux-Mers and Bordeaux Blanc
Model	Sancerre		
Grape	Sauvignon Blanc		
		Spain	Viura from Rioja (new-style)
		Portugal	Alvarinho from single estates Vinho Verde
		USA	Sauvignon from Pacific North-West and New York State, some Californian North Coast
		Australia	Sauvignon Blanc from Tasmania, Victoria, Western Australia
		New Zealand	Sauvignon Blanc, especially from South Island
		South Africa	Sauvignon Blanc estate wine (e.g. De Wetshof) Chenin from Fleur du Cap

> ## CHAMPAGNE
> There are no real challengers to true champagne, but the best are the top Californians, Bourgogne Mousseux, Pinot Bianco/Chardonnay champagne-method from north-west Italy and Australian champagne-method. The two most commonly quoted substitutes – Spanish *cava* and French Saumur – are good sparkling wines, but rarely achieve the classic balance of champagne-method wines.

		GOOD ALTERNATIVES	
Style	*Sweet dessert wines*	France	Muscat de Beaumes de Venise
Model	Sauternes or German Beeren-auslese	Italy	Moscato Naturale from Piedmont
Grape	Sémillon (Sauternes), Riesling (Germany)	Australia/USA	Beerenauslese or 'Botrytis affected', Rhine Riesling, Chardonnay and Sémillon
		Austria	Rust Beerenauslese

TASTING WINE

You take sugar in your coffee; I don't. You put salt on your sirloin; I don't. You put Tabasco sauce in your scrambled eggs; I don't. The reasons? We like different tastes. As simple as that. No-one would question your right to enjoy sugar, salt or chilli sauce. They would accept that those are flavours you have come to like through trial and error.

Now translate that to wine. You drink claret; I drink burgundy. You drink Chardonnay; I drink Sauvignon. You drink Chianti; I drink Beaujolais. The reason? Again, we like different tastes. But all of a sudden, the hot breath of prejudice swirls at you from all sides. Passionate defences of burgundy versus claret ensue from those who have made some study of either. Passionate denunciations of 'Wine Snobbery' and 'Hokus Pokus' erupt from those who've never tried to see the fairly obvious difference between Chianti and Beaujolais.

Obviously there has got to be a middle way, and we had better follow it, because wine, its flavours, and how to treat them, brings out both the best and the worst in people. There is no doubt that wine can create passionate comment, because the complexity and endlessly changing variety of flavours which wine offers is equalled nowhere in the world of food or drink. And inside broad swathes of taste, each as obvious and sharply defined as the side-swipe of a sabre, there is a myriad of differences, tiny, increasingly subtle, yet measurable. In one small village in one small vineyard in the Côte d'Or of Burgundy, an expert can take 12 different patches of vineyard land in the parish, with 12 different men tilling their soil and making their wine, and he can find identifiable differences between every single one.

If that sounds like a lifetime's quest, it is. But that needn't stop us taking the first few faltering steps down the path. As soon as we make the decision to try to understand a little more about wine we are immediately on the way to increasing our pleasure in wine quite out of all proportion to the effort we worry will be demanded of us. All that is demanded of us is that we 'think while we drink'. That, quite simply, is the essence of wine-tasting.

It's a bit like the difference between hearing and listening. On a spring morning we can hear the birds sing and not think much of it. Or we can pause for a moment from our chores, and *listen* to their tumbling cascade of sound, marvel at the pleasure it gives us, and continue working with a lighter heart and a flicker of a smile playing on our lips. So it is with wine. We can drink it every day, never much caring which bottle is ordered, being vaguely aware of the differences between sweet and dry, red and white, but taking most notice of how much of a dent it makes in our wallet and whether or not it gives us a headache. Or, each time we pour a glass of wine, we can pause for a moment, look at its colour, swirl it round, and breathe in its aromas, then take a mouthful and reflect for a second on the flavours it has. As we swallow it, we can just take passing notice of the pleasure it gives, as we resume our conversation just a tiny bit more contented because of the wine we have drunk.

And that, in its simplest form, is what wine-tasting is.

If we get to grips with even the most basic tenets of wine-tasting, it will help us to get the very best out of what our budget can afford – not wasting money unnecessarily for hopeful effect, not being stingy without cause for want of the confidence to know what the occasion demands. And it will show us that it is the *flavour* of a wine which matters, not the fancy artwork on a label.

I'm not going to go into the finer points of wine-tasting here, but I *am* going to state the basic points which you can at least make use of, tempering any excess according to whether you're with like-minded friends who have got together to really give a few bottles a good going over, or whether taking it too seriously would upset your guests when you're the host, or, worse still, your hosts when you're the guest. So here goes.

Looking Looking at a wine will tell you a good deal about whether it comes from a cool country or a hot one, a frail grape or a gutsy one, and whether the wine is young or old. This is all crucial in professional wine-tasting but not of great importance socially. Even so, looking *will* tell you whether the wine is clear or not; and sometimes the colour is so beautiful it's worth gazing at a while to heighten your expectations.

If you're looking at a wine critically, take a sheet of white paper under some clear light – daylight if possible, and definitely not neon – tilt the glass towards the paper and check the wine for colour and depth. If you're looking at a wine simply for pleasure, swirl the glass near any light source and watch the glittering range of colours a single wine can possess.

Smelling This is very important, for both criticism and pleasure. It is the first impression your 'olfactory' (i.e. taste and smell) senses will get, and, since our sense of smell is much underused, that first impression is very important. Swirl the glass gently, and take a good steady sniff, as if you'd leant over to smell a rose in the garden. Those initial split seconds of inhalation may reveal all kinds of familiar or unfamiliar smells. *Always* interpret them in words which mean something to *you*. Use the memory traces of everyday life. If the flavours remind you of honey, or chocolate, or curry and carrots, fresh apples, or rubber tyres – if those or any others are the smells you get – they are *sure* to be right for *you* because it is your nose doing the smelling. Another person may interpret the smells differently. That's fine. They're not using your nose. But it is only by honestly reacting to the stimuli of taste and smell in language that means something to us that we can build up a memory bank to judge future wines against.

For this reason, it is worth noting down those sensations on a piece of paper – a glance at what you wrote down at the time will bring the flavours careering back weeks later.

Tasting Take a reasonable draught of wine – so that your mouth is maybe one-third full, and then follow one of two courses. If you're by yourself, or with some friends or colleagues who are actively interested in wine-tasting, you can afford to pull a few faces and make some disconcerting slurping noises. The whole objective is to get the fumes from the wine which is in your mouth to rise up to your nasal cavity which is actually where the real tasting goes on.

What about the tongue? I hear you cry. Well, sadly, the tongue doesn't play a terribly big part in tasting anything, let alone wine. Think about it. When is the one time we all lose our sense of smell? When we have a cold, surely. And why? Because our nose is all blocked up. There's nothing wrong with our tongue, waggling away like nobody's business, to no avail, merely picking up the most basic sensations of

Stating the obvious: before you can do anything else you have to get the cork out.

The cork's out: I'm now pouring the wine carefully into the perfect-shaped tasting glass.

Checking the label of a very decent bottle of red Graves.

TASTING WINE

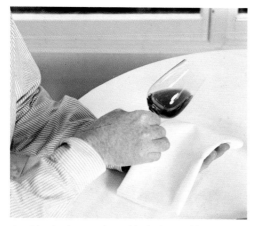

A white background – tablecloth, napkin, even a sheet of paper – and ordinary daylight are the best conditions in which to check a wine's colour.

I'm now showing Colette how to swirl the wine in the glass to release the aroma and bouquet.

My nose is now heading for the rim of the glass. A good sniff will give me all the wine's perfume.

sweet, sour, etc. It's dead easy to prove. Hold your nose, take a swig of wine, and try to experience its taste. Nothing. Release your nose, breathe out through it, and immediately there's a flood of flavour.

So – you have your mouthful of wine and what you need to do is, firstly to pick out any toughness or acidity, which you will feel in your mouth, and then experience all the personality and flavour, which you will 'taste' in your nasal cavity. Breathe out through your nose, if possible trying to draw a little air into your mouth without slurping the wine all over your shirt, and 'chew' it. Quite literally, 'chew' – as if you had a piece of meat between your molars! And concentrate. You want to clock, first your spontaneous impression, then the actual taste that will develop after the wine has been in your mouth a few seconds, and finally – after you've swallowed or spat out the wine – the persistent lingering taste which wine-tasters call 'the length'.

The flavours may blast you unchangingly from the first whiff, or they may shift as tantalizingly as sand under the rising tide. In either case, do make notes as you go. There's no better reinforcement of knowledge just gained than the 'I thought so', and the warm sense of achievement as you see your previous notes on a wine match up. This is the 'wine-taster' at work. At a social occasion, however, take the second course – no gurgling noises and grimaces, but just a few moments' quiet concentration given to the wine amidst the bustle of good conversation and appetizing food.

Apart from heightening the obvious enjoyment of the flavours, there is another reason to do all these things when buying wine, because each stage will help you *evaluate* the wine's quality, and its probable development. In this book you will often come across words like 'tannin' (the toughness in red wines) and 'acidity' (the slightly raw lemony edge, more marked in white wines, but crucial in both for a taste to be fresh and interesting). These are basic tasting terms. You will also come across much more far-reaching (far-fetched, you might say!) terms of description – flavours reminiscent of flowers, fruits, vegetables, meats, and a multitude of other everyday smells and tastes; these are my subjective views of flavour. They are there to give an idea of the most basic job a wine has – to taste nice and give pleasure – and these terms are some of the ones I use to describe how a particular wine sets about it. I hope you'll add your personal flavour reminders to mine as you go along, because it isn't that a wine necessarily tastes exactly like blackcurrants – chew a handful of blackcurrants and even the most blackcurranty Cabernet Sauvignon won't be a bit the same – no, it's just that the term for the wine merely reminds you of flavours drawn from all the smells and tastes you've experienced in day-to-day life.

If a wine straightway tastes delicious and you're happy with what it costs, it all seems plain sailing; descriptions flow, eyes sparkle. Yet wine isn't usually delicious from the first second it is made – and there are a couple of tasting points to remember, especially with immature wines.

Acidity A white wine, be it sweet, medium or dry, must have acidity. It is what keeps the flavour refreshing and also allows a wine to age. If you're buying a wine to mature for a bit, that lemony, steely sharpness is vital. Red wine, too, should have some sharp acidity if it is to age, but must have a noticeable fruity body and length as well. One acid you don't *ever* want is acetic. That's vinegar.

Tannin Tannic acid is the rasping, tooth-furring component which tea contains, and, when stewed for too long, seems to dry your mouth out with its bitterness. Red grapes have this in their skins and greater or lesser amounts of it are crucial if a wine is to age, but, again, an attractive sensation of fruit is also vital, even if it may be rather hidden. Heavy southern reds which taste of nothing but cold tea and pressed prune skins may age for an eternity, but still won't taste any better.

Colour A good big colour *is* a good sign, but is not necessary in all wines. The best cool country whites like Rieslings and Sauvignons often have almost no colour. With red wines, burgundy or other Pinot Noir wines, and good Rioja, very *rarely* have a deep colour, but may still be packed with flavour.

Fruit Fruit manifests itself in a thousand ways. Sometimes rich and grapy in German sweet wines, sometimes lean and green in a good Sauvignon, sometimes gurgling with fizzy newborn freshness in Beaujolais Nouveau. But in whatever form, fruit is crucial. Wine is made of fruit and, at any level of maturity, wine without fruit is dead wine.

We're not practising whistling or blowing kisses: I'm showing Colette how to suck in air while the wine is in her mouth, which releases extra flavours.

Colette is now rolling the wine round in her mouth and making up her mind.

Sorry, Colette, but spitting wine out is crucial if you don't want to be under the table.

PRACTICAL MATTERS

Laying down wine in a cellar. That phrase has a marvellous ring to it. I have visions of the butler gliding into the drawing-room of an elegant country house, purring into my ear 'Would sir come to view the cellar?'. I'm up in a flash, not even waiting to finish my Pimms or the article in *Vogue* on this year's croquet fashions, and pad eagerly after the keeper of the cellar. Down we go. The stairs get darker, danker, as we descend; cobwebs, the slight glistening of damp fungus on the stone – and then – the iron gate – the paradise. The great rusty key turns grudgingly in the lock, the squeak of the gate opening echoes like panicked bats in the gloom, and the butler lights an enormous tallow candle to reveal – as far as the eye can peer – bins and alcoves packed with every wine of every vintage I ever read about in the wine books of yore. And each bottle I touch in wonder – ancient Bordeaux, dust-covered burgundy, Sauternes whose golden richness stares beseechingly out of its cold clear glass – the butler silently lifts to transport back to the thin, clean air of the house above – where I shall try every single one at dinner. Each one will be perfect, and I shall be so imbued with superhuman powers that I shall drain every decanter (well, my hosts will have *some*) and yet my head will stay clear to the last drop of lees.

Mmmm! I'm still waiting, but most people who own big country houses with well-stocked cellars have got more sense than to invite me with my roving eye. But, seriously, the concept of laying down wine and the concept of building up a bit of a cellar both bear some examination. Laying down means buying your wine in advance, laying it on its side somewhere suitable and letting it mature and mellow. It is usually expected to entail some grand 20 year plan involving the whole gamut of the world's greatest wines. But that's not the whole story at all. As soon as you make the decision that you are not going to continue dashing into the wine shop on your way home, feverishly scanning the shelves at the same time as you eye your wrist watch and wonder whether, if you buy something more expensive than you meant, you'll get away with being late back for dinner again, you'll be ready for the plunge. Take the decision to stop and think. Do you usually spend more than you intend to? Does the wine taste all shook up when you open it after a mad rush from the wine shop? Is it always too warm or too cold – and no time to rectify matters short of the deep freeze or the microwave? And does it ever get you out of hot water for being late for dinner? If the answer's yes to the first three and no to the last, for the sake of your pleasure in drinking wine and domestic harmony, it's time to consider laying some wine down.

This simply means, begin to plan a little in advance. If you can afford to say, 'I'll buy a dozen of that wine I like, and I'll shove it under the stairs for a couple of weeks', you're laughing, you're on your way; you feel as though you're investing and collecting, both at the same time. But if that prospect is a bit daunting, what about buying an extra bottle next time you want some wine, putting it away somewhere dark and cool and forgetting about it for a bit? If it's any sort of red wine, and most sorts of white wine other than Liebfraumilch, the wine will taste better for having been laid down for a week or two at home. Get an extra bottle every month, maybe two, concentrating on red, but also maybe splash out on a Chardonnay or a Sauvignon Blanc. In no time you'll have a dozen bottles sitting there allowing you the luxury of pulling out the different wines, deciding which one to drink in good time, allowing you to cool it or warm it as gently as you wish and allowing you the pride of 'owning' a cellar.

The fact that a wine is always better after it's rested even for a few days should be enough to get you going, but once the collec-

Left *This shows the dregs of an old bottle of burgundy, which I've just decanted. By placing a light or a candle underneath the neck and pouring the wine gently, I can see the thin line of sediment slide up the bottle and I'll stop pouring just as it reaches the neck.* **Below** *The left hand glass contains the wine which is safely in the decanter.*

tor's urge grabs you – beware. You may be about to move on from laying down a few bottles for a simple extra pleasure, to setting aside a 'cellar space' in the house and buying by the case, to the ultimate involvement of purchasing fine wine for investment. There are two sides to the investment thing. If you decide to invest in pleasure – the pleasure of buying fine wine at its birth, maturing it yourself, and finally being able to offer to family and friends delicious mature wine which is worth a great deal more than when you bought it – then this is one of the most satisfying ambitions to have in wine. Fine wine does increase in value, and there comes a time when the wine approaches its peak, for example, at 10 to 15 years old, when the value surges ahead as restaurants and hotels clamour to buy – because they themselves didn't buy enough to start with. However, if you decide to buy wines purely to re-sell at a profit, purely as a paper investment, I can only say, Make sure your buying advice is very, very good. Classic wines from classic vintages have a rarity value straight away but we are talking of perhaps 100 wines at maximum in the world. The rest is speculation, and open to sharks and wide boys, boom and bust exactly the same as any other 'futures' market.

The best method of investment buying is *en primeur*, i.e. at first offering when the wine is still in the barrel. Increasingly, wine merchants and importers are operating schemes whereby they act for you in buying new wine direct from the property – usually in the spring following the vintage. These schemes are

highly advantageous, but since you won't see your wine for at least a couple of years after you've bought – it's still in the cask! – only buy from a company with an established track record. Never risk your entire investment for the sake of a few centimes saved.

WINES TO BUY EN PRIMEUR

Classed Growth and Good Bourgeois red Bordeaux wines.
Classed Growth Sauternes.
Northern Rhône reds and whites.
Red burgundy from a reliable producer.
White burgundy from a reliable producer.
Vintage ports.
Vintage champagne.
New-style Cabernets and other high-flying Vini da Tavola from Tuscany.

PRACTICAL MATTERS

California Cabernet, Zinfandel and some Pinot Noir from good wineries.
California barrel-aged Chardonnay and Fumé Blanc.
Australian Estate Cabernet, Shiraz and Chardonnay.

It's worth remembering that with many of the best Californian and Australian estates the only chance you'll get to buy the wine is to be on the mailing list and order by return of post when the wine is first offered. As you can see, given the range of the world's wine, that's a tiny proportion. These are wines that should improve for 5 to 15 years. Each of these wine types has 'lesser versions' which may not need more than a few months to soften and blossom. In Bordeaux there will be wines of poorer years, or less classy châteaux, in Burgundy the wines of the Côte Chalonnaise or the more obscure villages of the Côte d'Or, in California and Australia, the lighter 'non reserve' wines with more emphasis on fruit and less on barrel-aging. A few bottles of these put by for a month or two will give you a good sense of well-being and a better chance of a decent drink.

STORING WINE

But 'put by' where? Most of us don't own country houses with cellars hewn out of the rock of ages any longer. Well, for fine wine, it *is* a problem, and if you own valuable bottles, there is a strong argument for storing most of your stock with a wine merchant. You will have to pay a storage charge, but quality storage becomes increasingly important as wine gets older, and a good wine merchant will have the right facilities.

If you're improvising at home, there are four prerequisites to try to achieve – correct cool temperature, adequate humidity, relative

This is what happens if you drink champagne warm and shake the bottle about – the cork flies out and makes a hole in the ceiling and you waste half the wine as well as soaking the carpet.

darkness and relative stillness. This blend of conditions will age the wine slowly, which always results in a slightly more exciting end-product. Warm or unstable cellar conditions age wine faster, which almost always results in a less perfect balance of flavour at maturity. Some old houses will have cellars, and such lucky owners really don't have to look any further, but just check that the air isn't too damp, since, although that won't affect the wine, it will make the labels look pretty slimy and moth-eaten by the time you hope to carry the bottles proudly to table.

Most old houses will have nooks and crannies – under the stairs, old fireplaces, the back of the garage. These won't be ideal, but will at least provide fairly enclosed places where, if nothing else, you won't trip over the bottles on the way to bed. There are a variety of wine racks easily available in the shops which allow you to utilize unused wall space in any relatively quiet room. There is also a new 'spiral staircase' system whereby each step of a spiral staircase becomes a bin holding wine. It's highly efficient and stores a lot of wine – so long as (a) you've already got a spiral staircase and, (b) you've got somewhere for your spiral staircase to go to, apart from your ceiling/the floor of the apartment above, in the event of your ordering one. For long-term storage, the wooden boxes which major Bordeaux châteaux use for their wines are excellent, compact and durable.

Temperature This should be as stable as possible. And if there are going to be differences they should be of the gradual seasonal sort rather than jumps of 10° every time the central heating switches itself off or on. Ideally, the temperature should be between 10–13°C (50–55°F) which is rather less than most householders will tolerate just to keep some wine cool, so the wines are always best kept away from the main living area, and certainly out of the kitchen and not near a radiator. If they are stored at higher temperature the wines will certainly mature more quickly. But don't worry too much – most wine isn't supposed to age for more than a year or so, and will stand up to a few knocks.

Humidity is allied to temperature because temperature changes can tire a fine wine and shrink the cork, as can an atmosphere which is too dry. It isn't silly, if you have a very dry house, to get a humidifier. And your furniture will benefit too.

Darkness Bright light does have an oxydizing effect, especially on light white wines. Champagne is particularly susceptible and I always think Roederer Cristal in its clear white bottle is being especially daring. So if you are storing the wines in direct light, just get an old blanket and drape it over them. Not pretty, but effective.

Peace and quiet Vibration, too, tires a wine, but since half the best cellars in London are underneath railway arches which vibrate quite frighteningly every time the endless parade of commuter trains trundles above, perhaps it's not too serious. Even so, I should have thought any well-brought up bottle might quite justifiably react to a daily dose of Heavy Metal at full pitch. Mozart, however, well, that's quite another thing.

SERVING WINE

If we've managed to store the wine reasonably, it does make sense to be aware of a few things when serving it. Many ordinary wines couldn't care less how you serve them, and are just as happy out of a picnic mug in the middle of a football crowd as they are in polite company out of good crystal. But let's just lay down a few guidelines.

Atmosphere The commonest killer is tobacco smoke. You can't smell tobacco and wine at the same time. Some cooking smells, in particular highly spiced oriental food and greasy, oily fried foods, do leave a stench which will make it impossible to smell good wine. So with that kind of smell in the house, open all the windows or *don't* open anything special.

Foods Those spicy or fried foods aren't likely to do much for the taste of wine either, though I was amazed when, faced with a *chilli con carne* so hot I could feel it going down every inch of the way, my host offered me Zinfandel and Rioja. I was gasping for liquid, and gulped down both. To my amazement, their tastes came through quite plainly. Which is one up for the oaky Rioja and the brambly Zin, but still not a precedent to be followed.

Curries in general really do nothing for wine. Vinegar is pretty disastrous, as are mint and chocolate. These are the worst offenders, demanding your cheaper bottles or water.

Corkscrews There are a lot of pretty weird corkscrews about, which can rip out the centre of the cork, yet leave the sides clinging tenaciously to the neck of the bottle. Avoid ones where the blade looks too thick or too thin. Ideally, buy a screwpull.

Glasses Always err on the side of generosity. Preferably you want large glasses which have a good bowl and which narrow towards the top so that when you swirl the wine round, all the perfume and fragrance collects in the top of the glass.

When washing your glasses, it is important to do several rinses with hot water because any trace of detergent will affect the flavour of the wine.

Decanting Old wines may need it for separating the sediment many of them have from the wine, but don't give old wine too much air. The wines most likely to *need* decanting because of sediment are mature red Bordeaux, red burgundy, northern Rhônes and vintage or crusted ports. Although some Bordeaux reds may develop their bouquet during an hour or two in a decanter most burgundies are at their best very shortly after opening. It is better for you to develop a wine's bouquet in your glass than decant too early and find its flavour has dissipated by the time you come to drink it. In general, most wines don't need decanting, but if you've got a nice decanter, well, pour in the wine, red or white, perhaps an hour or so before serving. It'll look lovely and may even soften up a bit.

Temperature Don't subject the wine to sudden chilling or cooling. If anything, too cool is best, since you can warm the glass of wine up with your hands. Cool – about 10°C (50°F) – is best for good whites, and 15–18°C (60–65°F) for good reds. The worse the white, the colder it should be.

And one more thing – all red wine doesn't have to be warm, or 'chambré' – light, fresh young reds like Beaujolais, Loire reds, etc., are better slightly chilled.

HOW WINE IS MADE

The first wine wasn't made: it made itself. Well, we haven't actually got any scientific data which proves that conclusively, but what *is* likely is that for as long as grapes grew and ripened, and as long as man picked them, stored them and ate them, some wine was unintentionally made each year, because the transformation of a grape and its juice into wine is simplicity itself.

The grape ripens and fills with sugar. The yeasts which are present in a vineyard settle on the grape skin. In a warm climate, as soon as a single skin is broken, the yeasts begin to work on that grape, transforming the sugar into alcohol, and the juice into wine. End of story.

Wine is generally thought to have originated in the Middle East. Perhaps for years the palace housemaid would throw out the grapes which had begun to go 'off' in the heat and had started getting that sickly sour smell of fermentation. Until one day, she happened to eat a bunch or two, felt good, fell over, woke up with a headache and a mind full of dreams and put two and two together. She'd get her friends in, they'd tell their friends, and in no time at all everybody was keeping back a few of the grapes to see if they could go on a bender too.

PREPARATION

Red wines extract all their colour from a period of contact between the juice and skins after crushing. In general, white wines are removed quickly from their skins to avoid any coloration.

Reds and Rosés

The grapes are tipped into a machine which either crushes the grapes and pulls off the stems, or, alternatively, simply crushes the grapes, leaving the stems intact. This mixture of grape juice and skins and pips is called the must. A slight addition of sulphur dioxide acts as an antiseptic before fermentation. The mush of grapes and juice is pumped into a vat of wood, stainless steel, cement or fibreglass.

Exceptions to this method are wines made by the *macération carbonique*, or 'whole grape' method of fermentation.

Fortified

In port wines the grapes are still very occasionally trodden by foot in large stone troughs or *lagars*.

Whites

The grapes are always tipped into a machine which crushes and destems. According to the wine style required, there are then three main methods of preparing the juice:

(a) The grapes may 'macerate' on their skins, with fermentation kept in check by cooling the vat. This method is often used to draw out fruit flavours from relatively neutral grapes in hot climates. It usually takes about 12 hours, after which the juice and pulp are pumped to a horizontal press which gently squeezes out the juice, taking care not to crush the pips which contain harsh tannins. At this stage the pressed juice or 'must' is still full of some solid matter, which must be removed. This is done by either allowing the solids to drop naturally (known as *débourbage* or 'unmuddying') or through centrifuging the must. (A centrifugal force draws off all the solids to the sides of the tank, leaving the clear juice to drain out of the bottom.) The wine is then transferred to its fermentation tank or occasionally, as with top Chardonnays, to a small oak barrel.

(b) The grapes may be crushed, then left to drain so that a 'free-run juice' is obtained. This gives lighter and fresher wines. The remaining pulp is then pressed and the fuller-tasting juice mixed in – or not – according to the wine.

(c) The grapes may be crushed, pressed and immediately separated from their skins by the centrifuge. This usually results in clear but neutral wines.

> ### MACERATION CARBONIQUE
> Here the grapes are put whole into a vat. Obviously, the ones at the bottom get a little crushed, which means their juices begin to ferment in a normal way. However, the vat is sealed and carbon dioxide is pumped in. This causes fermentation to take place inside the uncrushed grapes; the colour is drawn off from the skins internally, but very little tannin. As they finish fermenting, the grapes burst and the juice is run off. The remaining pulp can be pressed and the juice added back for tannin and body or kept separate. This is a highly successful method for fruity wines in hot countries.

Well, maybe not, but no-one's come up with a more valid explanation. And, anyway most of the world's great inventions probably occur by chance when the inventor has his mind on something else. Newton certainly wasn't thinking about apples, Archimedes was probably looking for the soap, and Fleming was no doubt looking for a clean saucer to put the cat's milk in when he discovered penicillin.

But let's get back to the grape – the basis of all wines. The grape consists of water, sugar, acidity and tannin, and the way these four elements will combine will crucially influence the style of wines which result. All these four factors are influenced by the type of grape variety used, the soil of the vineyard, the climate and annual fluctuations in weather conditions – and, increasingly, by the wine growers' own intervention in the vineyard.

So, let's assume that we've got our grapes off the vine. The laden truck has just screeched up to the winery loading bay. What happens next?

Well, that will depend on whether the wine is red, rosé or white. But basically, all grapes/wines undergo four main processes: preparation, fermentation, maturation and bottling. These will differ according to the colour and style of wine.

FERMENTATION

All wines undergo two fermentation processes: the alcoholic fermentation (the transformation of sugar to alcohol) and the malolactic fermentation (the transformation of malic acid into lactic acid).

1. ALCOHOLIC FERMENTATION

This is the first fermentation. Precisely how it is achieved will radically affect the flavour of the wine. In simple terms, slow and cool will give fragrance and delicacy (most important in whites), quicker and hotter will give extract, colour and heaviness (most important in big reds).

Reds

In red wines, the fermentation usually takes place with the grape skins in large vessels of either concrete, wood or stainless steel. Very rarely, as on some Australian estates, small oak barrels are used.

Though natural yeasts will start the fermentation if the temperature is over about 18°C (65°F), nowadays cultured yeasts developed to suit a particular grape variety or wine style are added. In cool areas, the must may be heated to start fermentation. In Burgundy and northern Europe, it may be heated considerably to extract colour from unripe or rotted grapes.

One of three methods can then be used.

(a) The grapes may spend only a short period – two or three days – in the vat with their skins, before the still-fermenting juice is drawn off to finish the fermentation without skins. This method is used for light red wines.

(b) The 'whole grape' method of fermentation or macération carbonique may be used. (See p. 20).

(c) The grapes may sometimes have had a portion of stems left in the must. In such cases, the must will be left to ferment on its skins at a temperature of 24-26°C (75–80°F) for anything from one to two weeks. Hotter fermentation and longer skin contact will produce darker, more tannic, more highly flavoured wines. All the great classic reds and most other traditional wines follow this method.

During the alcoholic fermentation, the skins rise like a cap, or chapeau, to the top of the vat on a bed of bubbling carbon dioxide. This 'cap' should be continually churned back into the wine for two reasons: firstly because it contains the tannins and colouring extract, and secondly because, if it is left to sit on the top oxygen will affect it, giving a slightly 'bruised skin' taste to the wine, and the wild yeasts from the atmosphere may turn it vinegary, giving an acetic or 'pickled' taste.

When the weather is hot at vintage time, causing a violent, tumultuous fermentation, keeping the 'cap' submerged is of enormous importance. This is usually done by remontage, or 'remounting', whereby the fermenting must is regularly sprayed over the 'cap' to resubmerge it. Sometimes a grille is fitted just below the surface of the wine so that the 'cap' is always submerged. Sometimes it is pressed down by poles, as on the traditional Bordeaux and port properties.

New methods include enormous fermentation vessels called 'rotofermenters' which rotate slowly, continually immersing the 'cap', and autovinificators (used a great deal in Portugal and hot areas), whereby the pressure of

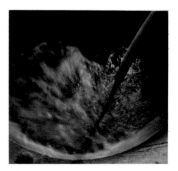

HOW WINE IS MADE

FERMENTATION

carbon dioxide inside a sealed vat is used to push out juice into a trough. At a certain point of pressure, the vacuum is broken and the juice all drains back into the vat, submerging the 'cap'.

Fermentation must be continuous, otherwise acetic bacteria will attack the wine to feed on the remaining sugar and the wine may turn into vinegar. When the sugar has been consumed to the last gram or so per litre, the fermentation is over. Most of the liquid, about 80 per cent, will by now have separated from the skins. This is drawn off and is called the 'free-run' wine. The remaining pulp is then pressed in two stages in a tough hydraulic press. The first pressing will produce darker, more tannic, but also more volatile wine. This 'press wine' is usually kept separate, to be added back as necessary to the 'free-run' wine for extra colour, tannin and staying power. The second pressing will yield harsh, tough wine not suitable for blending in.

When this alcoholic fermentation is over, most red wines will undergo malolactic fermentation.

Rosés

The juice will be drawn off the skins after a day or less, having taken a little colour from the skins, and the fermentation proceeds, usually at low temperature, as for white wines.

Fortified Wines

Fortified wines are created by the addition of brandy to the half-fermented must, which immediately raises the alcohol level

too high for yeasts to operate and preserves a rich, strong, sweet flavour in the wine. Sherry is slightly different in that the wine ferments right out and the brandy and any further sweetening or colouring wine is then added according to the style required.

Whites

White wines are increasingly fermented using specially cultured yeasts, at cool temperatures – between 15 and 20°C (60 and 68°F) – and for periods of at least a month. The fermentation usually takes place in large stainless steel, concrete or fibreglass tanks which are kept cool by various methods. In some cases, cold water is regularly trickled over the tank and down the sides; in others the vats have 'jackets' which can be filled with cooling agents rather similar to antifreeze. Alternatively, the wine is passed through a serpentine cooling coil, or 'heat exchanger', whenever the temperature rises. If all else fails, they can throw in blocks of ice.

The range of possible styles is wider for white than red wine, and at this stage the winemaker has several choices he can make:
(a) He can ferment at quite high temperatures in small oak barrels. This is common in Burgundy and may also be used for Chardonnay and, occasionally, Sémillon and Sauvignon wines elsewhere. This method will give a strong taste of oak which may be increased by charring the inside staves, or leaving some of the oak shavings in the barrels. (Also, the wine will have a close contact with its yeast deposits, which in some areas are later 'roused' or stirred up by the winemaker to fatten out the flavour.)
(b) He can use cool, slow fermentation down to 15°C (60°F) or less and lasting a month or sometimes more, preferably in large, stainless steel tanks. This will achieve the modern objective of dry, light whites. Air contact is

often avoided by laying a carbon dioxide 'blanket' over the surface of the wine. If, in addition, the vat is closed, this will have the effect of dissolving a little carbon dioxide in the wine, giving it an attractive prickle.
(c) If the winemaker wishes to achieve medium or medium sweet wines there are several options open to him or her. The objective is generally to stop the fermentation using up all the sugar, so that the resulting wine will be more or less sweet. Traditionally, this was done by pumping into the wine at a chosen point to stop the fermentation. These days the wine is cooled towards the end of fermentation and either a centrifuge or fine filter is used to remove the yeasts, thus preventing further fermentation. This effectively preserves fruit flavours.

Another method is to ferment out to dryness and then add back some sterilized grape juice to a certain level of sweetness. This will give a fresh, grapy style from almost any grape, and is the normal method used in Germany and in other countries like New Zealand and England wishing to imitate a German style.

The above methods can also be used to make fairly sweet wines, rarely with distinction.

Fine sweet wines are made from 'noble rot' infected grapes (see p. 26) or occasionally from shrivelled, raisined grapes. The sugar level in the grapes is so high that the yeast can only convert a maximum of 12–13° of alcohol before it is stifled and the unconverted sugar which remains will determine the sweetness of the wine. In Germany, California and Australia, alcohol levels will not even reach 12° as every effort is made to preserve the maximum amount of sweetness. Ideally, this fermentation takes place very slowly in oak barrels.

After the first fermentation, the winemaker must choose whether to use the malolactic fermentation.

Sparkling Wines

The base wine undergoes a first fermentation, which is fundamentally the same as for ordinary still white wine and ideally should yield a fairly light wine high in acidity. This still wine will then rest for a few months, usually in stainless steel tanks, before a second fermentation, in a sealed container, is started with added yeasts and sugar. The carbon dioxide caused by fermentation is unable to escape and so dissolves, thus creating bubbles.

The best wines are made by the champagne method (see p. 26) where the second fermentation takes place in the bottle, as against the vastly inferior *charmat,* or Cuve Close method, where the second fermentation takes place in a sealed vat.

There is a third method, the 'transfer' method, in which the second fermentation does take place in the bottle, but the wine is then filtered and 'transferred' under pressure to another bottle, thus avoiding the costly champagne methods of *remuage* and *dégorgement* to remove the sediment (see pp. 102-103).

2. MALOLACTIC FERMENTATION

The malolactic fermentation (or, more simply, 'the malolactic') is the second fermentation, this time of bacteria turning harsh malic acid to the softer lactic acid. The effect of this is to reduce the acid level in the wine, making it softer and rounder, and less overtly fruity. When it is not carried out, the sharp strong new fruit will dominate the flavour. If such wine is inefficiently stabilized by fine filtering or centrifuge, the malolactic may occur in bottle, causing the cork to blow off.

Traditionally, the malolactic occurred in the spring following the vintage, and it is still sometimes achieved by creating a 'false spring' – by raising the temperature of the cellar to about 21°C (70°F). But usually it is possible to inoculate the wine with the relevant bacteria.

Since malolactic fermentation lowers total acidity in the wine it is frequently arrested for white wines, especially in hot countries where the wines have a tendency to be flabby. It can be avoided altogether by filtering and centrifuging the wine, thus preserving the appley malic acid which adds a pleasant tart freshness. However, the great white wines will usually undergo the malolactic for the extra nuances of ripe flavours it seems to bring about.

Reds and Whites

In both reds and whites, there are two vital activities which affect quality and can be carried out during fermentation.
(a) *Chaptalization*. The adding of sugar during fermentation to increase the degree of alcohol, this process is named after the Napoleonic functionary who first authorized it. It is a crucial, sometimes misunderstood process – particularly vital in cool areas where the grapes are frequently insufficiently ripe to ferment properly unaided. Carefully done, preferably in several small doses, it should be beneficial. Carelessly done, it results in lumpish wine.
(b) *Acidification and Deacidification*. This is the upwards or downwards adjusting of acid in a wine. In cool countries, unripe grapes will often need to be de-acidified, for which a substance called Acidex is widely used. Grapes grown in warm countries don't have enough acidity, so tartaric (ideally), citric or malic (less good) acids can be added in. Acidification and deacidification should be carried out during fermentation.

MATURATION

Wine-making isn't finished when the fermentation finally gives out. In many cases the styling of the wine has only just begun. Everything will now depend on the length of maturation, the type of container used, the ambient temperature it takes place in and the degree of clarification, or 'cleaning up', before bottling.

Maturation is of greater importance with red wines than whites, which are usually bottled after a brief period of maturation.

Reds

Many modern red wines are made for early drinking and only mature very briefly. However, most red wines demand a period of time before bottling to lose their tannic bitterness and enhance their flavours.

There are various options:
(a) The wine can be filtered, centrifuged and bottled almost immediately as in Beaujolais Nouveau.
(b) The wine can age for anything from a few months to a few years in concrete or stainless steel. This will do little to change the taste though wines like Portugal's Dão do gradually soften.
(c) The wine can go into large old wooden barrels of thousands of litres capacity. These will age the

HOW WINE IS MADE

MATURATION

wine and reduce its fruit, rarely adding anything back. If kept too long like this – as traditional southern French and Italian reds are – the wines dry out, but retain both acid and tannin to no effect whatsoever.

(d) The wine may age in small barrels of 225 litres capacity. All the top reds of France, Spain, the USA and Australia are matured by this method, and it is increasingly used elsewhere too.

When the barrels are new, there is a wealth of flavour in the wood which the wine slowly sucks out. The most important of these is vanillin – the sweet, buttery, even honeyed taste many great reds have. Other tastes are less definable but have the herby, spicy flavours of fresh-cut timber in the carpenter's shop. The barrel wood also contains tannin, which is crucially important in giving the wine the backbone to age. So, from a base of the simple fruit flavours of a just fermented wine, an entirely different range of flavours develops, and this is further enhanced by the gentle effect of oxygen through the wooden staves. French barrels are the most highly regarded, followed by American and Yugoslavian. Each gives different perfumes and flavours. The amount of charring the wood underwent while the staves of the barrel were being flamed into shape also affects the flavour of the wine. Except for a few top properties, most winemakers only use a proportion of new barrels for each harvest.

Wine may be stored in oak barrels for as little as three months and as much as two to three years. The barrels lose their flavour as they get older, though the insides can be gouged out so that fresh wood is revealed and fresh flavours released. The hotter the ambient temperature in the cellar, the stronger the wood flavours. Nowadays there is a move towards wood maturation in cool temperature controlled rooms, which gives a far subtler flavour to the wine.

Rosés

Rosés are rarely kept in barrel, and rarely improve if they are. They should be treated as for fresh, young wines.

Fortified Wines

All good fortified wines are aged in barrel. These are usually much bigger than the 'Bordeaux' barrels of 225 litres used for the best table wines. The period of maturation may be short – two years for Vintage port – but is much more likely to be at least five years and often 10 to 20 as the wines lose colour and ferocity in the barrel and gain softness and perfume. Many commercial ports are now brought to a precocious maturity by chill filtering to below 0°C. This removes all chance of a sediment being thrown, and all chance of the port's developing its full personality in bottle.

Whites

Most whites are made to be bottled and drunk young, with as little air contact as possible. A few are made to mature and deepen in vats which will require contact with oxygen. The methods of maturation are as follows:

(a) **Sterile tank storage.** The wine is stored away from air contact. For the lightest, freshest types this may even include storing it under a blanket of nitrogen or carbon dioxide.

(b) **Non-sterile tank storage.** This is unlikely to improve the wine, especially if the tank is made of concrete or cement, but is often practised in southern Europe.

(c) **Big barrel storage.** In Germany, the finest Rieslings are often matured for a year or more in big wooden barrels and, given the cool climate, seem to gain flavour and complexity. In hotter climates it is likely to lead to rapid oxidation.

(d) **Small barrel storage.** Less important than for reds, but top burgundies and other Chardonnay wines, as well as good Graves and some Sémillon and Sauvignon (Fumé Blanc) wines, gain immeasurably in rich, fat, honeyed flavours from a period in barrel, rarely more than a year. Old-style white Rioja often has several years in barrel. The great sweet wines also gain enormously from small barrel-aging.

It is during the maturation period that any blending thought necessary between grape varieties and between different batches of wine will be carried out for reds and whites. Also, any malolactic not previously completed will take place.

Sparkling Wines

Ideally, all champagne and most good sparkling wines should be stored in cool cellars for up to two to three years in their bottles before *dégorgement* and also for a period of months after *dégorgement* and before sale.

Clarification – Reds

During maturation the wines will deposit sediment or lees (colouring matter, used yeast cells, tannin and acids). Red wine being stored must not stay on these lees or it will get a yeasty taste and before bottling any further solid matter must be removed. This is done in two stages: racking and fining or filtering (or both).

Racking involves drawing the wine off the barrel or tank just above the level of the sediment on the bottom of the container and transferring it to a clean container. If the wine needs oxygenating the racking may be done via an open bowl, otherwise it will be done by hose.

The next stage involves fining or filtering or both. **Fining** is a simple operation whereby a coagulant is added to the wine to cleanse it. The substance is poured onto the surface of the wine, where it forms a film which slowly descends through the suspended liquid, carrying with it all but the tiniest solid particles. Whipped egg white is still best for this.

Lesser wines will also be filtered to a greater or lesser extent.

Clarification – Whites

Except for certain wines which gain character from contact with their yeast deposits or lees, like good-quality Muscadet and burgundy, white wines are either centrifuged (again!), fine filtered, or 'fined' (see reds). A substance called Bentonite made from clay is most commonly used. The wines are then usually chilled to deposit tartaric crystals which may otherwise be precipitated in the bottle during cold weather. After this they are ready for yet another filtering – and bottling. All this activity is all right for cheap wines, but, when used on fine wines it strips the wine of character. Fine white wines will simply be left alone in oak barrels in a similar way to fine reds. In this case they will normally be racked (see reds).

Bottling – Reds and Whites

The next stage is bottling. Choosing the right bottling date is crucial. Bottling too early can kill the chances of a red wine developing a really exciting personality. Bottling too late may mean a light wine will have lost all its fruit. For most white wines bottling takes place within the first nine months after the vintage. Very few whites, save the finest dessert wines, will be bottled more than 18 months later. Reds may, similarly, be bottled very young to preserve fruit. Beaujolais Nouveau is bottled days, rather than months after the vintage, but the great reds often have two years in barrel. Some Italian reds like Brunello di Montalcino are not allowed to be bottled before they are four or five years old. Rioja Gran Reservas may stay in wood 5 to 10 years, going sweetish and tawny before being bottled.

The bottling must be sterile, and is usually done on enormous automatic bottling lines, which will employ one of two methods:
(a) Pasteurization or 'hot bottling'. This involves heating the wine to kill its harmful bacteria. It is detrimental to the wine's flavour and is becoming less common.
(b) Cold sterile bottling. Here the bottles are delivered sterile from the factory, injected with nitrogen, then filled with cool wine which therefore has a nitrogen lock between itself and the cork, thus inhibiting decay or infection.

All great wines will be bottled at their property, often by a mobile bottling plant. The objective will be to ensure cleanliness but not super-sterility, since any overuse of filters to remove the last particle of sediment is sure to remove personality too.

Bottling – Fortified Wines

These will not usually be bottled before five years of age.

Aging in Bottle

This is called reductive aging, because there is only a tiny amount of oxygen between the wine and the cork and the wine's reaction over a period will reduce this to nothing. Usually a wine of any quality becomes much more exciting with a period of bottling, developing most of its bouquet in bottle and most of its particular nuances in character. The finest wines can mature and improve in bottle for 30 years or more.

The supporting elements of tannin and acidity gradually soften, the flavours change from the strong primary flavours of fruit which characterize young Mosel or Beaujolais, to the deep, twining, endlessly varied traces of a host of flavours quite unconnected with their first rush of fresh fruit straight off the vat, which characterize white burgundy or red Bordeaux or Hermitage at their peak. A great wine is the most complex of all the world's liquids. Exactly how it changes in bottle is the subject of continued scientific controversy, but change it does, and for once it may be wise to listen to the romantics and dreamers rather than read the technical manuals. Ideally, take good advice, buy a few bottles young and be patient. Most of all, great wines will demand your time, to wait, to hope and finally to enjoy. But it may be a long wait.

ALTERNATIVE PACKAGING

There are a growing number of alternative packages for wine. The wine box or wine cask is increasingly popular. This is filled from the tank on a semi-automatic bottling line, and is prone to suffer from oxidation. The Tetrabrick or Combiblock is a plastic container, filled beneath the surface of the wine, and it seems to offer good hope of keeping the wine fresh and fruity over reasonable periods.

Some companies are also using cans and plastic bottles with seemingly good results.

GLOSSARY

acetic Vinegary. A sign that a wine is infected by acetobacters and only fit for the vinegar still.

acid/acidity Sharp, refreshing quality in wine.

acidification The addition of acid (usually tartaric) during fermentation, frequently practised in hot climates where grapes tend to overripen and become deficient in acid.

aging Alternative term for maturation. Sometimes term of criticism, as in aging prematurely.

alcoholic fermentation The process whereby yeast and sugar present in grapes react to produce alcohol, transforming grape juice into wine.

almacenista Spanish word for stockholder. Term used in Jerez for individuals maturing small individual barrels of sherry.

Amontillado A medium sherry.

AC Abbreviation of **Appellation d'Origine Contrôlée** – the French quality control designation. 'Controlled Appellation of Origin'. Also seen as Appellation Contrôlée and AOC.

atmosphere The pressure in a sparkling wine is measured by its number of 'atmospheres'.

Auslese German term meaning 'Selected'. Usually applied in Germany, Austria and Australia to sweet late picked whites, but in the Alto Adige, Kalterersee Auslese is a light red wine.

Beerenauslese German term meaning selected single berries. Used for sweet wines in Germany, Austria, Australia and USA.

Bereich German regional term for village or group of villages. Usually applied only to QbA wines.

blanc de blancs Still or sparkling wine made only from white grapes.

blanc de noirs Still or sparkling white wine made from black grapes.

bodega Spanish word for 'cellar'. Used to describe wine companies in Spain.

brut Term used to describe driest type of sparkling wines.

centrifuging Filtering out of yeasts and impurities by means of centrifugal force.

Champagne method Traditional method of making wine sparkle by inducing second fermentation in the bottle.

chapeau French for cap. The layer of grape skins which rises to the surface during red wine fermentation.

cuve close. Modern, inferior sparkling wine method using large pressurized vats.

chaptalization The addition of sugar during fermentation to increase alcoholic strength.

château French for castle. Term denoting a single vineyard, especially in Bordeaux.

chill filtering Severe but effective removal of solid matter – especially tartaric acid deposits – from wine.

claret English term for red Bordeaux.

clarification The removal of solid matter from a wine after fermentation.

classico Italian term for the original central part of a wine area.

clone Strain of grape species. Grapes like Pinot Noir have hundreds of clones.

cold fermentation Long slow fermentation at low temperature to extract maximum freshness from the grapes. Crucial for whites in hot climates.

commune French term for village. Often used, e.g. in Burgundy, where each major commune has its own appellation.

cool climate The areas at the coolest limits

of grape-ripening, e.g. Germany, England, Washington State in the north USA.

co-operative Grouping of growers which handles wine-making, and, increasingly, marketing, on communal basis.

courtier French term for broker, acting as middleman between grower and merchant.

crémant Sparkling wine style using less pressure (atmospheres). In Loire, Burgundy and Alsace a quality wine appellation.

cru Literally 'growth'. Term used to describe a single vineyard, usually qualified with a quality reference such as 'Grand Cru', 'Premier Cru' etc.

cultivar South African term for single grape variety.

cuvée Selection. Often, as in 'Tête de Cuvée', 'Cuvée Exceptionnelle', 'Cuvée De Luxe', implying a special quality.

demi-sec Semi-dry, but more accurately translated as 'demi-sweet' in most cases.

dégorgement Process in champagne of removing sediment from the bottle.

DOC Abbreviation of Denominazione d'Origine Controllata – the Italian Controlled Appellation of Origin system. Also seen as DO.

DOCG Abbreviation of Denominazione d'Origine Controllata 'Garantita' – the new top flight of Italian quality control for its most revered wines.

domaine French word for single vineyard.

dosage A sugar and wine mixture added to sparkling wine after disgorgement which affects how sweet or dry it will be.

dulce Spanish word for 'sweet'.

Eiswein Very intense sweet wine made from frozen grapes. Germany and Austria are the chief exponents.

estate A single property, though this may, as in Germany and Burgundy, encompass several different vineyards.

filtering Removal of yeasts, solids and any impurities from a wine.

fining Addition of albumen-type substances to surface of wine, which then descend slowly through the wine, taking any solid matter with them.

Fino The dryest type of sherry.

flor A film of yeast which forms on the top of Fino sherries, inhibiting oxidation and imparting the unique dry flavour to the sherry.

fortified wine Wine which has high strength spirit added, usually before the initial alcoholic fermentation is completed, thereby preserving sweetness.

frizzante Italian term for semi-sparkling.

garrafeira Portuguese term for superior wine which has had aging in bottle.

governo Traditional method of Chianti production involving addition of raisined grapes to soften and create a slight prickle.

grand cru classé 'Classed Great Growth'. Bordeaux has several classifications of quality, and this term is also occasionally used elsewhere, often without justification.

gran reserva Top Spanish table wine quality level involving long barrel-aging.

Grosslage A grouping of German vineyards under a single name.

imbottigliatto dal produttore all origine Italian term meaning 'Bottled by the producer at his estate'.

jug wine US term for basic table wine.

Kabinett German quality term for least ripe of the top flight. Kabinett wine cannot have sugar added in Germany (though it can in Austria).

Late Harvest The harvesting of wines after the ordinary harvest date to increase alcoholic strength or sweetness.

laying down The storing of wine which will improve with age.

lieu-dit Burgundian term for single vineyard below First Growth Standard. In Beaujolais, any single vineyard.

liqueur de tirage Sugar and wine mixture added to champagne after first fermentation to cause re-fermentation in bottle.

liqueur d'expedition The same as *dosage* (see above).

macération carbonique Fermentation of whole, uncrushed grapes in a closed container under a blanket of carbonic gas to produce light fruity red wine.

malolactic fermentation A secondary fermentation which converts malic acid to the softer lactic acid. Normal in reds, though hot country whites may arrest it to keep the wine fresher and more acid.

Manzanilla Very dry sherry.

marque French for 'brand' or 'trade name'.

maturation Positive term for the beneficial aging of a wine.

méthode gaillaçoise/rurale Fairly basic method of creating sparkling wine by bottling it before the first fermentation is fully over. Occasionally used in Blanquette de Limoux, Gaillac and Clairette de Die.

mise (en bouteille au domaine) 'Bottled at the property'.

mise (en bouteille sur lie) Muscadet term for wine bottled without filtering directly off its lees.

moelleux French term for sweet, though not quite so sweet as Doux or Liquoureux.

négociant/négociant éleveur French term for a merchant or shipper who buys wine from various sources, matures it, maybe blends it, and then sells it.

'noble rot' A fungus which, in warm autumn weather, can attack white grapes, shrivel them and concentrate the sugar.

non-vintage A wine without a stated vintage year, usually a blend of more than one harvest.

Oidium Powdery Mildew, a very dangerous vine disease which rots the stalks, shrivels the leaves and splits the grapes.

Oloroso Full, rich, aged sherry.

oxidation Over-exposure of wine to air, causing loss of fruit and bacterial decay.

pétillant French term for slightly sparkling.

Phylloxera A louse which attacks vine roots. All European vines are susceptible to it, so they must be grafted on to resistant American root stocks.

press wine The wine pressed from the skins after most of the wine has been drawn off after fermentation. Usually hard and dark, and used sparingly to beef up a wine.

prise de mousse The stage after **liqueur de tirage** (see above) when a wine re-ferments in bottles and the subsequent carbon dioxide is dissolved in the wine, creating bubbles or mousse.

QbA Abbreviation of Qualitätswein bestimmter Anbaugebiete (Quality Wine from a designated region) very broad German quality defininition.

QmP Abbreviation of Qualitätswein mit Prädikat. 'Quality Wine with Special Attributes' — the real German quality level embracing unsugared wines from defined areas between the light Kabinett level and the intensely rich Trockenbeerenauslese.

racking The gradual clarification of quality wine by the transferral of wine off its lees to another barrel.

récoltant manipulant Term for grower who also 'champenizes' his own wine.

remuage The riddling-down of sediment on to the bottle's cork, at which point it may be 'disgorged' with minimal loss of wine. Increasingly done by machine.

reserva Spanish definition for good quality with some wood aging.

reserve wine Older wine kept back to add class and maturity to non-vintage blends of champagne.

riserva Italian DOC definition usually referring to a minimum aging period before bottling.

sec 'Dry'. When applied to champagne it actually means medium dry.

'second' wines Wines not thought to be up to the level of a property's main production and sold separately.

Sekt German term for sparkling wine.

Sélection des Grains Nobles Alsace term for late picked wine similar to German Beerenauslese.

solera Spanish and Portuguese term for the systematic topping up of older barrels with younger wine of the same style, so as to ensure continuity.

Spätlese German term for 'late-picked' wine, usually slightly sweet.

sugar In areas where grapes do not ripen fully, sugar has to be added to the must to aid fermentation.

Süss reserve Unfermented grape juice, added to wine just before bottling to increase sweetness and fruit and create a 'Germanic' style.

Tafelwein German for Table Wine. Most basic quality designation.

tannin The bitter, mouth-drying component in red wines, derived from skins, stalks and sometimes wooden barrels, which is harsh when young, but crucial to a wine's ability to age.

Trocken German for dry. Applied to new-style German wines made completely dry in an effort to make them more suitable for meals.

Trockenbeerenauslese German term for selected shrivelled single berries. This describes the method of picking employed to create Germany's and Austria's sweetest wines. Occasionally found in Australia and California.

varietal A grape variety. Wines made from a single grape are called 'varietals' and labelled with the name of the grape.

VDQS Abbreviation of Vin Délimité de Qualité Supérieur ('Delimited Wine of Superior Quality'). This is the second rank of French quality control, between Appellation Contrôlée and Vin de Pays.

Vendange Tardive Alsace term for Late Harvest, similar to German Spätlese/Auslese.

Vin de Pays French 'Country Wine', a less stringent French quality designation than Appellation Contrôlée.

Vin de Table 'French Table Wine'. Basic quality designation.

Vinho Maduro 'Mature Wine'. Portuguese term for wines which undergo aging.

Vinho Verde 'Green Wine'. Portuguese term for unmatured wine, red or white.

vinification The process of turning grapes into wine.

Vino da Tavola Italian 'Table Wine'. Basic quality designation, but including some exciting non-conformist wines.

vintage The harvesting of the grape; used to describe the produce of a single year.

Vitis Labrusca American grape species which makes over-powerful flavoured wine on its own but is crucial in supplying phylloxera-resistant rootstocks for Vitis Vinifera.

Vitis Vinifera The species of grape which makes all the world's finest wines.

wood aging Aging of wine in barrels, casks or vats. Effects can vary from the highly beneficial to the disastrous.

Tasting Terms

aromatic Descriptive term for wines of a markedly flowery, spicy or grapy character.

beefy Term for reds meaning solid, chunky, 4-square.

buttery Often applied to white Chardonnay and sometimes red Merlot, Pinot Noir or Shiraz. Usually refers to the soft, rich vanilla flavour imparted by new oak barrels.

chewy Wine with a lot of tannin and strong flavour.

clean Wine with no bacterial or chemical faults and a simple, direct flavour.

clone Strain of grape species. Grapes like Pinot Noir have hundreds of clones.

deep Term for full-flavoured reds and whites, often applied to wines still not at their peak.

dusty Usually applied to hot country reds, in particular wines from the southern Rhône.

earthy A slight root vegetable, muddy flavour, not usually complimentary, except for wines made from the Cabernet Franc grape.

fat A heavy, sometimes slightly clumsy, wine, though if made from fully ripe grapes it can imply a rather unctuous richness in the wine, sweet or dry.

freshness The youthful aromas in a wine, usually associating good acidity with floral or fruit flavours.

fruit Term, literally, for the fruit element in a wine. It may not taste of grapes, but it will resemble a fruit of some kind – e.g. blackcurrant, strawberry, apple – and is crucial to the flavour of any wine.

fullness The feel, or weight, of a wine in the mouth.

grapy Quite rare flavour of the grape itself in wine. Commonest with Muscat, Gewürztraminer and Riesling.

green Unripe, or tart, not necessarily an unattractive taste in a light wine.

hard Usually applied to reds which have an excess of tannin. In young reds, this is often necessary to support the aging process.

honeyed Applied to ripe wines which, sweet or dry, have a taste of honey.

jammy Rather big, cooked sweetish wines, usually red.

length The way a good wine's flavours continue to evolve in the mouth even after swallowing.

nutty Usually for dry whites – a soft brazil or hazel nut flavour in Chardonnay, a woodier taste in Chenin or Sauvignon, and a dry richness in medium sherries or Madeiras.

oaky The slightly sweet vanilla flavour imparted by maturation in oak casks.

petrolly Applied to old Riesling wines.

plummy Often applied to big round ripe reds from Pomerol, St-Emilion, Côte de Nuits and Napa.

prickly A wine with slight residual gas left in it. Usually attractive in light young whites, but in reds it is often a sign of re-fermentation in bottle.

smoky Many wines do have a smoky taste, especially when slightly charred oak barrels have been used for maturation.

spicy Exotic fruit and spice flavours in whites, particularly Gewürztraminer, but also a peppery or cinnamony/clovy perfume in some reds.

steely Applied to top Riesling for the very dry, almost metallic flavour they develop.

stony Usually implying a rather dull, empty dryness in a red or white.

sweet Tasting term, applied not only to sweet wines, but also to the elements of ripeness or richness which good quality dry wines can often suggest.

sweet sour The slightly sour raisiny taste often found in Italian reds.

tart Green, unripe wine. Can be desirable in light, dry whites.

tough Usually implying too much tannin.

VINTAGE GUIDE

A vintage chart is of some relevance to about one percent of France's wine, and a good deal less of Germany's and Italy's. Any mark given to a vintage is a generalization. There are disappointing wines in brilliant years, and brilliant wines in difficult years. The highest marks are given to vintages where the **ripeness of the grapes is best balanced by the acidity of the juice – and, for red wines, the proper amount of tannin,** giving wines which have the potential to age. Until the 1970s it was quite possible for a vintage to be lost and merit a derisory mark, but nowadays, though it makes for a more boring vintage chart, the basic quality of vintages has risen enormously, usually to at least 5/10.

So use the chart only as a guide – *never* as a bible. Lower marks may give more pleasure, at lesser maturity and at a lower price, than the fabled vintages. This chart is here for you to enjoy, to agree with, to argue with, to berate as well as to admire. The arguments it causes are just as valuable as the advice it gives. (**Chart overleaf.**)

NR = Not Ready **JR** = Just Ready **AP** = At Peak **PB** = Past Best

BORDEAUX

RED	'89	'88	'87	'86	'85	'83	'82	'81	'79	'78
Pauillac, St-Julien, St-Estèphe	9NR	9NR	5NR	8NR	8NR	8NR	10NR	7JR	7JR	9JR
Margaux	8NR	7NR	5JR	7NR	8NR	9NR	8NR	7JR	7AP	8JR
Graves	9NR	9NR	5NR	8NR	8NR	9NR	9NR	8JR	7AP	8AP
St-Emilion/Pomerol	9NR	9NR	6JR	8NR	9NR	8JR	10JR	6AP	7AP	7AP

WHITE	'89	'88	'87	'86	'85	'83	'82	'81	'79	'78
Graves	8NR	8JR	6JR	7AP	7AP	8AP	6AP	7AP	8PB	7PB
Sauternes	10NR	9NR	4NR	10NR	6NR	9JR	5AP	6AP	5AP	4AP

BURGUNDY

Red burgundy is desperately unreliable so we rate the vintage according to what can be expected from a decent single domaine. White burgundy is more generally reliable.

RED	'89	'88	'87	'86	'85	'83	'82	'81	'79	'78
Côte de Nuits	8NR	10NR	7NR	6NR	10NR	7NR	6AP	3AP	6AP	8AP
Côte de Beaune	8NR	10NR	6NR	5NR	9JR	7JR	6AP	3PB	6AP	8AP

WHITE	'89	'88	'87	'86	'85	'83	'82	'81	'79	'78
Chablis	9NR	8JR	6JR	8AP	7AP	8AP	6PB	9AP	5PB	9AP
Meursault, Montrachet, Puligny-Montrachet	8NR	9NR	6NR	9JR	8JR	6AP	7AP	5AP	7PB	8AP
Pouilly-Fuissé	8NR	8JR	6JR	9AP	8AP	7PB	6PB	7PB	6PB	8PB

CHAMPAGNE

Vintages are usually only 'declared' in the best years, several years after harvest, but a few producers will make vintage wine every year.

	'89	'88	'87	'86	'85	'83	'82	'81	'79	'78
Champagne	9NR	8NR	4NR	7NR	9NR	8JR	9JR	6AP	8AP	7AP

LOIRE

In general Loire wines should be drunk young but some wines can age, particularly reds and sweet wines.

	'89	'88	'87	'86	'85	'83	'82	'81	'79	'78
Sancerre white	8JR	9JR	6AP	9AP	6PB	7PB	5PB	8PB	5PB	9PB
Sancerre red	9NR	8JR	4AP	8AP	7AP	8PB	7PB	6PB	5PB	8PB
Cabernet (Bourgueil, Chinon)	10NR	8NR	5JR	6JR	9AP	8AP	7AP	6AP	5PB	8PB
Sweet (Anjou, Vouvray)	9NR	8NR	4NR	6NR	10NR	9JR	7JR	5JR	6AP	5AP

RHONE

The reds of the northern Rhône take to aging extremely well, and white Hermitage can even outlive the red. Southern reds can age, but mature sooner.

	'89	'88	'87	'86	'85	'83	'82	'81	'80	'78
White Hermitage	8NR	9NR	8NR	7NR	8NR	9NR	8NR	6JR	6JR	9JR
Red Hermitage	9NR	9NR	6NR	7NR	9NR	10NR	7AP	4AP	7AP	10AP
Côte Rôtie	8NR	10NR	6NR	7NR	10JR	9JR	7AP	4AP	6AP	9AP
Châteauneuf-du-Pape	8NR	9NR	4JR	7JR	8AP	7AP	5AP	7AP	6AP	9AP

ALSACE

These should usually be drunk young, but the occasional Late Harvested wine merits keeping.

	'89	'88	'87	'86	'85	'83	'82	'81	'79	'78
Alsace	10NR	10JR	6AP	7AP	9AP	9AP	5PB	7AP	7PB	5PB

GERMANY

This chart only applies to the 'Prädikat' level of special quality wines.

	'89	'88	'87	'86	'85	'84	'83	'82	'81	'79
Mosel-Saar-Ruwer	10NR	9JR	4AP	5AP	8AP	4AP	8AP	4AP	5AP	5PB
Rheingau	9NR	9JR	4AP	5AP	7AP	3PB	9AP	5AP	6AP	5PB
Rheinhessen	10NR	9JR	5AP	6AP	7AP	4PB	9AP	6PB	6AP	6PB

ITALY

Though vintages are of considerable importance for the best Italian wines, wine-making methods differ so widely within the same DOCs that these marks are only approximations.

	'89	'88	'87	'86	'85	'83	'82	'81	'79	'78
Barolo	7NR	10NR	7NR	8NR	9NR	8NR	10NR	4JR	7JR	8JR
Brunello	5NR	9NR	7NR	8NR	9NR	9NR	8NR	6NR	6JR	8JR
Chianti Classico	5NR	10NR	5NR	8NR	10NR	8JR	8AP	5AP	6PB	7PB

SPAIN

Vintage charts are relevant to few Spanish wines.

	'89	'88	'87	'86	'85	'83	'82	'81	'80	'78
Rioja Reserva	7NR	7NR	6NR	7NR	8NR	7JR	8JR	6AP	5AP	7AP
Penedès red	8NR	7NR	7NR	6NR	8NR	6JR	8JR	8AP	9AP	9AP
Penedès white	8NR	8JR	6AP	7AP	6PB	6PB	8PB	9PB	7PB	8PB

PORTUGAL

Portugal is only just beginning to apply rigid vintage dating to table wines. Port, however, is one of the great vintage wines, though a vintage is only 'declared' in exceptional years. * = declared.

	'89	'88	'87	'86	'85	'83	'82	'80	'78	'77
Red Dao	7NR	4NR	3NR	4NR	8JR	9AP	4AP	7PB	6PB	5PB
Vintage port	8NR	6NR	6NR	*9NR	*9NR	*7NR	*8JR	6JR	*10JR	

USA

So many vineyard areas are still in the exciting development stage throughout the USA and I have concentrated on the best known of the top quality areas.

	'89	'88	'87	'86	'85	'84	'83	'82	'81	'80
Napa Cabernet	6NR	9NR	8NR	8NR	10JR	9JR	5AP	7AP	7AP	8AP
Napa Chardonnay	7NR	8JR	8JR	9AP	9AP	9AP	6AP	8PB	9PB	7PB
Sonoma Cabernet	7NR	9NR	8NR	8JR	10JR	9AP	6AP	7AP	7AP	9AP
Sonoma Chardonnay	7JR	9JR	8JR	9AP	10AP	9AP	7PB	8PB	9PB	8PB

AUSTRALIA

The world of wine is changing so fast in Australia that in most instances the skill of the winemaker is more important than the vintage. As new cool-climate vineyards come into maturity, vintage variations will become more marked. We list two great areas which are traditionally susceptible to vintage variations.

	'90	'89	'88	'87	'86	'85	'84	'83	'82	'80
Coonawarra red	8NR	6NR	8NR	8NR	8JR	9JR	10AP	4AP	8AP	10AP
Hunter Valley Semillon	6NR	7NR	6NR	8JR	10JR	8JR	7JR	8JR	7JR	7AP

FRANCE

Nobody can do it like the French. Many try, none quite manage it. But the very fact that all over the world, winemakers have taken the French model and are moving hell and high water to try to copy it must mean something.

It certainly does. By a mixture of historical chance, geological peculiarity and climatic conditions, she is still the world's greatest wine-making nation. The historical chance is that while her civilization was flowering and her vineyards developing she had a series of natural trading partners to the north for whose markets she specifically moulded her wines. (The Low Countries, Scandinavia, Germany and Switzerland are to this day her chief export markets. Italy and Spain, their natural trading areas being frequently under teetotal Moslem influence, did little but develop their own instinctive domestic tastes in wine.) Her geological and climatic position allows her to exploit some of the coldest as well as some of the hottest vineyards and consequently, in between these two are an array of wine areas where particular grapes can find virtually perfect conditions to ripen. Not to overripen; and this is the secret of France's success.

In the far north Champagne makes thin tart wines, but from classic grape varieties – the black Pinot Noir and Pinot Meunier and the white Chardonnay – and the hardly ripened wine which results is the perfect base for transforming into the greatest of sparkling wine – champagne.

Just to the east, a rainshadow under the Vosges mountains allows Alsace to look back to a history intertwined between German and French influence and to produce intensely perfumed yet dry wines from such Germanic grapes as Riesling, Gewürztraminer and Ruländer (Pinot Gris). While Germany's Late Harvested Rieslings have become the model for much sweet wine-making, it is the Alsace model the world follows when it wants to make anything Germanic but dry. Away from the German border, below Paris, begins one of the most contentious, passionately involving wine regions of the world – Burgundy. Her white wines, from the Chardonnay grape, begin in frosty, steely isolation in northern Chablis, then re-appear full of power, ripeness and beauty in the Côte d'Or

where the villages of Puligny-Montrachet, Chassagne-Montrachet and Meursault produce wines combining honeyed richness with savoury fragrance which have had two generations of New Wave winemakers across the world wearing their fingers to the bone trying to reproduce them in their own vinelands. It ends in overpriced but juicy renown in the Mâconnais – home of all-conquering Pouilly-Fuissé. The reds are centred on the Côte d'Or, where the Pinot Noir grape does its best to disprove its reputation as one of the two greatest red wine grapes in the world, but in the hands of a few growers prepared to cosset, bully, cajole and taunt this sulky grape the wines are of such a haunting, perfumed brilliance that one is almost prepared to forgive the many mediocre bottles which surround them. Burgundy growers are not alone in their frustration. Few winemakers elsewhere have yet got near the heart of the Pinot Noir and Burgundy, but that only makes them try all the harder. To the south, the Chalonnais produces some very good burgundy in miniature, and the Beaujolais region using the Gamay grape produces the archetypal fresh, bright, young quaffing red whose style has been copied all over the world.

A short leap south to the Rhône and it is the Syrah's turn. This dark, strong, pungent grape makes the great red wines of Hermitage and Côte Rôtie, as well as contributing to Châteauneuf-du-Pape and a host of others. Although Australia does great things in her own way with the grape (here called Shiraz), many Australians, as well as South Africans and Californians, are itching to get going on re-creating their version of Hermitage.

On the south-west coast is the mecca for red wine makers – Bordeaux. An astonishing amount of great wine is made from the Cabernet Sauvignon, Cabernet Franc and Merlot grapes. Any red wine maker who wishes to be admitted to the top rank of the New Wave must try his hand sooner rather than later at Cabernet and the ideal of the perfect Bordeaux recreated in his own backyard. The sweet wines of Sauternes are indisputably some of the world's greatest dessert wines and a few lion-hearts are beginning to tread this path too.

Finally, turning back north again, the Loire valley offers a wide range of wines from different grapes, but, above all, Loire Sauvignons have set the standard for sharp, tangy, fresh whites which every cool-climate wine-growing region in the world is now rushing to imitate and improve upon. None of these wines just occurred out of thin air, and though some of them, like Beaujolais and Sancerre, have only recently found fame and fortune, they are all the result of the distillation of centuries of trial and error with vineyard sites, grape types and wine-making methods. It is these considerations which, in 1932, formed the basis for the Appellation d'Origine Contrôlée Laws which are at the heart of French quality control, and which, except in Germany, have formed the basis for quality control systems in Europe, North America and the Southern Hemisphere.

CLASSIFICATION

There are three main levels of quality control, as follows:

Appellation d'Origine Contrôlée
Or just Appellation Contrôlée (AC). The top designation, it is based on any one, or a mixture of, eight factors.

1 Geography The most fundamental. Suitable sites, sometimes only small microclimates in a larger area, are singled out as having particular suitability. The judgement will usually be based on a mixture of soil evaluation and climatic conditions or micro-conditions.

2 Grape varieties Each appellation will have one or more grape varieties permitted according to proven suitability and historical practice.

3 Alcoholic degree All wines have a minimum alcohol degree, which in areas away from the south and southern Rhône can be achieved by a mixture of grape ripeness and addition of a strictly controlled amount of sugar.

4 Yield In general, the more grapes you allow a given patch of ground to produce, the less special the wine will be. Consequently, all appellations have maximum grape yields measured as hectolitres of wine produced, usually between 45 and 50hl per hectare, but reaching as low as 25hl in areas like Sauternes. However, this crucial quality criterion is being increasingly flaunted as the Institut National des Appellations d'Origine bows to local pressure and allows increases in yield. Local syndicates can apply for increases in the base yield each year, and then add to that a device called a Plafond Limité de Classement (PLC) – literally, the limited ceiling for each class – which can produce a further 20 per cent of wine. In some areas, like Champagne and Burgundy, it just becomes a joke, and 1982 in Burgundy saw the Grands Crus, whose legally ratified superiority has traditionally been based on single special plots of land producing strictly limited small quantities of wine, literally doubling their allowance overnight.

5 Vineyard practice Rules lay down the number of vines per hectare, the method of pruning and even (as in Sauternes or the Beaujolais Crus) the method of picking. With the advent of machine-picking in many areas, whose results are still causing much controversy, this section becomes increasingly important.

6 Methods of wine-making Traditional and modern wine-making methods are monitored, and such things as adding or taking away acids depending upon whether your grapes are too ripe or not ripe enough are controlled.

7 Analysis All appellation wines since 1979 have to be submitted to a tasting panel, which rejects faulty or untypical wines. You can present your wine twice. If you fail twice – that's it. Your finest Grand Cru vintage can end up as a mere table wine.

8 Bottling Some appellations, like Alsace, and, of course, Champagne, stipulate bottling in the region of production.

Vin Délimité de Qualité Supérieure (VDQS)
This is really a kind of 'Junior Appellation Contrôlée'. Some wines are VDQS rather than AC simply because the wrong grapes are grown in the right place; for example, Sauvignon de St-Bris is VDQS because it is from the Sauvignon Blanc grown in the Chardonnay and Aligoté-only Burgundy area.

In the Consumer
Checklists
Q = Quality
P = Price
V = Value

Other areas are VDQS because, despite many properties being of full AC quality, the overall level is still too erratic — such is the case with Côtes du Vivarais, an exciting but unproven mountain area in the Southern Rhône. In general, the regulations concerning yields, grape types and alcoholic strength, etc., are a little less strict than for AC wines, and it is regarded by many as being merely a stepping-stone up to full AC status. Every year two or three wines are 'promoted'.

Vins de Pays

Literally, 'Country Wines'. These were created by government decree in 1968 and 1973. They do have limits in the AC style, but are the laxest of the three groups. The intention was to take the large, anonymous areas of table wine production and give them regional identity. Consequently there are three levels of Vin de Pays.

1 Vins de Pays Régionaux Regional classifications covering wide areas. Vin de Pays du Jardin de la France, for instance, covers the whole Loire valley.

2 Vins de Pays Départementaux These cover the wines of a whole *département* or 'county', e.g. Vin de Pays de l'Aude.

3 Vins de Pays de Zone These cover wines of single communes or small areas, e.g. Vin de Pays de l'Uzège for wines from the locality of Uzès, which is in the Gard *département*.

Below the Vin de Pays designation is Vin de Table, or table wine, which is simply the uncontrolled production of the most basic wine.

Now let's take a closer look at the regions, their wines, and – most important – what they taste like!

BORDEAUX

Bordeaux is the greatest red wine area in the world. There was a time when such a bold statement would bring a chorus of dissent from the supporters of Burgundy, and the argument might well rest evenly balanced between the two as both camps agreed to differ. But as Burgundy's ability to produce a consistently high quality of wine in reasonable amounts becomes more questionable with every vintage and her supporters retire in aggrieved confusion, Bordeaux has gone from strength to strength, with every vintage producing yet another crop of wines clamouring to join the top levels of achievement. Indeed, if I were to look for people to refute my statement, I'd look for them in the Napa or Sonoma valleys of California, or the Coonawarra, Geelong and Yarra valley areas of Australia, not to the east in France.

While there is no doubt that Burgundy can make some stunning bottles, Bordeaux's position is so strong because of the enormous volume of tremendously high quality wine that she produces. This is chiefly red, but in fact, until recently, it was white which was the dominant style in many parts of the region. This is now on the wane as the demand for red Bordeaux grows at every level, and although the Graves and Entre-Deux-Mers regions do produce some fine dry whites, Bordeaux's reputation is really founded upon two main wine styles – the rare but brilliant sweet white wines of Sauternes and Barsac, and the numerous high-quality reds of the Médoc – in particular the Haut-Médoc – Graves, and Pomerol–St-Emilion.

The Bordeaux region is in the south-west of France on both sides of the Gironde estuary

APPELLATIONS CONTRÔLÉES

and straddling the Garonne and Dordogne rivers which join up to form the Gironde just below the city of Bordeaux. The region benefits from several different geological and climatic plus points. Firstly, her proximity to the Atlantic Ocean means that although she is on a similar latitude to the harsh dry vineyards of the Rhône valley, she has relatively mild winters and summers which are usually marked by few extremes of temperature. She also has a wedge of forest, the Landes, between her and the sea, which soaks off some of the seaside rain as well as stopping salt winds from blasting the vineyards. South of the city of Bordeaux the rainfall increases, and in the small area of Sauternes the ice-cold spring waters of the River Ciron join the warmer waters of the Garonne. Every day in late summer, this causes fog to rise off the rivers, to be broken up into a hazy warmth by the sun. Here, as in few other wine-growing regions, this warm, humid atmosphere creates the 'noble rot' fungus (see p. 26) which in turn creates the world's greatest sweet wines.

So the growing season is usually long and warm. But that wouldn't be enough without the soil being right. And, luckily, it is. The most important factor is the considerable quantity of gravel banks in the Graves and Médoc vineyards. In the best villages, like Margaux and St-Julien, this gravel topsoil can be about 1 m (3 feet) deep. Gravel not only drains well, but is poor in nutrients and retains warmth from the sun. The warmth helps to

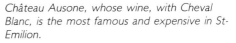

Château Ausone, whose wine, with Cheval Blanc, is the most famous and expensive in St-Emilion.

ripen the grapes while the lack of nutrients and the relative dryness force the vine roots deep into the subsoil for food. It is said that vines don't like having wet feet, but do like to be made to struggle; this gravel topsoil on a sandy/clay subsoil rich in minerals but well below the surface is ideal, and the Cabernet Sauvignon, which, of all the great grapes of the world, thrives on a good battle with its soil, is in its element. In Pomerol and St-Emilion on the north side of the Dordogne, clay is the dominant feature, sometimes mixed with gravel or limestone, sometimes packed with iron deposits. The quicker-ripening Merlot grape finds this cooler, damper soil suits it perfectly. And in the southern Graves and Sauternes, the soil is predominantly limestone and chalk, the two most suitable bases for great white wine.

GRAPE VARIETIES AND WINE STYLES
The red and white varieties have both evolved over hundreds of years into what are now regarded as classic recipes for each style. In both cases, almost all the wines are made by a blend of grapes, one variety's strength balancing another's weakness and vice-versa.
THE REDS
Cabernet Sauvignon Possibly the world's most famous grape variety, and planted in every

single country which has enough sun to ripen it. It has small, dark thick-skinned berries and ripens late, so it is ideal in the warm gravel soils of the Médoc and the Graves. The crucial factors in wine built to age well are balanced amounts of tannin, acidity, and the fruit to keep up with them. The Cabernet Sauvignon has all these in abundance. It gives dark, tannic wine with a strong initial acid attack, but when aged in new oak barrels it has a stark pure blackcurrant fruit and a cedary, cigary library-dry perfume which is stunning (new oak barrels give tannin to a wine, but at the same time the wine draws out delicious soft, vanilla and butter spicy softness from the wood). It is the dominant grape in the Haut-Médoc, but always blended to soften it.

Merlot Dominant in St-Emilion and Pomerol, and used to soften Cabernet in the Médoc and Graves. It ripens early and gives a gorgeous succulent minty, honeyed blackcurrant- or plum-flavoured wine, which explains why Pomerols and St-Emilions take less effort to enjoy than Médocs.

Cabernet Franc A lesser Cabernet, giving lighter-coloured, softer wines than the Cabernet Sauvignon, sometimes slightly earthy but also with good blackcurrant fruit. It is a blender in St-Emilion, Pomerol, Graves and Médoc, only being grown for its own virtues on the Loire to the north.

Petit Verdot A tough acid grape with a liquorice and plums taste, but not much planted.

Malbec A rather bloated, juicy grape, not much seen, though very important in Cahors where it is known as Auxerrois.

THE WHITES
Sémillon Bordeaux's great white grape, and the mainstay of all Sauternes and Barsac. It gives luscious, honeyed, lanolin-rich wines when affected by 'noble rot'. As a dry wine it can have an excellent full freshness like apple skins and cream.

Sauvignon Blanc Usually blended with the Sémillon, though sometimes nowadays it is made very dry and unblended for its sharp, green nettly freshness. However, it is best as a blender.

Muscadelle A musky, exotic grape traditionally used to create a sensation of 'false noble rot' in poor vintages and used in small quantities to add richness to the sweet wines.

These grapes are used in all the wines of Bordeaux, but with dramatically different results. Although Bordeaux does produce enormous amounts of fine wine, the majority of her production is honest but basic. In whites, less than 10 per cent of the 900,000 hl crop reaches the minimum requirements for the appellations of Sauternes, Barsac or Graves, while in reds, even grouping together all the vineyards of the Médoc, as well as St-Emilion, Pomerol and Graves, these wines make up less than 30 per cent of the total. The overall appellations Bordeaux and Bordeaux Supérieur (Supérieur simply means the wine has half a degree of alcohol more) account for over 40 per cent of the annual yield of about 2.5 million hl. The appellations gradually become more and more specific as quality increases. For instance, in the locality of Margaux village, the least suitable land would be AC Bordeaux, the fringes would be AC Haut-Médoc, and the best vineyards would be AC Margaux, even though they might all have the same postcode.

Yet, unlike Burgundy, where tiny plots of land have been designated Premier Cru (First Growth) or Grand Cru (Great Growth) and usually divided between many owners, the concept of top quality in Bordeaux is based around the 'château'. (*Château* literally means 'castle', but in Bordeaux the term is applied to the overall, single ownership of a property.) Thus a property can dwindle or expand in size, but so long as the deeds to the château – which may be a country house, a farm house, or merely a notional central point – are held, that property will retain its overall quality designation literally regardless of the vineyard land owned and worked at that time. In effect this means that a château proprietor owns a *marque* or 'brand'. Such concepts go beyond the Appellation Contrôlée laws, because, whereas in Burgundy the village appellation – e.g. Pommard or Vosne-Romanée – is the beginning of a carefully regulated appellation hierarchy which becomes more and more specific as the vineyard land improves, in Bordeaux, Château Lafite, for instance, one of the world's most expensive wines, will share the

same appellation – Pauillac – as the wine of a peasant proprietor with a few barrowloads of grapes he wheels listlessly to the co-op. It is the 'château' concept upon which quality differences have been built. Bordeaux, and in particular the Médoc, were lucky because they were primarily developed as large estates by monied interests and the nobility whereas Burgundy's current fragmentation can be traced back to the disintegration and redistribution of Church lands after the French Revolution to almost anyone who could hoe a row of vines. Thus the identity of a wine in Bordeaux immediately became associated with the owner and his château, not so much with different patches of field on a particular slope, as in Burgundy.

Bordeaux was superbly situated for developing an export trade with the critical northern European nations. Due to this importance as a trading port, her wines quickly acquired reputations and developed differentials in price so that by 1855, when a group of *courtiers*, or wine-brokers, wished to establish a classification of quality, there were a century's records of different properties, their owners and their prices for comparison. The 1855 Classification (see p. 36) has been one of wine's most absorbing bones of contention ever since, because the perception of quality had nothing to do with an officially sanctioned government hierarchy of vineyard

Castillon is chiefly famous for the battle at which England lost control of Bordeaux, but good lesser wines are made here.

quality but, rather, a haphazard grouping based on merchants' prices, which has been jealously guarded ever since by the châteaux which are 'classified', and bitterly resented by those which are not. The absurdity is shown by the fact that if I own a 'Classed Growth' (Cru Classé) Château X and buy land from the non-Classed Growth Château Y, that land immediately becomes classified because I am the possessor of a Classed Growth property deed or 'brand name'. If Château Y buys some of my Classed Growth land, it immediately loses its right to Classed Growth status because Château Y is not classified. The land is the same, the grapes are the same, but the overall property ownership, through a quirk of chance in 1855, is not a Classed Growth so, suddenly, nor is the previously Classed Growth land.

Even so, the concept of the château, centring all the production of a single wine in proper quantities, in single hands, is very much one of the chief reasons for Bordeaux's position at the epicentre of fine wine. It provides for reliability and consistency, and the development of a particular quality and style, since nowadays, on all leading properties, everything from the care of the vineyards to

BORDEAUX

the making of the wine and the maturing, bottling and sale is in the same hands.

Because red Bordeaux is a wine which, at the top level, takes a decade or more to mature, this trustworthiness has been the reason why people choose to invest in red Bordeaux and at every meeting of wine-lovers across the world, whatever the wines being drunk, the talk eventually veers to the Cabernet Sauvignon, the Merlot and the great red wines of Bordeaux.

Bordeaux, luckily, has fairly simple natural boundaries which means that each sub-region is quite self-contained. The Médoc is the whole region to the north of the city of Bordeaux on the Gironde left bank. The chief section is the Haut-Médoc, or 'Upper Médoc', which, as well as being an overall appellation, also contains the greatest wine villages of Bordeaux, each of which is dealt with separately. The appellation Médoc covers the less regarded but important northern section, traditionally called the Bas-Médoc, or 'Low Médoc'. St-Emilion and Pomerol make up the most important areas to the east of Bordeaux while Graves and Sauternes are situated close to each other south-east of the city. I have given the remaining appellations a separate chapter entitled 'Bordeaux's Other Wines'.

THE BORDEAUX CLASSIFICATION OF 1855

First Growths (Premiers Crus)
Château Lafite-Rothschild, *Pauillac*
Château Latour, *Pauillac*
Château Margaux, *Margaux*
Château Haut-Brion, *Pessac, Graves*
Château Mouton-Rothschild, *Pauillac*
(since 1973)

Second Growths (Deuxièmes Crus)
Château Rausan-Ségla, *Margaux*
Château Rauzan-Gassies, *Margaux*
Château Léoville-Las-Cases, *St-Julien*
Château Léoville-Poyferré, *St-Julien*
Château Léoville-Barton, *St-Julien*
Château Durfort-Vivens, *Margaux*
Château Lascombes, *Margaux*
Château Gruaud-Larose, *St-Julien*
Château Brane-Cantenac, *Cantenac-Margaux*
Château Pichon-Longueville-Baron, *Pauillac*
Château Pichon-Lalande, *Pauillac*
Château Ducru-Beaucaillou, *St-Julien*
Château Cos d'Estournel, *St-Estèphe*
Château Montrose, *St-Estèphe*

Third Growths (Troisièmes Crus)
Château Giscours, *Labarde-Margaux*
Château Kirwan, *Cantenac-Margaux*
Château d'Issan, *Cantenac-Margaux*
Château Lagrange, *St-Julien*
Château Langoa-Barton, *St-Julien*
Château Malescot-St-Exupéry, *Margaux*
Château Cantenac-Brown, *Cantenac-Margaux*
Château Palmer, *Cantenac-Margaux*
Château La Lagune, *Ludon-Haut Médoc*
Château Desmirail, *Margaux*
Château Calon-Ségur, *St-Estèphe*

Château Ferrière, *Margaux*
Château Marquis d'Alesme-Becker, *Margaux*
Château Boyd-Cantenac, *Cantenac-Margaux*

Fourth Growths (Quatrièmes Crus)
Château St-Pierre, *St-Julien*
Château Branaire-Ducru, *St-Julien*
Château Talbot, *St-Julien*
Château Duhart-Milon-Rothschild, *Pauillac*
Château Pouget, *Cantenac-Margaux*
Château La Tour Carnet, *St-Laurent*
Château Lafon-Rochet, *St-Estèphe*
Château Beychevelle, *St-Julien*
Château Prieuré-Lichine, *Cantenac-Margaux*
Château Marquis-de-Terme, *Margaux*

Fifth Growths (Cinquièmes Crus)
Château Pontet-Canet, *Pauillac*
Château Batailley, *Pauillac*
Château Grand-Puy-Lacoste, *Pauillac*
Château Grand-Puy-Ducasse, *Pauillac*
Château Haut-Batailley, *Pauillac*
Château Lynch-Bages, *Pauillac*
Château Lynch-Moussas, *Pauillac*
Château Dauzac, *Labarde-Margaux*
Château Mouton-Baronne-Philippe, *Pauillac*
(formerly known as Mouton d'Armaihacq)
Château du Tertre, *Arsac-Margaux*
Château Haut-Bages-Libéral, *Pauillac*
Château Pedesclaux, *Pauillac*
Château Belgrave, *St-Laurent-Haut Médoc*
Château de Camensac, *St-Laurent-Haut Médoc*
Château Cos Labory, *St-Estèphe*
Château Clerc-Milon-Rothschild, *Pauillac*
Château Croizet-Bages, *Pauillac*
Château Cantemerle, *Macau-Haut Médoc*

BORDEAUX/Médoc

THE GENERAL PICTURE

You can argue against describing the Médoc as the heart of red wine on emotional grounds, but not on the basis of hard fact. You may prefer the silky sweet perfumes of great burgundy, you may prefer the tough, black richness of Hermitage, the dry, chocolaty grandeur of Barolo or the exhausting concentrated fruit of great Napa wine, but those are all decisions of the palate and the heart. What cannot be denied is that for sheer acreage planted, volume produced and perennially exciting quality, the Médoc stands supreme in the world of red wine.

There are 10,000 hectares (25,000 acres) of vines in the Médoc, which stretches like a jutting lip to the north-west of the city of Bordeaux. It is flanked to the right by the Gironde estuary (formed by the confluence of the Garonne and Dordogne rivers), and to the left by the Bay of Biscay, which is sometimes turbulent, and prime mover in the heavy black banks of cloud which can roll sullenly in from the sea and wreck a vintage with their teeming downpour, but is far more important for the gentle moderating effect that proximity to water has on a climate, tempering high summer sun and staving off the harshness of mid-winter excess.

The Médoc is divided into two overall areas. Haut-Médoc is the southern part, closest to Bordeaux. This has all the greatest properties, and the most famous villages. Six villages have their own appellations, as follows: Margaux, St-Julien, Pauillac, St-Estèphe, Listrac and Moulis. Though the first four are famous in their own right, Listrac and Moulis, with the smallest production and least individual wines, are generally thought of as belonging to the Haut-Médoc appellation. These six total 4,850 hectares (12,125 acres).

The catch-all Haut-Médoc appellation, which applies to all wines in the less favoured pieces of land and one or two brilliant vineyards without a village to attach themselves to, is just over 2,500 hectares (6,250 acres). North of St-Estèphe, the Haut-Médoc comes to an end as the predominantly gravelly soil gives way to heavier clay soil. This is the Bas-Médoc, or 'Low Médoc', but because the growers said that 'low' sounded like a slight on the quality of their wine, they are allowed to call themselves Médoc. There is an increasing amount of good wine here, and, so far, 2,650 hectares (6,625 acres) of vineyard.

APPELLATIONS CONTRÔLÉES

Cos d'Estournel
Montrose

Médoc

Médoc

St-Estèphe ● St-Estèphe

Pauillac ● Pauillac

Lafite-Rothschild
Mouton-Rothschild
Latour
Pichon-Lalande
Lynch-Bages

St-Julien
Haut-Médoc

St-Julien

Léoville-Las-Cases
Gruaud-Larose
Ducru-Beaucaillou
Beychevelle

Listrac ● Listrac

Moulis ●

Moulis

Margaux

Margaux

Margaux
Rausan-Ségla
Lascombes
Giscours
Palmer

Château Margaux, one of the great edifices of Bordeaux, a magnificent, porticoed First Empire building down a long tree-lined avenue.

BORDEAUX/Médoc

THE IMPORTANT DETAILS

CLASSIFICATION

It just shows you should never refuse an invitation to a party simply because you can't be bothered. In 1855, Château Lanessan was regarded as one of the top wines of the Haut-Médoc, and was asked to submit samples for the World Exhibition in Paris, where a classification of Bordeaux wines was to be made. Lanessan would certainly have done very well, but the owner literally felt he had better things to do with his time. On such decisions, fortunes are made and lost. That Paris Exhibition produced the 1855 Classification, the most famous and enduring attempt ever made to give a hierarchy of quality to the wines of an area. Lanessan, overnight, was out of the Major League, and it has cost the château dear in reduced income in every single vintage since then.

There was no intention to create a timeless order of merit in 1855. The Bordeaux Chamber of Commerce simply wanted to put on a good show at the Paris Exhibition, and concentrated on the wines most highly regarded at that time – the reds of the Haut-Médoc, plus Haut-Brion in the Graves, and the whites of Sauternes. They collected up their samples, checked out the prices that the wines had sold for over the preceding vintages and put down five categories of wines, from First to Fifth Growth, based simply on price (see p. 36). They argued that the best wine would naturally achieve the highest price. In the modern world of high-pressure marketing and advertising, this would be a highly questionable premise, because even in wine, the person with the loudest voice is often presumed to make the best wine. Yet they can't have been that far wrong. At the beginning of the eighteenth century, the *London Gazette* carried advertisements for individual Bordeaux estates for the first time. Four wines were offered – Haut-Brion, Lafite, Latour and Margaux – the four First Growths (Premiers Crus) ratified in 1855, and today still regarded as supremely worthy of their position at the top of the tree.

However, there is no doubt that some fine vineyards were either excluded altogether, or given lower status than they deserved. The most famous example is Mouton-Rothschild, only classified as a Second Growth (Deuxième Cru) in 1855, but recognized throughout this century as a First Growth in quality, and finally

making it to official First Growth status in 1973. This is the only change in the classification. But there are many other properties which are now asserting their right to a more exalted position by the only expedient which counted in 1855 – they have made the effort to create a finer wine than their neighbours, and charge a higher price accordingly. *Plus ça change* . . . In today's investment-conscious world, the Fifth-Growth (Cinquième Cru) Grand Puy Lacoste or Lynch-Bages sell at the same price as a Second Growth, the Third Growth (Troisième Cru) sells at a price not far short of a First, and the Second Growths Ducru-Beaucaillou, Léoville-Las-Cases and Pichon-Lalande outprice all the other Second Growths with ease. Wines like these are establishing their own unofficial ranking on quality and price alone, the same criteria as were applied in 1855.

Almost since its creation, there has been talk of the injustices of the classification, and, particularly since 1959, when Alexis Lichine, one of Bordeaux's most influential winemakers and wine writers, actually published his revised list, with many châteaux shuffling positions, and some being demoted altogether. It all makes for excellent conversation and it's a great excuse to keep opening the bottles – just to compare, purely for academic interest, of course – but since fear of demotion is probably a greater spur than desire for promotion, little will change in black and white, though every vintage nowadays

Château Palmer is one of Bordeaux's fastest-rising stars. Its superlative wines are more expensive than any other Second or Third Growth. The lovely château has international ownership, with French, Dutch and British flags flying from the roof.

brings the exciting news that another château is emerging from the shadows and producing wine of the highest class again. Recent examples are Rausan-Ségla, Cantemerle, Léoville-Poyferré, d'Issan, Dauzac, Marquis d'Alesme . . . If we really do need a classification – and any wine buff's life would be simplified but impoverished without it – this one still does pretty well.

The only group of châteaux one does feel a little sorry for are those which were in a state of temporary decline in 1855. Several châteaux were unofficially classified before 1855 – the two most famous examples being d'Angludet and Lanessan – but were being badly run at that moment. Most of these are now making Classed Growth quality wine, but by no means all of them are achieving Classed Growth prices. Still, they do seem to make a living, and it provides claret-lovers with one of the few chances nowadays to pay less for a wine than its true worth. Unofficially these wines are called 'Crus Exceptionnels'. There are 13 of them, as follows: d'Angludet (Margaux), Bel-Air-Marquis d'Aligre (Margaux), La Couronne (Pauillac), Fonbadet (Pauillac), Gloria (St-Julien), Labégorce (Margaux), Labégorce-Zédé (Margaux), Lanessan (Haut-Médoc), Maucaillou (Moulis), de Pez (St-Estèphe), Siran (Margaux), La Tour de Mons (Margaux), Villegeorge (Haut-Médoc). Along with the Classed Growths, most of these châteaux make some of the Médoc's best wine.

The rest of the Médoc has always looked jealously on these Classed Growths, the privileged few. The other properties have had to make do with the scarcely heart-thumping communal title of 'Bourgeois' Growth for the bigger properties and 'Artisanal' or 'Peasant' Growth for the least 'worthy'. Hardly likely to inspire confidence in the product. Ever since 1920, when the Syndicat des Crus Bourgeois et Bourgeois Supérieurs du Médoc was set up the owners have been trying to improve their position. By 1977 they managed to come up with a classification of Bourgeois Growths. They named 68 Crus Bourgeois which have to be at least 6 hectares (17 acres) in size, have their own winery and make the wine at the château; 41 Crus Grands Bourgeois, which, in addition, have to use oak barrels to age their wine; and 18 Crus Grands Exceptionnels, which must age the wine in barrel, bottle it at the château, and must be situated in the Classed Growth area of the Médoc between Ludon and St-Estèphe.

This seems a plausible attempt at defining quality, but for several reasons it doesn't quite work. Firstly, none of the original 'unofficial' Exceptionnel châteaux has had anything to do with the classification, and therefore the new 'Exceptionnel' category cannot be assumed to include the best non-Classed Growth Médocs. Of these new Exceptionnels, only Chasse-Spleen (Moulis) without question, and perhaps Meyney, Phélan-Ségur, Marbuzet and Haut-Marbuzet (St-Estèphe), Cissac (Cissac) and Fourcas-Hosten (Listrac) regularly achieve an exceptional standard. Secondly, some of the best properties are doomed to miss out on Exceptionnel status because they don't lie between Ludon and St-Estèphe. The fine wines of Sociando-Mallet (St-Seurin de Cadourne), Potensac (Potensac) and La Tour de By (Bégadan) are examples. Thirdly, I have done various tastings across a wide range of all three new categories, and the differences in quality seem as vast as in the much-criticized 1855 Classification.

Inquiring into details after tasting I find everything is down to soil and quality of ownership – exactly as with the Classed Growths. If there are holes in that classification, there are holes in the 'Bourgeois' listing too, and I see no point in enshrining such a relatively arbitrary ranking. The taste of the

BORDEAUX/Médoc

THE IMPORTANT DETAILS

wine and the money demanded for it creates a quite fair enough criterion of relative merit. In passing, it is worth noting that this new 'classification' has not yet been accepted as official by the French authorities.

One other form of classification is beginning to emerge – that of the 'second wines' – in effect, a property's second-quality wine.

Single village appellations can be declassified to Haut-Médoc, which is further declassified to Bordeaux or Bordeaux Supérieur.

'Second' Wines

Increasingly, the top Médoc châteaux are taking their responsibilities to produce top wines at top prices seriously. This means that every vintage a good deal of wine is excluded from the final 'Grand Vin' blend as being either unsuitable or of too low a quality. These wines are then made, bottled and labelled under a separate label, which, however, usually bears enough tell-tale marks so that you can tell exactly whose cast-offs you're getting. From the top châteaux you get very classy cast-offs, and most of these wines are being snapped up very fast by a thirsty market. The result? Well, of course, if the quality is good, and the product relatively scarce, up goes the price, and, as in 1855, a 'ranking' develops which, again, defies legal definition, but exists regardless. Top wines to look for are:
Moulin des Carruades (Lafite-Rothschild)
Les Forts de Latour (Latour)
Réserve de la Comtesse (Pichon Lalande)
Clos du Marquis (Léoville-Las-Cases)
Le Sarget de Gruaud-Larose (Gruaud-Larose)
Le Connétable de Talbot (Talbot)
Haut Bages Avérous (Lynch-Bages)
Château Lalande Borie is a subsidiary wine made at Ducru-Beaucaillou but from a specific part of the vineyard.

ORGANIZATION/S

The dominant unit of production in the Haut-Médoc is the 'château'. In Bordelais terms this means a composite property, hopefully with some kind of house attached. These range from a few hectares' size, to the giants like Larose-Trintaudon with 160 hectares (400 acres). Ideally, a château is a compact piece of land, like La Lagune with 56 hectares (140 acres) in a solid chunk, but more frequently a château gradually acquires land over the generations and has blocks in all corners of the village, or commune. Sometimes, as with Pichon-Lalande, for instance, the château vineyards are in two different appellations (Pauillac and St-Julien). The château had to do some hard bargaining to swap land with neighbour Léoville-Las-Cases in St-Julien, but still has 13 hectares (32 acres) in St-Julien and 46 hectares (115 acres) in Pauillac. In true democratic style, it's all allowed the Pauillac appellation. The fragmentation of vineyards which all owners nowadays are trying to eradicate is well illustrated by two leading Margaux châteaux. Rausan-Ségla's 50 hectares (125 acres) at the turn of the century were in 215 plots, now gradually rationalized to a mere six. On the other side of the village, Lascombes blithely divides its 86 hectares (215 acres) between nearly 1,000.

The château is often owned by a single individual, sometimes by a shipper, and sometimes by a business consortium more or less concerned with wine. Increasingly, the wine is nowadays 'château-bottled', meaning that from the first pruning of the vine to the final despatch of the corked, labelled bottle, the wine has never been off the owner's premises, and so there is a guarantee of authenticity, which, as prices rise remorselessly, is very important. There is a diminishing trade in 'generic' Haut-Médoc with village names like Pauillac or St-Estèphe on the label. These are usually wines made from young vines, or vats of wine not thought good enough to go under a château label. Though these are very occasionally from a single château, they are usually blends made up by merchants who buy from the châteaux, or from the co-ops. These smaller wines may well be chosen by a broker who knows the localities well, and takes a commission from both sides. Fine wines are increasingly handled by commission agents who have no stock but simply a telex and a nose for a bargain. Though co-ops are less important in the Haut-Médoc than most other parts of Bordeaux, nonetheless they are not insignificant, and, particularly at Pauillac and St-Estèphe, they make large amounts of very good wine under a variety of labels.

THE GOOD YEARS

Increasingly, the differences in absolute quality between the sublime and the disastrous are being ironed out in the Médoc. Improved vineyard techniques have dramatically reduced the damage which a wet autumn can inflict through rotting grapes, thereby virtually eliminating any chance of awful results, like those of 1963/5/8. Indeed, only a dozen years ago it would not have been possible to produce the wines of 1977, 1978 and 1980, but anti-rot sprays allowed a healthy, and very late, vintage. Similarly there is a feeling that the truly astonishing quality levels of a vintage like 1961 may not be achieved again, as such wines were made with a view to maturing for at least 20 years, and nowadays, even at the top châteaux, the move is towards making fairly early-maturing wines. Yet brilliance will out, and the startlingly good 1982 vintage is showing signs of breaking all the rules and winning all the prizes.

In general, Médoc wines do take time to mature, because of the high proportion of tough Cabernet Sauvignon grapes in the blends, but when reading these vintage generalizations, remember that while a wine from the co-op might be ready to drink in three years and past it in five, a good Bourgeois château might be ready in five and going downhill in ten, while a top Classed Growth might be ready in 10 and still getting better in 20. All from the same vintage. The only really valid generalization is – you can't generalize. It used to be said that although it was easy to make poor wine in a great vintage, it was impossible to make a great wine in a poor vintage. In the modern Médoc it's more correct to say – it's difficult to make very good wine in a poor one.

1989 Incredibly hot year bringing in a super-ripe harvest at the earliest date since 1893. Although acidities are low and tannins can be high there will be some magnificently rich reds.

1988 A surprisingly cool finish to the season brought the grapes to maturity with tantalizing slowness, but the gentle pace of ripening has produced some of the most classic claret styles of the 1980s.

1987 Autumn deluges after a very hot run up to harvest spoiled chances of a greater vintage, but the best wines, from early-picked Merlot, are soft and round and very drinkable already.

1986 produced a very large crop indeed – as much as 19 per cent above the record in 1985. The wines are dark and strong, and fairly tannic. Those properties who have made a severe selection have produced long-lasting wines. Remarkably, the fourth fine vintage in five years.

1985 What a beauty. Gorgeous, rich, luscious wines looking better every time I taste them. The Merlot excelled this year and added a succulence rare in red Bordeaux and the Crus Bourgeois probably made their finest wines ever, as profits were re-invested in better wine-making. However, it was a record crop so strict selection of "best vats only" was necessary.

1984 A very difficult, rather cool year, with very little Merlot grape to soften the wine because it didn't flower properly in a cold, damp spring. The wines are dark, dry, not too charming, but reasonably interesting if you've got any money left after '83 and '82.

1983 A marvellous year, and quite unexpected. By September the vineyards were in a dreadful state, with soggy, rotted grapes struggling to remain on the vine. Then the sun came out and stayed out. Ripeness levels sped up like a gymnast off the trampoline and great

The heart of the Haut-Médoc. Château Beychevelle is on the left, with vineyards stretching right down to the Gironde River in the background.

BORDEAUX/Médoc

THE IMPORTANT DETAILS

wine was produced. It has lots of colour, is dry, firm and is going to be a long term triumph, even if it is drinkable quite early.

1982 Sensational wine – blown out of all proportion by the world's press until you taste the wines, reel back from their concentrated, gut-clutching flavours and find your vocabulary just isn't prepared for the barrage of taste sensations you're getting. Classed Growths and top Bourgeois should have made great wines, drinkable for their knockout fruit almost immediately, but better suited to cheering in the new century.

1981 This got lost in the rush for 1982. The Bordeaux trade was a bit stand-offish and haughty when we *did* want to buy them, and now there's so much else exciting doing the rounds, these have been forgotten. But they have all the marks of good claret – they're well-coloured, very dry, an austere cedary perfume already dominating some of the wines.

1980 If 1981 got lost in the rush, 1980 got obliterated. A poor vintage, people have said. Nonsense. The wines are relatively light, very fresh, with a dry, green, blackcurrant leaves fruit and often some decent vanilla-y oak – and they're absolutely delicious. Drink them in great draughts for their slightly raw but mouthwatering charms.

1979 I don't want to spend all my time disagreeing with accepted opinion, but here's another generalization I have to put the boot into. They said the 1979s were forward, light, rather soft and for quick-drinking. Well, that can apply to the lesser properties which *do* need drinking, but the leading châteaux have made big, dark, ripe wines, full of colour, fruit and tannin. They'll age for ages, and it's only a slight lack of the spark of genius which keeps them off the top line.

1978 This was the first of the 'miracle' vintages, usually characterized by incredibly late ripening under the gathering autumn storms, which went on till 1983. These are excellent wines with a most distinctive vintage characteristic of intense, juicy, raw blackcurrant fruit. They may peak quicker and fade faster than the 1979s, but at their peak they *will* have the spark of brilliance 1979 lacks.

1977 A late, cold vintage, not a lot of fun to pick the grapes, not a lot of fun to make the wine, and not a lot of fun to drink. But, if you don't mind the slightly harsh green flavours of fairly unripe fruit, a little maturity has brought out some good, lean character which may not be a barrel of laughs, but is a decent drink.

1976 Not really up to its claims. Most '76s have a rather indistinct character, the raisiny over-ripeness of the sun-scorched fruit put out of focus by the vintage-time rain diluting the grapes. There are some exceptions, but in general, they're beginning to fade – so drink them on down.

1975 Will it, won't it? Is it, isn't it? Will it what? Will it lose its tough tannic cloak for one thing (since these wines have had so much cold-tea tannin right from the start that if you swallowed some of them, you'd probably choke on their harshness and need a soothing glass of milk)? Some are going distressingly brown without budging their tannic overdose but there are some fine wines, slightly purple-dark and with enough fruit to begin to loosen the stays of their tannic chaperone. And is it another 1961, as they once said? No. Not a chance. It has none of the tumultuous rush of fruit that 1961 had to keep its tannin well-spoken. These will always be austere, but the successful wines will nonetheless be very fine, and still need keeping yet. But don't blithely rate it as a class vintage: it's far too patchy.

Older Vintages

1970 Everything went right in 1970 – loads of wine, tremendously ripe. Too much fruit, some said – not enough tannin; but such faint-hearts have no romance in their souls because these big, ripe wines have quite enough tannin to keep their gorgeous perfumy sweet fruit going for some time yet.

1966 This vintage has had its ups and downs, but it's up at the moment, very dry, still slightly reserved but the quintessence of the blackcurrant and cigar-box style of claret, with some way to go.

1961 Each Christmas, each birthday, each anniversary, keep praying for a bottle or two of 1961, because the stunning balance between cedary, lead pencil austerity, and the mint and spice and blackcurrant of great Cabernet Sauvignon fruit is something you must try. But start saving now. No, come to think of it, they're already too good to save for. Take out a second mortgage on the beach hut and blow the lot on '61.

Here are the main villages of the Haut-Médoc, starting with the most famous.

BORDEAUX/Médoc – Margaux

THE GENERAL PICTURE

This is the first of the great wine appellations on the road out from Bordeaux, where the gravel soil which marks out all the finest Médoc vineyards first spreads right across the landscape. It is the gravel which allows the vineyard to drain, and brings out the remarkable depth of flavour and perfume allied to relatively light body, which marks out the greatest clarets. Margaux is a village, dominated by its First Growth wine, **Château Margaux,** but the actual appellation spreads over five villages in all – Margaux itself with 326 hectares (815 acres), Cantenac with 376 hectares (940 acres), Arsac with 86 hectares (215 acres), Labarde with 115 hectares (287 acres) and Soussans with 143 hectares (358 acres), making 1,046 hectares (2,615 acres) in all. Margaux is thus the second biggest appellation – only just behind St-Estèphe – but it has the largest number of Classed Growths. There are two styles to the wine. The vineyards round Margaux itself are the finest, and can produce the most 'beautiful' of all clarets. The perfume of a good property like **Margaux, Palmer, d'Issan** or **Lascombes** can be ravishingly good. Certainly the flavour is based on blackcurranty fruit, but it's much, much more. It smells as though Christian Dior had sprayed the barrels with his most precious perfume essence, and then the winemakers emptied bottles of Crème de Cassis into them. That sounds a bit over the top, but, really, the perfume is astonishing. The Cantenac end of the appellation is usually a little fuller and less perfumed, but often with a marvellously plummy sweetness to mingle with the blackcurrant fruit. Margaux wines are often quite dry and hard to start with, but the wait for maturity is worth it. As well as harbouring many of the great clarets, Margaux has its share of disappointing châteaux. **Rauzan-Gassies, Durfort-Vivens, Cantenac-Brown** and **Boyd-Cantenac** are disappointing, while **Rausan-Ségla** is fighting its way out of a long, disappointing spell, as are **Marquis d'Alesme** and **Dauzac.**

THE IMPORTANT DETAILS

READING THE LABEL
Check to see whether the label says 'Propriétaire à Margaux', or one of the other four villages, since the actual Margaux wines have a more delicate, fragrant style. There are also many good non-Classed Growths in Margaux. Margaux vineyards ripen a week to ten days ahead of the rest of the Médoc, with unpredictable results. 1983 was a whopping success, 1988, 1982 and 1975 less so.

WHAT DO THEY TASTE LIKE?
From Margaux, the wines of Palmer, Lascombes, recent Rausan-Ségla and post-1980 or pre-1970 Malescot and d'Issan give astonishing, sensuous fragrance. Giscours can give remarkable wines as fine as the finest Pauillacs for sheer breed. Du Tertre, Prieuré-Lichine and Marquis d'Alesme give marvellous plum-rich gutsy wines, while from the hinterland an array of the best Bourgeois wines – d'Angludet, Siran, Labégorce-Zédé, La Tour de Mons, and others – combine silky perfume with stuffing and fruit.

ENJOYING THE WINES
The more fragrant Margaux don't want too much competition from the food. The fuller Cantenac wines are made of sterner stuff and could happily take on slightly more gamey, or spicy dishes. But, again – nothing too drastic. Some of the lesser Cantenac and outskirts wines can be drunk young and cool to some effect.

BORDEAUX/Médoc – Margaux

CONSUMER INFORMATION

AVAILABILITY

Quite a few Margaux châteaux seem to have exclusive or semi-exclusive distribution arrangements, and are rarely seen on the general market. But otherwise, there is a wider variety of wine from Margaux than from any Médoc appellation. Nearly all outlets will have several examples.

WHAT DO I GET FOR MY MONEY?

If you choose your château, there are both top-line performers charging a lot for fine wine, or some excellent undervalued outperformers. Top châteaux are **Margaux, Palmer, Giscours** and **d'Issan**. Good performers in their class are **Prieuré-Lichine, Kirwan, du Tertre, Malescot, Rausan-Ségla**. Outperformers are **d'Angludet, Siran, Labégorce-Zédé, Marquis d'Alesme-Becker, Dauzac, La Gurgue**.

Good Years Margaux wines do need a few years of maturity to reach their best – at least 5 for the lesser wines and 10 for the top ones. Recent successes: 1988, 1986, 1985, 1983, 1981, 1978.

Taste Notes Margaux wines are frequently the lightest of the major Médoc appellations, yet are often quite tough and dry when young. Given time to mature, they develop a wonderful exotic perfume and a fragrant fruit.

BORDEAUX/Médoc – St-Julien

THE GENERAL PICTURE

After the roaming excellence of the large Margaux vineyards, one turns the corner outside Soussans – and, suddenly, no vines! It's quite a shock, but also easy to explain. The gravel plateau was washed away thousands of years ago, and though it continues to troop through the woods a few kilometres to the west, it doesn't re-appear on the banks of the Gironde until St-Julien, 12 km (8 miles) further on. When it does re-appear with a slab of great Classed Growth land, just past a brook called the Chenel du Milieu, it rises and falls in an endless succession of fine vineyards till well past St-Estèphe to the north.

The old saying in the Médoc is that to make great wine you must be able to see the River Gironde from the vineyard, and this certainly applies to St-Julien. Every one of her great vineyards is on the pebbly ridge of land which sweeps down to the Gironde's sluggish waters. This is the smallest of the great appellations, with 744 hectares (1,860 acres), and there's really no village at all, the hamlets of Beychevelle and St-Julien being entirely unmemorable architecturally. But the wines are unforgettable, and often seem to be the most perfect of all clarets, mixing some of the perfume of Margaux with some of the firm body of Pauillac and adding to that a cedary, pine needles scent which is as dry as summer wind, yet as rich as a spice-ship's hold. When they are young, some of them have a creamy, honeyed softness, but this is all seductive puppy fat encasing the taut, pure brilliance of St-Julien when it is mature.

The foaming purple of the new wine contrasts brilliantly with the polished wood of the traditional vats at Château Léoville-Las-Cases.

THE IMPORTANT DETAILS

READING THE LABEL

There used to be a lot of 'St-Julien' of very dubious quality sold without the château name. One look at the map will show that this is as unlikely as it is uncalled for, since this small appellation is packed sardine-tight with great vineyard names. So only go for Château wines. The one exception to this is the excellent 'second' wine of Léoville-Barton which is labelled simply 'St-Julien'. Also, nearly all the land is classified, but the few non-classified properties are mostly worth a try. Beychevelle is the name of a château as well as the little village in the south.

WHAT DOES IT TASTE LIKE?

The most immediately classic, cedar-fragrant wines are those of Léoville and Langoa-Barton. The most succulently rich, which will be brilliantly drinkable at 10 years old but which will repay keeping are Léoville-Las-Cases, Ducru-Beaucaillou, Gruaud-Larose, Talbot and Branaire-Ducru. Beychevelle develops a distinct and fascinating plummy fragrance, while Lagrange and Léoville-Poyferré are sloughing off a long lacklustre period and heading for the cedary mainstream once again. St-Pierre is one of the deepest, shyest, yet most beautifully made wines in the Médoc. There is a little white 'Caillou Blanc' from Talbot.

ENJOYING THE WINES

Drunk young, the relative fatness of the wines means that they go very well with heavy duck or wild boar roasts and casseroles, but as they age, the food should get simpler and more refined – beef and lamb, carefully roasted, or even free range poultry, roasted and served simply in its juice.

CONSUMER INFORMATION

WHAT DO I GET FOR MY MONEY?

St-Julien wines are expensive, and although **St-Pierre** and **Lagrange** used to be undervalued, new owners have put a stop to that. In terms of value, the great wines of **Langoa-Barton**, **Léoville-Barton**, **Gruaud-Larose** and **Talbot** are never overpriced. **Léoville-Las-Cases** and **Ducru-Beaucaillou** are brilliant and more expensive than any other Second Growth wine. Outperformers would include the excellent, non-classified **Hortevie** and **Terrey-Gros-Caillou**, and the 'second' wines of **Léoville-Las-Cases**, **Gruaud-Larose**, **Talbot** and **Léoville-Barton**.

AVAILABILITY

There is never enough St-Julien, because demand is very high, but, despite the prices, the great wines feature on any wine list of quality.

CONSUMER CHECKLIST

Château Léoville-Las-Cases 1982	Q: 1 2 3 4 5 6 7 8 9 **10** P: 1 2 3 4 5 6 7 8 9 **10** V: 1 2 3 4 5 6 7 **8** 9 10	
Château St-Pierre Sevaistre 1981	Q: 1 2 3 4 5 6 7 **8** 9 10 P: 1 2 3 4 5 6 **7** 8 9 10 V: 1 2 3 4 5 6 7 8 **9** 10	

Good Years St-Juliens benefit enormously from aging. In general they are reliable in lesser vintages, and outstanding in great ones. Recent successes 1989, 1988, 1986, 1985, 1983, 1982, 1981, 1979, 1978.

Taste Notes There are two styles to St-Julien – one soft, honeyed and almost slightly sweet, the other dry, taut, perfumed in a sandalwood and cedar way, and as close to class in claret as you can get.

BORDEAUX/Médoc – Pauillac

THE GENERAL PICTURE

Pauillac is separated from St-Julien by the width of a country lane, the width of an old stone wall or the width of a stream, depending where you're standing. But that insignificant boundary line separates two very distinctive wines, for Pauillac is the focal point, the quintessence of red Bordeaux, and its principal grape, the Cabernet Sauvignon, summons all its strength in Pauillac to produce wine of great power and remarkable beauty, an unlikely combination which is achieved surprisingly frequently. Certainly the style is stark, it is often unbending, it is aggressive and uncompromising, it doesn't count on your favours, but in its arrogant way, it knows that sooner or later, you will come to recognize it for what it is – one of the great flavours of the world. The fruit seems to be all blackcurrant, sometimes thickened with blackberry or raspberry or plum, but at the same time made haunting and memorable by the twining fumes of lead pencil shavings and late evening cigars which side with the fruit. Of all clarets these last the longest and from a hard roughnecked youth they can tangle tastes almost sweet and perfumed and quite beyond words as they age. Pauillac is a big commune – with 7,000 inhabitants the Médoc's nearest thing to a town centre. Its 957 hectares (2,392 acres) not only harbour good minor châteaux, but also 18 of the Classed Growths (only Appellation Margaux has more with 21), and three of the five First Growths in **Latour**, **Lafite-Rothschild** and **Mouton-Rothschild**, and from First Growth to Bourgeois one can see the toughness turn to gentleness with age.

THE IMPORTANT DETAILS

The pebbled vineyard of Mouton-Rothschild.

READING THE LABEL
A large number of Pauillac wines are Classed Growths, but only the First Growths state their full rank on the label. Otherwise, with the exception of Pichon-Lalande and Pichon-Baron (Second Growth) and Duhart-Milon-Rothschild (Fourth), they are all Fifths. This looks like overcompensation for the predominance of First Growths, and several are of Second Growth quality (Lynch-Bages, Grand-Puy-Lacoste, Mouton-Baronne Philippe). But others like Croizet-Bages, Pédesclaux and Lynch-Moussas struggle to hold their own against the good Bourgeois.

WHAT DO THEY TASTE LIKE?
Latour is renowned for its massive structure, and rich blackcurrant fruit backed up by that lead-pencil perfume (the French call it *goût de capsule* after the smell of the lead capsule around the bottle). Mouton-Rothschild is the other way round, with the pencil shavings fragrance backed up by blackcurranty fruit, while Lafite treads a somewhat dainty path between the two. Other properties of the 'blackcurrant and pencil shavings' style are Pichon-Baron and Pichon-Lalande, Lynch-

Bages, Mouton-Baronne-Philippe and Grand-Puy-Lacoste, and the 'second' wines Les Forts de Latour and Moulin des Carruades. There is also a plummier, broader less perfumed style which is still extremely good, and epitomized by Batailley, Haut-Bages-Libéral, Grand-Puy-Ducasse, Fonbadet and Haut Bages Avérous.

ENJOYING THE WINES
The classic accompaniment for mature Pauillac is Pauillac lamb. Rare ribs of beef are good too. The Bordelais might well eat steak grilled over vinecuttings – and a young, sturdy Pauillac would be delicious with this as well as with full-flavoured pheasant and hare.

CONSUMER INFORMATION

WHAT DO I GET FOR MY MONEY?
The whole gamut. Although the First Growths are as expensive as any wine in France, and **Pichon-Lalande, Grand-Puy-Lacoste** and **Lynch-Bages** are pricier than other wines of their level, some Pauillac is relatively cheap. **Batailley, Pédesclaux, Pontet-Canet, Grand-Puy-Ducasse, Haut-Bages-Libéral** and even **Pichon-Baron** are all cheap inside their rankings as are **Fonbadet, Pibran, Haut-Bages-Avérous. Haut-Bages-Monpelou** and the co-op wine **La Rose**.

AVAILABILITY
The First Growths' availability is governed purely by your wish to spend that sort of money. Most wine-sellers have at least one, but usually far too young and very dear. The other Classed Growths are much better value. Pauillac's Bourgeois wines are rarely seen but worth seeking out.

CONSUMER CHECKLIST		
Château Latour 1975	Q: 1 2 3 4 5 6 7 8 9 **10**	
	P: 1 2 3 4 5 6 7 8 9 **10**	
	V: 1 2 3 4 5 6 7 8 **9** 10	
Château Lynch-Bages 1970	Q: 1 2 3 4 5 6 7 8 **9** 10	
	P: 1 2 3 4 5 6 7 8 9 10	
	V: 1 2 3 4 5 6 7 8 9 10	

Good Years Pauillac takes longer to mature than St-Julien and Margaux, yet reaches the highest peak. Even Bourgeois Growths often need 10 years, and Classed Growths often need 20. Recent successes: 1989, 1988, 1986, 1985, 1983, 1978, 1970, 1966.

Taste Notes Even the lighter Pauillacs should have an intense, concentrated character. They are dark, plummy and tough when young, and as they mature manage to combine a rich blackcurrant fruit with a unique 'cigar-box' or 'lead-pencil' fragrance.

BORDEAUX/Médoc – St-Estèphe
THE GENERAL PICTURE

The famous Haut-Médoc appellations end, as they began at Margaux, in a huddle of hamlets and fields loosely drawn together round a single name – that of St-Estèphe. The finest vineyards look out across a mere dip in the land to the glories of Château Lafite-Rothschild in Pauillac, but two sharp twists in the road and you feel you have cut all ties with the glitzy showbiz world of Pauillac and returned to the humdrum, labouring life.

There is much truth in this. St-Estèphe *is* the least glamorous of the main appellations, and makes the least glamorous wine. It has no First Growths and only five Classed Growths, covering 230 hectares (575 acres) out of the total of 1,105 hectares (2,760 acres). Indeed,

the area was planted later than the rest of the Haut-Médoc, and many of the top vineyards were still young and relatively unknown in 1855, when the Classification was drawn up.

But the lack of Classed Growths has another cause. The soil is different. Those great banks of gravel are becoming exhausted and diluted with clay by now. Clay is colder, drains far less well, and ripens grapes less easily; the wine is heavier, more acid, more likely to have a clumpy solidity than a swishing beauty, to satisfy with fistfuls of flavour rather than thrill and tingle with genius. That said, not only is there fine wine in St-Estèphe, but there is re-soundingly trustworthy wine too, and almost always at a fair price.

BORDEAUX/Médoc – St-Estèphe

THE IMPORTANT DETAILS

WHAT DO THEY TASTE LIKE?

The finest of the wines is without doubt Cos d'Estournel, Lafite-Rothschild's neighbour across the brook. This is fine, rich, long-lasting wine, full of fruit and body, its perfume strong rather than beguiling. Calon-Ségur and Montrose are the next most important. They seem to be trying to modernize their style, but at heart St-Estèphe is an old-fashioned village and it shows. Lafon-Rochet is a little-known rapidly improving wine, while Cos Labory is slightly uncertain of itself.

To go with these, the top Bourgeois Growths of De Pez, Haut-Marbuzet, Meyney, Les-Ormes-de-Pez and Phélan-Ségur are often of Classed Growth quality – a little sturdy, even earthy sometimes, but often dragging enough blackcurrant and vaguely tobacco-y cedar perfume from the soil to make fine claret that is only a little bit short on magic and dreams.

READING THE LABEL

Since St-Estèphe is the home of the Bourgeois growth, a large number of unfamiliar labels regularly appear. They may sport a variety of terms like Grand Vin, Grand Cru, Cru Exceptionnel, but they are still 'Bourgeois'. Apart from the growths mentioned below they are unlikely to be brilliant, but, since they're not expensive, worth trying as solid simple claret.

ENJOYING THE WINES

St-Estèphes are very adaptable. Even the finest wines like Cos d'Estournel can partner fairly highly seasoned dishes, and a St-Estèphe might well be first choice for a heavy Sunday lunch. Kidney, liver, tongue and ham are not ideal for showing wine at its best, but these wines aren't worried by them. Claret is blunted by cheese, but mild Dutch cheese is very popular in Bordeaux and St-Estèphe is the best type of claret to go with it.

CONSUMER INFORMATION

WHAT DO I GET FOR MY MONEY?

Value for money all the way. Even **Cos d'Estournel**, usually the equal of **Ducru-Beaucaillou** in quality, is relatively cheap. **Lafon-Rochet, Cos Labory, Les-Ormes-de-Pez, Meyney, Andron-Blanquet, Haut-Marbuzet**, are all wines which have a good price-quality ratio. **Le Prieuré de Meyney** is Meyney's 'second' wine, **Marbuzet** is Cos d'Estournel's. Both are good value.

AVAILABILITY

Availability is fairly good. A lot of St-Estèphe is made, and most outlets will have an example. If a particular château is not available, with the exception of top wines like Cos d'Estournel, an alternative will probably show similar style.

CONSUMER CHECKLIST												
Cos d'Estournel	Q:	1	2	3	4	5	6	7	8	9	**10**	
1982	P:	1	2	3	4	5	6	7	8	**9**	10	
	V:	1	2	3	4	5	6	7	8	9	**10**	
Château	Q:	1	2	3	4	5	6	7	**8**	9	10	
Meyney 1982	P:	1	2	3	4	5	**6**	7	8	9	10	
	V:	1	2	3	4	5	6	7	8	9	**10**	

Good Years In the ripe years St-Estèphe wines mature slowly, and need as long as Pauillac to soften. In lighter years, the wines are often drinkable quite young.

Recent successes: 1988, 1986, 1985, 1983, 1982, 1981, 1979, 1978.

Taste Notes The St-Estèphe wines rarely achieve the heights of memorable flavours which mark out the best Pauillacs, but even so they do reach a full and lightly plummy even cedary style which is deeply satisfying.

BORDEAUX/Haut-Médoc

THE GENERAL PICTURE

This means 'High Médoc', and it does sound grand, yet the reality may be rather more down to earth because this is the appellation which covers the vast southern chunk of the Médoc peninsula, and consequently, since the major villages have their own jealously guarded appellations, most of the best properties only use Haut-Médoc as an alternative appellation for their less successful vats which they wish to de-classify. Yet this rather haphazard gathering of the less glamorous villages does boast five Classed Growths, and two of the supposedly backwoods villages do have their own appellation – Listrac and Moulis. Listrac has a good deal of the gravelly soil and many vineyards are being replanted with considerable success so far.

The Haut-Médoc as a geographical definition runs from south of Margaux near Bordeaux to north of St-Estèphe and accounts, with Moulis and Listrac, for about 3,500 hectares (8,750 acres). Mostly it applies to vineyards a few kilometres back into the pine forests away from the Gironde estuary, but between Margaux and St-Julien and again for the final gravelly fling north of St-Estèphe, the vineyards do reach down to the estuary, although not sufficiently impressively to have caught the imagination of the 1855 Classification pundits. However, **La Lagune**, at Ludon, and **Cantemerle** at Macau are great wines in search of a commune appellation. They used to be described as Margaux, yet now their name and quality is so renowned they have no need to borrow another village's name. Inland from St-Julien, the village of St-Laurent has three Classed Growths (**La Tour-Carnet, Belgrave** and **Camensac**), all till recently dismissed as non-performers, yet all now showing that they have class, and the determination to prove it.

Between Margaux and St-Julien, Arcins, Lamarque and Cussac make relatively light wine, but of a good, fruity style, and north of St-Estèphe, the last gravel outcrop at St-Seurin de Cadourne, led by **Sociando-Mallet**, shows that the Haut-Médoc doesn't go down without a struggle, as a crop of quality-conscious châteaux put up their own personal rebuttal of the village's exclusion from consideration in 1855.

THE IMPORTANT DETAILS

READING THE LABEL
The great majority of Haut-Medóc wines are not Classed Growth. Since the appellation covers so much land, the address of the châteaux at the bottom should give some idea of style. Ludon has several good soft châteaux: Arcins, Cussac and Lamarque wines are mostly light and slightly earthy but with a quick-developing blackcurrant perfume, and St-Seurin de Cadourne combines full, strong fruit with a definite tannic bite. Where new oak is used to age the wine, it will have a softer more buttery flavour.

WHAT DO THEY TASTE LIKE?
The taste varies widely. La Lagune is one of the most sumptuous of all Médocs while Cantemerle is rich but very restrained and dark to start. In general, though, there is an earthiness to the Haut-Médoc taste, sometimes improved by fruit and perfume as in St-Laurent, Moulis and Listrac or between Margaux and St-Julien. It is not as reliable an appellation as the smaller village ones, simply because it *is* a catch-all, and the fine wine eccentrics are judged alongside the town toughies.

BORDEAUX/Haut-Médoc

THE IMPORTANT DETAILS

ENJOYING THE WINES

Haut-Médoc is largely all purpose, reasonably tannic and somewhat earthy. With the exception of Chasse-Spleen and Clarke, the wines are best with fairly full-flavoured food.

CONSUMER INFORMATION

WHAT DO GET FOR MY MONEY?

The Classed Growths are all fairly priced. Clarke is the only really high-priced label, but the wine is good. Chasse-Spleen makes some of the best wine in the whole of the Médoc and it isn't expensive. For cheap, simple claret, Appellation Haut-Médoc is usually less good value than Appellation Médoc.

Best wines: La Lagune, Cantemerle, Clarke, Chasse-Spleen, Fourcas-Hosten, La Tour Carnet, Cissac and Sociando-Mallet. Good outperformers: Belgrave, Camensac, Lanessan, Villegeorge, Maucaillou, Lamothe-Cissac, Malescasse, Victoria, Ramage La Batisse, La Tour du Haut Moulin, La Rose-Trintaudon, d'Agassac, Beaumont, du Castillon, Peyrabon and Brillette.

AVAILABILITY

La Lagune, Cantemerle and Chasse Spleen are quite widely available, and most outlets have examples of the châteaux above.

CONSUMER CHECKLIST		
Château La Lagune Cru Classé 1982	Q: 1 2 3 4 5 6 7 8 9 **10**	
	P: 1 2 3 4 5 6 7 **8** 9 10	
	V: 1 2 3 4 5 6 7 8 9 **10**	
Château Chasse Spleen 1985	Q: 1 2 3 4 5 6 7 **8** 9 10	
	P: 1 2 3 4 5 **6** 7 8 9 10	
	V: 1 2 3 4 5 6 7 8 **9** 10	
Ramage La Batisse 1986 Bourgeois	Q: 1 2 3 4 5 **6** 7 8 9 10	
	P: 1 2 3 4 **5** 6 7 8 9 10	
	V: 1 2 3 4 5 6 **7** 8 9 10	

Good Years Vintage variation is considerable. In general, the hotter years produce measurably finer wines, though there are some good 1987s. All but the best will mature fairly quickly.

Taste Notes The Classed Growths, along with Chasse-Spleen, Sociando-Mallet and Clarke, are often very exciting, with a full oaky softness balancing excellent fruit.

BORDEAUX/Bas-Médoc

This is the northern end of the Médoc, jutting upwards into the sea, and called the Bas, or 'Low' Médoc. The growers don't like the sense of inferiority which 'Bas' gives but the simple fact of the matter is that in a region committed to great wines based on the remarkable combination of gravel soil and Cabernet Sauvignon, this is an inferior region. The gravel outcrops are decidedly few and far between, and the soil is increasingly a rather sickly pale clay.

But that's enough criticism. What this area does better than the haughty Haut-Médoc is provide juicy, fruity, slightly earthy claret based in general on the softer Merlot grape rather than the tougher Cabernet Sauvignon, which predominates in the Haut-Médoc. Most appellation 'Médoc' wine is fairly light, not too tannic, but with a grassy, blackcurrant fruit which is a bit reminiscent of the sharp, tangy reds of the Loire, yet is softer, smoother, riper, as though someone had added a blob of glycerine to the wine at the last moment before bottling. Most of the names on the label will not be familiar, and many of the wines will come from one of the co-ops at Bégadan, Prignac, St Yzans, Queyrac or Ordonnac. The co-operative movement is very important and the standard is usually high.

The other important influence in the area has been investment in large properties by the mainstream Bordeaux trade. Initially led by Loudenne and La Tour St-Bonnet, and backed up by Castéra and La Tour Prignac, the waves are now being created by the wonderfully consistent and drinkable La Tour de By and Patache d'Aux and the remarkable Potensac. With the same ownership as Léoville-Las Cases, this marvellous oaky, blackcurranty wine shows that genius can be transferred a few miles downriver from the fat upland meadows of the Haut-Médoc.

BORDEAUX/St-Emilion

THE GENERAL PICTURE

St-Emilion is riddled with wine. Literally. This gorgeous, twisting, tumbling cluster of hill-houses on the hillside is the only genuinely picturesque town in all of Bordeaux and has been a wine centre since Roman times. Squashed into a fold in the steep slope of limestone which marks the southern edge of the St-Emilion/Pomerol plateau, the town is a hive of cellars and tunnels burrowing through the soft rock and many as full of wine now as when the Romans struck camp. It is a wonderful, untidy, timeless town, and happily the wine area to which it has given its name is one of the greatest of France. St-Emilion.

Immediately the name conjures up the acceptable face of red Bordeaux. The softer, juicier fruit, the quick-maturing, rather jammy, tastes which are delicious years before the Médoc wines have shifted an ounce of their tannin, these are the flavours which have made St-Emilion world-famous. And while neighbouring Pomerol offers similar pleasures, Pomerol is a small area, sorely tested to meet demand. St-Emilion has no such problems. With over 5,200 hectares (13,000 acres), this single area fanning out on all sides from the town is appreciably bigger than the entire Côte d'Or in Burgundy which has just under 4,040 hectares (10,100 acres). In 1979 it produced 20 per cent more wine than all the major Haut-Médoc appellations put together. The vast majority of this St-Emilion acreage is simply producing pleasant enough soft red wine which is easy to drink and sell at a fair profit. The true greatness of St-Emilion, upon whose reputation the whole enormous area feeds, is a small stretch of land around the town, with the finest vineyards clambering up and down the steep south-facing slopes, and a further stretch of gravel outcrops running like billowing waves in a sea swell up to Château L'Evangile across the Pomerol border.

GRAPE VARIETIES AND WINE STYLES

Except for a sparkling wine made primarily for tourists (of whom between 200,000 and 300,000 visit the town each year) in the cellars under the ancient Couvent des Cordeliers, St-Emilion is primarily red wine country, and the dominant grape, as in Pomerol, is the Merlot, assisted by the Cabernet Franc and Malbec and, only to a small extent, by the Cabernet Sauvignon. This is because much of the area is sand and clay, which the Cabernet Sauvignon

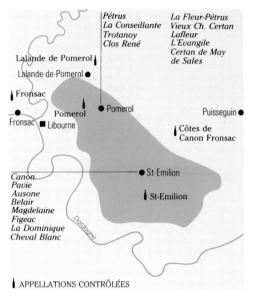

| APPELLATIONS CONTRÔLÉES

doesn't like, and on the sun-baked 'Côtes' (slopes) near the town, the limestone soil produces dull Cabernet Sauvignon but excellent Merlot.

There are three main areas. The most important, giving nearly all the great wines is the 'Côtes' St-Emilion. This area, made up primarily of limestone and clay, has its prize properties on the steep plateau edge, but is generally reckoned to run a good way back from this front line. As red wines go, they can be succulently rich, with properties like **Canon, Pavie** and **l'Arrosée** able to conjure an amazing honeyed sweetness out of their grapes, but they do also usually have a tannic toughness which makes them a lot finer than simply gooey, butter-soft reds for gulping. **Ausone, Belair, Magdelaine** and the controversial **Beauséjour-Bécot** combine honeyed ripeness with a sometimes minty, eucalyptus fragrance, and a tannic grip.

The second major area is the 'Graves' St-Emilion. The name implies gravel soil, but most of the area is sandy, with the only decent gravel nourishing the small stretch of vines at **Cheval Blanc** and **Figeac**. These are two great wines. The gravel allows Cheval Blanc to have two-thirds Cabernet Franc, and Figeac 35 per cent each Cabernet Franc and Cabernet Sauvignon. The result is powerful, blackcurranty wine, with the Merlot adding a minty perfume to the blockbusting mouthful of ripe fruit. Of the other 'Graves' properties, only **La Dominique** really excels.

BORDEAUX/St-Emilion

THE GENERAL PICTURE

Vineyards in Puisseguin-St Emilion.

Thirdly, the 'Sables' – or 'sands' – St-Emilion, are the flatter, sandier areas, usually down near the River Dordogne. It is these wines, pale red, quickly turning to orange but with a brief, delicious burst of soft fruit, butter and honey which have given St-Emilion its name for light, easy wine. **Monbousquet** is the finest property; the wine is soft, plummy but with something almost meaty to make it more exciting. Apart from these more or less defined areas, there is a large hinterland to the north-east and south-east of the town.

Much of it has the appellation St-Emilion, but there are four so-called satellites which can hyphenate their names to St-Emilion. These are Lussac, Montagne, Puisseguin and St-Georges. There are over 2,800 hectares (7,000 acres) of these vineyards! In general, the wines are fairly strong and plummy, without being terribly exciting. Wines like **Château St-Georges** in St-Georges-St-Emilion are the exception.

THE IMPORTANT DETAILS

CLASSIFICATION
Up till 1984, the St-Emilion classification was a bit of a joke. It was set up in 1954, and provided St-Emilion with four appellations – St-Emilion Premier Cru Classé subdivided into two 'A' châteaux and ten 'B' châteaux; St-Emilion Grand Cru Classé, which numbered 72 properties; St-Emilion Grand Cru, for which a château could apply each year by submitting a sample of wine for testing: this usually amounted to between 150 and 200 or more châteaux; and finally St-Emilion. This completely debased the idea that 'Grand Cru' or 'Great Growth' was a term applied to a special patch of land of historical wine-growing excellence, and meant that as many as one-third of the 1,000 proprietors of the whole area might be Grand Cru! This charade finally came to an end in 1984 when the four

appellations were reduced to two – St-Emilion Grand Cru, comprising at most 90 top properties, and plain St-Emilion. The two descriptions Premier Grand Cru and Grand Cru Classé cease to be appellations and become subdivisions of Grand Cru, which are re-examined every year and for which properties must apply, subject to various requirements including a lower yield than St-Emilion, compulsory château bottling, a commitment not to change the shape of the property in the ensuing ten years (a condition with which many famous Médoc Classed Growths would be unable to comply), and an undertaking that at least 50 per cent of the wine comes from vines 12 years old or more. (In the 1984 re-examination, one Premier Grand Cru was demoted, ten Grands Crus Classés were demoted, and one Grand Cru was promoted to Grand Cru Classé.) There is also an Association de Propriétaires de Grands Crus Classés de St-Emilion which comprises 27 of the châteaux just below the very top rank who are committed to improving their image and quality through voluntary restriction of yields in the vineyards, compulsory aging in oak barrels and similar assurances of a quality-first approach. It is about time the 'Grands Crus' of St-Emilion became a little more demanding in their specifications, and these encouraging moves look to be bearing fruit. St-Emilion wines may be de-classified to Bordeaux or Bordeaux Supérieur.

ORGANIZATION/S
The estates are not in general all that large in St-Emilion. About 1,000 growers share the 5,200 hectares (13,000 acres), and even the major Classed Growths are small by Médoc standards. The lesser properties frequently sell their produce to the local Libourne merchants in bulk, or to one of the five co-ops. The central one, at St-Emilion, is the second biggest in Bordeaux, and vinifies various single properties as well as supplying much of the Libourne and Bordeaux trade in bulk.

READING THE LABEL
Judging the standard of a St-Emilion is complicated by the wide-ranging Grand Cru system (see above). However, from the 1984 vintage the term Grand Cru on the label should confirm a definite quality level. We shall see. Several good properties are owned by Libourne merchants and the wine is bottled there rather than at the château.

WHAT DO THEY TASTE LIKE?
Soft, round, rather generous wines are the norm in St-Emilion. They don't always have the minerally backbone of Pomerol, and the sweetness is usually less plummy, and rather more reminiscent of butter, toffee or sometimes raisins. The Great Growths add a minty, blackcurrant depth to this which confirms them as some of Bordeaux's finest wines.

THE GOOD YEARS
The following notes are applicable to both St-Emilion and its immediate neighbour, Pomerol. The vintages in St-Emilion and Pomerol do not always correspond to those of the Médoc in style or quality, due to differing soils, differing balances of grape varieties and a generally earlier vintage date. The wines, particularly of St-Emilion, easily achieve a higher natural alcohol than Médoc wines. Despite the lower tannin and acid levels, this allows them to mature as effectively, while the mellow Merlot influence makes them drinkable much younger. Lesser St-Emilions and Pomerols are often ready at only three to four years old, and even the great wines are usually delicious in six to seven years.

1989 Tremendous early torrid vintage producing exciting rich reds when the tannins and acids are also in balance.

1988 Great potential spoilt in some cases by overproduction. Even so, some superb wines of perfect balance.

1987 The harvest was largely in when the rains came and wines are soft and forward, already very attractive to drink.

1986 The ripeness levels were in some cases even higher than the remarkably successful 1985s, and, even if the 1986s are not quite so deep coloured and concentrated, they are still very fine, although some properties have spoilt it by making too much wine.

THE IMPORTANT DETAILS

1985 The wines are even better here than in the Médoc with the soaring richness of the super-ripe Merlot grape abundantly in evidence. Again there was too much wine, so strict selection was necessary, but when it was achieved, many 1985 Pomerols and St-Emilions are, remarkably, even better than the 1982s.

1983 A fine vintage, but slightly less good than in the Médoc since the Merlot grape suffered from rot. Some of the wines are slightly lean, but this means they should age well.

1982 Brilliant. One of the greatest years for St-Emilion and Pomerol this century. The Merlot grape shot to unprecedented ripeness levels, produced sumptuous, bursting flavours which will age very well but give a memorable blast of flavour right from the start.

1981 Rather swept aside by the blockbusting 1982s, which is unfair, because the 1981s, though less ripe and concentrated, have produced delicious, slightly austere wines, more akin to the Médoc in style, and good for aging.

1980 In general, less successful than the Médoc, since many St-Emilions in particular are too green, but Cheval Blanc, La Dominique and Magdelaine are fine wines, while many Pomerols are also good.

1979 This is a big soft vintage, initially hailed as

Right *The Merlot grape provides much of the softness and richness in red Bordeaux.*

superior to 1978 because of the ripeness of the Merlot. The gap is closing, but these are lovely wines, fragrant, soft, and slightly sweet.

1978 Rather hard and lean at first, these wines have come out of their shell and provide some very fine fairly dry drinking. Figeac is one of the most perfect wines of the year.

1976 Hailed as a great Pomerol and St-Emilion vintage because of the hot summer, the wines in general have a rather over-rich raisiny sweetness, but some châteaux, like Ausone in St-Emilion, and Petit-Village and Pétrus in Pomerol, have produced fine wines.

1975 This is less hard and exacting than in the Médoc but even so the wines are mostly fairly tough still. However, the best wines, in particular properties like La Grave Trigant de Boisset and Petit-Village, are beginning to soften as they lose hold of their youthful fruit.

1970 A great year. Wonderful rich, balanced wines, delicious now, but still with time to go.

ENJOYING THE WINES
The richness and softness of many of the wines gives them a similar role to Pomerol in being drunk with pâtes, cheeses and spicy foods and many of the Burgundian specialities go well with St. Emilion.

CONSUMER INFORMATION

WHAT DO I GET FOR MY MONEY?
There are relatively few bargains in St-Emilion since the well-known châteaux are much in demand, the outperforming lesser properties don't remain unknown for long, and the basic generic wine is always fairly highly valued. However, here are some outperformers you might catch if you hurry. L'Arrosée, Larmande, La Dominique, Balestard La Tonnelle, Canon La Gaffelière, Fombrauge, Dassault, Leydet-Figeac, La Tour-Figeac, Fonplégade, Fonroque, Monbousquet, St-Georges.

AVAILABILITY
There is always a St-Emilion of some sort available in a retail outlet, but only rarely will it be one of the top properties, since their output is small, and much of it is bought direct in France.

CONSUMER CHECKLIST		
Château Figeac 1982	Q: 1 2 3 4 5 6 7 8 **9** 10	
	P: 1 2 3 4 5 6 7 8 **9** 10	
	V: 1 2 3 4 5 6 7 **8** 9 10	
Château Fombrauge 1985	Q: 1 2 3 4 5 6 **7** 8 9 10	
	P: 1 2 3 4 5 **6** 7 8 9 10	
	V: 1 2 3 4 5 6 7 **8** 9 10	

Good Years St-Emilions mature more quickly than Médocs because of the far higher proportion of Merlot in the vineyard, but they can last at least as well as all but the greatest Pauillacs. Off vintages can sometimes be a little raw. Recent successes: 1989, 1988, 1986, 1985, 1983, 1982, 1979, 1978.

Taste Notes Frequently there is an almost sweet flavour to St-Emilions, a gentle, buttery, even honeyed softness because of the predominance of Merlot.

BORDEAUX/Pomerol

THE GENERAL PICTURE

It's no use looking on any ordinary map for the village of Pomerol, because there isn't one. No town, no village, and, as far as one can tell from the map, no natural boundaries either, because Pomerol is a block of fields on the north side of the Dordogne River 40 km (25 miles) east of Bordeaux which, not that long ago, no-one had ever heard of. On the surface it still seems to be a featureless, flattish plateau of rather heavy dull vineyard land, just past the small wine-town of Libourne, with none of the slopes and escarpments which are supposed to presage great wine. Pomerol *does* have natural boundaries, but they lie underneath the surface of the soil, and in certain places these natural features combine with human skill and commitment to produce what are possibly some of the greatest red wines in the world. The subterranean boundaries are dictated by the limits of her most unusual subsoil, of dark packed clay, shot through with a remarkably high iron content.

For a couple of hundred hectares in the centre of the area the land rises slightly, as though the dark, packed clay subsoil was pushing its way to the surface. It very nearly does. In the finest vineyards this subsoil is only just over half a metre down. The Merlot grape feeds on this heavy soil like a pirate on rum and brave braggart wines result.

GRAPE VARIETIES AND WINE STYLES

Pomerol is small but absolutely solid with vines. Out of 700 hectares (1,750 acres) of land within the appellation, nearly 650 hectares (1,625 acres) are planted with vines, which doesn't leave a lot of room for back gardens and cabbage patches. The dominant grape here is the Merlot, even more than in St-Emilion, Pomerol's neighbour. **Château Pétrus**, which in some vintages makes a finer red wine than any other vineyard in the world – there is no other vineyard for which I would make such a claim – is 95 per cent Merlot on a soil of virtually pure clay and iron.

The next most important grape is the Cabernet Franc, and occasionally the usually dismissed Malbec, but many vineyards have none at all of Bordeaux's most famous grape, the Cabernet Sauvignon. Clay soil is cool and damp and the Cabernet Sauvignon, which ripens much later than the Merlot, often doesn't ripen at all in clay.

There are no white grapes. The area divides into three approximate styles, according to soil. To the west the soil is sandier, and the wines are lighter, but still have a brilliant sweetness, almost sinfully delicious even when very young. Wines like **Clos René, de Sales** and **l'Enclos** epitomize this style. Running across the southern part of the region is a much more gravelly soil which links almost imperceptibly with St-Emilion. The resulting wines are drier, tougher when young, which is *not* a normal Pomerol attribute, and rarely get quite the juicy, plummy richness of the typical Pomerol. However, they have some of the cedary austerity of the Médoc which is otherwise lacking in Pomerol. The gravel also means a lower proportion of Merlot is grown. Good examples are **Petit-Village, La Conseillante** and **Beauregard**.

Between these two areas is the heart of Pomerol where a succession of small properties make sensational wine on their iron-clay soil. There is no question that there is a mineral taste to Pomerol from this iron, and it adds an extra dimension to the rich, ripe plump fruit, the wonderful buttery sweetness of new oak barrel aging, and the silky, perfumy 'well fed prelate' feel of great Pomerol. The best wines are so sumptuous you can't decide whether to concentrate on the experience or laugh out loud with pleasure. **Pétrus** is the greatest, followed at a respectful distance by a host of others including **Trotanoy, La Fleur-Pétrus, Vieux Château Certan, Lafleur, La Grave Trigant de Boisset** now renamed **La Grave à Pomerol, Latour à Pomerol, Le Pin, L'Evangile** and a gaggle of others nearly as good. There is also a 'subsidiary' area, Lalande de Pomerol, to the north. It isn't cheap but is generally good, soft plummy wine.

BORDEAUX/Pomerol

THE IMPORTANT DETAILS

CLASSIFICATION

There is no classification in Pomerol. This may seem remarkable for an area with so many great wines, but Pomerol's fame is astonishingly recent, post World War Two, which must give heart to areas like Fronsac which are tantalizingly close to breaking into the big time. A Professor Roger did classify 63 châteaux in 1960, but the only universally accepted decision is that Pétrus is out on its own. There follow a good dozen very fine châteaux, led by Trotanoy, La Fleur Pétrus and Vieux Château Certan, and perhaps 40 others which usually make wine up to Médoc Classed Growth standard.

Pomerol wines may be de-classified to Bordeaux or Bordeaux Supérieur.

ORGANIZATION/S

There are 180 growers in Pomerol with one-third of them owning less than $1\frac{1}{2}$ hectares ($3\frac{3}{4}$ acres). There are only a couple of properties over 40 hectares (100 acres) and a few châteaux are big enough to have 'second' wine labels. Despite this fragmentation, there is no co-operative. The smaller growers sell their grapes or wine to merchants in Libourne, two of whom are called Moueix. A. Moueix owns several properties; however it is J-P. Moueix, led by the deeply quality-committed Christian Moueix, who matter most. They are the largest proprietors in Pomerol, owning and managing many of its greatest vineyards, including Pétrus, and are chiefly responsible for strides towards greatness the area as a whole has so recently taken. Other important merchants are Audy, Janoueix, Querre and d'Arfeuille.

READING THE LABEL

The labels of Pomerol often have a slightly old world' look, as though they're not yet affected by the world of high finance and marketing men. Several of them use titles like Grand Cru and list medals of bygone days. A more reliable pointer is to follow any château with J-P. or C. Moueix on the label.

WHAT DO THEY TASTE LIKE?

Often described as a cross between the Médoc and St-Emilion, but the description is not exact. Few of them have the lean clear definition of top Médocs, yet most have a deeper, rounder flavour than St-Emilion, the plummy fruit going as dark as prunes in great years, but with the mineral backbone of toughness preserving it for a very long time.

THE GOOD YEARS

The vintages are treated in detail under the St-Emilion section, since they are usually similarly affected by the year's climatic conditions. Pomerols are easy to drink when they are only four to five years old, due to the plummy richness of their fruit. However, they have excellent keeping qualities and at the top level can last better than most Médocs due to their concentration of finely balanced fruit.

More specific information on good years is given in the section on St-Emilion.

ENJOYING THE WINES

These wines have such a rounded rich fruit to them, that, of all clarets, they are some of the easiest to enjoy without food. At the very top level of Pétrus, Trotanoy, etc., there are few foods which would not be overwhelmed by their sheer bravura intensity. However, this 'plummy' roundness can also be turned to good account. The spicier game dishes, whether strongly herbed terrines and pâtés, or birds such as pheasant, pigeon and duck, blend beautifully with these wines, and the raw Bayonne ham from south of Bordeaux is much better with Pomerol than with most wines. Big casseroles using a lot of red wine in their preparation will also benefit from the sweet-fruit edge of Pomerol.

95 per cent of the vines planted at Château Pétrus are of the Merlot grape. Pétrus is noted for the high proportion of clay in its soil.

CONSUMER INFORMATION

WHAT DO I GET FOR MY MONEY?

There is almost no such thing as a cheap Pomerol: the area's wines are in far too heavy demand. Yet, thankfully, the standard of wine-making here is tremendously high, so there is little chance of poor value either. The famous châteaux at inflated prices and the unknown ones at marginally extravagant prices both, in the end, deliver the goods.

AVAILABILITY

Not good. There isn't a lot of wine and there are a huge number of thirsty enthusiasts. Specialist wine outlets will be able to secure the top wines – but at a price. The lesser wines are not often seen, the chief reason being a very high level of direct sales to private individuals particularly in northern France and the Low Countries.

CONSUMER CHECKLIST		
La Fleur Pétrus 1985	Q:	1 2 3 4 5 6 7 8 **9** 10
	P:	1 2 3 4 5 6 7 8 **9** 10
	V:	1 2 3 4 5 6 7 **8** 9 10
Clos René 1985	Q:	1 2 3 4 5 6 7 **8** 9 10
	P:	1 2 3 4 5 **6** 7 8 9 10
	V:	1 2 3 4 5 6 7 8 9 **10**

Good Years These usually resemble the good years in St-Emilion. They are also easy to drink young, but can age well. Lesser vintages are often successful in Pomerol. Recent successes: 1989, 1988, 1986, 1985, 1983, 1982, 1981, 1979.

Taste Notes Although there is a lot of resemblance between St-Emilion and Pomerol, the latter have a big plummy richness backed up by a positively mineral backbone which is tremendously satisfying.

BORDEAUX/Graves

THE GENERAL PICTURE

Harvesting at Château Carbonnieux, one of the bigger and better known Graves properties.

To those of us brought up on the idea that most Graves is white, flabby, sulphurous, and likely to put us off our food, it is a little difficult to grasp, firstly, that most Graves wines, and nearly all the best wine, is now red, and secondly that for the 300 years between 1152 and 1453 during which Bordeaux owed allegiance to the English Crown, it was red Graves wine, and red Graves wine alone, which the English came to love as claret. The Graves area is the original fine wine area of Bordeaux. The Médoc, which now bristles with superstars, was merely swamp. Indeed, the first Bordeaux wine ever to be recorded under its own name was the top Graves wine – Haut-Brion – which the diarist Samuel Pepys went wild about in 1663. The reason is that the area surrounds the town of Bordeaux and in days when travel was tricky, the nearer to the city that you could grow the wine, the better. But Bordeaux was rapidly expanding and most of Graves's original vineyards are now lost under the urban jungle of tarmac and brick, but Haut-Brion still survives, hemmed in on all sides by housing estates, and La Mission Haut-Brion is still there sliced in two by the main Paris to Madrid railway line. These have only been able to fend off the property-developers because of the very high price their wine fetches, and the owner of La Mission Haut-Brion is rather fond of his urban surroundings, since he reckons that the houses raise the average temperature of his vineyard by nearly 2° and allow him to call up great flocks of grape-pickers at the last possible moment as the autumn suns turn gold then cool. Nowadays the Graves region stretches mostly to the south of Bordeaux, some 56 km (35 miles), but it still encircles the whole city, and technically starts north of the city at Le Taillan, the boundary with the Médoc. There are 43 communes or villages included in the area, of which 37 are more or less active in wine-growing, but only six are regular producers of top-quality wine. These are all in the north of the region (though south of Bordeaux), and are as follows: Pessac, Talence, Villenave d'Ornon, Léognan, Cadaujac and Martillac. Though the Graves is a large region, it is nothing like as committed to vineyards as the Médoc, and the whole region only has about 3,000 hectares (7,500 acres) of vines, much of the remainder being forest and mixed farmland. The movement from white to red is still continuing, despite the improvement in white wine-making techniques. In late 1987 a new appellation was created in the north and better end of Graves. Called Pessac-Léognan, it distinguishes Ch. Haut-Brion and 54 other estates from the rest of the large Graves region. 1986 was the first vintage to use the new name.

GRAPE VARIETIES AND WINE STYLES
The red grape varieties are the same as for the Médoc – Cabernet Sauvignon, Cabernet Franc, Merlot, Malbec and Petit Verdot. There is a little less emphasis on Cabernet Sauvignon, and a slightly bigger Merlot presence which makes for slightly softer styles of wine. Indeed, the Graves reds really do run the whole gamut of claret flavours, and are less easy to generalize about than any of the other main regions. This is partly because

while the properties near Bordeaux mostly have good gravelly (*Graves* means 'gravel') soil, there is also a good deal of clay about, and, further south, a fair amount of sand too.

However, the more important influence is the attitude of the proprietor in his choice of grape varieties and method of vinification. The description 'earthy' which is often applied is a fair one for many of the wines, because there is an indistinct, dry backbone to the fruit which stops them being razor-sharp in their flavour-definitions as the great Médocs often are. Yet they do often have the blackcurrant and cedar flavours of the Médoc, as well as having a little of the full, plummy roundness of Pomerol. For blind winetasters they are an endless tease, and frequently the rule followed is – if it seems like Médoc, but not quite, and yet seems like Pomerol, but not quite – plump for Graves.

The dry whites are made from Sémillon and Sauvignon. There has been a rush to uproot Sémillon and replant with the more fashionable Sauvignon, but, with a couple of exceptions like Malartic-Lagravière and Couhins-Lurton, Sauvignon doesn't perform at its best by itself in Bordeaux, often giving a rather muddy, tough wine. Sémillon, on the other hand, is well suited to the area, and gives a big, round wine, slightly creamy but with a lovely aroma of fresh apples which is very exciting. Ideally, the two should be blended, with Sémillon the dominant variety. White Graves is still often a dull wine, but if it is fermented at a low temperature, and if new oak barrels are used, sometimes for the actual fermentation (as at Couhins–Lurton), but crucially for a 6- to 12-month aging period, the result is a wonderful, soft, nutty dry white, often going honeyed and smoky as it ages to a maturity of perhaps 7 to 15 years as one of France's great white wines.

Some semi-sweet and sweet whites are made under the Grave Supérieures appellation, but, with the exception of a rare wine like Clos St-Georges, the quality is unlikely to be thrilling.

THE IMPORTANT DETAILS

CLASSIFICATION

The top Graves château, Haut-Brion, was the only non-Médoc red wine classified in the famous 1855 Classification. The rest of the Graves is classified according to a 1959 ministerial decree. The châteaux are in alphabetical order, and are marked R or W according to whether they were honoured for red, or white, or both. The Graves is the only place in Bordeaux where red and white are equally highly regarded.

Bouscaut **R & W**
Haut-Bailly **R**
Domaine de Chevalier **R & W**
Carbonnieux **R & W**
Couhins **W**
de Fieuzal **R**
Haut-Brion **R & W**
Malartic-Lagravière **R & W**
La Mission-Haut-Brion **R**
Olivier **R & W**
La Tour-Martillac **R & W**
Laville-Haut-Brion **W**
Smith-Haut-Lafitte **R**
La Tour Haut-Brion **R**
Pape-Clément **R**

There is also a 'Union des Grands Crus' which is an organization for promoting Bordeaux's Classed Growths, but three other Graves châteaux do belong – Ch. Rahoul, Ferrande and Larrivet-Haut-Brion.

Graves wines may be de-classified to Bordeaux Supérieur or Bordeaux.

ORGANIZATION/S

There are relatively few famous properties in the Graves, and the majority of wine has traditionally been handled fairly anonymously by the Bordeaux trade. At one time every wine list would sport an indeterminate 'Graves' in the white wine section, and this would be a blend made up by Bordeaux merchants to a low price specification. However, Graves has now become a relatively expensive appellation, and there are fewer shippers' blends about. Only local experts like Yvon Mau and Pierre Coste make a particular point of them, and for red and white their 'house blends' can be outstanding. In general, the wine which is not sold for merchants' blends is château-bottled, though some merchants like Coste, Eschenauer and Kressmann

THE IMPORTANT DETAILS

who have close contacts in the area, will bottle single property wine at their own cellars.

READING THE LABEL

With relatively few famous wines, it is worth studying the label, because if possible, when the wine is from a single property, it should come from one of the six villages where the overall quality is highest (see p. 58). However, Portets, with Chx. Rahoul, La Vieille France, La Tour-Bicheau and Millet, and St-Pierre-de-Mons near the important town of Langon, with Ch. Magence, can produce good wines of either colour. Fieuzal and Smith-Haut-Lafitte, though unclassified for white, nonetheless produce good white wine. Check for château or merchant bottling. In generic wines, the best are from Coste and Mau. Graves Supérieures are usually fairly sweet.

WHAT DO THEY TASTE LIKE?

From a region whose name means 'gravel' it is easy to pretend to detect something earthy or stony in the flavours, yet the reds do often have a rather attractive earthiness, and the whites, if not enriched by the use of new oak barrels, often have a very stony dryness. The top reds divide fairly evenly between those with a sweet juicy fruit and lots of buttery oak, and the more reserved, aquiline styles of cedary fragrance and dry fruit. Below the top wines, the reds don't often have a great deal of colour but they usually do have a fairly chunky full flavour which is enjoyable rather than memorable. The top whites, with the vanilla of the new oak barrels adding perfume and depth do combine quite brilliantly the apple freshness of the fruit and the sweetness of the oak, becoming honeyed and almost oily as they age. Lesser whites are best when marked by the strong sharp green tastes of modern ice-cool fermentation methods.

THE GOOD YEARS

In general, the Médoc and Graves produce very similar vintage patterns, and therefore the Médoc vintages on p. 41 can also be applied to the Graves. This is because the weather variations seem to coincide with whether or not you are north or south of the Gironde, and both the Médoc and the Graves are on the southerly left side. One thing which does affect the Graves more than the Médoc is the higher incidence of spring frosts because of the amount of woodland there is, but this is balanced by a slightly earlier ripening date because of the more southerly latitude. Most so-called 'poor' years can produce some fairly good wines in the Graves, while the hottest years, like 1989 and 1982 may produce slightly baked wines. Red Graves are ready to drink earlier than Médocs, but when well made, will last as long. Some châteaux are experimenting with producing very quick-maturing reds with some success.

Except for the fabled few, most white Graves is at its best two to three years after vintage. The fabled few will age as well as their red counterparts.

ENJOYING THE WINES

Red Graves are extremely adaptable food wines, able to partner the classic 'Médoc wine' hams, beef and freshly-killed game, as well as the richer dishes associated with Pomerol and St-Emilion of well-hung game, casseroles and the less pungent cheeses. And they are particularly suited to the Bordeaux speciality – lampreys in red wine sauce.

White Graves of the fresh variety have enough body for the local fish and seafood, as well as being good by themselves. Great white Graves almost need drinking by themselves or with simply grilled fish to get the full beauty of the flavour.

CONSUMER INFORMATION

WHAT DO I GET FOR MY MONEY?

The top white Graves are very expensive, as are the top six or seven reds, but the quality is uniformly high. The middle rank of white Graves is often rather dull, and only good value if vinified in a modern way to preserve all the fruit of the grape. Red Graves from lesser châteaux or made under a merchant's label is usually pretty good and fairly cheap.

For the reds, top performers are: **Château Haut-Brion** (brilliant, fragrant, almost creamy red of the highest class); **Domaine de Chevalier** (the most elegant and cedary of all the Graves, brilliant, unfleshy classic claret); **Pape-Clément** (also dry and light in the Médoc style as it ages); **Haut-Bailly** (a sweeter, juicier style); **La Mission-Haut-Brion** (massive, aggressive, unrelentingly imposing claret). Outperformers are: **Malartic-Lagravière** (very dry, austere even, but a beautifully balanced long-distance runner); **Fieuzal** (rich, exotic fruit and great personality); **La Tour-Martillac** (taut, restrained, eventually delicious cedary wine).

For the whites, top performers are: **Château Haut-Brion**, **Domaine de Chevalier** and **Château Laville-Haut-Brion** (three of the greatest dry white wines of France, honeyed, slightly resinous, nutty and bursting with old-fashioned class); **Château Couhins-Lurton**, **Château Malartic-Lagravière** and **Château Rahoul** (very attractive oaky, soft whites); and **Fieuzal**, **Carbonnieux**, **Montalivet** and **La Louvière** (fresh, bright, fruity wines).

AVAILABILITY

Except for the ubiquitous white 'Graves' which is pretty widely available, but only good from a specialist *négociant* like Coste, availability isn't brilliant. The top estates' wines are much sought-after, and the amount of wine otherwise marketed under a single-estate name is not vast and is by no means generally available.

BORDEAUX/Sauternes

THE GENERAL PICTURE

Although I can state without fear of contradiction that the Sauternes and Barsac areas 40 km (25 miles) south-east of Bordeaux produce the greatest sweet wines of France, and frequently of the world, this pre-eminence is a comparatively recent thing, and is pre-dated by Germany in particular by a considerable period of time. Although the Sauternes region had made some fairly hefty Muscat wines in the seventeenth century in an attempt to rival Spain's rich Moscatels, it wasn't until 1836 that a German winegrower called Focke noticed that the autumn weather was warm and humid, and that the fogs steamed up off the River Ciron much as they did in his homeland of the Rhine, where he made sweet wine by the 'noble rot' method. He applied his Rhine methods to his Château La Tour Blanche. This involved leaving the grapes on the vine well into the autumn when this mixture of late summer warmth and steamy morning damp infected the grapes with a fungus called 'noble rot'. This is a close relation to 'grey rot', which turns grapes to a soggy, stagnant pulp, but 'noble rot', instead of simply pummelling the ripening grapes into a squashy sodden submission, is rather more selective. It sits on the grape skins and feeds on the water in the grapes, leaving the sugar and acid comparatively untouched, so that after a few days of this parasitical existence,

These horrid shrivelled berries are the basis of great Sauternes; they are infected with 'noble rot' which concentrates the sugar.

BORDEAUX/Sauternes

THE GENERAL PICTURE

Autumn at Château Climens, a few kilometres from the town of Barsac.

the grape is shrivelled, ugly, but full of an intensely sweet 'essence' of grape juice, increasing in concentration day by day as more and more water is sucked out.

This is the *only* way it is possible to make great sweet wine without the addition of brandy to half-fermented grape juice (as in port) because the natural acidity in the grape remains high while the sugar and glycerine become more concentrated inside the grape. Without acidity, sweetness is gross and exhausting. Just think. If you take a glass of water and add spoon after spoon of sugar to it, the result is sickly and undrinkable. But if you squeeze a lime or a lemon into it, suddenly it becomes refreshing as well as rich. However, this natural 'noble rot' phenomenon is very tricky to harness and, in many vintages, the crucial combination of heat and humidity just doesn't occur. Sometimes the sun doesn't shine, sometimes it even shines too much, and frequently autumn rains arrive just too soon for the pickers to gather all the grapes.

Also, the grapes may not 'rot' at a uniform rate, so teams of pickers have to comb the vineyard time and again only picking off the single berries which are properly shrivelled, or, when the owner cannot afford this expense, at least the bunches which are most affected. The top few properties may do this

between five and ten times, depending on the vintage. These grapes are incredibly high in sugar content, often reaching 20° of potential alcohol. However, the yeasts which cause fermentation can only operate up to about 13–14° of alcohol, at which stage the alcohol strength puts them to sleep. So any sugar left unconsumed by the yeasts is straight sweetness, balanced by natural acidity. From grapes picked at 20° of potential alcohol, this will leave between 80 and 100 g of sugar per litre. Yet this tortuous, slow creative process has taken its toll. The yield is about one-sixth of the normal yield a vineyard could produce, and it has probably taken six times as much care and expense to gather the grapes and make the wine. Do the producers get six times the price? Hardly ever.

GRAPE VARIETIES AND WINE STYLES
Sauternes is the overall appellation for a group of five villages in the south of the Graves region which comprise just under 2,020 hectares (5,000 acres) of vineyards. The villages are Sauternes, Bommes, Fargues, Preignac and Barsac. Barsac wines may use their own village name if they wish. The soil at Preignac and Barsac is quite chalky and the vineyards are flat, while the other villages, a little further south, are hillier, and the soil is a mix of sand, gravel, clay and limestone. In general this difference produces lighter wines in Barsac and richer, more succulent ones in Sauternes, Bommes and Fargues. The most important grape is the

Sémillon. This is very susceptible to 'noble rot' and imparts a rich, lanolin feel to the wine, while the Sauvignon adds acidity and freshness. There is a little Muscadelle, quite useful for its heady perfume.

What these grapes combine to produce is a wine quite surprisingly lacking in any ripe fruit taste, yet brilliantly rich and glyceriny, coating the mouth with a sticky lanolin fatness, and combining honey and cream and nuts when young with something oily and penetrating as it ages and the sweetness begins to have an intensity of 'volatile' flavours rather like a peach, bruised and browned in the sun. The colour goes gold with age to a heavenly burnished hue, as the wine sheds sugar yet keeps a toffee-intense beauty for decade after decade. These are the fine wines of the great châteaux. Sadly, economic pressures mean that few proprietors can make the commitment to create such wines, and, outside the top growths, much Sauternes is made sweet simply by the addition of sugar to the juice and the brutal arrest of fermentation with a massive slug of sulphur. These wines, usually without a property name, have nothing in common with true Sauternes or Barsac and should not be allowed to use the name. There are several areas nearby, less favoured by 'noble rot', which nonetheless usually make attractive sweet wine. The best of these is **Cérons,** inside the Graves appellation, and both **Ste-Croix du Mont** and **Loupiac** over the River Garonne do fairly well when they try. Many Sauternes proprietors also produce red and dry white wines, rarely of any great quality, simply to try to pay the bills.

THE IMPORTANT DETAILS

CLASSIFICATION

Sauternes was also classified, along with the Médoc, in 1855 (see p. 36). Château d'Yquem is accorded First Great Growth Status, after which there are 11 First Growths and 14 Second Growths. There were originally nine of each, but some properties have split. The Second Growth Myrat has replanted its vineyards. The finest First Growths are Rieussec, Guiraud, Suduiraut, Climens, and Lafaurie-Peyraguey. The best Second Growths are Doisy-Védrines, Nairac, de Malle Doisy-Daëne and Broustet. There are quite a number of Bourgeois Growths, but with the creation of true Sauternes being so expensive, few of these are really good. Exceptions are the excellent de Fargues and Raymond-Lafon, and the good Bastor-Lamontagne, Liot, St-Amand, Chartreuse, Guiteronde, Cantegril, Ménota, Gilette and Piada.

ORGANIZATION/S

Most Sauternes is sold under the generic label, blended to a price by *négociants*. It is rarely good. The great wines are from individual properties, bottled at the château, but almost all the proprietors have other occupations and many make dry wine as well, because the market will not pay a high enough price for fine Sauternes. Predictably, there is no co-op.

READING THE LABEL

You should be able to tell if the wine is of the lighter (Preignac, Barsac) or heavier style (Bommes, Fargues, Sauternes) by checking at the bottom of the label to see which village the property is in. There are some very dull, young wines sold under château labels. Apart from the wines listed above, approach the unclassified lesser known names with caution.

BORDEAUX/Sauternes

THE IMPORTANT DETAILS

Picking off the sweet noble-rotted grapes in Sauternes in late October.

WHAT DOES IT TASTE LIKE?

The wine should be luscious. Whether it is intensely, overpoweringly so, or delicately, fragrantly so will depend on the vintage and the style of wine-making chosen. Because Sauternes wines have less obvious fruit flavours than most sweet wines yet have a full, sometimes thick richness to them, they are the best sweet wines to go with food.

THE GOOD YEARS

Vintages are of crucial importance in Sauternes. If the weather doesn't produce at least some 'noble rot' in the vineyards, there is not a lot even the finest winemaker can do. In difficult years, the best winemakers will ruthlessly 'select' only the very sweetest vats from their entire crop for their final château label wine. This may mean they end up making less than 10 hl per hectare in some years. Sauternes is ready to drink young, but good ones will improve over 10 to 20 years.

1989 D'Yquem said the conditions were the most perfect ever experienced for making great sweet wine. Sounds exciting – and expensive.

1988 Superb year, beautifully balanced, lusciously sweet from the noble rot in the vineyards. Classic wines.

1987 The rains came too early and spoiled the crop, but there were some interesting wines made by freeze-concentrating the juice of the grapes.

1986 After the nearly-but-not-quite 1985 vintage when the hoped-for greatness just didn't materialize, 1986 produced the goods. There was just the right mixture of rains, mists and sunshine to produce some memorable noble-rotted wines.

1985 Not bad but certainly not brilliant because the hoped-for noble rot only surfaced in dribs and drabs – the weather was too good for it to develop, and by the time it did arrive, most people had picked.

1983 Wonderful year, probably the best since 1967. The vineyards were full of 'noble rot', and those who waited till the last moment to pick made stunning, intense, almost painfully honeyed wines. Significantly, this was the first year the speculators began to show an interest in Sauternes's investment potential.

1982 Nearly very fine. The grapes reached super-ripeness and were infected by 'noble rot' simultaneously. The first *'tries'* of the pickers brought in marvellous grapes. (*Trie* is the French word for each separate excursion the pickers make through the vines). Then it rained and rained. Suduiraut produced great wine. Most other '82s lack a little richness.

1981 A pleasant but not intensely 'rotty' year. Some wines are sweet and balanced.

1980 A good year and the wines, though light, have that lovely, dangerous lime-acidity bite to spice up a good sweetness. Underrated.

1976 Big, brawny, intensely fat ripe wines, yet this richness is due to grapes literally roasted to ripeness by the sun; it was almost too hot for 'noble rot'. The wines are tiring and, though fairly rich, just lack the final spark.

1975 A lighter year, but beautifully balanced, the sweetness is still all golden honey and no decay. Lovely, classic wines.

1971 Similar to 1975, not heavy or intense, but lovely, gently sweet wines of great style.

1970 Marvellous big strong year, full of honeyed sweetness and a rich, lanolin ripeness.

1967 Wines of enormous power and memorable beauty.

ENJOYING THE WINE

Sauternes is more adaptable than people think. It is the best of all wines with desserts, although going even better with fresh fruit or fruit tarts and puddings, than with cream and chocolate-based concoctions. It is wonderful with nuts and is one of the only wines which can successfully partner blue cheese or *foie gras*. The French drink it as an aperitif.

CONSUMER INFORMATION

WHAT DO I GET FOR MY MONEY?
Although **d'Yquem** is very expensive by any standard, it is also possibly the most expensive wine in France to make. Other top châteaux are not expensive, given their quality and the Bourgeois mentioned above are positively cheap. Avoid generic Sauternes – it's cheap, and tastes it.

AVAILABILITY
The quantities of the great wines are always small and so they are not easy to find. Most good outlets will have one or two proper château wines which are worth buying; all outlets will have one or two commercial generic blends, which are not.

CONSUMER CHECKLIST

Château Rieussec 1983	Q: 1 2 3 4 5 6 7 8 9 **10**
	P: 1 2 3 4 5 6 7 8 9 **10**
	V: 1 2 3 4 5 6 7 8 **9** 10

Château Bastor Lamontagne 1986	Q: 1 2 3 4 5 6 **7** 8 9 10
	P: 1 2 3 4 5 **6** 7 8 9 10
	V: 1 2 3 4 5 6 7 8 **9** 10

Good Years Good years are less frequent than for almost any other French wine, but lesser years will often give pleasant wine. Recent successes: 1989, 1988, 1986, 1983, 1980, 1976, 1975, 1971, 1970, 1967.

Taste Notes The flavours are honeyed, lanoliny and sometimes nutty, but balanced by good acidity.

BORDEAUX/Other Wines

It really isn't a sign of unpardonable historical bias to suggest that Bordeaux is the greatest wine-producing area in the world. She manages to attain astonishing heights with her red wines, her dry whites and her dessert wines. The wines whose names we know, whose prices we quail before, are the great Classed Growths of the Médoc, Graves, Sauternes and Barsac and St-Emilion, and the rightly vaunted top wines of Pomerol. Yet these star wines only account for just 2 per cent of Bordeaux's output even though they capture 99 per cent of the headlines. Even the entire produce of those famous regions is only one-third of the Bordeaux total. Outside these privileged leading appellations there is an enormous amount of wine looking for a direction to run in. The Burgundy region is lucky that her basic wines are given such a lead by Beaujolais Nouveau. This side of France has nothing so publicity-conscious to play with.

The finest of Bordeaux's 'other' wines are red, so following the pattern of the region as a whole. Indeed, Bordeaux is one of the only major regions in the world where there is a movement towards uprooting white vines and replanting red. This is because basic Bordeaux Rouge does at least have a fairly buoyant market as a good-quality quaffing red, and, as the prices of the famous appellations shoot up, there is also sure to be a demand for seriously vinified single property wine at a sensible price. Yet the baffling mystery is why white Bordeaux has so totally failed to tap what is the fastest-growing market in the wine-drinking world – off-dry, light, fresh whites at a low price. The great hinterland of Bordeaux, epitomized by Entre-Deux-Mers, was an enormous grape basket of white varieties like Sauvignon, Sémillon and Muscadelle which were crying out for modern vinification methods to make them into the light, simple, gently fruity styles they were most suited to. Yet for too long these wines had earned a fully deserved image as being heavy, dirty and sulphurous. The very names Entre-Deux-Mers and Bordeaux Blanc reeked of dull, tired wine-making. A few pioneers have been making excellent dry white for years, but until recently the price of Bordeaux Blanc remained as low as any appellation wine

A traditional vinatage meal in Entre-Deux-Mers – hunks of bread, bowls of soup and enormous pitchers of rough red wine.

in France. Still, there are signs of better things. A pure Sauvignon Sec appellation has had some success, though, to be honest, Bordeaux Sauvignon by itself isn't half the wine it can be when blended with Sémillon. And Entre-Deux-Mers is beginning to find a way to market its very attractive name – 'Between Two Seas'.

Which leaves the sweet wines. Sauternes and Barsac are no longer struggling to sell. Yet all along the Premières Côtes de Bordeaux there are vineyards like Loupiac and Ste-Croix du Mont which have traditionally produced unrehearsed understudy imitations of the great sweet wines. There's no market for them at the price they must command to survive and many vineyards are uprooting white vines and turning to red, or at very least having a go at producing dry white, hoping for more success than the guys who are already doing that. So 'below stairs' in Bordeaux, life is a bit of a struggle, but the inherent quality of the region as a wine-producer should pull the minnows through with the giants, so let's try to unravel the world of the 'other' wines of Bordeaux.

FRONSAC AND CANON-FRONSAC

These red wines have been rising stars for so long that one wonders if they are ever going to burst upon the scene. Hopefully, the golden touch of Jean-Pierre Moueix of Château Pétrus in Pomerol who is now taking a keen interest in the area, will at last bring the rewards the area deserves. The Fronsadais is a small area just a few kilometres west of Pomerol. Its larger appellation, Fronsac, is about 685 hectares (1,712 acres), and the smaller Canon-Fronsac is just over 280 hectares (700 acres), making an area about the size of Pauillac in the Médoc. The wines, particularly of Canon-Fronsac, have tremendous quality. They have the plumminess of Pomerol, and the mineral dry background but also something more elegant, cedary and Médocain in style. Prices are quite low, but availability is still poor. Yet I'm constantly amazed that we should still be listing an area of obvious high quality amongst the 'miscellaneous' regions of Bordeaux.

Good Properties: Canon, Canon de Brem, Junayme, Moulin-Pey-Labrie, Mayne-Vieil, de La Dauphine, La Rivière, Vincent and Vrai-Canon-Bouché.

CÔTES DE BOURG

Bourg is a small region, primarily of red wines, bang opposite the Haut-Médoc on the north bank of the Gironde. Her wines were known and sought after long before the great Médoc vineyard was more than a twinkle in its mother's eye. It is this great past which is a mere twinkle in the eye of the Bourg growers now, yet their wines are still undoubtedly good. They have a fairly full rather raisiny flavour, but backed up by good tannin and acidity which make them resemble Pomerol, though less successfully than the Fronsac wines. The best wines are from the properties on the banks of the Gironde looking across to Margaux. Prices are fairly low, and distribution is reasonably good.

Good Properties: de Barbe, du Bousquet, Guerry, Haut-Rousset, Sauman, Mendoce, La Croix de Millorit, Haut Guiraud. The co-op at **Tauriac** is one of the best, offering much high quality wine, e.g. **Châteaux Nodoz, Marzelle, Domaine de Bouche**.

BLAYE

Blaye is a large but rather diffuse area also looking out towards the Médoc, and immediately north-west of Bourg. There seems no clear pattern to the wine-making, except in the hinterland where the co-ops which control two-thirds of the region make a disturbing amount of heavy lifeless white. The best wines are red and are accorded the appellation Premières Côtes de Blaye, but they usually have a rather hot jammy taste which isn't terribly refreshing. Things are improving and better balanced wines are appearing.

Good Properties: Le Menaudat, Haut-Sociondo, Grand Barrail, Loumède, Barbé, Peybonhomme-les-Tours and Grand-Pierre.

COTES DE FRANCS

This is a tiny, almost unknown area to the north of Castillon which is already producing fine wine and will, within 10 years, be producing some of the great wines of Bordeaux. Watch this space.

Good Properties: de Francs, La Claverie, Puygueraud.

PREMIÈRES CÔTES DE BORDEAUX

The Premières Côtes consist of a 50-km (30-mile) long thin sliver of land stretching down the right banks of the River Garonne to the south-east of Bordeaux, which gazes jealously, longingly at the respected and well established vineyards of Graves, Barsac and Sauternes within spitting distance over the water, and at the same time feels the threat of a sleeping giant throwing off its sour sulphurous cobwebs at its back – the enormous Entre-Deux-Mers hinterland. Caught between these two, it has not found it easy to establish an identity, but, after spending a long time rather pallidly aping the rich sweet wines of Sauternes, it's now doing rather better by turning its hand to dry reds and whites in the Graves style. Much replanting of white with red wine varieties has gone on. Indeed, in the last 10 years, the production of white wine has halved. Sweet wines are on the decline, because they were never very satisfyingly sweet, but the dry whites being made are some of the best of the New Wave dry whites, showing that the soil is basically fine, and only needs a bit of gentle prodding. Reds also can be excellent, the earthiness balanced by a big, raisiny fruit, and, now and then, some real Cabernet blackcurrant.

Good Properties: Reynon, du Juge, Lamothe, Auniche, Domaine de la Meulière.

ENTRE-DEUX-MERS

This is a 'white only' appellation, but increasingly properties are making red as well, which

only qualifies for Appellation Bordeaux or Bordeaux Supérieur. Entre-Deux-Mers used to be terrible dull stuff, seemingly designed to repel all boarders who might want to give white Bordeaux a try. But with new, modern winemaking, white coats and stainless steel brushing aside the faded blue overalls and heirloom wooden vats, these wines are increasingly good, dry, slightly neutral, but fresh and fairly full bodied. The reds, although sometimes a bit earthy, can also be sharp, dry, and very good for just about any food you might care to throw at them.

Good Properties: Toutigeac, Reynier, Grand Puch, La France, Camarsac.

BORDEAUX AND BORDEAUX SUPÉRIEUR

These are two catch-all appellations, with 'Supérieur' meaning that the permitted yield of juice per hectare of vines is lower, and the minimum alcohol is higher. Reds and whites rely completely on the skill of the winemaker or merchant, but can represent excellent value for money. A few areas within this wide appellation do make better than average wine. Cubzac is one, on the Pomerol side of the Dordogne river, which makes good, rather sweet but beefy claret, and Castillon is another, stretched along the low ridge between St-Emilion and Bergerac, which can give a very good, slightly minty, blackcurranty wine, interestingly at its best in the less ripe vintages.

Good Properties: Parenchère, de Belcier, Moulin-Rouge, Lagrange Monbadon, Pitray (Castillon), and Timberlay, Terrefort-Quancard (Cubzac).

BURGUNDY

Burgundy has two stories. One is of unrivalled success, with a world clamouring for her wine, paying money heedlessly and without complaint for the succession of fine to great wines which her vineyards can produce. This is the story of the white wines, from the Chardonnay grape, as sought after as any wines in the world, more frequently copied and with greater success than any of the world's great wines have ever been. This story stretches from the northern tip of Chablis to the southern fields of the Mâconnais, and it has made a million drinkers happy and a thousand growers rich.

Her other story is of passion and pain, of brilliance shadowed by mediocrity, achievement humbled by greed, of great, tangled flavours, more sensuous and exotic than words can cope with – too often diluted and cheapened to such an extent that to waste words on such charmless, one-dimensional tastes seems a disheartening and needless exercise. This story of troubled brilliance, of greatness beyond belief and mediocrity past relief, is the story of her red wines from the Pinot Noir grape. History, chance and fashion have made the red wine names of her Côte d'Or, her 'golden slope', more famous than any in the world. When we catch a glimpse of the towering splendour of fine Chambertin, the musky fragrance of Musigny or the mouth-filling beauty of Corton, we find wines for which any price seems worthwhile, and any words inadequate. However, when we

are faced with the tart anonymity of a blended Nuits St-Georges or the sickly bull-necked attack of a rogue's Pommard at a price which would shock the pips from a pomegranate, then we are in a world of exploitation and callous disregard which for generation after generation has nonetheless exercised a fatal fascination over any lover of red wine.

And, just as the great winemakers of other parts of the world have attempted with enormous success to ape and even improve upon the white wines of Burgundy, so the sullen, arrogant yet hauntingly beautiful Pinot Noir has refused to give up its secrets to any but a scattered few across the world. The creation of an Australian Chambertin or Californian Corton is still a wraith which dissolves in the winemaker's fist every time he thinks he has found the solution.

Burgundy is in essence a long, thin streak of land, heading south down the Saône valley from Dijon to Lyons. The only exception is the clutch of northerly vineyards below Paris near Auxerre which make up Chablis. The Saône valley is wide and fertile. In normal areas you would expect vineyards to feature quite prominently in this valley economy. But burgundy is no ordinary valley wine, and, while the white Chardonnay grape is both relatively adaptable and easy-going, the red Pinot Noir is demanding and pernickety far beyond the behaviour of any other great grape. Were it not that the Pinot Noir can occasionally produce wine of peerless beauty, the local Gamay grape, which gives little trouble, but less fine wine, would have taken over the vineyards long ago.

As it is, the Gamay is banned from the good vineyards of the Côte d'Or and only flares to a certain fame in Beaujolais and the Mâconnais to the south. Otherwise red wine comes from the Pinot Noir, and a quick drive south from Dijon towards Nuits St-Georges, Beaune and Chagny will show both the heart of Burgundy and the root of its problems, because the very first thing that strikes you is how small the area is, yet how many famous names are squeezed into its narrow confines. To the left, an enormous wide valley plain stretches across to the Jura mountains and Switzerland – and is almost completely devoid of vines! Although some small patches do cluster close to the road, these, with a couple of unimportant exceptions, do not qualify for the right to use their nearby village names. And to the right, there is a gently rolling valley hillside, facing east to south-east. Sometimes, as when the great vineyards of Chambertin appear just past the village of Gevrey-Chambertin, this blanket of vines stretches for only about a kilometre before the shrub-covered brow of the hill cuts like a furrowed forehead across the land and the vines abruptly stop. Sometimes, as in the fine Nuits St-Georges vineyards of Clos Arlots or Clos de la Maréchale, the thin band of vines shrinks to less than 200 m (656 ft) in width. Further south, between Beaune and Pom-

The village of Fleurie, home of one of Beaujolais's most important Crus.

BURGUNDY

mard, the vineyards stretch briefly to their widest at all of 1,200 m ($\frac{3}{4}$ mile). Within these limits are the Grand Cru, or 'Great Growth' (the best) and the Premier Cru, or 'First Growth' (the next best) vineyards upon which Burgundy's reputation rests. They exist in closely regulated form only in the central to upper parts of what is anyway a very shallow slope and a very short one too. Even the most cautious driver can cover the 50 km (30 miles) from Dijon to Chagny in less than an hour, and that is the length of the entire Côte d'Or, comprising the Côte de Nuits as the northern half and the Côte de Beaune as the southern half.

Below this quality level, as the vineyards flatten towards the road, and then peter out on to the valley floor, the wines may either take their village name, or simply what are called 'generic burgundy' titles for the lowest quality wines (see p. 98). Some of these wines may be good, but already they are beginning to trade on the names of the few finest vineyards. Indeed, most of the villages have been doing that since the nineteenth century. You will notice that most of the important Burgundy villages have hyphenated names – like Gevrey-Chambertin, Chambolle-Musigny and Puligny-Montrachet. The first word is always the original name of the village. The second word is the name of that village's most famous vineyard, which is snapped on to the village name to catch some reflected glory. Nowadays, the most prestigious of these vineyards are enshrined as 'Grands Crus'. They do not have to use their village name on the label, but they cannot stop the village using their name, hyphenated, on the run of the mill wines.

These Grand Cru wines, whose names of Chambertin, Romanée-Conti, Montrachet and the like, are amongst the most famous in the world, produce tiny amounts of wine, for which there is an insatiable demand. Prices are sky-high and a queue quickly forms to buy the few bottles they produce.

It would be nice to state in black and white exactly why these favoured vineyard sites consistently produce the most remarkable wines, and an army of geologists and viticulturists have tried to analyse the soil, the angle of vineyard, and the micro-climate without conclusive results. Certainly the mixture of marl and limestone which dominates

the central band of the Côte de Nuits seems perfect for red wine, and the starker limestone outcrops of the Côte de Beaune are wonderful for white, but since parcels of land inside the same plot, with seemingly identical soil make-up can produce widely differing qualities, one has to say that in this difficult and relatively northerly vineyard area, the balance of micro-climate is always poised on a knife-edge and something as slight as a marginal increase in the angle of the slope or a momentary dip in the field, giving to a little patch an unwanted greater susceptibility to spring frosts or autumn rot, is the almost unclassifiable truth behind which pieces of land are born great, and which are not.

And then there is man. If ever there were an area where it is more important to know who made the wine than where it minutely comes from, it is Burgundy. Quite simply, supply cannot hope to meet demand. This is true for all the fine reds and whites of Burgundy, in particular the Grands Crus and Premiers Crus of the Côte d'Or, but also for the village wines whose names, if not whose qualities, have become famous along with their most special vineyards. It is also true for the wines of Chablis, although feverish re-planting of vineyards is attempting to satisfy the surge in interest there; and for the Mâconnais to the south – traditionally an area where the majority of the wine was red and undistinguished, but where now the white wines such as Pouilly-Fuissé can rival the wines of Meursault in price.

Indeed, buying burgundy at present, one has the feeling of being swept up in a gold rush. With the heady stench of the massive profits to be made clouding the air, it is difficult to remember that Burgundy has always been a land of low yielding vines and irregular vintages. It is estimated that the Pinot Noir only ripens properly, and only produces a decent quantity, in one vintage out of four. It is those one-in-four vintages upon which the fame of her wines was originally built, but you don't make much of a living by only producing saleable wine once every four years. So ways of increasing the strike rate had to be found. The ideal red wine was reckoned to be big, dark, full of rather heavy plummy fruit. This is the kind of wine that the thin-skinned, basically pale, Pinot Noir produces not one year in four, but about once a decade. However, further south, in the Rhône valley or even in the vineyards of North Africa, big, rich red wine was made, and in varying degrees the less rich years of Burgundy were made to resemble the ripest, most alcoholic vintages by the addition of these heavy reds which not only came from different regions of the world, but also from different grapes. To say that many people nowadays pine for such 'old-fashioned' burgundy, is to say that such people may be pining for a very good drink, but it is not the natural produce of the Pinot Noir grape in Burgundy which they are missing, more likely, a mixture of Hermitage, Châteauneuf-du-Pape and all stations south.

With the tightening-up of restrictions since 1973, modern red burgundy is at least closer to the produce of the permitted grape varieties in the properly delineated vineyards. However, the need to stretch the tiny produce of Burgundy has not diminished. So subvarieties, or 'clones', of the Pinot Noir grape, which ripened more regularly and produced larger crops, were planted and modern fertilizers helped swell the volume. The resulting wine was genuinely pale in colour, but pale in flavour too, yet at least a certain spurious body could be obtained by adding large amounts of sugar to the grape musts so that the wine was sweetish and alcoholic but completely lacking the delicate, lingering perfumes which even quite humble Pinot Noir wine will have if honestly made. Adding sugar is a perfectly normal device in northern vineyards. It is done at the beginning of fermentation and, carefully carried out, it will help to round out and stabilize the wine. But if profligately added to thin light wine from overproductive vines it will reduce what flavour there was and leave you with a dull, vapid wine which feels thick in the mouth when you drink it and which leaves you feeling thick in the head the next morning.

Red burgundy has lurched from a reliance on the heavy reds of the sunny south to a reliance on inferior productive 'clones' of Pinot Noir – in particular the respectable-sounding Pinot Droit, or 'Upright Pinot' (merely a comment on its straight-backed appearance rather than overabundance of moral rectitude) – and a heavy hand with the sugar shovel. Yet the signs are that the warning signals have been heeded by the good growers. The growers are already deserting

Nuits St-Georges' finest vineyards slope up from the Beaune road to Les Vaucrains just below the forest.

the traditional outlets for their wine in droves as they decide to stop selling in bulk to merchants and control their own wine's destiny from the budding of the vine right through to the final bottling and sale of the wine. Until recently this had been the employ of the numerous merchants, or *négociants-éleveurs* (the people who deal in and 'raise' the wine) up and down the Côte d'Or. Mostly they ran profitable businesses, but few of them showed more than scant regard for the true flavours of their wines, or the heights of beauty the wines could achieve. For them, burgundy wine was a commodity in which to trade. But increasingly it is being realized that red burgundy demands a closer, more personal relationship between a winemaker and his vines than any other wine, based on intimate knowledge and devotion to that quest for perfection for which the grower alone is equipped.

It is red wines which show up Burgundy's problems, particularly in the Côte d'Or, but also in the much less renowned Côte Chalonnaise just to the south.

White burgundy is much less of a problem. White wines ripen far better than red in cool climates, as is shown by the minor importance and quality of red wines further north, in Alsace, Luxembourg, England and Germany. Indeed, in the last 15 years, there has not

BURGUNDY

been one single write-off vintage for white wines. Even 1975, which was fairly close to a disaster for red burgundy, and in which the whites struggled too, in fact produced one of Chablis' greatest recent vintages. The Chardonnay is a reliable, healthy grape able to give good wine even at its unripest in cool damp years, when the red Pinot Noir fails to ripen, and able to overcome the hottest vintages by producing something buttery and rich, luscious yet totally dry in a unique way.

It is at its greatest in the Côte de Beaune. In the villages of Meursault, Puligny-Montrachet and Chassagne-Montrachet many growers both ferment and age their wine in small oak barrels (sometimes charred on the inside, to add an extra smoky flavour) which adds a unique savoury spiciness to the wines; the result is dry white wine at its most spectacular. Yet the demand and the prices are such that shortcuts are taken by the less scrupulous. Yields are pushed up, wooden barrels are dispensed with in favour of concrete tanks, and sugar is added randomly to these fermenting vats too. Although such procedures dramatically reduce the brilliance of the wine, the Chardonnay grape still manages to produce white wine which is good, if distressingly

expensive. The vineyards of Chablis are taking full advantage of the craving for white burgundy with expanded vineyards and a powerful flow of fine, dry white wine.

The Mâconnais in the south is less honourable. Pouilly-Fuissé and the wines from the surrounding villages, with hardly a wooden barrel in sight and prodigious yields in the vineyards, nonetheless manage to obtain some of the highest prices in France for wines which range from small amounts of the very good to a veritable flood of the fattest, dullest wine the long-suffering Chardonnay produces anywhere in France.

For such a small region Burgundy is relatively complicated. We've divided up the wine areas as follows: Chablis, the Côte d'Or, the Chalonnais and the Mâconnais. The Côte d'Or is the heart of an understanding of Burgundy, containing almost all the greatest wines and vineyards, and therefore each village is treated separately, with all the Grands Crus listed where applicable as well as the best of the other single vineyards. Beaujolais, although technically in the Burgundy area, uses a different grape, the Gamay, and has different traditions, and so we deal with this last, followed by 'generic Burgundy'.

BURGUNDY/Chablis

THE GENERAL PICTURE

Chablis is probably the most famous white wine in the world, and seen in larger quantities than any other wine. That's the fiction.

Now the fact. Real Chablis is only made in one small fold in the hills where the River Serein glides through the small town of Chablis between Paris and Dijon. It is made from the Chardonnay grape, it is white, and no other wine produced anywhere else has the right to call itself Chablis. Sadly, however, the word Chablis has been debased in so many countries for so long that there's no point in the real Chablis producers gnashing their teeth, they must simply grin and bear it. After all, they're making a high-quality dry white wine in the north of Burgundy from the Chardonnay grape in a world which is gasping for Chardonnay and white burgundy as though it were the elixir of life. Yet, in-

terestingly, the more sophisticated markets of North America and northern Europe are more circumspect: it is the newer markets for whom an order for Chablis is almost an importer's first act. One grower spoke of his excitement at receiving a 900-case order from Benin for immediate dispatch, cash on the nail. It was only as the cases were being loaded on to the truck, that he noticed the small print – equal amounts of white, rosé and red Chablis, with a particular interest in the rosé!

GRAPE VARIETIES AND WINE STYLES

There is only one grape used for Chablis and that is the Chardonnay, here often called the Beaunois. There are other grapes in the area, but they cannot make Chablis. What influences the style is firstly the positioning of the vineyards, and secondly the method of vinification and maturation of the wines.

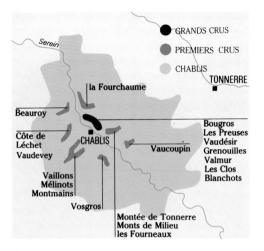

Winter pruning at Les Grenouilles (the town of Chablis is in the background).

Traditionally, true Chablis comes from a relatively small group of vineyards which are based on Kimmeridgian limestone. All the great Grand Cru and Premier Cru vineyards are from Kimmeridgian soil. Vineyards are now being expanded on to Portlandian limestone soils which seem to produce a less distinct wine, and used to be classified as Petit Chablis, or 'Small Chablis'. There is something of a war between the traditionalists who say the marvellous flinty, glinting green flavours of Chablis only come from Kimmeridgian soil, and the revisionists, who, purely by chance, mostly own estates away from the centre of Chablis, who argue their wine is as good as anyone's. Perhaps one should go back to the original classifications. All the best vineyards have always been on Kimmeridgian soil. That won't change. Yet no area, be it Burgundy, Bordeaux or the Napa Valley, lives by its Grands Crus alone, so expansion of the basic Chablis appellation should be for the general good. It is when you see woodland being cleared and classified as Premier Cru and old,

derelict vineyards which bear names like 'Champs des Navets' ('Turnip Fields'), or 'Verjus' ('Sour Grapes') being promoted that you wonder about the integrity of the exercise. Also, there is a marked, but less bitter difference of opinion between producers who swear Chablis should be fresh, bright, and lean, and drunk as young as possible, and those who think it is capable of greater things. The first group use stainless steel and concrete to vinify and mature their wines. The second group is less rigid. Some very serious producers, with Grand Cru vineyards, think wooden barrels add too much taste to the stark, pure flavours of their wines. Others are convinced that only by the vanilla-y influence of newish oak, and the less clinical surrounds of a wooden barrel can Chablis ever get past being merely good to the sumptuous, golden glories of a Grand Cru from a great vintage in full flight.

THE IMPORTANT DETAILS

CLASSIFICATION

Chablis is like a microcosm of Burgundy, and its classification system in general works better, with far less variation due to human factors. There are seven Grands Crus, all on the steep slopes looking out south-west over the little town of Chablis. These often produce wines of such power and depth, yet always holding on to a steely acidity, that for once

there is no argument about their Grand Cru status. The seven Grands Crus are Blanchots, Les Preuses, Bougros, Grenouilles, Valmur, Vaudésir and Les Clos. (There is one anomaly, a *cru* called La Moutonne, which straddles the Grands Crus of Les Preuses and Vaudésir.) There are 30 different vineyards traditionally rated as Premiers Crus, with one new creation, Vaudevey, yet to prove itself.

BURGUNDY/Chablis

THE IMPORTANT DETAILS

They are grouped under 12 names to simplify commercialization. These are frequently very good but rely far more on the attitude of the grower than do the Grands Crus. As the Premiers Crus are expanded to unproven vineyard sites, it will become necessary to choose the vineyard site and grower with care. The groupings are Fourchaume, Montée de Tonnerre*, Monts de Milieu, Vaucoupin, Les Fourneaux, Beauroy, Côte de Léchet, Vaillons, Mélinots, Montmains*, Vosgros and Vaudevey (* = the most reliable).

Ordinary Chablis, despite recent price rises, is still the most dependable and most fairly priced of all white burgundies. However, its classification is becoming very diffuse. Originally only wine from Kimmeridgian clay could be included, the remainder being Petit Chablis, but the recent expansionist movement which has doubled the vineyard area to over 1,600 hectares (4,000 acres) has mostly taken place on soil which was previously Petit Chablis. The result has been a slight loss of definition in the taste. Petit Chablis is an unpopular appellation because it sounds derogatory and the declining acreage is now hardly more than 80 hectares (200 acres).

ORGANIZATION/S

It is not often that a co-operative dominates a fine wine area, but it does in Chablis. The reason is that until recently Chablis growers frequently had a real struggle to make a living and the co-op protected them from the worst ravages of poor weather and indifferent market. The La Chablisienne co-op has 250 members, controlling 500 hectares (1,250 acres). The wines are sometimes sold under La Chablisienne's own name, and, confusingly, sometimes under the supposed estate name of a member. Mostly, however, they are sold in bulk to *négociants* locally and elsewhere, or under 'own-label' to brewery and retail groups. Ten per cent is sold in bottle, 20 per cent to local merchants in bulk and 70 per cent to other merchants in bulk. The French *négociants*, in particular Drouhin and Bichot from Beaune, who own vineyards in Chablis, handle about 50 per cent of all sales. There are five local Chablis *négociants*; they are increasingly important, handling 35–40 per cent of the Chablis market. The growers bottle and sell 10–15 per cent of the crop, depending on the vintage.

READING THE LABEL

The co-op's policy of allowing its members, whose wines are made in the communal vat, to put a 'Domaine-bottled' title on the label is an unnecessary confusion in reading a Chablis label. It is worth looking for a local *négociant's* name on ordinary Chablis or for Drouhin of Beaune. For Premiers Crus and Grands Crus the best wines are from single growers. Chablis Premier Cru by itself on the label will be a blend of several different Premier Cru wines.

WHAT DOES IT TASTE LIKE?

Ideally, Chablis at every level should have a steely freshness about it, even though Grand Cru wines from fine years can approach the Côte d'Or wines in their marvellous blend of lusciousness and nuttiness, with an austere savoury bite. Basic Chablis is a little less stark in taste than it used to be but is still one of the driest of all wines made from the Chardonnay. The use of oak barrels to age the wines makes them considerably fuller.

THE GOOD YEARS

In the past the area's proneness to spring frosts often meant the virtual destruction of a year's crop. Now, modern frost prevention techniques mean there is a fair to excellent crop every year. Normally, straight Chablis should be drunk within two to three years, though the wine will age longer, particularly from acid years. Premier Cru and Grand Cru wines *must* be aged to develop their exciting personalities.

1989 is ripe and fat, but excellent from the best producers, 1988 is a little more classic while 1986 is dry and intense. Only the best vineyard sites produced good 1987s, but 1985 and 1983 are round and full. 1982 is soft and easy and ripe, 1981 is splendid, deep, exciting wine. 1978 was remarkable, intensely rich.

ENJOYING THE WINE
Chablis' reputation as a seafood wine, particularly an oysters wine, was founded on its sharpness and relatively unripe flavour.

Modern Chablis is rounder and fatter than before, but is still one of the best whites for the job. Indeed, simple Chablis can perform the same Jack-of-all-trades task as Muscadet can, but with a bit more style.

Premier Cru and Grand Cru Chablis are fine enough to go well with any simply prepared fish, and also plain roasts of poultry or white meat, but are not quite up to the richer concoctions.

CONSUMER INFORMATION

WHAT DO I GET FOR MY MONEY?
Prices are apt to see-saw in Chablis, with periodic attempts to achieve stability being cast aside as soon as demand hots up. There have been recent price rises, but basic Chablis still offers excellent value for money. Some **Premiers Crus** are surprisingly cheap, while **Grand Cru** wines are only half the price of their Côte d'Or equivalents.

AVAILABILITY
Amazingly Chablis is not widely available in France, but elsewhere, ordinary Chablis is reliable and easy to obtain. Premier Cru wines are less common, and Grand Cru wines are rare and usually only from specialists.
Good Producers:
Merchants: La Chablisienne, Henri Laroche, Regnard/Pic, Simmonet-Febvre.
Growers: Jean Brocard, René Dauvissat, Paul Droin, William Fèvre, Louis Michel, Louis Pinson, François Raveneau, Philippe Testut, Robert Vocoret.

<table>
<tr><td colspan="2" align="center">CONSUMER CHECKLIST</td></tr>
<tr><td>Chablis 1989</td><td>Q: 1 2 3 4 5 6 **7** 8 9 10
P: 1 2 3 4 5 6 7 **8** 9 10
V: 1 2 3 4 5 **6** 7 8 9 10</td></tr>
<tr><td>Chablis 1er Cru
1989</td><td>Q: 1 2 3 4 5 6 7 **8** 9 10
P: 1 2 3 4 5 6 7 **8** 9 10
V: 1 2 3 4 5 6 7 **8** 9 10</td></tr>
</table>

Good Years Chablis is very susceptible to frost, as the winter of 1985 showed.
Therefore vintage size fluctuates wildly. The hottest vintages produce nutty, honeyed wines to drink young, the cooler vintages steelier, harsher wines which demand aging. Recent successes: 1989, 1988, 1986, 1985, 1983.

Taste Notes Ideally Chablis should be the driest of all classic Chardonnays. It is frequently made without oak, and the result, even in ripe years, is very dry, nutty but not rich. Oak adds a creamy softness when used.

RED WINES

There is *no* red Chablis. But there *is* red wine in the vicinity which is individual and good. At a time when the Pinot Noir vineyards of Burgundy's Côte d'Or are being rightly criticized for making much pale, characterless wine, this difficult grape finds unlikely champions in the scattered growers of Burgundy's northernmost region. Chablis is centred on the River Serein, but to the west in the Yonne valley near Auxerre, and to the east in the Armançon Valley near Tonnerre, there are pockets of red wine. The wines are largely Pinot Noir, sometimes considerably beefed up by an addition of tough, dark wine from the César grape. **Irancy** is the finest wine, rarely deep in colour, but always perfumed, slightly plummy, and attractive. **Coulanges Les Vineuses** is a little rougher, and **Epineuil,** near Tonnerre, is light, but fragrant with strawberry fruit.
Good Producers: Bienvenu (Irancy), Simmonet-Febvre (Irancy and Coulanges), Hugot (Coulanges) and Michaut (Epineuil).

BURGUNDY/Côte d'Or

THE GENERAL PICTURE

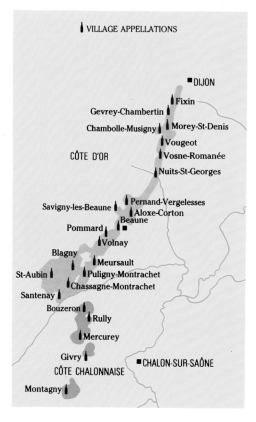

Pruning over, the branches are burned in a bruette (burner barrow) at Dujac in Morey St-Denis.

Here we are in the heart of Burgundy. This thin 50-km (30-mile) stretch pumps the blood of the grandest name in wine. Because Burgundy *is* a grand resonant name, reverberating with rich plummy purple tones, and the wines which have woven the magic over the centuries are all from this tiny allotment of soil. The name 'burgundy' has been seized by every other red wine producing country to describe heavy, chewy, sweet-fruited reds, satisfying, corpulent, thick-necked reds – but is burgundy like that? The answer is – almost never. Burgundy's reputation was made by the occasional vat of splendid richness in the occasional superheated vintage. Yet in this northern region it is impossible consistently to repeat that by honest means, and the majority of the red wines of the Côte d'Or are in fact *light*. Fragrant, yes, marvellously perfumed with cherry and strawberry fruit, sometimes meatier, sometimes intensely spicy, but light. Modern-day burgundies have gone too far down this road, in the same way as *méthode ancienne* ('ancient method') burgundies went heavy-footed into numerous gross misinterpretations of that handful of famous wines. Due to incessant demand, the growers have always felt they can sell all they make, and their vineyards have been seriously overcropped, leading to thin, pallid wines. If we were talking of some out-of-the-way wine region, we could shrug our shoulders and look elsewhere, but Burgundy stands at the core of the great French traditions of food and wine, and the Côte d'Or, right at the heart, is where the most callous abuse takes place. Even so, let us look at the area dispassionately, aware of its greatness, yet also taking note of its weaknesses. The Côte d'Or is divided up into two smaller areas, the Côte de Nuits and the Côte de Beaune.

CÔTE DE NUITS
The Côte de Nuits is almost entirely devoted to red wine, from the Pinot Noir grape, and contains the most famous of all Burgundy's vineyards in the Grands Crus of Gevrey-Chambertin, Vougeot and Vosne-Romanée. The vineyards used to stretch right up to Di-

jon, but now, except for a couple of small vineyards at Chenôve, the vines really start at Marsannay. Going from north to south, the villages are as follows:

Marsannay

In 1987 a new appellation for reds, whites and rosés replaced the old **Bourgogne Rosé de Marsannay,** pleasant rosés from the Pinot Noir grown on the outskirts of Dijon. An increasing number of light but well-flavoured red wines are now emerging and this is an appellation to watch. Producers to note are **Clair, Fougeray, Huguenot** and **Quillardet.**

Fixin

Fixin and Marsannay are chalk and cheese, because Fixin makes strong, tough red wine. It is little known as a village, which is a good thing in Burgundy, because there is less incentive to 'stretch' the wine. Usually the wines are chunky, fairly tough, lacking a little excitement, but if you want to feel you're drinking Gevrey-Chambertin without shouldering the cost, Fixin fits the bill. The best vineyards are **Perrière** and **Clos du Chapitre** (both Premiers Crus), with Gelin and Molin the most successful growers. There is a **Clos Napoléon,** but Napoleon's real love was Chambertin just down the road and the slightly jilted taste of the Fixin wine reflects this.

Gevrey-Chambertin

Now we're into the big time. Gevrey has been famous for its wine for over 1,000 years, and its eminence is marked by the village possessing eight Grands Crus. Two of them, **Chambertin** and **Chambertin Clos de Bèze,** can be some of the greatest of wines. They have a rough, plumskins and damson strength which is fierce when young but assumes a brilliant wafting perfume and intense plum richness as it matures. A Chambertin from a good vintage should need 10 to 15 years aging, yet, because of the popularity of the name, many are made far too light. The same can be said of all the other wines in Gevrey, which, without having the largest vineyard area, has the largest production. This is very sad, because a strong sensuous Charmes-Chambertin or a fragrant exotic-scented Griotte-Chambertin is intensely delicious. Chambertin was Napoleon's favourite wine, and its popularity is undiminished since then, so it is essential to buy this village's wine from a serious grower. The following can make fine wine – Burguet, Rousseau, Bachelet Faiveley, Camus, Trapet, Magnien, Rossignol, Joseph Drouhin, Jacquesson, Domaine des Varoilles, Antonin Rodet, Boillot.

Grands Crus: Chambertin, Chambertin Clos de Bèze, Chapelle-Chambertin, Charmes-Chambertin, Griotte-Chambertin, Latricières-Chambertin, Mazis-Chambertin, Ruchottes-Chambertin.

Good Premiers Crus: Combe-aux-Moines, Lavaut, Clos St-Jacques, Véroilles.

Despite the strictures, great Chambertin is great wine, and is worth a few risks to find.

Morey St-Denis

Morey used to be famous for being the least famous of the Côte de Nuits villages, and consequently was always singled out as being particularly good value. This isn't the case any more. The wines are expensive, and the wines in general suffer badly from overproduction and oversugaring. The vineyard area is relatively small, but it has four Grands Crus and part of a fifth. These should produce wines with less body and more perfume than Gevrey-Chambertin, and a slight meatiness blending with a rich chocolaty fruit as they age. Most modern Morey wine is far too light for any of those adjectives to apply. Luckily it does possess a small number of outstanding growers, whose names are more important on the label than the vineyard designation: Bryczek, Dujac, Lignier, Marchand, Ponsot and Tardy.

Grands Crus: Bonnes Mares (part of), Clos des Lambrays, Clos de la Roche, Clos St-Denis, Clos de Tart.

Chambolle-Musigny

This is famous as the lightest, the most fragrant, the most delicate of burgundies. The scent of a fine Chambolle-Musigny is cherry sweet and as come hither as roses in bloom – and that's only part of it, because the smoky, dark side of the Pinot grape also adds a fascinating slight shadowy depth to this heavenly scented wine. At the present time this is largely memories, since most Chambolle-Musigny is inexcusably gooey and thick, which is terribly sad. If I go on saying how sad I am, my tears will make the ink run.

Grands Crus: Bonnes Mares (the majority), Musigny.

BURGUNDY/Côte d'Or

Good Premiers Crus: Amoureuses, Charmes.

Good growers: de Vogüé, Dujac, Grivot, Roumier and Ghislaine Barthod. De Vogüé makes a little **Musigny Blanc** which is very dry and light, good but not thrilling.

Vougeot

The village of Vougeot is completely dominated by its Grand Cru, **Clos de Vougeot,** the 50-hectare (125-acre) walled vineyard which seems to many to epitomize burgundy. Indeed it does, for here, above all, the name of the grower is crucial. Over 80 growers share this enclosure, and while the land at the top is very fine, the land by the road is not. Somehow no-one ever admits to owning any of those roadside hectares. The rare bottle of good Clos de Vougeot is a wonderful fat burgundy, rich, strong, rather unsubtle but exciting for its grandness. The château at the Clos de Vougeot is the centre of the Chevaliers du Tastevin, a remarkably successful public relations organization formed to promote burgundy wines. There aren't many vines outside the walls, but they're still pretty good and **Clos de la Perrière** and **Clos Blanc** often give good wines.

Good growers: Bertagna, René Engel, Henri Lamarche, Mongeard-Mugneret.

Vosne-Romanée

Vosne-Romanée is the greatest Côte de Nuits village. Its Grands Crus have more renown, and sell for more money than any red wine on earth, except for Château Pétrus in Bordeaux, and, remarkably for Burgundy, they are dominated by a single estate, the

Dinner at the Clos de Vougeot, headquarters of the Chevaliers du Tastevin.

Domaine de la Romanée-Conti. Romanée-Conti itself is a single vineyard of almost 2 hectares (5 acres), capable of a more startling brilliance than any other burgundy, and possibly than any other red wine of France. La Tâche, Richebourg, Romanée-St-Vivant and Grands Echézeaux all follow close behind, producing flavours as disparate yet as intense as the overpowering creamy savouriness of fresh *foie gras* and the deep, sweet, liquorous scent of ripe plums and prunes in brandy. There is also something smoky, something spicy, altogether something as memorable as it is beyond words. These are the great wines, but in addition there are Premiers Crus which also have the compelling mixture of savoury richness and sweet fruit. The village wines are rather overshadowed by this parade of the immortals and they are not so reliable as once they were. Even so, they can still reflect their leaders, and sometimes add a delicious minty, eucalyptus scent too.

Grands Crus: Echézeaux, Grands Echézeaux, La Romanée, La Tâche, Richebourg, Romanée-Conti, Romanée-St-Vivant.

Good Premiers Crus: Beaux-Monts, Clos des Réas, Grande-Rue, Malconsorts, Suchots.

Good producers: Domaine de la Romanée-Conti, Engel, Grivot, Jean Gros, Henri Jayer, Henri Lamarche, Latour (for Les Quatre Journaux), Méo-Camuzet, Rion and Rouget.

Flagey-Echézeaux is a village just over the road on the valley floor. Its best wines are Grand Cru, with a little wine qualifying for the Vosne-Romanée appellation.

Nuits St-Georges

Nuits St-Georges has been one of the most abused of all Burgundy's names, largely by the English trade, presumably because the St George in the title warmed the cockles of the patriotic burgundy drinker. However, following its virtual disappearance from the export market, it has begun to reappear, expensive, but measurably better. It has no Grands Crus, but some very good Premiers Crus increasingly squeezed between roadside and scrubby hill brow, in this longest but narrowest of communes. The Pinot Noir is a savage, turbulent grape, and at its greatest it often produces a rotting, burnt, decayed kind of flavour which sounds horrible, but is at the heart of great burgundy. In Nuits St-Georges, this is frequently encountered but this whiff of a cabbage left too long at the bottom of the vegetable tray is balanced by a plummy, pruny sweetness and a brown, smoky depth which can make fine Nuits St-Georges one of the most fascinating of all red burgundies. **Prémeaux,** to the south, uses Nuits' name. There is a little white wine in Nuits St-Georges, the best made in the La Perrière vineyard from a mutation of Pinot Noir producing white grapes! It is sappy, savoury, and remarkably like a red wine to taste.

Good Premiers Crus: Chaignots, Clos de la Maréchale, Perrière, Porets, Pruliers, Les St-Georges, Vaucrains.

Good producers: Jean Chauvenet, Chevillon, Jayer, Grivot, Labouré-Roi, Michelot, Rion.

Côtes de Nuits-Villages is an appellation covering the three southernmost villages of Prissey, Comblanchien and Corgoloin and Brochon and Fixin in the north, though Fixin usually sports its own name. Its wines are beginning to assert themselves as stylish burgundy when made by decent producers. Usually fairly light and dry, they can nonetheless conjure up the cherryish perfume and 'delicious decay' of good Côte de Nuits red.

Good producers: Chopin-Groffier, Durand, Rion, Rossignol, Tollot-Voarick.

CÔTE DE BEAUNE

The Côte de Beaune is far more evenly divided between red and white wine, and while it has relatively few of the most famous red wine sites, it has all of the greatest white wine sites. When people say that white burgundy is the world's greatest dry white wine, they are thinking of the Grand Cru and Premier Cru wines from the villages of Aloxe-Corton, Meursault, Puligny-Montrachet and Chassagne-Montrachet, and made from the Chardonnay grape. Going from north to south, the villages are as follows:

Aloxe-Corton

The Côte de Beaune starts with a bang because Aloxe-Corton has the only Grand Cru red in the Côte de Beaune – **Le Corton** – as well as one of its most famous white Grands Crus – **Corton-Charlemagne** – both smothering the famous dome-shaped hill of Corton. Ideally, red Corton should have something of the savoury strength of Vosne-Romanée to the north and something of the

The heart of the Corton-Charlemagne vineyard. Over the road, in the background, are the good but less exciting vineyards of Pernand-Vergelesses.

mouth-watering, caressing sweetness of Beaune to the south. In fact, however, Le Corton has often been strangely insubstantial in recent vintages, and wines from subdivisions of Le Corton, such as **Corton-Pougets, Corton-Bressandes** and **Corton-Clos du Roi** more regularly reach this ideal. White **Corton-Charlemagne** which occupies the upper half of the hill where the first of the Côte de Beaune's limestone outcrops becomes apparent, is almost entirely Chardonnay, but a little Pinot Blanc or Pinot Gris (here called Beurot) is found which can add an intriguing fatness to the wine.

Corton-Charlemagne can be a magnificent, blasting wall of flavour, not big on nuance but strong, buttery and ripe enough to blank out any argument. However, it does need to age, and the increasing number of disappointingly stolid wines in recent vintages may open out with time.

The village wines of Aloxe-Corton are overwhelmingly red, and they only too rarely show the marvellous savoury flavour which used to make them some of Burgundy's finest 'commune' wines.

Grands Crus: Corton-Charlemagne (white), Le Corton (red).

Good Premiers Crus: Chaillots, Meix, Vergennes.

Le Corton is sometimes subdivided and Bressandes, Pougets and Clos du Roi are par-

ticularly good – often better than Le Corton.
Good producers: Chandon de Briailles, Chevalier, Drouhin, Louis Jadot, Louis Latour, Senard, Tollot-Beaut, Voarick.

The village of **Ladoix-Serrigny** includes some Corton and Corton-Charlemagne vines in its boundaries, but wines under its own name are rarely seen.

Pernand-Vergelesses

This is a pleasant little village, snuggling in the lee of the hill of Corton, and until recently only known as the producer of a good chunk of the less remarkable Corton wines. However, the village's own wines can be good – it has some of the best Aligoté (see pp. 98-9) in Burgundy. The white Chardonnays are of the straight, stony type, while the reds have a fair amount of body and a rather rich strawberry fruit pastille taste.
Good producers: Dubreuil-Fontaine, Laleure-Piot, Pavelot, Rapet, Rollin.

Savigny-Les-Beaune

A higgledy-piggledy village up a side valley, Savigny affords the first welcome sight of a vineyard on the thirsty drive from Paris. The wine is almost entirely red, and, while it isn't usually very full, it does have quite an attractive earthiness which backs up the gentle strawberry fruit. With Pernand-Vergelesses, Savigny gives good-quality wine at a fair price.
Good Premiers Crus: Dominodes, Guettes, Marconnets, Vergelesses.
Good producers: Bize, Ecard-Guyot, Guillemot, Pavelot-Glantenay.

Beaune

Beaune, from having been one of the most flagrantly devalued wine names in Burgundy, has pulled itself back to being one of the most reliable communes in the region, giving a very representative range of wines which show burgundy at its most enjoyable, and sometimes at its most impressive. This is excellent news for the drinker, because Beaune, which is the centre of Côte d'Or trade, and a sizeable town, has the largest acreage in the Côte d'Or, and also because the vast majority of vines are owned by the merchants and so their wines are frequently easy to find. There are no Grands Crus, but a large number of good Premiers Crus. The wines are nearly all red, and have a lovely soft, 'red fruits' sweetness, usually backed by a slightly mineral toughness, which makes them ripe and perfumed yet just sturdy enough to play the burgundy role in all the big eating the area loves.
Good Premiers Crus: The majority are good, and quite plentiful: Avaux, Bressandes, Cent Vignes, Clos des Mouches, Clos du Roi, Fèves, Grèves, Marconnets, Teurons, Vignes Franches.
Good producers: Joseph Drouhin, François Germain, Louis Jadot, Jaffelin, Lafarge, Leroy, Morot, Moillard, Tollot-Beaut.

The few outlying vines of the town can be called **Côte de Beaune**, surprisingly, a very rare appellation not to be confused with Côte de Beaune-Villages, which is a blend of wine from various villages. Chantal Lescure is a good producer, of red and white.

All along the Côte d'Or are fine examples of Flemish Burgundian architecture with its distinctive features of turrets and multi-coloured roofs.

BURGUNDY/Côte d'Or

CÔTE DE BEAUNE

The village of **Chorey-Lès-Beaune** can also produce some very attractive perfumy reds, particularly from Tollot-Beaut and Germain.

Pommard

While Nuits St-Georges became the Englishman's idea of the archetypal burgundy, Pommard filled the same role for the USA. For a small village to satisfy the expectations of an entire nation cannot be healthy, and standards must suffer. In Pommard they certainly have, and amongst Burgundians, the quality of the village's wheeler-dealing is often more praised than the quality of the wine. Even so, Pommard *does* have good producers, and there can be a strong meaty sturdiness, backed by a slightly jammy, but attractive plummy fruit which may not be subtle, but is many people's idea of what red burgundy should be.

Good Premiers Crus: Arvelets, Epenots, Pézerolles, Rugiens (Haut & Bas).
Good producers: Ch. de Pommard, Comte Armand, Gaunoux, Lahaye, Jean Monnier, de Montille, Mussy, Parent, Pousse d'Or.

Volnay

Volnay's reputation has traditionally been for producing the lightest wine in the Côte d'Or, but with overproduction going on on all sides, this is no longer a boast to be proud of, and in any case, it isn't that accurate. Up to the eighteenth century, Volnay *did* produce particularly pale wine, and the top part of the vineyard has a great deal of chalk which reduces colour, though not alcohol strength. However, it might be truer to say that Volnay is one of the most perfumed red burgundies, having a memorable cherry and strawberry spice to it, but also, in its Premiers Crus, being able to turn on a big meaty style without losing the perfume. Also, though regarded as a quick developer, from a good grower, bottles last well.

Good Premiers Crus: Bousse d'Or, Caillerets, Champans, Clos des Chênes, Clos des Ducs, Fremiets.
Good producers: Domaine de la Pousse d'Or, Clerget, Lafarge, Marquis d'Angerville, Montille.

Monthélie

It seems to be a rule in Burgundy that if your village is in one of the folds of the hill, rather

HOSPICES DE BEAUNE

Many of the finest wines in the Côte de Beaune sport the Hospices de Beaune labels. The Hospices are charitable institutions, which since 1443 have largely supported themselves by various bequests of vineyard lands.

Over the centuries, the Hospices holdings have grown to 57 hectares (143 acres) – which is bigger than the Clos de Vougeot! Each year on the third Sunday in November the famous Hospices de Beaune sale is held, amidst a great deal of brouhaha. It used to be thought that the prices for the lots were an accurate reflection of how burgundy prices in general were moving. Since they are virtually guaranteed to rise, regardless of quality, you could be excused for saying it's all good publicity, great fun – but – what is its relevance? Frankly, the sale has little relevance, save for providing the burgundy trade with an excuse for price hikes and presenting a rosily prosperous face to investors, bankers and the like. However, the Hospices de Beaune wines themselves are nowadays made with tremendous skill, and Bernard Porcheret, in charge of the cellars, consistently produces a range of wines whose quality is as high as any in Burgundy. Indeed, in a difficult vintage like 1984, the Hospices wines were some of the most skilfully made in the entire Côte. Sadly, these fine wines cease to be the responsibility of the Hospices after they are auctioned. Many *négociants* who subsequently 'raise' and label the wines finally offer for sale products bearing little resemblance to the original barrels they bought. Given the quality of the original wine, that is little to be proud of.

than on the main slope, your wine, however good, will not be well-known, because in olden times the wines would have been sold quite happily under the name of the nearest famous neighbour. Monthélie is no exception, sharing boundaries with Volnay and Meursault, but fame with neither. It's a red wine village, and the wine deserves recognition since it is full, dry, rather herby or piny in

BURGUNDY/Côte d'Or

CÔTE DE BEAUNE

taste, but with a satisfying rough fruit. Often a good buy.

Good producers: Deschamps, Potinet-Ampeau, Suremain, Thévenin-Monthélie.

Auxey-Duresses

Even further round the corner than Monthélie, Auxey-Duresses has never been renowned, but has always had some reputation for full-blooded red and soft, nutty whites. Recently, with a few notable exceptions, there seems to have been a slump in quality and a certain loss of direction, the tough but attractive reds becoming more sugary and flabby, and the nutty whites becoming tired and fat. Hopefully, the handful of good growers will pull the wines back into a position where they can take advantage of burgundy's booming popularity.

Good producers: Diconne, Duc de Magenta, Leroy, Roulot, Roy, Thévenin.

Meursault

White wines finally take over from red in the village of Meursault, and they take over in the most spectacular way with by far the largest white production of any Côte d'Or village, and a general standard which is remarkably high. It is *much* easier to make good wine from Chardonnay than from Pinot Noir and there has not been a disastrous vintage in Meursault for 20 years. The limestone runs in a broad band through the middle of the sloped vineyards, and the result is wines of a delicious, gentle lusciousness, big, nutty, sometimes even peachy and honeyed. They perform the great white burgundy trick of seeming rich and luscious, yet being totally dry.

There is an air of commercial zeal abroad in Meursault, but you should never be jostled into buying, because Meursault has more producers bottling their own wine than any other village, so there's plenty of choice.

Meursault has no Grands Crus, but some good Premiers Crus, situated to the south of the village:

Good Premiers Crus: Bouchères, Charmes, Genevrières, Goutte d'Or, La Piece-sous-le-Bois (Blagny – see below), Perrières, Poruzots.

Good producers: Ampeau, Buisson-Battault, Coche-Dury, Comte Lafon, Jobard, René Manuel, Matrot, Michelot-Buisson, Pierre Morey, Millot-Battault, Prieur, Roulot.

The hamlet of **Blagny** is situated up the hill on the boundary with Puligny-Montrachet and usually markets its slightly harder wine under that name or Meursault's. Meursault red exists, either simply as Meursault, or as Blagny. But the best is called Volnay-Santenots from vineyards on the Volnay boundary, yet within Meursault, which have claimed the historic right to the classier red wine name of Volnay.

Puligny-Montrachet

Meursault may have the approachability of style and the high overall standard, but the brilliance, the genius of everything which Burgundy and the Chardonnay grape stands for comes firmly to roost in Puligny. The great vineyards cling to the upper edge of the hill while the lesser vineyards slip away towards the village some half a mile away on the flat. Le Montrachet is a peerless wine, showing in the most perfect way how humble words like honey, nuts, cream, smoke, perfume, and all the rest do no true service to a white wine which seems to combine every memory of ripe fruit with a dry savoury tang that leaves your palate restless, your mind amazed and your expectations satisfied. There are several other Grands Crus, less intense, but whose wines buzz with the mingling opposites of coffee and honey, smoke and cream. And, of course, there is a range of Premiers Crus as well. While 'Village' Meursault may be good, it is always worth buying a single vineyard wine in Puligny-Montrachet.

Grands Crus: Bâtard-Montrachet, Bienvenues-Bâtard-Montrachet, Chevalier-Montrachet, Montrachet.

Good Premiers Crus: Champs Canet, Clavoillons, Combettes, Folatières, Pucelles.

Good producers: Bachelet-Ramonet, Carillon, Chapelle, Louis Jadot, Laguiche, Leflaive, Ramonet-Prudhon, Rodet, Sauzet, Thénard.

Chassagne-Montrachet

Chassagne also has a chunk of the great Montrachet vineyard, so it's a bit of a shock to discover that Chassagne is basically a *red* wine village, only 40 per cent of her produce being white. Although the standard of her Grands Crus is sky-high, neither the red nor white Premiers Crus dazzle in quite the same way as Puligny's. If anything the taste of the whites is a little chunkier, inclined just to stop short when you hoped it might reveal one more nuance of flavour. As with Puligny, you should buy single-vineyard wines, and you should get a full flavoured, slightly nutty, dry white of considerable quality.

The reds are a puzzle. Because they are reasonably priced I am always seduced into trying yet one more, and I am usually disappointed by the rather hot plum skins and chewy earth flavours. Even so, I'll keep trying while my money lasts.

Grands Crus: Bâtard-Montrachet, Criots-Bâtard-Montrachet, Montrachet.

Good Premiers Crus: (red and white) Boudriotte, Cailleret, Clos St-Jean, Grands Ruchottes, Morgeot.

Good producers: Colin, Gagnard-Delagrange, Laguiche, Duc de Magenta, Albert Morey, Ramonet, Ramonet-Prudhon.

St-Aubin

The Route National 6 slices between the villages of Puligny and Chassagne-Montrachet, and after a dangerously sharp turn at the misleadingly-named hamlet of Gamay, St-Aubin appears rather diffidently on the right. Again, a village with no reputation, used to declassifying its reds and whites to AC Bourgogne, but again, a backwoods village of very strong, tasty, proud Pinot Noir, and full, racy Chardonnay. Two-thirds of the vineyards are Premiers Crus, and the wines represent some of burgundy's best value.

Good producers: Colin, Clerget, Duvernay, Jadot, Jaffelin, Lamy, Roux, Thomas.

St-Romain

Even more out of the way, north of St-Aubin and west of Auxey-Duresses, St-Romain doesn't produce a lot of wine, although Francois Frères, one of France's most famous barrel-makers, selling to Domaine de la Romanée-Conti and California's Mondavi is here, sheltering under the high hills. But the full, rather broad flavoured, cherry-stone dry red, and the flinty dry white are fine wines sold cheaper than they deserve.

Good producers: Bazenet, Buisson, Thévenin, Thévenin-Monthélie.

Santenay

The end comes rather suddenly in the Côte de Beaune. One moment you are flirting with immortality in Chassagne-Montrachet and a few hundred metres later, the hills veer away to the west, the village of Santenay grabs what it can of the disappearing slopes, and that's just about it. Santenay used to be more famous for its Casino, and wine was largely sold as Côte de Beaune-Villages. However, the wine is better than that. It used to be amongst the meatiest of burgundies, having a strong savoury flavour and a good ripe strawberry fruit. In general, the savouriness has been replaced by a gentler, fruit pastille softness which is attractive without making you leap up and down with excitement. Even so, the general standard is fairly good, and vineyards like **Clos des Tavannes, Gravières** and **La Comme** (Premiers Crus), can give you a bit of the beef as well.

Good growers: Belland, Domaine Lequin-Roussot, Mestre, Morey, Pousse d'Or, Prosper Maufoux, Prieur-Bonnet, Roux.

Maranges

A new AC covering the string of vineyards drifting away to the west of Santenay. Few signs of much quality yet.

Côte de Beaune-Villages

This is a catch-all red wine appellation for 16 villages on the Côte de Beaune. Only Aloxe-Corton, Beaune, Volnay and Pommard cannot use the appellation. It used to be utilized by growers and merchants who had small amounts of several villages' wine to blend together, or by lesser-known villages unable to sell under their own name.

Leflaive's Puligny-Montrachet Les Pucelles: wines seldom have a mechanical vintage in Burgundy.

BURGUNDY/Côte d'Or

THE IMPORTANT DETAILS

CLASSIFICATION

Basically, Burgundy has five different levels of classification, all relevant to the Côte d'Or:

Non-specific general appellations, with no geographical definition, e.g. Bourgogne. Inferior, damp valley land in the Côte d'Or may be lumped in this, as may the produce of young vines.

Appellations Régionales, or 'Specific Regional Appellations', e.g. Côte de Beaune-Villages. Usually a blend of one or more village wines made by a merchant for commercial reasons.

Appellations Communales or 'Village Commune wines'. Each village has its vineyards legally defined. This category applies to vineyards which have not established any special reputation over the years, and are thus usually blended together under the village name. However, there is a growing move towards even relatively unknown vineyards appearing on the label. These 'non-classified' vineyards are called *'lieux-dits'* or 'stated places'. They can only appear on the label in letters half the size of the village name.

Premiers Crus or 'First Growths'. Typically in Burgundy, first growth means second growth, because these are the second best vineyard sites. Even so, they contain some of Burgundy's finest wines. In many villages, the majority of vineyards are classified as first, which can devalue the title somewhat, and the lesser known vineyards can be lumped together and sold as Premier Cru, e.g. Beaune Premier Cru. If the vineyard name is used, e.g. Beaune-Grèves, the vineyard name (Grèves) must follow the village name (Beaune) but may be printed the same height.

Grands Crus or 'Great Growths'. These are the real top growths, the cream of the vineyards.

Not every village has a Grand Cru. The reds are concentrated in the Côte de Nuits, the whites in the Côte de Beaune. They are the vineyards which, traditionally over hundreds of years have consistently produced the finest wines in the village, and have become renowned under their own, rather than under the village, name. Indeed, during the nineteenth century, many villages added on the name of their most famous vineyard to promote their more general wines. So the village of Gevrey took the name of its greatest vineyard, Chambertin, and called itself Gevrey-Chambertin, effectively reflec-

ting the great vineyard's glory. These Grands Crus may appear on the label as names and appellations in their own right, with no reference to village name.

The last three of these classifications are made with two criteria to the fore. Firstly, those pieces of land which have shown varying aptitudes to produce great wine: the Grand Cru soil and aspect is the best, the Village or Commune wine is less particular, though still worth more than a general 'Bourgogne' appellation. Secondly, quality of wine is reckoned to be directly affected by type of grape variety and yield of grapes per hectare. Pinot Noir makes the red, and Chardonnay, with a little Pinot Blanc, makes the white. However, Pinot Noir is a notoriously rogue grape. The great wines have always been produced by various stubby, irregular, unreliable strains called 'Plant Fin' or 'Fine Plant'. Yet other types of Pinot Noir called 'Pinot Droit', or 'Straight Pinot', which grows straight and handsome and yields large regular amounts of patently inferior grapes, are permitted too.

Which brings us to the subject of yield. Technically, Grand Cru vineyards are not allowed to give more than 35 to 40 hectolitres (1 hectolitre = 100 litres) of juice per hectare (2.5 acres) of vineyard. Even village wines are only supposed to give 45 hl per hectare. With these new strains, both Pinot Noir and Chardonnay can yield much more than that. So now the local growers' body can decide each year what the yield should be. In a perfect world, why not? They know the vineyards best. Yet in a grasping commercial world the honest voices of caution will always be swamped by the hoots and cackles of greedy men. In 1982 Montrachet could technically have produced 72 hl to the hectare, the red Côte de Nuits Grands Crus over 60. In the Côtes du Rhône such yields are never allowed, even for regional wine.

So does it debase the idea of 'Grand Cru'? Of course it does. The honest growers who

limit their yields suffer at the hands of the unscrupulous. Does it affect quality? Of course it does, particularly in the reds, since the Pinot Noir is too delicate a grape to take such dilution. And does it affect prices? Of course not. They continue to rise, endlessly testing what new limits the market will bear.

ORGANIZATION/S

Remarkably, the organization of the Côte d'Or is still strongly influenced by the French Revolution! The great reputation of burgundy had been built up by ecclesiastical domaines (*domaine* is the Burgundian word for 'estate') and these were confiscated, split up, and sold off. Over the years vineyard ownership became ridiculously fragmented. The average holding for one grower is 2 hectares (5 acres), which would probably be divided between two or three different vineyard sites in two or three different villages. So he or she might have up to a dozen wines, all in tiny quantities. From the point of view of trying to cash in on the reputation of a village or a famous vineyard, this meant that the vineyard might have 10, 15, 20 different owners, all making their own wine their own way. Because of burgundy's historical fame, this led to the rise of *négociants-éleveurs*, merchants who deal in and 'raise' the wines in their cellars. These merchants would buy up quantities of a village's wines in barrel from different growers, mix it all together, bottle it, and offer it as 'Maison X's Gevrey-Chambertin' or 'Maison X's Le Chambertin'. As these merchants' businesses prospered, the pressure on supply in a tiny area like the Côte d'Or became intense and many shamefully dishonest wines were sold under famous names.

For a time this made them good profits, but in 1974 there was a general tightening-up on fraud in Burgundy at the same time as the American market was becoming interested in fine burgundy. The USA demanded authen-ticity. The one way to guarantee authenticity is to buy a grower's wine, bottled at the domaine. The fact that only small amounts of each wine were available didn't matter as burgundy specialists made a point of how limited production was as against the merchants' previous boast that they could always guarantee supply.

Now the Côte d'Or is increasingly in the hands of the growers, and foreign and domestic buyers are going direct to the vineyard to purchase, bypassing the *négociant* houses. In 1970, 95 per cent of Côte d'Or wine was handled by *négociants*. By 1989 it was less than 50 per cent, with the growers now bottling and selling the majority of their wines themselves. The role of the *négociant* as a 'department store', offering all the top names in burgundy is at an end. Those who do not own vineyards themselves will find it difficult to survive, because they cannot buy enough good wine, with the decent growers increasingly bottling and selling their own. The *courtier*, or 'broker', used to act as intermediary between grower and *négociant*, but has now spread his activities to include direct contact with foreign buyers more in the role of a 'commission agent'. As one might expect in an area where profits are easy to come by, the co-ops are not strong and one of France's smallest is at Gevrey-Chambertin, where 139 member growers cultivate 60 hectares (150 acres). The most important is the Caves des Hautes-Côtes, south of Beaune.

READING THE LABEL

The Côte d'Or label should be a model of intelligible information, given the comprehensive classification of the vineyards. Unfortunately, although it can tell you which vineyard site the wine is from, it cannot say whether the Pinot used is good or bad, whether the crop was heavy or light, whether the winemaker added sugar liberally or frugally. However, there is an increasing amount of

BURGUNDY/Côte d'Or

THE IMPORTANT DETAILS

burgundy bottled by the grower, so, following the list of growers given with each village, one can spot their names on the label. If the wine is from a merchant the name will be accompanied by 'Négociant-Eleveur', otherwise look for 'Mise en bouteille au domaine' or some variant on that theme. In such a difficult world as burgundy buying, it is at least a start.

WHAT DOES IT TASTE LIKE?
White Côte d'Or burgundy is rarely poor, and can go from good, bone-dry, slightly one-dimensional commune wine, through to the glorious honeyed, rich yet dry, luscious yet savoury flavours of the top wines. Red burgundy is much more of a problem. A lot of the wine is pale, short, vaguely strawberry-scented wine, pleasant at a low price, outrageous at a high price. Yet the infrequent great wines of Burgundy combine a soft ripeness with a perfumed, exotic fruit, sometimes a dry chocolaty trace and, ideally, a smoky, rotting compost richness which is one of the most exciting, unexpected flavours the whole gamut of red wine has to offer.

THE GOOD YEARS
Vintages are of enormous importance in the Côte d'Or, but so is the name of the producer. In so-called great years, poor producers will offer wines completely lacking the expected characteristics. In so-called bad years the good producer will salvage a decent wine. Which means, always trust the good winemaker more than the reputation of the vintage. It is much easier to make white wine in a cool year than red. In general, the whites can be drunk after two or three years but the best ones really should be kept for ten. Sadly, many red wines can also be drunk after two to three years and often don't keep for ten. Properly made red burgundy should still be fairly tough when young and improve noticeably after a few years in bottle.
1989 A very early, super-ripe vintage, but the

vineyards didn't suffer from drought and the reds and whites, while certainly plump and juicy, have a lovely early-drinking style to them.
1988 A great year for reds. Intense colour, intense fruit, intense perfume. Will rival, if not exceed, 1985. Whites suffered from high yield, but are also very attractive fruity wines of good balance.
1987 Low yields enabled good dry reds to be made despite unfavourable weather. Whites are quite good but they are still not entirely ripe.
1986 A massive vintage – which was necessary to damp down a dangerously overheated market. The wines aren't too bad, but they just lack real generosity and fruit. There was a fair amount of rot, which you can often taste, and most wines are a bit lean and tannic. The whites are a totally different story. Beautifully concentrated, fresh, exciting fruit perfectly balanced by thrilling acidity. The best vintage of the 1980s.
1985 Fabulous. The vintage even the Burgundians couldn't spoil. Rich, fragrant wines, all perfume and fresh juicy fruit flavours. Marvellous to drink young, marvellous to age, probably the best red burgundy for 20 years. The whites are impressive – big, almost oily, rich and alcoholic, but they don't quite "sing". They fill your mouth OK but don't make your eyes shine.
1984 A difficult vintage. Light, but tasty, pleasantly fruity reds for early drinking, and some fairly decent, fresh whites.
1983 A very difficult vintage, largely because the potential for quality was tantalizingly great, yet demanded fine wine-making skills. A very hot summer brought in black grapes at record ripeness levels and the good guys will have made great wine. But torrid heat at vintage time and sweeping rot in the vineyards means many winemakers blew it. White wines are sometimes a sensation but often are just too strong, and, not

infrequently, rotty.

1982 A massive quantity. The reds are mostly distressingly light but when properly made are soft and fruity. The whites are in general round, ripe and easy.

1981 A few surprises, but mostly uncharming, with whites better than reds.

1980 This vintage was disgracefully written off by the experts. So let's put the record straight. The Côte de Nuits, in particular, and to some extent the Côte de Beaune, produced some of the best red burgundy of recent years. Dry, closed, but well coloured, with a deep satisfying fruit now evident, they are fine, austere burgundies. Whites are less good and now aging fast.

1979 A big vintage of wines which initially seemed forward and soft but actually kept their fruit for some time and many reds are still good.

1978 Hailed as a great year, in the right hands it certainly is. Both red and white looked superb to start with, yet many whites have developed a strong, thick, chunky taste, impressive yet not beautiful. The reds, again, go from Grands Crus kissing their nearest and dearest premature farewell to marvellously full, beautifully balanced classics from lesser vineyards.

1976 The trumpets brayed long and hard over this vintage, proclaiming it one of the all-time greats. Old burgundy hands growled into their beards and said Let's wait and see. The red wines are big, tough, and strong, yet there really is too much tannin for the fruit. As always, good growers coped and have produced some rich, deep, demanding wines, which are just beginning to soften and open out. The whites were certainly the supporting act in 1976, yet in their rather heavy, chubby way, they've been extremely good, fat burgundy.

Older vintages
1972 Written off as a disaster, this proved to be one of the most successful red vintages of the decade!

ENJOYING THE WINE
White Burgundy is the finest of all white wines, either to prepare the palate and whet the appetite for red to follow, or simply for itself, with the marvellous savouriness, weighty yet fresh, which most of them have. The richer fish dishes of French *haute cuisine* are almost impossible to partner except with white burgundy and many of the poultry and lighter meat dishes go brilliantly with it too. As a wine to turn a snatched mid-day snack into a gastronomic experience, there's nothing like it.

Red burgundy is traditionally though of as a 'game' wine – for venison, pheasant, hare – as well as for 'hearty roasts'. Yet many light modern burgundies would have little to offer such rich-tasting food and would be at their best with simple lamb or port. Despite the importance of cheese in Burgundy, a good red is wasted with cheese, though some of the rough reds might actually benefit from the combination.

CONSUMER INFORMATION

WHAT DO I GET FOR MY MONEY?
The greatest wines are very expensive, but worth the money for the inimitable sensations they give. However, without getting good unbiased advice, or embarking on a costly 'trial-and-error' exercise, the good wines are not self-evident from their labels. The top vineyards will always be expensive and any attempt to get a bargain is almost certain to land you with a mediocre wine. However, the lesser villages have not enjoyed/suffered the same price explosion as the front line villages and any quest for quality at a reasonable price should take in the following – **St-Romain, St-Aubin, Monthélie, Savigny-Lès-Beaune, Chorey-Lès Beaune** — and **Beaune** itself. **Côte de Nuits-Villages** and **Hautes Côtes de Nuits** and **de Beaune** should also be tried.

BURGUNDY/Côte d'Or

CONSUMER INFORMATION

AVAILABILITY

For such a small area there are a suspiciously large number of 'Côte d'Or' burgundies in virtually every form of retail outlet. Many of these will be dull blends of overpriced and underexciting wines. Though there are an increasing number of 'estate' wines, not all these are good and to find the distinguished, memorable bottles, well made from good vineyards, is a difficult task, best pursued with the small number of merchants who really bother to seek out the best wines.

CONSUMER CHECKLIST

Meursault 1988	Q: 1 2 3 4 5 6 7 **8** 9 10		Gevrey-	Q: 1 2 3 4 5 6 7 8 9 **10**
	P: 1 2 3 4 5 6 7 8 9 **10**		Chambertin 1er	P: 1 2 3 4 5 6 7 8 9 **10**
	V: 1 2 3 4 5 **6** 7 8 9 10		Cru 1988	V: 1 2 3 4 5 6 7 8 **9** 10

Good Years The white Chardonnay grape produces fair to excellent wine almost every year. Recent successes: 1989, 1988, 1986, 1985, 1982, 1979, 1978.

Taste Notes From hot vintages the flavours of good white burgundy are succulent, rich, creamy, honeyed, incredibly gentle to drink, yet always balanced by acidity. From lesser years, the wines are sharper, more appley, but usually softened by oak barrel aging.

Good Years Red burgundy is not so much bedevilled by poor vintages as poor wine-making; even in the best vintages wines can be poorly made and overpriced. Recent successes: 1989, 1988, 1987, 1985, 1983, 1980, 1978.

Taste Notes At its best Côte de Nuits are wonderfully plummy, rich, perfumed – exotic. Tough when young but maturing over 10-20 years to flavour of incomparable beauty.

HAUTES CÔTES DE BEAUNE AND HAUTES CÔTES DE NUITS

Behind the line of famous villages and vineyards there is a large, somewhat ramshackle area of hills, forest and valleys which has a long tradition of wine-making, but which had until recently fallen into decay. The 28 villages of this hilly backwater comprise the Hautes Côtes, and they are rapidly assuming a considerable importance once again as the suppliers of that elusive commodity – affordable burgundy of a reliable standard. During the 1960s, two important growers, Hudelot and Thévenot, re-established large estates in the Hautes Côtes de Nuits – Thévenot being particularly impressive and even making a smoky Pinot Gris white – and the merchant house of Geisweiler followed suit.

In the Hautes Côtes de Beaune it was more a case of re-motivating existing vineyard owners, a task much aided by the establishment of a new co-op in 1968, and by the efforts of such growers as Mazilly, Joliot and Chalet to produce consistent, light strawberry-flavoured Pinot Noirs, sharp, tasty Aligotés and fresh, appley Chardonnays.

BURGUNDY/Chalonnais

THE GENERAL PICTURE

The Chalonnais, or, to give it its proper name, the Côte Chalonnaise, has until recently been the forgotten area of Burgundy, with much of its wine going to make up merchants' blends – usually under the generic appellation Bourgogne. However, since 1973, with the newer and more strictly regulated approach to burgundy labelling, anywhere with a legal right to a Burgundy appellation, and vineyards already planted with Pinot Noir and Chardonnay, has suddenly become an attractive proposition. A great upsurge in activity in the 1970s and the 1980s culminated in 1990, with the new AC Bourgogne – Côte-Chalonnaise for the whole area. The villages of Mercurey and Rully have greatly increased their productions and the many new hillside plantings are sure to yield good wine.

The Côte Chalonnaise lacks the well-ordered compactness of the Côte d'Or. Its vineyards are splattered rather than spread along the numerous ins and outs of hillside between Chagny, just below the southern end of the Côte de Beaune, and Montagny about 24 km (15 miles) south. So, as usual in Burgundy, we are talking about a tiny area. The grapes are primarily Pinot Noir – which in general here produces a very attractive rather light strawberry red, but sometimes a wine positively rich and perfumed – and Chardonnay, usually stony and dry due to the relative absence of oak barrel aging in the area, but again, sometimes a soft vanilla succulence creeps over the acid fresh wine when a grower decides to invest in a few barrels.

Bouzeron

Geographically in the Chalonnais but only accorded AC Bourgogne is Bouzeron, which has recently emerged from the shadows because a substantial estate is owned there by M. de Villaine, co-owner of Burgundy's richest hectares, the Domaine de la Romanée-Conti. Some of the glitter has rubbed off on Bouzeron where the very good sharp Aligoté is now at least marketed under its own appellation, (Bourgogne Aligoté Bouzeron), and the red and white Pinot and Chardonnay of M. de Villaine are the quintessence of light burgundy.

Rully

Bouzeron's neighbour is Rully, which is where the Chalonnais proper starts, although there is no great difference in style. The whites are best, with the Chardonnay giving a pale, nutty wine which is both soft and fresh. Lovely light white. The reds can be a little too light, but do well in a wispy strawberry way. Delorme is the biggest producer, but Noël-Bouton, Chanzy, Dury, Jacquesson, Jaffelin and Rodet are also good. Remember that Delorme's sparkling Crémant is extremely drinkable.

Mercurey

Mercurey, the next village, is a positive giant in Chalonnais terms, producing over half the region's total, and there has been pressure to re-name the Côte Chalonnaise the *région de Mercurey*. This is very much a red wine centre, and the whites are usually rather flaccid afterthoughts from the less good land. There are numerous good growers as well as several large merchants. The wines have considerably more body than Rully, but still manage to retain the strawberry fruit, adding a little smoky spice along the way. They are probably the closest to the Côte d'Or in quality, and the quality is helped by having the lowest permitted yield of anywhere outside the Côte d'Or. Names to look for are Faiveley, Antonin Rodet, Delaunay, Chartron et Trebuchet, Suremain, and Juillot.

Givry

Givry is a relatively small vineyard area, likely to get smaller as the suburbs of Chalon-sur-Saône make increasing demands on available land and on growers' scruples. However, the wine is sure to survive, and when well made is the biggest and richest of Chalonnais reds. Decent aging adds a plummy perfume to the strawberry fruit. The best wines are from Thénard, Mouton and Ragot.

Montagny

Montagny produces some of the driest, chalkiest Chardonnay south of Champagne, and that is all. The appellation only applies to white Chardonnay, not red Pinot Noir. It is excellent bone-dry food wine, but since I am paying burgundy prices, I'm glad they are now using a little oak to deepen the taste! Louis Latour and the co-op at Buxy are good labels.

THE IMPORTANT DETAILS

CLASSIFICATION

There are four village appellations, Rully, Mercurey, Givry and Montagny, as well as the new AC Bourgogne-Côte Chalonnaise. Mercurey does have five Premier Cru vineyards, while Montagny gaily calls any wine Premier Cru which achieves a half degree more of alcohol than the legal minimum, which is pretty silly. Villages outside this group must use AC Bourgogne (see p. 98).

ORGANIZATION/S

The most frequently met wines are from merchants who control about three-quarters

BURGUNDY/Chalonnais

THE IMPORTANT DETAILS

WHAT DO THEY TASTE LIKE?

Chalonnais wines used to be called the poor man's burgundy, and this is a fair generalization, since the flavours are certainly less intense and individual than on the Côte d'Or. The reds can have a special red-fruit fragrance to them, but the whites, though fresh and bright, could sometimes use a little more depth. Oak aging is now improving the best.

THE GOOD YEARS

Traditionally one could say that Chalonnais wines are ready to drink sooner than Côte d'Or wines, yet with the pallid offerings of much of the Côte d'Or this generalization can't be adhered to. Chalonnais whites are ready in two to three years, if only because they rarely have the structure to deepen and change. Reds from Givry and Mercurey can age eight to ten years from good vintages like 1978, 1985 and 1988, if they are from a serious grower.

of the distribution. There are co-ops too, with the Buxy co-op near Montagny being one of the most go-ahead and effective in Burgundy. However, particularly good Mercureys will normally be from growers.

READING THE LABEL

Some wines will bear vineyard names, but, except in Mercurey, these are not necessarily better in legal terms. However, mention of a vineyard is always an indicator of a more serious producer. Mercureys may have a 'Chante-Flûte' motif on the label, meaning that the local growers' association has given that particular wine a special award for quality.

ENJOYING THE WINES

The whites of Rully and Montagny are almost too dry for apéritif drinking, but make excellent all-purpose whites, dry enough for seafood, shellfish and local trout, cutting enough for snails, frogs' legs and fatty terrines. The reds, with their perfumy fruit, are better with simple meats and some of the gentler cheeses.

CONSUMER INFORMATION

WHAT DO I GET FOR MY MONEY?

Chalonnais value for money used to be excellent, since the wines were good and prices well below Côte d'Or levels. However, prices have risen fast recently, and, except from the best growers who don't stoop to over-sugaring, they are verging on the expensive. The commercial wines of Delorme, Rodet, Jaffelin and Jadot and the co-op wines of Buxy are still pretty good value.

AVAILABILITY

This is Burgundy's smallest area, so availability is not brilliant, but Latour's Montagny, Jadot's Rully and Bouchard Père et Fils' Bouzeron Aligoté are quite well distributed. Any burgundy specialist should have some growers' wines, and they are worth a try.

CONSUMER CHECKLIST		
Givry 1988 (red)	Q:	1 2 3 4 5 6 7 **8** 9 10
	P:	1 2 3 4 5 **6** 7 8 9 10
	V:	1 2 3 4 5 6 7 **8** 9 10
Rully 1988 (white)	Q:	1 2 3 4 5 6 **7** 8 9 10
	P:	1 2 3 4 5 **6** 7 8 9 10
	V:	1 2 3 4 5 6 **7** 8 9 10

Good Years The vintage years are similar to the Côte de Beaune. As wine-making techniques improve, the vintage variation is less dramatic.

Taste Notes The whites are usually very clean, dry and slightly nutty. The reds have a delicious fresh strawberry flavour.

BURGUNDY/Mâconnais

THE GENERAL PICTURE

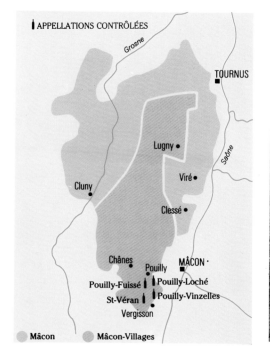

Jutting out over the vineyards of Pouilly-Fuissé, the rock of Solutré is Mâcon's most famous landmark.

With the usual 60 per cent up 60 per cent down price roller-coaster for Pouilly-Fuissé confounding our reason, and the thought of large numbers of Pouilly growers laughing their way to the bank till the tears run down their cheeks (and, hopefully, into the wine, to give it a touch of savoury Chardonnay depth which it will otherwise signally lack), let us step back briefly from the mindless mêlée and work out what this area consists of.

So. It is in southern Burgundy, starting almost at the borders of the Côte Chalonnaise near Buxy, and spreading south until it mingles with the frontiers of Beaujolais just south of its main town Mâcon. It is easily the biggest producer of white wine in Burgundy, primarily using the Chardonnay grape and claiming nearly half of the annual total. Pouilly-Fuissé is certainly the most famous of these wines, but two-thirds of the production is of simple, unmagical Mâcon Blanc.

Mâcon also produces a fairly hefty amount of red wine, for which it used, once, to be more renowned. It doesn't fetch an enormous price but it does sell fairly well, and, despite Mâcon's image being overwhelmingly for white wine, the standard of basic red wine here is probably higher than the standard of the basic white.

GRAPE VARIETIES AND WINE STYLES

Although there is a little Pinot Noir, red Mâcon is almost always from the Gamay grape. It is usually sold anonymously, although the co-ops at Igé and St-Gengoux have developed reputations for the slightly green, earthy wine they produce. It's often used as a Beaujolais substitute but is drier and rougher and less absurdly attractive. There is also a rare but reasonably good Mâcon rosé.

However, above basic level, the field is rapidly left to the whites. There is a whole list of Mâconnais appellations, and the Institut National des Appellations d'Origine has actually turned down requests for more saying there are too many already. Basic Mâcon Blanc is usually a dull wine, okay with food, but somewhat tart and earthy. You need to get to Mâcon Blanc Villages before you begin to see the signs of honey and fresh apples and nutty depth normally associated with good Chardonnay. 'Villages' wine is limited to 43 communes with the best land. Some of these add their own village name, and quality can really take off here. From a village like Viré, Clessé, Prissé or Lugny, the white wine can be

BURGUNDY/Mâcon

THE GENERAL PICTURE

full, buttery yet fresh and some of the best value in Burgundy. If anything, the wines may be a little fat. This is sometimes because the Chardonnay, which originated in the Mâconnais village of Chardonnay, has developed a rather exotic, spicy strain in some vineyards, fine in small doses, overbearing by itself.

By now we're closing in on Pouilly-Fuissé, but first we get to St-Véran, created in 1971 to bridge the gap between ordinary Mâcon Blanc Villages and the stars of Pouilly. It sandwiches Pouilly north and south, where it even manages to include some of the vineyards of the St-Amour Beaujolais Cru. These wines are usually soft, quick-maturing, but very attractive rather honeyed burgundy.

And then there's Pouilly. Two villages, Loché and Vinzelles, have hyphenated their names to Pouilly with resonable effect, but actual Pouilly-Fuissé comes from four mini-regions round the original village of Pouilly. It's mostly sold by the Chaintré co-op, without any oak from overproductive vines, and as such ends up as undistinguished and over-priced merchants' blends. However, from a grower who uses oak barrels like Corsin, Noblet, Feret, Guffens-Heynen and Vincent at Château Fuissé – this expensive wine can achieve a delicious deep, honeyed flavour up to the standard of a good Meursault. As I say, just from a small handful of committed growers, not the general run.

THE IMPORTANT DETAILS

CLASSIFICATION

Mâcon classification is an example of a regional wine gradually evolving its own particular hierarchy, and then attempting to consolidate these gains: from the catch-all Mâcon Blanc to the more specific Mâcon Blanc Villages from specific villages, and then to particular appellations grouped round one village's reputation. Curiously, it was Vinzelles which tried to delineate its vineyards before Fuissé, but it is Pouilly-Fuissé, now covering the produce of five different villages, which has hit the jackpot. St-Véran, already covering six villages, would like to be next.

ORGANIZATION/S

The co-operative movement is more effectively organized, and to a higher standard, here than almost anywhere else in France. There are 18 different organizations, covering over half the production and the standard of their wines, up to St-Véran level, is first rate. Pouilly-Fuissé is best from a single grower, if you can find one. Merchants often buy from co-ops, but the co-op's own label is often more trustworthy.

Despite sky-high prices, Pouilly-Fuissé properties still look peaceful and sleepy.

READING THE LABEL

It is worth looking out for stickers announcing medals awarded at Wine Fairs, since they are taken very seriously in the Mâconnais. Mâcon Supérieur merely shows that an ordinary Mâcon has attained an extra degree of alcohol. Don't be worried by seeing Pinot-Chardonnay Mâcon; this isn't a new mutant of Pinot and Chardonnay, it just means a Mâcon which could be made from either, but in practice is always Chardonnay.

WHAT DO THEY TASTE LIKE?

The reds are in general a little astringent, and lack the juicy fruit of good Beaujolais. The whites are the opposite, sometimes too soft and dull-edged, but rising to a lovely, gentle honeyed style in single village wines.

THE GOOD YEARS

In general, these are wines to drink young. Though Chardonnay usually demands time to develop its flavours, Mâconnais Chardonnay is immediately attractive and can quickly tire. Pouilly-Fuissé, properly made, repays keeping. The hottest years are not the best, so, while 1988 is delicious, and 1987 wasn't bad, 1989 and 1985 can seem rather overblown.

ENJOYING THE WINES

The reds need food, and their rather rough hewn flavours are ideal with *andouillettes*,

rillettes and *boudins*. The good whites have a softness which may slightly blur their personality, but which makes them very good all-purpose wines, even going well with chicken, veal and pork. The soft but fruity Crémants make ideal apéritifs.

CONSUMER INFORMATION

WHAT DO I GET FOR MY MONEY?

Mâcons veer from very cheap to very expensive, from rotten value to bargain buys. Cheap **Mâcon Blanc** is rarely very pleasant, and **Pouilly-Fuissé** is rarely worth the price, but single commune **Mâcon Villages** like **Mâcon Lugny/Prissé/Viré** and **St-Véran** can offer decent value for good-quality burgundy.

AVAILABILITY

Mâcon Blanc and Mâcon Blanc Villages are universally available. However, the higher up the quality scale you go the more elusive they become. St-Véran should ideally be more available, and top-line Pouilly-Fuissé is in great demand and rarely seen outside leading American outlets.

CONSUMER CHECKLIST		
Mâcon Viré **1989**	Q:	1 2 3 4 5 **6** 7 8 9 10
	P:	1 2 3 4 5 6 **7** 8 9 10
	V:	1 2 3 4 5 **6** 7 8 9 10
Pouilly-Fuissé **1989**	Q:	1 2 3 4 5 6 **7** 8 9 10
	P:	1 2 3 4 5 6 7 8 **9** 10
	V:	1 2 3 **4** 5 6 7 8 9 10

Good Years Nearly every year produces decent wine, with the white wines achieving most of the personality. The wines are usually ready to drink within the year. Recent successes: 1989, 1988, 1987, 1986.

Taste Notes These are the softer white burgundies. The straight Mâcons should have a gentle appley flavour, while the single village wines have a creamy, round honeyed taste.

BURGUNDY/Beaujolais

THE GENERAL PICTURE

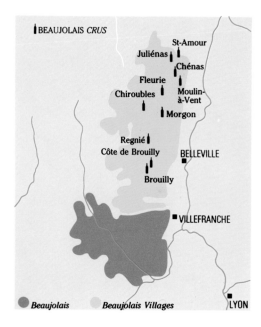

Beneath the magical Beaujolais hills the grapes wait in the vineyards to be carried into the winery.

Is there any wine more French than Beaujolais? Any name which conjures up so potently our visions of bucolic, moustachioed Frenchmen with obligatory beret and blue-and-white striped tee-shirt; of girls, flirtatious and frisky, in fishnet stockings and steeple-high heeled shoes, carousing carelessly with their flagons of foaming red? All the good, clichéd foreigners' fantasies about the French revolve around this splashing, irreverent red from the southern end of Burgundy.

Of course, it isn't really in Burgundy – the grapes are different, the soils and wine-making methods far removed. But in periods of shortage and high prices in the real burgundy world, further north round Beaune, it has been possible, with a judicious dollop of sugar and a good deal of stirring, to get a soupy, doltish burgundy look-alike.

That's all changed. Enthusiasm is very much the name of the game now, because with the general tightening-up of EEC laws about ten years ago, we're back to the bright-eyed basics once again – and the basics in Beaujolais are the rivers of juicy, gurgling, brand new wine which pour out of these hills and valleys above Lyons every year. We call it Beaujolais Nouveau; to the locals it's always been simply Beaujolais. And those locals have a massive thirst for one of the most unpretentious, open-faced wines we're lucky enough to possess.

The people of Beaujolais are all richer and rather more sober now that the rest of the world has taken to their local wine in such a big way. They can afford to sit back and enjoy the beauty of those winding hill valleys which make the region one of the most heart-softening and romantic of the wine areas to visit. And since the export market now gets much of the best Nouveau each year, we can get a taste of their good life too.

Beaujolais Nouveau is an astonishing marketing success, and has allowed the rest of Europe, and even the USA and Australia, to experience something of the wild excitement which flows with the broaching of the first wine of a year's harvest. And as such it shouldn't be scorned. It is an emotional moment when you take your first gulp of the fruits of a year's long labour, when you draw the cork from a bottle of wine which was ripe clusters of purple grapes sagging heavy on the vine just two months before – and few red wines retain the fizzing, grapy freshness of the recent harvest like Beaujolais Nouveau.

GRAPE VARIETIES AND WINE STYLES
There is in fact some *white* Beaujolais, and it is usually quite good, having a stony dryness

which is rather closer in style to the northern wines of Chablis than the fatter, softer, sunny wines of southern Burgundy. And the grape is Burgundy's finest white wine variety – the Chardonnay. You can actually make white Beaujolais out of the black Gamay grape, and one lone grower does, but the Gamay has a more important job in hand than making white wine. It is the one and only grape allowed to make 'le Beaujolais', which in the eyes of the whole world is red, red, red.

The Gamay grape is not one of France's noblest. It produces pretty dull stuff in most other areas, and can yield an unattractively hard, tart wine if grown any farther north than in Beaujolais. But somehow, on these granite slopes chiselled back towards the Massif Central from the Saône valley, the coarse Gamay grape manages to give one of the juiciest, most gulpable, gurgling wines the world has to offer.

Since the Gamay has no pretensions as a grape, Beaujolais should have none either. It should be drunk as young as autumn allows in great draughts of pleasure, preferably without being bottled at all. Although a few of the top wines of the top villages do improve with age, the vast majority of the region's 11 million cases per year do not improve. And they don't get a chance to either – over half the total production is drunk by Christmas as Beaujolais Nouveau.

THE IMPORTANT DETAILS

CLASSIFICATION
This is very important in Beaujolais, which is divided into three geographical categories.

Beaujolais or Beaujolais Supérieur
This covers all the basic wines and refers to the produce from the flatter, southern part of Beaujolais, stretching down towards Lyons. Supérieur simply means that the basic alcoholic degree is higher; it is rarely seen on the label, and does not ensure a better wine. Up to two-thirds of this harvest is now made into Nouveau, including most of the best stuff. So run-of-the-mill Beaujolais, apart from Nouveau, is nowadays likely to be pretty thin, reedy stuff, or beefed up with something altogether different.

Beaujolais-Villages
There are 39 villages, mostly in the north of the region, which are reckoned to make better than average wines, and can use this communal title. The wines certainly are better, and the cherry-sharp fruit of the Gamay is usually more marked. However, look for a wine bottled in the region, and preferably from a single vineyard, because an anonymous blend of Beaujolais-Villages may simply mean a heftier version of an ordinary Beaujolais.

The Ten 'Crus', or 'Growths'
These are the top villages, and *should* all have definable characteristics. *Should,* because the produce of different vineyards and growers is too often blended to a characterless mean by merchants based anywhere in France. These villages are grouped in the north of the region on steep hillside sites. Starting from the south they are:

Brouilly The flattest vineyards and usually one of the lightest 'growths'. It rarely improves much with keeping; in fact it makes a very good Nouveau! A few properties make a bigger, more peachy wine to age, but not for long – nine months to a year is quite enough.

Côtes de Brouilly The hill slopes in the centre of the Brouilly area. These wines are fuller and stronger-tasting, since they largely come from the exposed slopes of the Brouilly mountains which lap up the sun. The strawberry or raspberry fruit which can make Beaujolais such an enticing wine is often found in Côtes de Brouilly wines.

Regnié The new 10th 'Cru' came into force in 1988. Although in good warm years Regnié is attractive and perfumed – rather like Brouilly – the wines don't ripen too well in cool years, which is why it wasn't a 'Cru' in the first place.

Morgon These wines *can* be some of the great glories of Beaujolais. They can start out thick and dark, and age to a sumptuous chocolaty, plummy depth which resembles Côte de Nuits burgundy and yet is still definably Beaujolais. Sadly, Morgon is more susceptible to

BURGUNDY/Beaujolais

THE IMPORTANT DETAILS

Chénas Another strong, tough wine, from the smallest of the 'growths'. It can easily be as good as Moulin-à-Vent, but again, if you age it, it will taste more like burgundy than Beaujolais. Good value.

Juliénas This *can* be big wine, but many of the best more closely resemble the mixture of fresh red fruits and soft chocolaty warmth which marks good Fleurie. It can age, but is better young, and is rarely expensive.

St-Amour Amongst the most perfect Beaujolais, this pink-red wine from one of the least spoilt villages usually has freshness and peachy perfume and good ripe fruit all at once. It isn't that common, but is frequently the most reliable and the most enjoyable 'growth'.

ORGANIZATION/S
In general the merchants are the most important part of the Beaujolais scene. However, there are both good and bad merchants. Most good ones will specify which vineyards their best wines come from and if you want a 'growth' it really is worth seeking out these single vineyard wines. A few growers bottle their own wines, though this is not necessarily better than the wine from a good merchant in the area. The co-operatives are important, selling much of their wine to the merchants and to visiting tourists. Sometimes it is bottled separately and can be fairly good.

READING THE LABEL
The labels are straightforward but, except for Beaujolais Nouveau, when you simply want to see the merchant's name – and the vintage date to be sure it's this year's – the more information the better. A label showing a single vineyard name is a good sign.

WHAT DOES IT TASTE LIKE?
From top to bottom, the most important thing in Beaujolais flavours is not the differences between the various villages but the similarities the Gamay imposes. Gamay produces a gushing, purple-red, frothy-fresh wine. It reeks of cherries and raspberries and peaches, sometimes it's even slightly fizzy, and it has that rare quality for a red wine – it is thirst-quenching. Anyway, you should be knocking it back so fast and so carelessly that you haven't time to ponder on the taste.

'La Mode' than most of the 'growths'. 'A la mode' just now means light and quick-maturing.

Chiroubles Of all the 'growths', this best suits the early drinking fashion. The wines are naturally light, similar to a Beaujolais-Villages in weight, but with a perfumy, cherry fragrance which makes Chiroubles France's favourite Beaujolais 'growth'.

Fleurie Another lovely name, suggesting bright perfumed red wines, to laugh with and to tumble down your throat. Fleurie is usually gentle and round, its sweet cherry and chocolate fruit just held firm by a touch of tannin and acid but nowadays too expensive.

Moulin-à-Vent Enter the heavy brigade. These wines should be solid and strong, and should age very well for three to five years, sometimes longer. What one wants here is a big, plummy, slightly burgundian style, and the toughness of young Moulin-à-Vent doesn't give you much option but to wait. It rarely resembles anyone's view of straight Beaujolais; it takes itself far too seriously.

THE GOOD YEARS

In the majority of cases the most recent year is the best. 1989 is in any case a lovely Beaujolais year, but 1988 can still be gorgeous. This of course only applies to the 'growth' wines, because most Gamay wine is at its best purple-fresh, pumped full of fruit. That fruit can quickly fade, and then, whatever it says on the label, you just won't feel you're drinking Beaujolais any more.

ENJOYING THE WINE

Simply drink it whenever you want, however you want, with whomever and with whatever you want! Beaujolais, and in particular Nouveau, is the rule-breaker. You don't even need wine glasses – paper mugs, tea cups or glass slippers will do. You can drink it warm or cold – I'd go so far as putting it in the fridge, or even throwing a lump of ice in it. And you can drink it with anything, except perhaps chocolate cake and treacle tart. Just don't make the mistake of stopping to think about it.

What is Beaujolais Nouveau?

Nouveau is the 'new' vintage wine of Beaujolais, released in the same year as the grapes are gathered. A French government decree of 1951 prohibits release of this 'new' wine before 15 November of the year of the vintage. Criticism that the wines were too acid and slightly fizzy were met by a decree of 1980, limiting maximum acidity levels and ensuring that any second fermentation (the cause of the fizziness) has already taken place.

The wine is often only two months old when it is released, the grape harvest usually taking place mid-September. Consequently it will normally improve for several months in bottle. Many 1989 Nouveaux were at their best between Christmas and Easter. The firmer 1988s, however, often only reached their peak during the summer.

CONSUMER INFORMATION

WHAT DO I GET FOR MY MONEY?

There's a very wide quality span, because there's often a lot of duff Beaujolais on the market when Nouveau's finished, and in the hands of a careless merchant, those nine 'growths' don't always live up to their reputation either. But – fresh, fruity Beaujolais, frothing and tumbling from the jug? Well, sometimes, on a lazy summer Sunday lunchtime, or a foggy November night, or at any café table from Paris to Marseilles, it can be, just for a fleeting moment, the best red wine in the world.

Beaujolais *can* be overpriced, particularly Nouveau, and especially in the face of the competition from farther south in France. Yet there is always cheap Nouveau around, and it is frequently as good as stuff twice the price. The 'growths', from a single domaine, won't be that cheap, but from a good year they are normally a much better buy than an equivalent-priced burgundy.

AVAILABILITY

Universal. Nouveau has spread across the world like a spring tide, and we should lap it up gratefully. Virtually every shop and restaurant will have it in November and December. For the rest of the year, the good Villages and 'growths' which represent decent drinking are much less widely available, but should be sought out.

CONSUMER CHECKLIST

Beaujolais-Villages 1989	Q:	1	2	3	4	5	**6**	7	8	9	10	
	P:	1	2	3	4	**5**	6	7	8	9	10	
	V:	1	2	3	4	5	**6**	7	8	9	10	
Morgon Single Domaine 1989	Q:	1	2	3	4	5	6	7	**8**	9	10	
	P:	1	2	3	4	5	**6**	7	8	9	10	
	V:	1	2	3	4	5	6	7	**8**	9	10	

Good Years There is good wine every year, although wet years may produce thin basic wine. In general the wines should be drunk within a year, though top wines may age for three to four years. Recent successes: 1989, 1988, 1987, 1985.

Taste Notes Most Beaujolais is best very young for its delicious burst of purple-fresh, peppery, cherryish fruit. Top wines can age to a deep, chocolaty, plummy style.

GENERIC BURGUNDY

Although Burgundy is above all a region which packs as many famous names as possible into its fairly limited space, there are vineyards which do not qualify for the top honours and have to content themselves with a more humdrum title. This occurs for several reasons. Either the wrong grape is growing, which means Gamay in Pinot Noir land or Aligoté in Chardonnay land. Or the land is off the main slopes, either in the hinterland behind the Côte d'Or, or in the heavy flat land below the villages and away from the hillside. Or it may be that a good grower practises a form of self-denial, not putting wine from his young vines or his less successful vats in with his main production. These fall into two groups – the generic appellations, or region-wide general titles with no district identity, and the rather more specific general appellations with a wide reaching but defined catchment area.

GENERIC APPELLATIONS

Except in an excessive year like 1982, when there is gross overproduction to be soaked up, these appellations rarely reach 10 per cent of the harvest, unlike Bordeaux, where the basic Bordeaux Rouge and Bordeaux Blanc are the largest single appellations. It is interesting that burgundy has created such a ritzy reputation for itself that these cheaper wines often have difficulty finding buyers, while people are falling over themselves to buy the more expensive wines. But then, as the basic wines of the region, these are *not* cheap, sometimes being twice the price of basic Bordeaux or Rhône.

Bourgogne Grand Ordinaire/Ordinaire

This title uneasily mixes the optimism of 'Grand' with the dismissiveness of 'Ordinaire'. The clumsiness of the title usually slops over into the style of the wine. It can be produced throughout the region from virtually any grape found growing in most vineyards. The bulk of the red is based on Gamay, and the bulk of the white on Aligoté. I have yet to find one of more than passable, and easily forgettable, quality.

Bourgogne Passe-tout-grain

Often lumped in the same cart as Bourgogne Grand Ordinaire, this is a far superior product, and can achieve a delicious cherry-fresh burst of fruit which isn't all that common in modern-day burgundy. There is a little rosé made, but basically this is a red wine appellation. Legally, it should be two-thirds Gamay and one-third Pinot Noir, but with the increasing prevalence of big yields from the Pinot grape, the proportions in a year like 1982 can actually be reversed with Pinot Noir the dominant grape. Since few growers are replanting Gamay, preferring to increase their holdings of the more valuable Pinot Noir, the Gamay content is often from old vines yielding good rich wine to combat the frequently pallid Pinot Noir. Although this appellation is often dismissed as coarse, in a ripe year like 1988 or 1989, it can make excellent perfumed red to drink young, which will also age well – often to a gentle softness putting some classier burgundies to shame. From a grower like Thomas or Rion, or a shipper like Chanson or Leroy, these wines are undervalued and worth seeking out.

Bourgogne Aligoté

The Aligoté is Burgundy's secondary white grape, giving rather a lot of fairly acid wine. Even so, there are times when it suits the mood better than the superior Chardonnay wines. It mixes particularly well with the local fruit liqueurs to make Kir (with the local blackcurrant liqueur Cassis) and Mure (with the blackberry liqueur Murelle). With the oilier dishes like snails it is also sharp and good. Aligoté from the villages of Pernand-

grapes can include the César and the Tressot with their Pinot Noir. While in the Côtes d'Or and Chalonnaise the Pinot is used. Some of the Yonne wines from Epineuil, Irancy and Coulanges Les Vineuses are extremely good light reds. The Chalonnais, too, produces a fair amount of gentle, fragrant Pinot. When aided by aging in oak barrels as at the excellent Buxy co-op, the result is fine burgundy. However, the best is from the Côte d'Or. Good merchants do try to keep a good quality of basic Bourgogne, with recognizable Pinot Noir fruit, and companies like Jadot, Drouhin, Jaffelin, Rodet and Leroy usually succeed. But, again, it is the growers who vinify grapes from young vines separately, or take good care of their lesser vineyards who make the finest wine – Parent in Pommard, Pousse d'Or in Volnay, Jacques Germain in Chorey-Les-Beaune and Rion in Nuits St-Georges. Wines such as these can be the quintessence of perfumed, strawberryish burgundy – utterly delicious. In general, though, it isn't worth buying the cheap, blended offerings because there's a lot of poor, lifeless Pinot Noir about, and anything which can't be squeezed into a more expensive appellation will pay its dues in a vat of Bourgogne Rouge.

Vergelesses in the Côte de Beaune, and Bouzeron in the Côte Chalonnaise are the most famous, with Dubreuil-Fontaine in Pernand and de Villaine and Bouchard Père et Fils in Bouzeron being especially good. Indeed, Bouzeron is now allowed to include its name on the label along with Bourgogne Aligoté. Ideally, good Aligoté should have a smell of buttermilk soap, yet be tart and lemony to taste.

Bourgogne Blanc

This is the ordinary wine from the Chardonnay grape, sometimes with some Pinot Blanc too. Much of it comes from the Mâconnais where it is primarily used by dealers as a lower-priced alternative to the starry names of Pouilly. In the Côte d'Or, all merchant houses offer one, since there is frequently overproduction in the lesser vineyards which needs mopping up. From a good merchant it can be high-quality wine, and Jaffelin, Labouré-Roi and Jadot with their 'Couvent des Jacobins' are always enjoyable. However, the finest come from growers who make the produce from their young vines or outlying vineyards with as much care as their great wines. From a top grower like Coche-Dury or Millot-Battault in Meursault, the wine is rich, buttery, and a joy to drink at a fair price.

Bourgogne Rouge

This is a more complicated appellation than Bourgogne Blanc, since its objective is to soak up the excess grapes, and each district uses different ones. Beaujolais, for instance, can use this appellation for wine from its nine 'Cru' villages, which will be Gamay. In theory only Chénas makes much of this Gamay-based Bourgogne Rouge, sometimes as much as half the commune's crop.

In the Yonne, far north round Chablis, the few vineyards which commercialize their red

---

SPARKLING WINE

There is a large non-champagne-method industry in Burgundy, of which Kriter is the most famous example, but far more importantly, the area makes some of France's best champagne-method wines (see p. 102). At Chablis, Simmonet-Febvre and Caves Bailly make good dry wine, the rosé from Bailly being first class. The Côte d'Or has various firms making white and red, with Nuits St-Georges being the most important centre, and in the Chalonnais Veuve Ambal and Delorme in particular have long been famous for their fizz. The Burgundian sparkling wine industry was started there in the village of Rully in 1820. The Mâconnais makes a softer, but very drinkable style. The basic appellation for these is Bourgogne Mousseux, but the stricter and more come-hither title of Crémant de Bourgogne is increasingly popular.

CHAMPAGNE

THE GENERAL PICTURE

There's no conjuring act like it. From some of the rawest, sourest still wine in all of France they dip their hands into the magician's hat and draw out the most sumptuous, glittering creation in all the world of wine. From the most northerly windswept vineyards in France they bring out a parade of gorgeous fizzy flavours more reminiscent of the sunshades in the warm south of the French Riviera or the ritzy closeness of nightclubs, theatre dressing rooms, and 'dinners for two' of the slightly after-hours sort. And from a sea of vines which, come vintage time, are mostly weighed down with bunches of dark black grapes, tough and chewy to the taste, comes a foaming golden wine as far removed from a tart black grape as a geisha girl is from a heavyweight boxer.

How does it all happen? It needed a remarkable combination of natural climate and geological formations along with a stiff leavening of human ingenuity and good luck. The natural phenomenon could be described as a mixture of chalk and chill. The chalk cliffs which stare at each other over the English Channel between Dover and Cap Gris Nez are part of a long billowing seam roaming across southern England and northern France. There's nothing light white wine seems to thrive on as much as chalk, and round the cathedral city of Rheims, north-east of Paris, the chalk manages to find those deep cleft river valleys and tucked-away microclimates which can ripen wine grapes. Just. This is the Champagne region – the only one – and it has an average annual temperature just one degree above what is needed to ripen wine grapes. Many years it is a close-run thing. In some years, like 1987, the grapes just never get warm enough to ripen. But this 'risk' element is crucial to the eventual character of the wine, since, when they do ripen, the struggle has given a fresh fruit and a lingering depth to what is still a light wine in much the same way as a cool climate apple or pear or plum, fighting eternally against wind and rain, will always taste more interesting than the fat-cat table fruit from sunny climes.

That word 'champagne'. It doesn't just mean a style of wine. It doesn't simply mean something fizzy and fun. It can only legitimately apply to the wine coming from a very distinct, carefully delimited, part of France. The fact that this local wine has been such a

whopping international success has meant that 'champagne' is a term often used to describe any sparkling wine. This is neither accurate nor honest. Champagne can only come from the chalky, chilly hills and valleys centred on the River Marne. But the champagne 'method' *(méthode champenoise)* can be applied all over the world, wherever you want to make a still wine sparkle, so let's take a look at what this 'method' is.

'Make a still wine sparkle' is the key phrase here, because champagne, and all the wines made sparkling by the champagne method, are naturally still. Champagne is so far north that the wines ferment very slowly in the late autumn, and, if left to their own devices, usually fail to finish off the job before the icy winter winds freeze the cellars and so put the yeasts into limbo. Traditionally, most wines everywhere used to be made to be drunk within a year of the vintage; you had a vintage every 12 months, so why should you keep the wine any longer? This meant that the wines of Champagne were shipped off in barrels during the winter, to Paris first, and later to London. Spring came, the weather warmed up, and

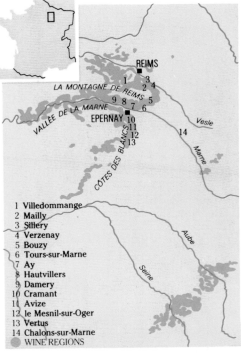

1 Villedommange
2 Mailly
3 Sillery
4 Verzenay
5 Bouzy
6 Tours-sur-Marne
7 Ay
8 Hautvillers
9 Damery
10 Cramant
11 Avize
12 le Mesnil-sur-Oger
13 Vertus
14 Chalons-sur-Marne
● WINE REGIONS

The pickers are sorting through the black grapes at vintage time to check for rot and disease. Few companies still do this.

the yeasts, which had gone into a kind of hibernation, woke up and returned to the task of fermenting out the sugar in the juice. Nobody quite realized why this was, but it meant that a creamy, foaming mousse appeared in the wine around Easter, and for six to eight weeks into the early summer, this laughing, gurgling liquid cascaded and frothed out of the barrels. Louis XIV's court loved it. Madame Pompadour declared that it was the only way to get sozzled and stay sexy.

The trouble was that the wine lost its fizz by June; it lay in its barrel, merrily bubbling away for a bit, and then just stopped. Yeast and sugar at a warm temperature react to create alcohol and carbon dioxide, and the yeasts had quite simply eaten up all the sugar. So once the yeasts had warmed up and devoured the rest of the sugar, that was it. Dry still wine. Until a local monk called Dom Pérignon came along and in effect 'invented' champagne as we know it.

What he did was to harness those bubbles and keep them dissolved in the wine. He noticed the way the wine frothed every spring, and also realized how much better it

tasted while it was still frothing. Luckily he had two fairly recent innovations to help him – new, high-quality glass bottles from England, and stoppers made of cork bark from Spain. He worked out how to bottle the wines with their fizz still in them, admittedly making a fair mess of the kitchen while he did it, because once you try to capture those bubbles and dissolve the gas in the wine, the pressure inside the bottle can build up to five or six atmospheres (an atmosphere is 1 kg per sq cm), and a lot of those early bottles burst.

The ones that survived produced a wine full of sparkle and also far richer in fruit and perfume than the thin, still wines they'd been used to knocking back in Champagne. The 'champagne method' had been born. Today, the champagne method means the inducing of a second fermentation of the wine inside the bottle, and the consequent dissolution of carbon dioxide in the wine. Cheap sparkling wines are either virtually pumped full of gas or subjected to the *charmat* method, i.e. fermented in enormous pressurized tanks. Sounds nasty? It is. Only the champagne method really delivers the goods.

CHAMPAGNE

CHAMPAGNE METHOD

Let's look in more detail at how champagne is made (much of this will also apply to other champagne method wines). The grapes are brought in and carefully pressed – and I mean carefully, since most of the grapes in Champagne have black skins, and the objective is to press them quickly and gently so that the juice is as pale as possible. These basic wines are then fermented out to dryness, and then wines from various vineyards are expertly blended into a single style. These blends are called 'Cuvées', and many champagnes have 'Cuvée' in their title, which denotes the particular blend of the house.

So you now have a satisfactory blend – of totally still champagne wines. And this is when the champagne method gets going, with three crucial stages to follow. The first stage is creating the bubbles. This blend is bottled in the spring with a little *liqueur de tirage* of yeast and sugar added to re-start the fermentation. A strong cork or metal stopper is shoved in the bottle, and the yeasts begin eating up the sugar again. Creating alcohol. Creating carbon dioxide, which, since it can't escape, dissolves in the wine, biding its time until it reappears as that beautiful twining and twisting tangle of bubbles when the wine is finally poured. To get good bubbles, you want this *prise de mousse*, or 'moussetaking', to last a fair while – two or three years certainly, longer if possible.

But while this second fermentation has been creating the bubbles, it's also been behaving in a less attractive way. It's been depositing used-up yeast cells as a thoroughly unprepossessing light brown gunge on the side of the bottle. Not the right image at society weddings or luxury liner launchings, but it is crucial for imparting flavour.

Let's think about it. There's sludge in the bottle. The bottle only has one opening, so that's the exit the sludge will have to leave by. There's a cork in this opening. If the bottles were tipped upside down, the sludge would drop on to the cork in a little dollop. Well, some would, some wouldn't, which leads us to the second principle – *remuage*, or 'removal'. If you gradually tipped the bottles from horizontal to upside down, giving the bottles a slight turn and a slight knock every day or two for weeks on end, the sludge which clung to the bottle's side would be jogged and gradually slip on to the cork.

Then comes the dénouement, *dégorgement*. With a certain amount of practice and a deft flick of a well-turned wrist, you pull out the cork, and simultaneously flip the bottle upright, removing the plug of yeast sludge and probably a few drops of wine too. Those few drops are a small price to pay for a totally clear wine, and while the cork is out you can add back a little sugar and champagne (*liqueur d'expédition*), according to how sweet you want your champagne.

Here we have the three fundamental principles of the champagne method. The first,

Top left *Rheims is riddled with Roman chalk pits which make cool, natural cellars for gently maturing the wines.* **Middle** *The second fermentation inside the bottle causes a thick sediment to form.* **Below left** *Remuage is a dying art as it's now increasingly carried out by machine.* **Below** *Most 'disgorging' of the champagne sediment is also now done by machine, but occasionally one sees the froth and spray of a craftsman doing it by hand.*

and obviously most crucial, is getting those bubbles into the wine. The second process, shifting the sludge, was invented by Veuve Clicquot, the greatest of the many indomitable widows who have forged the modern champagne industry. She invented a kind of two-sided desk with holes in it called a *pupitre*. Shove the bottles in the holes, go through the tilt-and-tap routine for three months and you're ready for the third principle – the *dégorgement*. There are new mechanical *pupitres* now – great big metal palettes of bottles clicking and clunking the sediment on to the cork, and though many companies swear they'd never replace the cold damp tunnel workers with their flailing fingers who can tear through 40,000 bottles a day, most of them will in the end. It's a sad fact, but efficiency comes before romance. Anyway, it must be a rotten job, and I should think arthritis is top of the bill of occupational hazards for those 'removal men'.

The *dégorgement* is literally the 'disgorging' of the muck. It used to require a large number of men with strong wrists and fast reflexes, popping corks and ejecting sediment, but now the neck of the bottle containing the deposit is frozen, the tight, chill pellet is whipped out on a machine production line, and the *dosage* is added. Less wine lost, more romance lost.

A word about the *dosage*. After the *dégorgement* the wine is still totally dry, since any sugar will have been eaten up by fermentation, which is also, of course, what has caused all those bubbles. Remembering that the basic wine of Champagne is fairly harsh and raw, there are very few champagne houses which don't add some sugar back after disgorging, to take the edge off the wine's acidity. Even Brut champagnes, usually the driest a house offers, will have some sugar added back, usually at least 6 g per litre. The sweetest may have more like 50 g. Only a very few rare brands, often called Brut Zero or something similar, have none at all.

Then the special triple-strength champagne cork is rammed in. This usually consists of three layers of high-quality cork fixed horizontally on to a good chunk of composition cork, made up of little chips of cork and glue. The high-quality end is jammed into the bottle, and the cheaper end is left out. When we remove a champagne cork it looks like a mushroom. This is because the cork is actually wider than the neck of the bottle. Compress it, shove it two-thirds in, and the bit in the bottle will strain to expand, thus preserving a total seal against the carbon dioxide panting to get out. Gradually the cork in the bottle will weaken and shrink, while the part outside stays the same shape, which produces the mushroom effect. And that's it! The champagne method! Put a wire over the cork just in case the wine gets over-excited, doll it up with gold foil, age it if you can – but, whatever happens from now on, you've just made a champagne-method wine!

CHAMPAGNE

THE GENERAL PICTURE

GRAPE VARIETIES AND WINE STYLES

The grapes of Champagne are primarily black! About two-thirds of the vineyards grow black grapes. Luckily, however, although the skins are black, the juice is white. The chief grape is the Pinot Noir, which makes all the finest red burgundies. It has difficulty ripening in Burgundy, and further north in Champagne it almost never attains any great depth and strength of colour or alcohol. Which is fair enough, because, with the exception of the occasional rosé champagne, or the rare, non-sparkling **Coteaux Champenois,** the general idea is to produce a *white* sparkling wine. Very careful pressing of the grapes in enormous square vertical presses is the best way to draw off the juice as pale as possible. Even so, the black grape juice does have a fairly big feel to it, and a champagne relying largely on black grapes is certain to be heavier and take longer to mature. The other black grape is the Pinot Meunier, which makes a softer, fruitier style, important in producing easy, forward wines. The white grape is the Chardonnay of white burgundy fame. This produces a lighter, fresher juice, and the resultant champagnes are certainly the most perfumed and honeyed. They have been criticized as lacking depth and aging potential. Not true; good **Blancs de Blancs** have a superb exciting flavour which is only improved by aging.

Champagne is basically produced in several styles, which are as follows:

Non-vintage The ordinary, most basic blend. Many houses used to pride themselves on providing a continuous house style through the judicious blending of various vintages. Some would even occasionally go to the extent of not declaring a vintage in a good year if they wanted to use the wine to keep up the standard of their non-vintage. Sadly this happens far less nowadays. Although a little older 'reserve' wine is added to smooth out the edges when the blend is being put together, most non-vintages are now released for drinking heavily dependent on a single year's harvest of perhaps two or three years' age, and some less scrupulous, or less solvent, producers, will offer wine not much more than a year old.

Vintage Wine of a single, usually good-quality, year, although the law allows a little flexibility here (!) – usually fuller, deeper, and a definite leg up the quality scale from non-vintage, but not necessarily more enjoyable for that. Certainly these are less effective as 'spontaneous celebration' wines, so save your money at parties! To get the best out of a vintage champagne it's worth taking your time.

Cuvée de Prestige/De Luxe A special, highly prized, and certainly highly priced, blend, usually vintage, but not always. It encompasses some great wines and some gaudy coat-tailers. There seems to be a virtual rule that the wines must come in silly bottles – wines like Bollinger RD are an honourable exception. Certainly some lovely wines, but at fabulous prices.

Crémant A champagne with only half the normal amount of fizz. If the base wine is good, that's still quite enough.

Coteaux Champenois Still wines, which can be either red or white. They sometimes come with a village name, like Bouzy or Cramant.

Rosé Rosé is an increasingly important sector. Traditionally the pink colour is gained by a careful and short maceration of the black Pinot Noir and Pinot Meunier skins with the juice. However, this method is unpredictable and usually a little red Bouzy wine is added to normal white champagne just before bottling. The wines are usually aromatic and fruity, but must be drunk young.

Blanc de Noirs This rare style is made from 100 per cent black grapes. The wine is white, usually rather solid, but can be impressive if aged long enough.

Blanc de Blancs An increasingly common style, from white Chardonnay grapes. The style is usually fresh and bright, and many De Luxe champagnes are now labelled Blanc de Blancs.

THE IMPORTANT DETAILS

CLASSIFICATION

The classification system in Champagne is based on vineyards, although the winemaker, according to his decisions regarding the eventual description of the quality and style of the final blend will also add a second, unofficial, classification. The approved areas for vineyards are strictly demarcated, and although small vintages up to 1981 caused an expansion to be sanctioned, this dispensation only applied to land which had originally grown grapes and had fallen into disuse. Vineyard land is graded according to suitability for black and white grapes, going from 100 per cent for the 17 traditionally finest Grand Cru villages, through 99-90 per cent for the 40 Premier Cru villages and on to 80 per cent for the least favoured.

Each year the growers all meet and fix the price they want when they sell their grapes to the champagne houses. If the price is 20 francs per kg of grapes, a 100 per cent village grower receives the full 20 francs. An 80 per cent grower will only receive 80 per cent – 16 francs – and so on. Champagne houses boast how high their 'average percentage' of grape is. One wonders who buys the rest. Some champagnes will have words like 'Premier Cru', or '100%' and a village name like Avize on the label. This shows that the wine comes from that single top village.

The second, unofficial 'classification' comes from those styles described in Grape Varieties and Wine Styles.

ORGANIZATION/S

Until fairly recently, one could have said that the leading champagne houses or companies controlled the whole operation. The most important companies are a group called the 'Syndicat de Grandes Marques' or 'Syndicate of Great Brands'. These 'Grandes Marques' still maintain the dominant position in the export market, but not in France.

This is because, with expanding world demand, and some dreadfully small harvests, the growers suddenly found the tables turned. The businessmen from the merchant houses had an urgent need for growers' grapes. The growers gained the upper hand, first by charging enormously inflated prices for their precious grapes, then by beginning to make their own champagne, something until then regarded as the merchants' prerogative . . . These so-called 'grower champagnes' now lead the French market. Surprisingly, however, the growers' own wine is not as good as the merchants', although it is usually cheap because the greatest champagnes are marked by a skilful blend of different village wines. Co-operatives such as Mailly and Avize are also very important in Champagne, often not merely handling the grapes, but increasingly making wine too. Many of the cheaper blends on the market come from one of the big co-ops. The standard is unusually good, and the prices keen.

Syndicat de Grandes Marques

Ayala et Montebello	Moët & Chandon
Billecart-Salmon	G. H. Mumm
J. Bollinger	Perrier-Jouët
Canard-Duchêne	Joseph Perrier
Deutz & Geldermann	Piper Heidsieck
Heidsieck & Co	Pol Roger
Monopole	Pommery & Greno
Charles Heidsieck	Ch. & A. Prieur
Henriot	Louis Roederer
Krug	Ruinart
Lanson Père et	A. Salon
Fils/Massé	Taittinger/Irroy
Laurent Perrier	Veuve Clicquot-
Mercier	Ponsardin

READING THE LABEL

Apart from the various descriptive terms on the back of the label, the letters in small print at the bottom will indicate the type of producer and the numbers following will identify

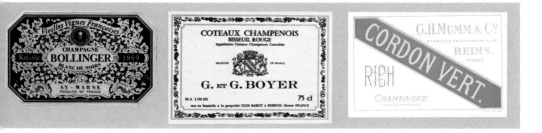

CHANGPAGNE

THE IMPORTANT DETAILS

each different winemaker. Main letters are as follows: **RM** (*Récoltant-Manipulant*, or 'Harvester-Handler') indicates that the wine is from a single grower; **RC** (*Récoltant-Coopérateur*) indicates a grower selling wine produced by a co-operative. **CM** (*Co-operative-Manipulant*, 'Co-operative-Handler'): this means that the wine comes from a co-operative; **NM** (*Négociant-Manipulant*, or 'Merchant-Handler') – merchants' wines: traditionally the most powerful and famous part of the champagne trade, their wines are likely to be of the highest standard; **MA** (*Marque d'Acheteur*): these letters appear when a merchant sells his wine under other, subsidiary labels to satisfy an export buyer's wish for a 'special selection', or to avoid conflict with his chief brand.

Sometimes the *Récemment Dégorgé* ('Recently Disgorged') appear on a label. These bottles have lain on their yeast deposits for much longer than usual, gaining depth and flavour from the living organisms. The disgorging only takes place shortly before the wine is sold, to preserve the maximum freshness. Such wines are frequently of De Luxe standard.

WHAT DOES IT TASTE LIKE?

What does it feel like? How does it make you feel? These might be more natural ways of looking at champagne and its flavours, since it is the effect of champagne and its bubbles that most people are after.

However, this would be to say that champagne is just 'another sparkling wine'. It is not. It is the most original, and the best. In terms of feel, champagne best promotes the heady, hectic sensations of good fortune and good company. That's because the carbon dioxide in it is absorbed at a particularly frantic rate by the stomach wall, which startles and livens up the circulation, which carries the alcohol to the brain at a far faster rate, which makes you feel friskier, brisker . . . Yes, *that's* the simple explanation why champagne really does make a party go with a bang – whoops! – pop.

The taste. Well, firstly there is some 'still' champagne wine, red and white, called Coteaux Champenois. It's rarely brilliant, and usually tastes a little thin and unripe; in fact it demonstrates precisely why they go to such

Winter in Champagne can be damp and bitterly cold. The vines nevertheless have to be pruned.

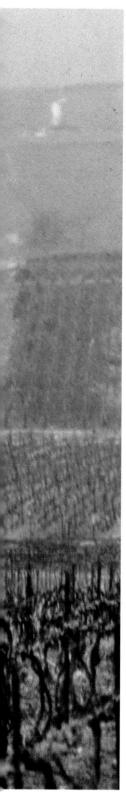

lengths to make it sparkle. The fizzy stuff ranges from the very green and rasping fresh, to the deep, honeyed, excitingly soft ripe wines of high quality when given perhaps ten years' aging.

This ability to age sets champagne apart from other sparkling wines, and is the result of the blending skills of the top champagne makers. As many as 30 or 40 different wines from all around the region may be used in a single final blend. Almost no single wine is as fine as the eventual resulting blend. And almost no wine would age as well by itself. From fairly tart, light beginnings, champagne can achieve remarkable rich flavours, and it is worth giving it time to prove it.

THE GOOD YEARS

1989 The tremendous heat produced a good crop of super-ripe grapes. This will be vintage wine for sure.

1988 An average crop of well balanced, classic-flavoured wine, which will be long lasting yet drinkable quite young.

1987 Large, tasteless, low acid crop, very feeble flavours, but useful for blending.

1986 Champagne needed a big harvest in 1986, but only got a fair one. There was enough wine to cover sales requirements, but not enough to build up big reserve stocks. The quality was impaired by late summer rains but is still goodish and of fair vintage standard.

1985 Not a great deal of wine, because Champagne got walloped by winter frost, but the wine is ripe and good and is already drinking beautifully.

1984 Hopeless as far as vintage prospects are concerned. The wines are light and feeble, and had enough trouble even getting their own fermentation going, let alone being considered for single vintage release. You shouldn't see *any* wines under this vintage.

1983 A wonderful year, and it's difficult to believe that Champagne will ever again be so lucky. The area made 300 million bottles, and the grapes were picked in superb condition. That 300 million represents the biggest harvest of all time in Champagne. Plus fine quality? Undoubtedly, but they are all being drunk far too young.

1982 Almost the same story as 1983; 295 million bottles of gorgeous, soft, ripe wines. 1982 followed several years of short, small harvests, so much of the wine will be used for

CHAMPAGNE

THE IMPORTANT DETAILS

reserve stocks. The vintage wines have been soft and easy right from the start but are aging beautifully.

1979 A very big crop of ripe grapes, which was lucky, because they were running out of wine in Rheims! Although a lot of it went into building up stocks of non-vintage blends to a safe level, the vintage wines are very good. Sadly they've mostly been drunk, although they're now at their peak.

1976 A 'nearly but not quite' vintage. For once there was actually too much sun in Champagne, and many of the wines taste as though they'd ripped off their coat and tie and basked for far too long in the unaccustomed warmth, before staggering back indoors with severe cases of sunburn and heat exhaustion. Champagne needs its acidity to be refreshing and exciting, and to enable it to age and any remaining 1976s will probably taste a bit past it.

ENJOYING CHAMPAGNE

I drink champagne just about any time I can get my hands on some. There's no drink more likely to put snap back into the fingers and bounce back into the feet, sparkle back into the eyes, and gurgling, flirting laughter back into the throat. Champagne is a wine which has no rules, except perhaps the general feeling that it should be chilled down rather than lukewarm. But even lukewarm, the whoosh of bubbles and the sharp-edged flavour mean it's easy to make the best of a bad job.

That said, it really does come into its own whenever there's a need to gee things up. If you want to get things moving with a well-aimed kick in the pants – stick to cocktails and hard liquor. Champagne is the conspiratorial nudge, the whispered aside, the encouraging flutter of the eyes, the hand held moments too long and too tight. If you want a civilized apéritif or don't feel your bottle is too special you could mess it about a bit. You could add a tiny dash of *cassis* or *mûr* or *framboise* liqueur, but *don't* – as so many bars do – use *sirop*. Adding some fresh orange juice makes Buck's Fizz, although both the fresh-pressed orange juice and the champagne are so good on their own that I'd keep the champagne separate and take alternate mouthfuls! And the same goes for Black Velvet (an unbeguiling mixture of champagne and Guinness).

And with food? Yes, of course, it *does* go with food. It is rarely the perfect taste combination, but since it is frequently the perfect complement to your mood one could say, 'Yes, it goes brilliantly with caviar, *foie gras,* salmon, roast venison, fish and chips and a bacon double cheeseburger (go easy on the ketchup) – so long as your mood is right.' Even a dry champagne can cope with rich cakes and puddings though a 'rich' style might be better. Otherwise, champagne is at its best with the lighter starter dishes rather than with heavy grand creations. The finely tuned flavours of *nouvelle cuisine* often defy traditional wine partnerships: champagne fits that bill very well indeed.

Left *Champagne suffers from two natural foes – birds which blithely eat the grapes in autumn, and frosts that can kill the buds in spring. Here the bird netting covers a rusting antifrost burner.*
Top *Perfect white grapes that will eventually be transformed into sparkling, golden wine: champagne.*

CONSUMER INFORMATION

WHAT DO I GET FOR MY MONEY?

In general terms, you get great value. Champagne *is* expensive, but show me be a substitute which is half as good. For basic celebrations, the own-label non-vintage blends are almost all improving now that the good 1988 vintage is being blended in. The top houses' **(Veuve Clicquot, Pol Roger, Taittinger, Lanson, Laurent-Perrier, Joseph Perrier)** non-vintages are usually 20-30 per cent more expensive and usually pretty good, but the great leap in quality comes with a vintage date. Sadly, vintage wines are all released for drinking far too young. Most vintages need eight to ten years to show their honeyed, perfumed best. The De Luxes are hardly brilliant value, though some are very exciting and one or two, like **Bollinger RD, Clicquot Grande Dame, Laurent Perrier Grand Siècle, Taittinger Comtes de Champagne, Krug Grande Cuvée** or **Roederer Cristal** are so classy, one might be tempted. Might.

AVAILABILITY

Champagne must be the most generally available wine in the world – that is, the non-vintage blends of the major champagne houses – which is normally exactly what we want. The straight vintage styles and the razzamatazzy De Luxe styles are much less widely available and thus more expensive – as they're supposed to be 'special', 'limited edition' creations. Single-domaine champagnes are rare outside France. Still Coteaux Champenois wines are rare anywhere.

CONSUMER CHECKLIST		
Non-vintage Pol	Q:	1 2 3 4 5 6 7 **8** 9 10
Roger	P:	1 2 3 4 5 6 7 8 9 10
	V:	1 2 3 4 5 6 7 **8** 9 10
Vintage Veuve	Q:	1 2 3 4 5 6 7 **8** 9 10
Clicquot	P:	1 2 3 4 5 6 7 8 **9** 10
	V:	1 2 3 4 5 6 **7** 8 9 10
Laurent Perrier	Q:	1 2 3 4 5 6 7 8 **9** 10
Grand Siècle	P:	1 2 3 4 5 6 7 8 **9** 10
	V:	1 2 3 4 5 6 7 **8** 9 10

Good Years 1986, 1985, 1983, 1982, 1979, 1975.

Taste Notes All champagnes should have a clear, clean fruit, not aromatic, but very fresh when young and going honeyed and mellow as it gets older. The higher quality the champagne is, the deeper and more thought-provoking the flavour should be.

THE 'AGING' CONTROVERSY

Let's get one thing straight – champagne *does* age. There's a rumour going round Champagne at the moment that their wine should be drunk young and tart, and as soon as it is put on the market. Rubbish! Sorry, all you PR wizards, but to deny that champagne ages is to gainsay the one thing that unarguably sets champagne apart from all other sparkling wines. The natural acidity in the grapes *must* be given time to soften, and because two of the world's greatest grapes – the white Chardonnay and the black Pinot Noir – are involved, you are certain to get the benefit of softer, richer, gentler flavours.

Time was when the champagne houses released their wines on to the market only when they were ready to drink – before high interest rates and an accountant on every board took their toll. This probably meant that vintage wine was released at seven to eight years old, and non-vintage at three to four years. Nowadays, vintage wine is more likely to be five years old, can be four, and non-vintage blends can be as little as two, but to bring out champagne's special characteristics these shorter periods just aren't sufficient.

Certainly there are some relatively low-priced champagnes around, and, even green and unready, they're better than any other equivalents. Also, the price differential between cheap champagne and expensive champagne-method wines is now relatively slight. If you want to drink them sharp and tangy and bursting with froth, fine. Just remember, though, that you've paid a high price. If only you gave it six months' aging, even the cheapest champagne would be transformed and become palpably superior to its rivals in the fizz market.

RHÔNE

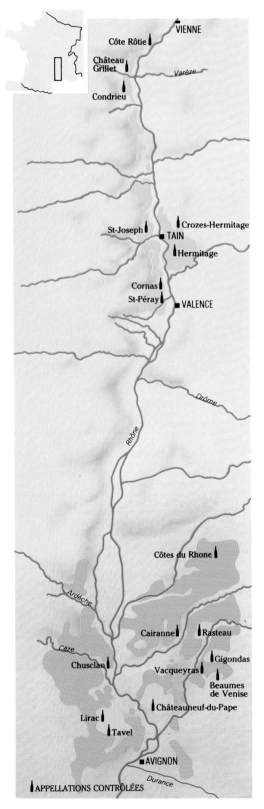

It's not till you've painfully negotiated the wretched highway system in Lyons, plunged south through the sour-smelling parade of grimy factories and refineries for the next 30 km (18 miles) and, gasping for the hot, fresh country air, swung the car over the two bridges spanning the Rhône near Vienne, that you know that you're in the South of France. From that moment on, every sign of civilization will seem to be rudely carved by the demands of the beating Mediterranean sun and the harsh summer winds.

The Rhône valley is both the beginning of the vast drab vinelands of the south, and the pinnacle of their achievement. Beginning with a sliver of narrow, precipitous vineyard rockface tumbling down to the river bed at Côte Rôtie in the north, and spreading to the immense tarpaulin of stubby, ugly vines carpeting the flat, arid land 150 km (93 miles) to the south round Avignon, this is one of France's most important regions, pumping out more wine than Beaujolais and Burgundy, and nearly as much as Bordeaux.

That's a lot of wine. But the Rhône valley has always been strangely unable to profit from its success. It harbours one of the world's most famous and abused wine names – yes, good old Châteauneuf-du-Pape – but cite me another household wine name from the Rhône. Apart, of course, from equally 'good old' Côtes du Rhône, which can cover just about every eventuality from half-hearted rosé to thick paintbrush bristle red palate-bashers, what else is there? Well, a good deal. It is remarkable how the Rhône's famous names have slipped from view in the past, but now they've finally had enough of the sideline shadows and great names like Hermitage, Côte Rôtie, Condrieu, Tavel, and even Châteauneuf-du-Pape are at last standing up for their birthrights as some of France's finest wines. And less fabled names like St-Joseph, Crozes-Hermitage, and Muscat de Beaumes de Venise are heralding an entirely new generation of stars. Many of these are from the thin, northern river-slope slice of the region, whose whole tradition is more geared to the production of high-quality, hand-crafted wines, and whose styles are markedly more reserved and 'cool climate' than the sweltering produce of the south. So let's divide the Rhône into north and south and try to see what makes each tick.

RHÔNE/The North

THE GENERAL PICTURE

GRAPE VARIETIES AND WINE STYLES

The northern section is chiefly red and is dominated by one grape – the Syrah. Along with Cabernet Sauvignon, Bordeaux's great grape, the Syrah makes the blackest, most startling, pungent red wine in France and, although it is grown elsewhere, it is here that it is at its most brilliant. The greatest wines are Hermitage and Côte Rôtie, two tiny vineyard areas less than a fifth the size of any of Bordeaux's great wine villages. **Hermitage** is one of France's burliest wines, while **Côte Rôtie,** by the judicious admixture of juice from the white Viognier grape, is one of France's most perfumed and fragrant reds. The wines of **Cornas,** black and tarry teeth-stainers, and the wines of **St-Joseph,** almost smooth and sweet by comparison, are also fine, and the large appellation of **Crozes-Hermitage** provides a lot of 'Hermitage-type'

In the northern Rhône valley, the river flows directly beneath the best vineyards, characteristically terraced on the steep slopes which are such a feature of this region.

wine – fairly strong and a bit tough, but good value nevertheless.

Despite red dominance, there is a white presence. The Viognier grape makes **Condrieu** and **Château Grillet,** two dreamy-tasting rarities, and the Marsanne and Roussanne grapes not only make white Hermitage and Crozes-Hermitage, but also St-Joseph and the rather forgotten **St-Péray.** And if you take a long hike eastwards from Valence, you'll eventually get to the River Drôme, where, twined high in the foothills, the Muscat and the Clairette grapes make **Clairette de Die Tradition** – delicious, light, super-fresh fizz.

RHÔNE/The North

THE IMPORTANT DETAILS

Left *The great hill of Hermitage climbs high above the riverside town of Tain. Some of France's greatest reds and whites come from this vineyard.* **Right** *Vineyard workers binding the vines in St-Joseph. The steeper sites like this one produce the best wine.* **Far right** *Château Grillet, France's smallest Appellation Contrôlée in its own right, produces white wine from the Viognier grape. The vines are planted on the terraced slopes high above the right bank of the Rhône.*

CLASSIFICATION

Classification in the northern Rhône is largely a matter of simple geographical delineation of vineyard areas around a single name. A couple of producers label their wines 'Grand Cru', but there isn't a *cru* or 'growth' system as such, and there's no Bordeaux-style official classification. A kind of pecking order is established: (a) through certain parts of some vineyards, like Côte Rôtie and Hermitage, having some particularly favoured patches (which, however, hardly ever appear on the label), and (b) through trade marks or traditional titles – like La Chapelle for Jaboulet's best Hermitage, for instance – which are only applied to particularly good wines. In any case, most northern Rhône wines are a blend of several wines from within the single vineyard appellation.

ORGANIZATION/S

The northern Rhône is one of the few areas where one could say that the honours are fairly evenly shared between merchants' blends and individual growers' wines. Most leading merchants own numerous plots of land, and in difficult vintages may even have the upper hand due to their ability to balance their wines through 'inter-plot' blending. This

applies chiefly to various Hermitage producers and to the firm of Guigal in Côte Rôtie. Otherwise one should follow a grower's reputation. These are difficult vineyards to work, back-breaking and spirit-bowing. A few generations of family pride in the small plot of land which you own and your forbears owned is a great incentive to strike out for quality and excellence. There are a few co-operatives and the best of these is probably at St-Désirat-Champagne.

READING THE LABEL

Rhône labels are fairly easy to interpret. They follow the Burgundian pattern of a general area name or single village name, but don't go in for the Grand Cru routine. Some basic wines will be offered without a vintage. There are some very good bottlings by merchants.

WHAT DO THEY TASTE LIKE?

You'd better be sitting down when you start reading this, because the purple prose may begin to flow like a breached dam at any moment. The red Syrah and the white Viognier, hidden in their steep-sided, twisting river valley below Lyons, pour out two of the most startling taste sensations the world of wine has to offer. The white Viognier, virtually ex-

clusive to Condrieu and Château Grillet, has such a steamy, exotic flavour of apricot, fresh, and bursting with the muskiness of ripe autumn fruit, that you gasp at the sheer unexpected beauty of the thing.

You gasp at the Syrah too. In young Hermitage and Cornas, this massive brute of a grape shoves aside the niceties of taste and bellows its presence, rasping with tannin and tar and woodsmoke, and the deep ungainly sweetness of black treacle. Leave it a while. Five years, maybe ten, then try again. The wine will have undergone a sea change. The almost medicinal edge will still be there, but those raw fumes will have become sweet, pungent, full of raspberries, brambles and cassis. There! I warned you about the purple prose, but good Syrah wine is *so* good, I thought I'd risk going over the top a bit – just to tempt you to try it. And drink it sitting down too – just in case you find it as exciting as I do.

Château Grillet A single property, and the smallest Appellation Contrôlée in France, at only 3 hectares (7.5 acres). Actually, there are several *grands crus* in Burgundy with their own AC which are even smaller! This white should have that magic reek of orchard fruit

and harvest bloom about it. If it does, the huge asking price is almost worth it.

Condrieu This is pretty minute too – only 20 hectares (50 acres), situated on the bend of the river just above Château Grillet, but at least there are quite a few different chaps giving it a go, and most of the best Viognier now comes from Condrieu, usually at less than half the price of Château Grillet. It is an amazing taste. That apricot scent leaps out of the glass at you, and the balance between succulent sweet fruit and gentle nipping acidity in a big, fairly dry white wine is worth all the effort and expense to root out.

Côte Rôtie The northernmost Rhône area, 'roasted slope' is an apt name for the baking cliff-like slopes which offer the best wines. It's another tiny area, with, traditionally, only about 100 hectares (250 acres) of vineyards. Sadly, there has been a massive and callous extension of appellation rights on to the ambling plateau land behind the river bend. Unless something is done to differentiate 'slopes' wine from 'flatlands' wine, the reputation of this highly priced, highly prized vineyard will be in tatters. At its best, from a few individual growers like Jasmin and Guigal and Jamet

RHÔNE/The North

THE IMPORTANT DETAILS

Côte Rôtie can be a most fragrant scented red, the fierceness of the Syrah grape tempered by a little white Viognier sweetness. Rare and delicious.

Hermitage The hill of Hermitage broods over the town of Tain, so steep and pointed that it would seem hardly possible to cultivate it. But those 125 hectares (310 acres) produce the Rhône's greatest reds and fine whites too. The manliest wine of France, it was once described as. Men should be so lucky, to combine such strength and fiery toughness when young with such a rich, brooding magnificence when mature. There is always a stern, vaguely medicinal or smoky edge to red Hermitage, but the Syrah also possesses a depth of raspberry and blackcurrant fruit no other grape can touch. White Hermitage is often a bit heavy and dull, but was once regarded as France's greatest white wine, and, curiously, ages tremendously well to a soft, content nuttiness.

St-Joseph Another appellation suffering from wanton expansion of vineyard into unsuitable terrain. Even so, good St-Joseph is a delicious wine, gentler and lighter than Hermitage, and stacked with blackcurrant fruit in a good year.

Cornas Closer to Hermitage in weight, but lacking a little of the fresh fruit which makes Hermitage so remarkable. Usually rather hefty, jammy even, and needing a fair bit of patience or a good dentist.

Crozes-Hermitage A potentially massive area of wine production, mostly red, which is usually solid, straight, rather dry and smoky Syrah, and always keenly priced. The white is dullish in comparison.

St-Péray This was once France's most famous sparkling wine after champagne. Not any more. Although it's quite good, it always seems rather stolid and short of freshness. The still whites also suffer from an honest toiler's dullness, which they'll have to overcome if they want to cash in on the modern boom in white wine drinking.

Clairette de Die Tradition A delicious, Muscat-scented sparkling wine of high quality. Other local wines are not so hot.

THE GOOD YEARS

It's as if the gods have taken pity on those back-bent winegrowers of the northern Rhône in recent years, trailing painfully up and down their steep and stony vineyard rows, because there has been a run of fine vintages to reward their efforts, including three which may stand up and be counted with the finest of the century. In previous times these strong stubborn reds would have been carted all over France to try to beef up various famous yet meagre reds. Happily they're now too precious and too rare in their own right.

1989 The torrid summer produced some memorable wines – when the acid and tannin were in balance.

1988 Wonderful vibrant classics, they are already delicious but they're also ready for the long haul.

1987 Adequate flavours for quick-drinking, but nothing special.

1986 Fairly good wines but not as good as 1985.

1985 Some classic wines, with wonderful Côte Rôtie.

1983 These are not ready as yet, but the wines are classics in the making, both red and white.

1982 Another brilliant year, thick with fruit and deep late-summer ripeness. Again they're only just ready, but will still make a mouthful worth hanging on for.

1978 Wonderful stuff. This is the vintage which set the whole world talking about Hermitage again. Sweet, concentrated, already absurdly delicious for a tough red style, but also capable of long aging. The whites are pretty exciting too.

ENJOYING THE WINES

Without exception the reds and whites of the north have uncompromising, unsquashable flavours, and they'll summarily brush aside any dull Lenten fare. The reds are quite superb with the most lordly of roasts and game, but are perhaps more used to the highly flavoured stews and charcuterie of their own region. The whites are more difficult to match with food, since they are relatively short on the cutting acid edge which makes white wine so refreshing. But simply prepared chicken, pork, and the local fish go well with most of them. The Muscaty Clairette de Die Tradition is a marvellously grapy apéritif.

RHÔNE/The South

THE GENERAL PICTURE

GRAPE VARIETIES AND WINE STYLES

The south is awash with permitted grape varieties, barely tolerated grape varieties and distinctly frowned upon grape varieties. Add to this a total change of terrain from the precipitous, crag-topped vineyards of the north to the sprawling flatlands of the south, with only the best villages pulling a few suitable slopes out of the bag, and a climate which, even as early as March, makes you reach for the sunhat or the tanning lotion – and you have a recipe for full, strong, indistinct flavours, big on guts, but going easy on the finer points. That, basically, is the south, but it's worth reminding ourselves, before we get too critical, that the Rhône is the best of

Wide-spaced vineyards like this one in the southern Rhône often stretch for miles across the landscape.

the south, and as you go further towards the Mediterranean and across to the Pyrenees, you'll pine for the positively sophisticated flavours even of the southern Rhône.

The only white grape of any distinction is the rare **Muscat,** centred round Beaumes de Venise. Other white grapes, for what it's worth, are Clairette, Roussanne, and Bourboulenc. In reds, the oomph is provided by the dark, tough Syrah or, sometimes, the recently-back-in-favour Mourvèdre, while Grenache and Cinsault provide the soft, juicy tastes which mark out the best wines.

THE IMPORTANT DETAILS

CLASSIFICATION

Basically, classification is similar to the northern Rhône except that the majority of southern Rhône wines come under the all-embracing Côtes du Rhône classification. The wines may be red, white or rosé but specific appellations may limit the colour of wines. The addition of 'Villages' to the title Côtes du Rhône will usually mean a considerable upward jump in quality and character. Otherwise, Tavel applies only to a small area of rosé wines; Châteauneuf-du-Pape is for red and white, while Gigondas applies to red and rosé, but you'll be hard-pressed to find anything but red. Two curiosities are the *vins*

doux naturels. Fortified with brandy rather than being naturally sweet, they are from the red Grenache grape in Rasteau and the white Muscat grape in Beaumes de Venise.

ORGANIZATION/S

The co-operative movement has made a dramatic contribution to the quality of the wines – co-ops like Chusclan, Beaumes de Venise, Cairanne and Vacqueyras now make some of the best in the region. In general, commercial blends are of a lower quality so, for real character in Châteauneuf-du-Pape, Lirac, Tavel, and Gigondas Côtes du Rhône Villages – go for a single grower.

RHÔNE/The South

THE IMPORTANT DETAILS

READING THE LABEL

The same applies as for the north. Particularly in Châteauneuf-du-Pape, it is important to check that the wine is domaine-bottled. In Côtes du Rhône and Côtes du Rhône Villages, a co-op bottling can be very good. Below are some examples.

WHAT DO THEY TASTE LIKE?

Châteauneuf-du-Pape This is the great name of the south, and is where the Appellation Contrôlée designation was first tried out in 1923. There are 13 different red and white grape varieties permitted in the vineyards, and the result is a slightly indistinct but extremely satisfying full red, with a characteristic dusty taste on top of the sweet juicy fruit. They're low in acidity, mature quickly, and have a brief burst of almost chocolaty richness at their peak. There is also a little surprisingly good white.

Gigondas This is often likened to Châteauneuf, but there isn't much similarity. Gigondas is usually bigger, beefier, and more ragged at the edges, more likely to have that strong, tough, southern taste of pressed grape skins warring with the admittedly considerable fruit.

Lirac An excellent and often underrated area just south-west of Châteauneuf. The reds and rosés are packed with fruit, often tainted with a not unwelcome mineral edge and the rosés are remarkably fresh for so far south. And they're cheap.

Tavel Always rosé, the wine is quite expensive, very tasty, and packs rather more of a punch than you'd expect.

In Châteauneuf-du-Pape these big stones litter the vineyards, retaining heat and bringing the grapes to 'super-ripeness'.

Côtes du Rhône Villages Usually red, from specific higher quality villages, the wines combine the rather earthy, dusty southern heat with a good deal of vaguely raspberryish fruit. Mostly good value chunky reds.

Côtes du Rhône The basic appellation. Again, mostly red, the wines can be tremendously fresh and fruity, like a rather softer version of Beaujolais, or they can be fierce black grape skins and alcohol monsters. I'd increasingly go for the former style as a source of good cheap reds but, since the label gives no clue, it's trial and error or merchants' recommendation.

Rasteau (vin doux naturel) Worldwide interest in sweet red wines is even lower than in rosés. Rasteau makes decent dry red, but is famous for some strong out-of-mode fortified red which I've never known what to do with.

Muscat de Beaumes de Venise (vin doux naturel) This sweet white wine is absolutely coining it in as a real fad drink. Luckily for us – it's delicious! Grapy, fresh, rich but not cloying.

THE GOOD YEARS

It used to be said that vintages didn't much matter in the southern Rhône, but they've been wildly inconsistent recently and in 1984 the French government had to declare the area a Disaster Zone!

The chief problem has often been the failure of the most important grape variety – the Grenache – although weather has also been a recent problem (they had summer fogs during 1987 at Châteauneuf-du-Pape). Even so, the 1989s and 1988s are extremely good, 1987 lacked a bit of ripeness and the 1986s were good if tough. 1985s are lovely and already drinkable. Of older vintages there are some classy 1981s while 1978 is still a real stunner.

ENJOYING THE WINES

These southern reds are rarely for pondering over, mind full of romance and poetry. No. Knock them back; use them as high-class quaffing wines for rough and ready foods – stews, grills and stinky cheeses. Good Lirac and Châteauneuf, as well as some 'Villages' wine, bear a bit more contemplation – but they'll still be happiest with chunks of lamb and slabs of goat's cheese rather than dainty morsels eaten off the best Wedgewood dinner set. The whites are usually dull, but a few attempts at a 'modern' style, while lacking apéritif freshness, are good first course wines. Chilled Muscat de Beaumes de Venise is wonderful grapy stuff at any time before or after a meal, or even with the sweet course.

CONSUMER INFORMATION

WHAT DO I GET FOR MY MONEY?

With the wines of both north and south, you get value. With the exception of the almost unobtainable, overpriced **Château Grillet**, and the violently expensive **Condrieu**, these classic wines are cheap. **Côte Rôtie** may seem expensive until you realize that the good growers are producing one of France's finest wines from one of her most tortuously tricky vineyard sites, and that equivalent wines from the kindergarten slopes of Burgundy and Bordeaux are far higher in price. **Hermitage** is often better than Côte Rôtie and is still underpriced. The lesser northern names like the cheap **Crozes-Hermitage** and its understudies of **St-Joseph** and **Cornas** are never expensive. Seek them out.

In the south **Châteauneuf-du-Pape** prices, despite the crisis of a tiny 1984 crop, have remained fair and from being an overpriced sham, original-bottled Châteauneuf has become one of France's best quality red wine buys. **Gigondas** rivals Châteauneuf in price, but doesn't really deserve to, while the wines of **Lirac** are almost always cheap for the quality. **Tavel**, sadly isn't. The sweet Muscats of **Beaumes de Venise** are France's best, though the price is high. Basic **Côtes du Rhône** is too prone to volatile reaction to price rises in Beaujolais and ordinary Bordeaux. When it is at its cyclical low price, it's good value, straight red. The 'Villages' wines are almost always worth the extra franc or so a bottle.

AVAILABILITY

Straight Côtes du Rhône is one of the world's most generally available wines. However, availability isn't brilliant for the top names because in this mass production orientated area, the islands of excellence are often small and isolated. Serious merchants worldwide will stock at least some of these wines.

CONSUMER CHECKLIST												
Côtes du Rhône/	Q:	1	2	3	4	5	**6**	7	8	9	10	
Côtes du Rhône	P:	1	2	3	**4**	**5**	6	7	8	9	10	
Villages 1988	V:	1	2	3	4	5	6	**7**	**8**	9	10	
Châteauneuf-du-	Q:	1	2	3	4	5	6	7	**8**	9	10	
Pape 1988	P:	1	2	3	4	5	6	7	**8**	9	10	
	V:	1	2	3	4	5	6	7	**8**	9	10	
Crozes-	Q:	1	2	3	4	5	6	**7**	8	9	10	
Hermitage 1988	P:	1	2	3	4	5	**6**	7	8	9	10	
	V:	1	2	3	4	5	6	7	**8**	9	10	
Hermitage	Q:	1	2	3	4	5	6	7	**8**	9	10	
1988	P:	1	2	3	4	5	6	7	8	**9**	10	
	V:	1	2	3	4	5	6	7	8	9	**10**	

Good Years North: 1989, 1988, 1985, 1983, 1982, 1980, 1978. South: 1989, 1988, 1985, 1981, 1980, 1978.

Taste Notes Rhône reds are usually strong, gutsy wines. Whites are mostly a little dull, with exceptions in Lirac, Châteauneuf, Hermitage, and the brilliant Condrieu.

LOIRE

The Loire valley pours in a great arc across the centre of France, and to a visitor seems to embrace so much of what we all like to think of as the great romantic soul of the country, in its history and architecture, its lush agriculture, and the natural French facility for an endless parade of different wines and different foods to match. Just as the food in the Loire valley swings from the heights of Michelin-starred gastronomic fare to some of the best café eating and simple market produce in the whole of France, so the Loire wines span the great sweet wines of Anjou, the super-trendy, sharp, tasty wines of the upper reaches round Sancerre and Pouilly, the dry, but piercing Cabernet Franc reds of Touraine. And always there's a great wash of café wine, red, white and rosé, from Muscadet, Anjou, Touraine, and numerous little vineyard areas dotted about the region. Altogether there are about a hundred different wines being made along the Loire's 1,000-km (620-mile) course.

But not a hundred different styles. The grapes which predominate are not on the whole France's most versatile or winsome. The white Chenin, though it does (with lots of time) make some wonderful sweet wine, can be unrelentingly harsh in its normal dry state. The Sauvignon Blanc is a simple grape, with a simple, highly attractive taste, at its green-grass best in the Loire, and the Muscadet prides itself of tasting of very little indeed. In the reds we have got the Cabernet Franc

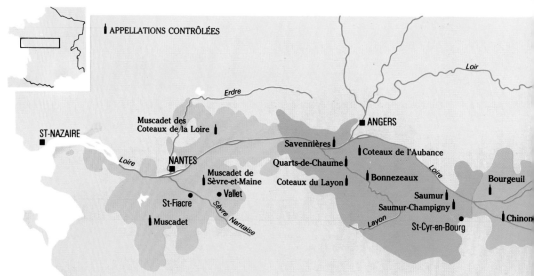

and the Pinot Noir, but both almost beyond their northern limits of ripening properly. The same could be said of the heavily planted Gamay (the grape of Beaujolais), and the pale Groslot, both of which make a fair amount of dullish, tart red, and a lot more indeterminate rosé. In all these, there are probably only six or seven truly different wine styles, so let's try to simplify the Loire by slicing it broadly into four regions with definable styles, plus, of course, the great (but, undeservedly, little known internationally) sweet whites.

Three of the four regions do divide roughly into grape types. Certainly the Muscadet region at the mouth of the Loire is completely dominated by the Muscadet grape. Anjou-Saumur's white production is heavily slanted towards the Chenin, and its red production towards the Gamay. Only small outcrops of Sauvignon and Chardonnay help to ameliorate the Chenin's generally charmless white. Cabernet Franc is the quality red producer, but very much in a minority. It is in Touraine-Vouvray that the Sauvignon at last shares the spoils with Chenin and the Cabernet slowly gets the better of Gamay, but it is not till we attain the upper twisting reaches of the river around Sancerre that the white Sauvignon finally takes over and the Pinot Noir takes up the endless battle to produce decent red Loire wine.

The River Loire has come a long way by the time it enters its final stage near Champtoceaux on the edge of the Muscadet region.

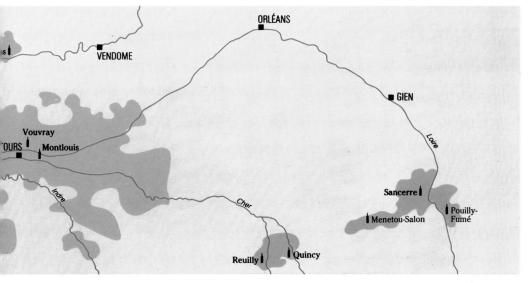

LOIRE/Sancerre

THE GENERAL PICTURE

Some areas seem to have all the luck. In many parts of France, generation after generation of winegrowers slave away, painstakingly building a reputation on an endless round of back-breaking labour and dedication, the struggle passing on from father to son. In others, no reputation is striven for, none is won, and the grapes are lovelessly grown and anonymously sold to the handiest bidder. And then there's the little enclave in the upper reaches of the Loire, centred round one of the wine world's most charmed names – Sancerre. Sancerre has the golden touch – in red, white and rosé – and there can be few luckier regions in the whole of France.

Only a quarter of a century ago, the villages of Sancerre, Ménétou-Salon, Reuilly, Quincy and Pouilly, were largely unknown. The vineyards were in decline and patchily planted on the hill of Sancerre and in the ragged fields spreading out east and west from the River Loire, here still toiling north, before its long arc westwards to the Atlantic coast. A fair amount of dull white and a surprising amount of rather thin red and rosé were made. And just a little of one of the sharpest, freshest, most startlingly dry white wines in France.

It was Sancerre's luck that these few top Sauvignon Blanc wines were stumbled across by Paris journalists in the 1960s, because the same tangy dry whites were the perfect drinking partners for a world keen to brush away the cobwebs surrounding food and drink. While Beaujolais Nouveau was hauling red wine into the era of the Beatles and the Rolling Stones, white Sancerre was being snapped up as the elegant 'in' drink of the swinging sixties sophistiqués, with their expense-account lunches and their self-conscious, slimline gourmandizing. It hit Paris like a whirlwind, and the neighbouring villages, in particular Pouilly, were quick to follow suit, hotfooting it up the N7 to the capital city.

By the late 1970s, the region's run of luck was still on course as its rosés and its reds were seized upon by the exponents of *nouvelle cuisine;* for a time you could hardly find a wine waiter in Paris who wouldn't

These wintering vines are in the best part of Sancerre, with the town itself in the background.

recommend red Sancerre with the fish! It's a fad which has made a lot of the area's winegrowers into wealthy men. Yet it is a dangerous fad, vaunting red and rosé wines which are at best quite attractive, at the expense of the fine white Sauvignon wines which are the prototype for a whole generation of winemakers, desperate to achieve lightness, and zingy, thirst-quenching fruit in their white wines. In short, when they're good, the dry white wines of this region are the best suited of French wines to satisfy the world's present craving for modernity – freshness, youth and big, bold, unashamed strokes of flavour.

GRAPE VARIETIES AND WINE STYLES

The whites are generally made from the Sauvignon Blanc grape, though a little wine called **Pouilly-sur-Loire** is made from the dull Chasselas grape, which makes good eating but not memorable drinking. The wines are lightest and most fragrant in **Ménétou-Salon** and **Reuilly**; most brilliantly balanced between sharpness and ripe, round body in **Sancerre** and **Pouilly Fumé**; and most assertive, almost overly so, in **Quincy**.

The reds are almost entirely Pinot Noir. Rosés are also usually Pinot Noir, except for some rather superior Pinot Gris in Reuilly.

THE IMPORTANT DETAILS

CLASSIFICATION

Classifications are not of great importance here, since there is no *cru*, or hierarchical vineyard site system. Even so, there are many well-known vineyard sites – such as Clos du Chêne Marchand or Monts Damnés in Sancerre, and Les Loges or Les Berthiers in Pouilly – which make the best wine.

ORGANIZATION/S

Nearly all the best wine comes straight from the growers and is bottled at the domaine, but there are some 'merchants', like Cordier, Aimé Boucher and Prosper Maufoux who make decent wine. The co-ops are of only middling quality.

READING THE LABEL

The labels for white wine simply state the village name, with a vineyard name if appropriate. Except for the above-mentioned Pouilly-sur-Loire, they will all be Sauvignon. Red wines may mention Pinot Noir, as may rosés, but the grape *is* always Pinot Noir, except in the case of some Pinot Gris rosé from Reuilly, which will be stated. The most impor-

tant thing to look for, as a mark of authenticity, is 'Mis(e) en bouteille au domaine' – domaine-bottled.

WHAT DO THEY TASTE LIKE?

Neither the reds nor the rosés in general have any very memorable flavours, though the red Sancerre of Vacheron does display a lot of strawberryish Pinot fruit plus some soft oak, and the Reuilly rosé of Robert Cordier is delicious.

The white wines go through a whole range of flavours connected with tangy, fresh green memory traces – from asparagus, through gooseberries, to nettles and fresh-cut grass. In the best examples all these flavours mingle, and there's even a slight whiff of newly-roasted coffee sometimes. The wines are said to smell of gunflint – Pouilly Fumé, in particular, is so-called because of its smoky smell. Being of a non-violent disposition I find this difficult to prove, but perhaps it's that pungent coffee smell they're talking about . . . What you *don't* want is any smell of sulphur, or anything meaty or flabby. Sancerre wines live by their freshness.

LOIRE/Sancerre

THE IMPORTANT DETAILS

Sancerre has a pale, chalky soil which the Sauvignon grape particularly enjoys. Except on the slopes around the town, vines share the land with other crops.

THE GOOD YEARS
These wines are not always at their best in supposedly classic French years. 1989 is good, but broad, 1988 is ripe but better balanced, 1987 is adequate but tiring, while 1986 can still be fabulously good. None of these wines really improve with much keeping, and the amazingly fierce-smelling Sauvignon can end up quite bland and well-behaved after a few years.

ENJOYING THE WINES
The white wines are brilliantly adaptable. They have the bite and sharpness to partner quite rich fish dishes and yet their character isn't suffocated by vegetable *crudités* or by seafood – two dishes which make many wines taste sour. The strong gooseberry-fresh taste also makes them refreshing apéritifs.

The rosés are best as apéritif or picnic wines, and the reds rarely have enough style to go with anything except light meat dishes.

CONSUMER INFORMATION

WHAT DO I GET FOR MY MONEY?
The white wines are relatively dear, but often worth it because of their inimitable flavours. **Sancerre** is the trendiest name, but, as is often the case, this affects its quality and value. **Pouilly Fumé,** fuller in style and becoming more expensive, is thought by many to be the best wine the Sauvignon makes in the whole of France. Reds and rosés are usually overpriced.

AVAILABILITY
Although the area is not enormous, the distribution of white Sancerre and Pouilly Fumé is good. Virtually all merchants, restaurants and wine bars will have at least one example. Reuilly, Ménétou-Salon and Quincy are rare but worth seeking out.

CONSUMER CHECKLIST

Sancerre Les	Q:	1 2 3 4 5 6 7 **8** 9 10
Perriers 1989	P:	1 2 3 4 5 6 7 **8** 9 10
	V:	1 2 3 4 5 6 **7** 8 9 10

Good Years Sancerre is best drunk young, but occasionally, like in 1986 and 1978, wines are made which develop an intense gooseberry fruit with age. Very hot years like 1989 may produce some flabby wines.

Taste Notes Sancerre should be soft and reasonably full, as well as having a very grassy, even blackcurrant or gooseberry (or even asparagus!) green bite which is quite delicious.

LOIRE/Muscadet

THE GENERAL PICTURE

Muscadet isn't the most exciting of wines. It doesn't have flavours which burst and glitter in the glass and have you lunging for your dictionary of quotations in search of a description. Yet it is an incredibly important part of the Loire winescape, because, with Sancerre at the distant upper end of the river, it is the Loire's most famous wine. Sometimes it seems that all the racy upriver excitement is mirrored in Sancerre, while the heavy sluggish spread of muddy waters into the Atlantic estuary past Nantes is epitomized by the dull, undemanding character of most Muscadet.

Well, there is some truth in this, but only for the dumb, deadened commercial blends of Muscadet, which, indeed, may well come from the slabby flatlands towards the river mouth. The true virtue of Muscadet is discovered in the Sèvre-et-Maine district further inland, and in particular in the twisting, hilly vineyards round St-Fiacre and the more meadowy vineyards of Vallet. In this core of the Sèvre-et-Maine region, the best growers get to work to produce a fine wine which has managed to make a positive virtue out of its relative neutrality.

GRAPE VARIETIES AND WINE STYLES

There is only one grape, and its name is the **Muscadet** – the same as the wine. There used to be others, and at one time the area was largely given over to black grapes, which can't have been very exciting. But Dutch traders, looking for a light white wine which they could then distil, persuaded growers to plant something simple and innocuous, and the grape they finally settled on was the Melon de Bourgogne, or Muscadet, a vine long since kicked out of Burgundy as having no class and lowering the tone of the place. But it suited the growers at the mouth of the Loire. It had almost no discernible flavours, and ripened very early. Although initially grown for brandy distilling, it quickly earned itself a reputation as the perfect quaffing wine for all the local seafood, and it might have remained just a pleasant, bright, sharp local white, if the Beaujolais Nouveau in Paris of the 1950s hadn't decided it needed a white stable mate to slop over the bistro tables. The light, early picked and rather low-in-acid Muscadet was the perfect wine. Remarkably, it is this *lack* of flavour, this simple neutrality of style, which has made Muscadet famous!

As always, this success has led to the more serious growers deciding to try harder, and there are now many domaine-bottled Muscadets which, while remaining fairly neutral, can develop a peppery, even peachy fruit in the mouth. For once, this upping of a basic wine into something more sophisticated seems to have worked, and the general level of domaine-bottling is good. The best have 'Mis(e) en bouteille sur lie' on the label. This means the wines have lain in the vat or barrel on the dead yeast cells which have been deposited after fermentation and they are bottled directly off these lees. The fellows who still do this properly are now in a minority, but the *sur lie* designation on a label should nonetheless ensure a fresher, fruitier, perhaps very slightly *pétillant*, wine.

A storm brews in the background over the vines at Vallet, one of the best wine villages in the central Muscadet area of Sèvre-et-Maine.

LOIRE/Muscadet

THE IMPORTANT DETAILS

CLASSIFICATION
There are three Appellations Contrôlées for Muscadet:

Muscadet – the general appellation; the wine is usually pretty basic and dull;

Muscadet des Coteaux de la Loire – a small area; the wine is rarely seen, but it can be okay;

Muscadet de Sèvre-et-Maine – the biggest and best central area.

ORGANIZATION/S
Surprisingly, the co-operative movement has never gained any sway in Muscadet, and is of little importance. This is the land of endless small, proprietor-run vineyards. However, the vast majority of these are only a few hectares, and many are run in tandem with other crops. The merchants are also very important, owning or controlling through contracts about 30–35 per cent of the vineyards. Though their basic blends may be dull, when they make an effort with single-domaine wines, the results are often good.

READING THE LABEL
That 'Sèvre-et-Maine' title is important on the label, as is the *sur lie* tag. Preferably buy domaine-bottled wine, and check the address at the bottom, looking out for St-Fiacre and Vallet, two of the best villages.

WHAT DOES IT TASTE LIKE?
Simple, fresh, thirst-quenching, unquestionably dry, yet, for a wine which has built its reputation on its dryness, there is remarkably little rasping acidity. A good Muscadet may taste slightly nutty, even honeyed, but never heavy – it is the only appellation in France to impose a *maximum* alcohol degree (12.3°).

THE GOOD YEARS
Unless you have good reason, it's advisable to always buy the most recent vintage. Although it is true that some Muscadets can age rather well, in general terms, you should try to catch them as young as possible. Of recent years, 1988 and 1989 are undoubtedly the best.

ENJOYING THE WINE
Above all, this wine is a perfect complement to seafood. Offer me champagne with my oysters, Chablis with my clams, and I'll spurn them all for a good Muscadet. This dry but neutral taste even copes with the seaweedy greenness of Brittany oysters. Otherwise, it's dry and light and fits in easily as a cheap white compromise in most situations.

CONSUMER INFORMATION

WHAT DO I GET FOR MY MONEY?
You'll rarely be overcharged for Muscadet; indeed, the basic stuff is one of France's cheapest white wines. Unless you happen to be in the area, don't go for the cheapest because the price/quality ratio for a single-domaine **Sèvre-et-Maine** is reasonable.

AVAILABILITY
Excellent. You'll see the ordinary stuff everywhere, and any decent outlet will have at least one proper Sèvre-et-Maine.

CONSUMER CHECKLIST

Muscadet de	Q:	1 2 3 4 5 **6** 7 8 9 10
Sèvre-et-Maine	P:	1 2 3 4 **5** 6 7 8 9 10
sur lie 1989	V:	1 2 3 4 **5** 6 7 8 9 10

Good Years Muscadet is usually best at only a year old. 1989 is a particularly good recent year.

Taste Notes Muscadet is basically a dry, fairly neutral white wine.

LOIRE/Anjou

THE GENERAL PICTURE

Anjou is most famous for its rosé. Most infamous, perhaps I should say, because rosé is a wine style which used to be held up as a gently fruity, vaguely sweet all-purpose wine for those who were just dipping their toes into the wine drinking lake. As such it was useful, since there were few light soft wines around to get started on. But the advent of an entirely new, modern, stainless-steel-and-white-overalls kind of wine-making in the last ten years or so has flung up numerous wines to fit that bill, and from numerous countries. The beginner doesn't need Anjou rosé any more, and the wine hasn't yet really discovered a new identity for itself.

In red and white, too, Anjou is struggling to rid herself of a depressed downmarket image, while in sweet wines (see p. 129) she has some of the most exciting and least appreciated wines in all of France. And as a producer of sparkling wine, based around the town of Saumur, she sometimes produces a plausible rival to champagne.

GRAPE VARIETIES AND WINE STYLES

Though rosé accounts for over half of Anjou's wine production, there are no less than 25 appellations, and the most interesting wines are white, with the Chenin grape being of almost overriding importance. The late-ripening Chenin is often shown at its most curst and mean-minded as **Anjou Blanc**. It is one of France's cheapest Appellation Contrôlée wines, and often deserves no better in its sulphured, sour state. Yet it *can* deliver the goods. The tiny **Savennières** appellation from estates like Coulée de Serrant of Mme Joly,

and the **Roche aux Moines** of La Bizolière, just north of the Loire, produces some of the steeliest, diamond-dry wines in the world; the eventual honeyed fullness of the wines still only glinting coldly through the acid after a dozen years and more. Anjou growers like the Domaine Richou who are beginning to mix Sauvignon, and, more importantly, Chardonnay with their Chenin, are now realizing the potential of the area for good fresh whites.

Rosé wines are mainly from the Gamay or Groslot grape, although the better, drier wines are made from the Cabernet Franc. Since rosé is a declining market, many growers now make red wine, much of it raw and Gamay-based, but some light and sharply-fruited Cabernet reds (e.g. Richou) have started to appear. As with the white Chenin, modern vinification methods such as those used at Domaine Richou are drawing out exciting, unthought-of fruit flavours from both these grapes. **Saumur-Champigny,** particularly from Filliatreau, is probably the best of the Cabernet reds.

The sparkling wines are Chenin-based but unless softened by Chardonnay, or even the black Cabernet Franc, they can be a little fierce. Gratien et Meyer and Langlois-Château are two of the most stylish. All the best is champagne method, and the most carefully made can use the title 'Crémant de Loire'. This involves more restricted yields from the vineyards, gentler pressing and a longer maturation period.

The Anjou vineyards are soft and gently rolling, though the vines often struggle to ripen.

LOIRE/Anjou

THE IMPORTANT DETAILS

CLASSIFICATION

The dominant appellation is simple 'Anjou' with the appellation 'Anjou-Villages' covering the best villages. Inside the small Savennières appellation exists the tiny enclave of Savennières Coulée de Serrant. Saumur-Champigny holds a similar pre-eminence among the reds. Sparkling wine is chiefly AC Saumur, with some Crémant de Loire.

ORGANIZATION/S

The large merchant houses are by far the most important influence in Anjou, yet much of what they produce has a predictable and indistinct personality. Where growers do bottle their own wine it is well worth paying the little extra. Co-ops are also important, one at St-Cyr en Bourg producing the best dry and medium rosé, and others making considerable percentages of each harvest with some success.

READING THE LABEL

Despite unspecific labels, the whites will in general be dry, the rosés medium, and the reds either raw or sharp but tasty. With sparklers, 'Brut' means very dry, and 'Sec' means medium.

WHAT DO THEY TASTE LIKE?

These are true northern climate tastes. The single most obvious flavour factor is acidity. With a good winemaker this can be an advantage, but in lazy hands reds, whites and sparklers alike can be too severe. Rosés should be light, appley, and slightly sweet.

THE GOOD YEARS

Vintage is crucial in Anjou. Without a fair amount of luck, those black grapes just won't ripen at all, and the white Chenin is a particularly slow ripener too. The excellent summers of 1989 and 1988 produced lovely wine, 1987 was meagre but 1986 and especially 1985 were good to excellent as was 1983. For reds, and white Savennières, other good years are 1982, 1981, 1978, 1976, 1975, 1970.

ENJOYING THE WINES

These are very much food wines. Even the sparkling wines have a kind of extra acid attack which demands something to nibble and soothe the beleaguered gums. That said, the good whites go well with the local river fish dishes, as can the reds, chilled down.

CONSUMER INFORMATION

WHAT DO I GET FOR MY MONEY?

Well, except for **Savennières** and **Saumur-Champigny,** no-one is asking you to pay all that much for these wines. Sparkling Saumur used to be a very cheap fizz and several champagne houses like Bollinger invested in Saumur companies as cheap alternatives to champagne. They're no longer so cheap, though the best ones are still good value.

AVAILABILITY

Anjou rosé is everywhere, but the interesting wines are as yet in short supply. There is very little Savennières and Saumur-Champigny. The exciting new-style appellation Anjou wines are mostly from individual growers, and will take some seeking out.

CONSUMER CHECKLIST		
Cabernet d'Anjou 1988	Q: 1 2 3 4 5 **6** 7 8 9 10	
	P: 1 2 3 **4** 5 6 7 8 9 10	
	V: 1 2 3 4 5 6 **7 8** 9 10	

Good Years Cabernet doesn't always ripen in the Loire and needs a warm vintage and a good winemaker. 1989, 1988, 1985, 1983 and 1982 all produced good ripe wine.

Taste Notes Red Cabernet d'Anjou has an earthy flavour and tart acidity which needs ripeness. However, in hot years, it can develop a delicious raw blackcurrant flavour and, from a domaine like Richou, may even develop over 5 to 6 years.

LOIRE/Touraine

THE GENERAL PICTURE

The high and mighty of France have always seen Touraine as their personal, private vacation spot, and this central swathe of the Loire valley is dotted with many of France's greatest and most breathtaking castles. But it wasn't just the landscape which lured them. The climate is one of the mildest and softest in the country and the gentle hills and valleys tumble and flow with fruit and vegetable produce, the rivers teem with fish, and the forests used to be congested with game. So, of course, there is wine here too, but these are not regal wines to match the castles and their history. Rather, Touraine wines are a good example of wine primarily blending with the local food. Although often similar to Anjou's offerings, Touraine wines are just that bit riper, that much more fruity – and there is another crucial difference. We see less of the rather tricky, charmless Chenin and Gamay grapes, and a good deal more of the finer Sauvignon Blanc and Cabernet Franc. There are famous names here – Vouvray is one, and red Chinon is another – but in general the pleasure of Touraine is the abundance of fresh, straight red and white wine with no pretensions to drawing-room elegance, and there's even a little rosé, dry and sappy, to keep the balance.

GRAPE VARIETIES AND WINE STYLES

The dominant white grapes are the Sauvignon Blanc and (still) the Chenin, with, encouragingly, a little Chardonnay growing as well. Chenin produces **Vouvray** and **Montlouis,** from bone-dry to full and sweet, to fizzy, and sometimes appears labelled 'Pineau de la Loire'. In the tiny area of **Jasnières,** the wine it produces is stark and dry. The Sauvignon, while lacking a single famous wine name to lean on, produces delicious grassy-green wine across Touraine, and frequently behaves like a Sancerre, without actually having the gall to ask a Sancerre price.

The best reds are based on Cabernet, and are found near the Anjou border in **Chinon** and **Bourgueil.** They are usually quite light and very dry, but can have a piercing blackcurrant fruitiness, sharp and thirst-quenching, which especially with Chinon, can age remarkably well, and end up resembling a particularly pure red Bordeaux. Elsewhere there is still a lot of Gamay, and the best is made by modern 'Beaujolais-type' methods to produce a similar young fruity wine. The rosés are often dry and good, which is a relief, and the sparkling wine companies of Vouvray, Montlouis and straight Touraine lap up the unwanted acid Chenin grapes and transform them into a good sharp fizz.

Every village in the Touraine area has its own café where the local wine is dispensed freely in rough tumblers.

THE IMPORTANT DETAILS

CLASSIFICATION

Touraine, like Anjou, is riddled with little appellations, like Touraine Amboise and Touraine-Mesland – both good for reds; Touraine Azay-le-Rideau – good for whites and rosés; and Jasnières, white again. The only evidence of a meaningful classification is thus when a single village or area achieves sufficient reputation to get its name on the label, rather than simple Touraine. The best Chinons, Vouvrays and Bourgueils are certainly Touraine's finest wines, but much dull stuff is sold under these labels, and simple Sauvignon de Touraine or Touraine Mousseux are the most reliable, reasonably priced wines.

ORGANIZATION/S

This differs dramatically from village to village within the region, but in general it is the merchants who are in command. It is difficult to find a single-domaine Vouvray, and most

LOIRE/Touraine

THE IMPORTANT DETAILS

Chinon and Bourgueil appear as commercial blends, yet the truly fine wines from these villages are single-domaine wines like Chinon Clos de l'Echo and Domaine du Grand Clos. Although co-operatives do exist here, they are most important further upriver, and at Oisly et Thésée, in the heart of the appellation Touraine, the co-op is one of the best in France. Throughout the region it is worth seeking out single growers.

THE GOOD YEARS

Touraine can produce pleasant Sauvignon almost every year, and in vintages like 1988 it is outstanding. In general, drink the reds and whites young – within two years. But good Vouvray should age, and anyway needs a warm vintage – otherwise the fizz-makers have to take the strain. Years like 1989, 1988, 1985, 1983, 1978, 1976, 1970, 1959, and 1947 produced great sweet wines. These years also produced fine Chinon Bourgueil and from such vintages good Bourgueils and Chinons can age 20 to 30 years.

ENJOYING THE WINES

The otherwise adaptable whites actually have too much fruit to be ideal with seafood. But the reds, often best slightly chilled, do go well with the local fish. The fizz? Drink it any time.

READING THE LABEL

For white wines and sparklers, check to see if the label has the words 'Sec' (vaguely dry), 'Demi-sec' (vaguely sweet) or 'Moelleux' (sweet). Otherwise the wines should be dry. On red wines check for the grape variety in the various Touraine appellations. Cabernet will usually be better than Gamay.

WHAT DO THEY TASTE LIKE?

Most Touraine wines are certainly tart and green, but have a lot of fruit. The acidity is a plus – ' thirst-quenching rather than gum-searing. Most of the Vouvray we see is mediocre – sadly, since the appellation can produce some of the finest Chenin. The sparkling wines often have more fruit than Saumur.

CONSUMER INFORMATION

WHAT DO I GET FOR MY MONEY?

In general the wines are fairly cheap, though not the Loire's cheapest. Yet it is usually worth paying a little more than the base price, since much of the wine is carelessly traded under merchants' labels from all over France. The Touraine Sauvignons and sparkling wines can be particularly good value.

AVAILABILITY

Good, but not brilliant. There is much mediocre Vouvray around and little of the best. Touraine Sauvignon is gradually and deservedly becoming better known. Many of the other wines are rare and difficult to locate except in the immediate vicinity.

CONSUMER CHECKLIST

Touraine	Q:	1 2 3 4 5 6 7 **8** 9 10
Sauvignon	P:	1 2 3 4 5 6 7 8 9 10
1986	V:	1 2 3 4 5 6 7 8 **9** 10

Good Years Touraine Sauvignon is best from warm but not super-hot years and rarely improves after a year. 1988 was excellent. 1989 was very good, if a little weighty.

Taste Notes Touraine Sauvignon is a tangy, green-tasting wine, grassy and refreshing when very young, and there's little point in aging it.

LOIRE/Sweet wines

THE GENERAL PICTURE

Anjou has a secret. It makes some of the greatest sweet wines in the world. Why is it a secret? Quite simply, because nobody seems to want to know. There the growers are, in their little river valleys of the Layon and the Aubance, toiling away at one of the riskiest, most expensive and exhausting challenges the world of wine possesses – the production of naturally sweet, 'noble-rot'-affected sweet wines, continuing picking late into November, doing several trips up the foggy, chilly vineyard slopes to pluck the last ounce of overripeness from their grapes, and at every harvest time risking autumn's storm and tempest, and the destruction of their crop. They're probably so whacked by this commitment that they haven't got the energy left to shout.

Well, in that case, *I'd* better shout. Quarts de Chaume and Bonnezeaux make two of the world's finest sweet wines; they're succulent and rare, yet the price they command is pathetic. If it weren't for many vineyard owners having other incomes, and all of them being afflicted by this marvellous mad passion to create great sweet wine, it's difficult to see how they'd survive. So, not only should we buy these classics, but we should willingly pay a higher price for them, or else they will quite simply go out of business. And there are other sweet wines, good, and cheap, made in Anjou. Coteaux du Layon, and Coteaux de l'Aubance are sweet, but in a crisp, fresh way. Moulin Touchais is a remarkable deep, sweet wine from the Anjou hinterland. And in Touraine, Vouvray can produce some exciting, chunky sweet wines, with Montlouis trailing in a little way behind.

GRAPE VARIETIES AND WINE STYLES

The Chenin is the only grape used. This rasping, harsh grape, which makes some of France's least charming whites in the surrounding areas, finds its vocation in no uncertain terms in the pursuit of great sweet wine. In the damp, warm valley-slope vineyards, as the autumn draws in, it is likely to be affected by the *pourriture noble* or 'noble rot'. This curious phenomenon is a kind of mutation of a nasty grey fungus which can eat and destroy a vineyard in record time – yet this particular manifestation thins the grape skins, sucks out the water and leaves the sugar! The Layon valley is one of the few places in the world where 'noble rot' appears naturally, and luckily the Chenin grape is easily afflicted.

The style of wine produced ranges from the pleasantly fresh, vaguely sweet fruity wines of most **Coteaux du Layon** and **Coteaux de l'Aubance** through the concentrated, though rarely luscious, wines of Vouvray, to the gorgeous, peachy, quince-rich wines of **Quarts de Chaume** and **Bonnezeaux**. Yet, through all these different wines, the fierce acidity of the Chenin grape is never lost. Balanced by sweetness, the acidity acts as a freshener and preservative, as well as fighting off the wine's decay and decline.

THE IMPORTANT DETAILS

CLASSIFICATION

The two most important appellations, often accorded a Grand Cru status, are Quarts de Chaume and Bonnezeaux. Other appellations to look for are Coteaux du Layon, any of the seven Coteaux du Layon 'Villages', Coteaux de l'Aubance, Vouvray and Montlouis.

ORGANIZATION/S

Making sweet wine demands rare dedication. Indeed, these winemakers have an almost eerie commitment to their wine. The majority of good wine comes from growers. Some merchants, like Brédif in Vouvray, both own land and make good wine, but do avoid an anonymous Vouvray with only a merchant's name on the label.

Anjou and Touraine are often thought of firstly as the land of the châteaux of the Loire and, only secondly, as wine regions.

LOIRE/Sweet wines

THE IMPORTANT DETAILS

READING THE LABEL

With Quarts de Chaume or Bonnezeaux on the label you should get as sweet a wine as the vintage has allowed. Coteaux de l'Aubance and Coteaux du Layon will imply a reasonably sweet wine. Sweet Vouvray and Montlouis should have 'Moelleux' on the label. If not, these wines could be dryish.

WHAT DO THEY TASTE LIKE?

Sweet Loires have a long, slow development of flavour. Because the acidity is so high, even the sweetest great wines don't always taste that sweet when young. Coteaux du Layon and Coteaux de l'Aubance are usually crisp-apple sweet rather than luscious. Great Chaumes and Bonnezeaux need 10 to 15 years to show their flavours, which then become intensely peachy, apricoty perhaps, and never cloying. The high acidity and a slight bitter twist make them some of the most refreshing of sweet wines.

THE GOOD YEARS

Vintages are very important for these wines. Most years can produce something vaguely sweet, and so ordinary Layon and Aubance should simply be drunk fresh and young without too many questions asked. Chaumes and Bonnezeaux wines are only at their best in noble-rot-affected years, and they take a long time maturing. 1947 is an all-time great, but 1959, 1964, 1969, 1970, 1976, 1983, 1985, 1988 and 1989 are good years.

ENJOYING THE WINES

The lighter wines can be delicious as apéritifs, since the strong acidity doesn't spoil the palate for any dry wine which may follow. Even the sweetest wines are good by themselves, are marvellous with fresh fruit, *foie gras* or fresh blue cheese, and can also go with the local river fish and chicken dishes. If you are prepared to give sweet wines a chance, these are some of France's most versatile.

CONSUMER INFORMATION

WHAT DO I GET FOR MY MONEY?

Tremendous value! In fact, the value is too good. They're remarkable bargains at every level. **Coteaux du Layon** and **Coteaux de l'Aubance** are *always* cheap and reliable, sweet **Vouvray** is rare but not too expensive, and **Quarts de Chaume, Bonnezeaux** and **Moulin Touchais** are great sweet wines selling for far less than their true worth.

AVAILABILITY

Except for Moulin Touchais, availability is very poor – there is so little of the best wine it can't be otherwise – but it's worth badgering specialist wine merchants to obtain some. However, Coteaux du Layon is quite widely available, and will give some idea of the styles of the other, rarer wines.

> #### CONSUMER CHECKLIST
>
> **Bonnezeaux** Q: 1 2 3 4 5 6 7 **8 9** 10
> **1985** P: 1 2 3 4 5 6 **7** 8 9 10
> V: 1 2 3 4 5 6 7 8 **9 10**
>
> *Good Years* Bonnezeaux cannot be made sweet and luscious every year, since the sweetness-concentrating 'noble rot' can appear only in warm, humid autumns. Sweet Loire wines need a long time to show their best. They are usually at their peak between 15 and 30 years old. 1985 and 1983 will be fine 1989 and 1982 good. 1988, 1976, 1970, 1964, 1959 and 1947 are highly successful.
>
> *Taste Notes* Bonnezeaux is a succulent wine, with a lovely perfume of peaches, but the acidity of the Chenin stops it cloying.

ALSACE

THE GENERAL PICTURE

The forested hills above the timbered, gabled towns in Alsace are studded with castles and fortifications.

When you go to Alsace, you may think yourself in an eater's and drinker's paradise. The food is wonderful and everywhere you turn there are vineyards and winemakers offering their wares. The local fare includes such great dishes as *choucroute alsacienne,* the well-bred glutton's favourite meal, as well as *pâté de foie gras, truite au bleu, tarte à l'oignon, coq au Riesling,* various kinds of mountain game, and the redoubtable, terrifying Munster cheese. There's only one problem. A good half of these dishes cry out for a good burly red wine, or an intense, lingering, fragrant one – and Alsace, despite all its efforts with the white wines, can't produce one.

When I've been in Alsace I've actually found myself dreaming of a jug of foaming, purple-red new Beaujolais above almost anything else – only dreaming, because this is white wine country, too far north to give anything more than a nod towards decent red, with its pale, though pleasant enough Pinot Noir. Thankfully, Alsace whites are some of the most adaptable the world offers.

The Alsace wine region is a long strip of land centred round the French towns of Colmar and Strasbourg, creeping up into the French Vosges mountains to the west, and stretching out to the German Rhine in the east. Its history has always been confused, and never more so than since 1870, when it was annexed by Germany. World War One surged and ebbed relentlessly across the region, but in 1918 Alsace became French again – for a mere 22 years. World War Two saw Alsace returned to the thick of the fighting, her vineyards churned into muddy wastelands and many of her most beautiful towns razed to the ground.

Looking back now, however, the mixture of German and French influences has created a remarkable people, mixing warmth and good humour with hard work and dedication. They are proud too, and the towns which were destroyed have been rebuilt in their ancient manner as far as possible. The towns that survived the war are so awash with narrow cobbled streets, high overhanging gabled houses and Romanesque or Gothic churches that they allow a rare glimpse of history still being put to work today, because these little towns and villages are now as broadly dependent for their living upon wine and its mysteries as they have ever been.

ALSACE

THE GENERAL PICTURE

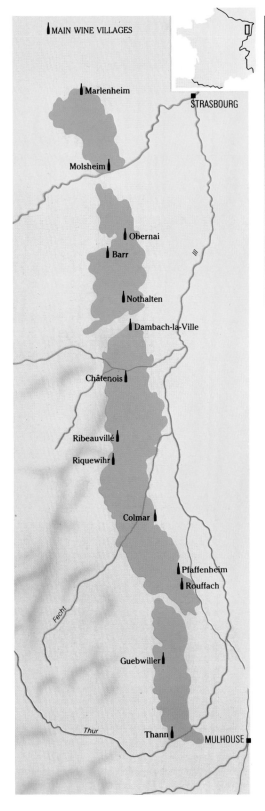

MAIN WINE VILLAGES

Marlenheim

STRASBOURG

Molsheim

Obernai

Barr

Nothalten

Dambach-la-Ville

Châtenois

Ribeauvillé

Riquewihr

Colmar

Pfaffenheim

Rouffach

Fecht

Guebwiller

Thur

Thann

MULHOUSE

Above *Alsace is full of beautifully preserved wine towns and Riquewihr is one of the most perfectly intact.* **Right** *The vines grow fairly tall and the Alsace vintage can be harvested without the workers spending all day crouching. The traditional grape baskets are sadly giving way to modern (though more hygienic) plastic varieties.*

GRAPE VARIETIES AND WINE STYLES

The image of Alsace is of fresh, briskly attractive white wines, balanced between the fruity fragrance of the German wine styles, and the commitment to dryness of the French mainstream.

In general these are some of the most trustworthy wines to be found in a restaurant or wine shop, though this overall reliability is sometimes at the expense of the brilliant, dangerous tastes which often mark out the truly great wines.

Above all, the image is of quality and adaptability. The white wines range from the light frothy-fresh and almost neutral wines of the **Chasselas** and **Pinot Blanc** grapes, through the remarkable austere steeliness of **Riesling,** to the mouth-filling, musky delights of **Tokay d'Alsace** (Pinot Gris) and **Gewürztraminer.** And if you think that all sounds like a curious blend between French and German grape varieties – you're right, it is!

Alsace wines are known by their varietal names and more details of the individual wines will be found below, under What Does It Taste Like?

CLASSIFICATION

Alsace classifications are a mix of both the French and German traditions, involving demarcation of the vineyard site (the French way), and categorization according to the amount of sugar in the grapes at vintage (the German system).

Alsace makes about 20 per cent of France's white Appellation Contrôlée wine, and although it only received its own appellation late, in 1962, it followed this by becoming the first French region to demand that all its wine be bottled *in* the region itself – a considerable weapon in cutting down on fraud and adulteration.

The appellation for the whole region is simply 'Alsace', and is normally used in conjunction with a grape name, thus: 'Riesling: Appellation Alsace Contrôlée'.

There are a number of historically excellent, but only recently classified, vineyard sites which are allowed to call themselves 'Grand Cru', or 'Great Growth'. There seems little doubt that the Grand Cru vineyards do deserve their title and *can* produce the finest wines. The Premiers Crus are less obviously

superior. However, as in Burgundy, it is only the best growers and merchants who will make the best of these regulations and realise the Crus' potential. Traditionally, descriptions such as Réserve, Réserve Exceptionnelle, and Cuvée Exceptionnelle have been used, without force of law to describe a grower's or merchant's best wines.

In the Germanic mould, there are two 'super-ripe' legal descriptions based on very high sugar content in the grapes, and these will certainly be bigger than is usual, and may even be sweet – rare in Alsace. They are the 'Vendange Tardive', or wines from late-picked grapes, and the 'Sélection des Grains Nobles', or selection of single, super-ripe berries, corresponding to a German Beerenauslese in ripeness and price, though rarely in sweetness.

ORGANIZATION/S

The co-operatives are very important, and their products are of good quality. However, the finest quality will come from the growers or from the best merchants. Wines from these merchants' own domaines will almost always be of a higher quality than their blends.

ALSACE

THE IMPORTANT DETAILS

READING THE LABEL

Most Alsace labels are simple to read, and will usually say Alsace, or Vin d'Alsace, followed by the name of the grape variety, the name of the shipper or grower, and the vintage.

Some special wines will also show a vineyard or domaine name. Other top selections will show a classification described on p. 133.

WHAT DOES IT TASTE LIKE?

An old winetaster's rule is that if it smells sweet and tastes dry it's probably from Alsace – and that's fairly accurate. Most of the wines do have a slightly spicy, grapy smell, but they are nearly always bone-dry. Here's a run-down, in ascending order of quality.

Edelzwicker This is the name for a blend of the less interesting grape varieties, in particular Chasselas, Pinot Blanc and Sylvaner. Usually it is fresh and nothing more. Just occasionally it is spicy, and then much more interesting.

Sylvaner Light, slightly tart and slightly earthy. It sometimes achieves rather more class than this, but usually tastes a bit empty and one-dimensional. If you leave it too long, it begins to taste of tomatoes.

Pinot Blanc This is taking over from Sylvaner as the basis for Alsace's bright and breezy young whites. It's a much better grape, giving clean, rather appley wine – light, quite acid, sometimes with a whiff of honey.

Riesling This is the grape that produces the great juicy-sweet wines of Germany. In Alsace it is usually startlingly dry – as austere and steely as any wine in France. Indeed it is particularly *unfruity* here but, for such a dry wine, it is often quite full-bodied to balance the starkly green, lemony acidity. In the best ones there is just a little honey to give this very dry wine a strangely rich flavour. As it ages it goes petrolly, a taste which is surprisingly delicious!

Muscat Light, fragrant, wonderfully grapy. Imagine crushing a fistful of green grapes fresh from the market and gulping the juice as it runs through your fingers. That's how fresh and grapy a good Muscat is – yet again, it is completely dry.

Pinot Gris The Alsatians prefer to call this wine Tokay d'Alsace. It is sumptuously honeyed at its best, and in such an obvious way that the flavour really can resemble a quick lick of the honeypot spoon. Even the light, young Tokays have a lusciousness lingering behind the basically dry fruit.

Gewürztraminer It is sometimes difficult to believe these wines are dry because they can be so fat and full of spice. But, with few exceptions, dry they are, yet big, very ripe, and with all kinds of remarkable, exotic fruit tastes – lychees, mangoes, peaches – and, if you're lucky, finished off with a slightly rasping twist, just like the perfumy tang of black pepper straight from the pepper mill.

Pinot Noir The Burgundy grape, which here makes light reds and rosés. It often achieves quite an attractive perfume and a light, strawberryish flavour, but is rarely worth seeking out that keenly.

THE GOOD YEARS

The lighter Alsace styles, like Pinot Blanc and Muscat, are ready within a year of the vintage, and most wines are at their best within two. Few Alsace wines demand aging, though some Rieslings and Tokays are improved by it. Of recent years, 1989 and 1988 are absolutely wonderful for everything, from Edelzwicker to 'Sélection des Grains Nobles'. 1987 and 1986 made a huge quantity of pleasantly fruity wines, while 1985 and 1983 were of a high quality.

ENJOYING THE WINES

Alsace wines go very well with food. There is almost no classic 'white wine' dish which will not be a good partner for Pinot Blanc or Riesling. And Tokay and Gewürztraminer have the weight and flavour to go with such tricky dishes as smoked fish or *choucroute*. And as for Muscat, I'd drink it by itself out in the garden on a summer evening.

Since the wines in their homeland *have* to accompany all the multi-faceted dishes of Alsace cuisine, you too can use them to break preconceived rules about red wines going with certain dishes. These wines can practically, if not ideally, act as apéritif, fish course, main course and even dessert wine!

The artist Hansi decorated many old wine towns with these wrought iron signs in the early 1900s.

CONSUMER INFORMATION

WHAT DO I GET FOR MY MONEY?

Alsace tastes do differ widely, and in general they are marked and obvious, often quite fiercely so. However, their flavours would be more concentrated and sharply defined if the vineyards did not produce so much wine.

Even so, it is worth choosing Alsace wines as they are almost always good value. The basic wines are of fair quality at a fair price, and the 'special selection' wines are often cheap for what they represent. But they are never available at rock-bottom prices. The 'Sélection des Grains Nobles' is rarer than German Beerenauslese and just as expensive.

AVAILABILITY

Very good. After all, there's a lot of wine – Alsace represents one-fifth of France's entire white Appellation Contrôlée crop. But this wide availability only applies to the basic styles of Edelzwicker, Pinot Blanc, Riesling and Gewürztraminer. The Muscats, Tokays and Pinot Noirs, as well as the 'special selection' wines, are only to be found on specialists' lists.

CONSUMER CHECKLIST											
Pinot Blanc 1989	Q:	1	2	3	4	5	6	7	8	9	10
	P:	1	2	3	**4**	5	6	7	8	9	10
	V:	1	2	3	4	5	6	7	**8**	9	10
Gewürztraminer 1988	Q:	1	2	3	4	5	6	7	**8**	9	10
	P:	1	2	3	4	5	**6**	7	8	9	10
	V:	1	2	3	4	5	6	7	8	**9**	10
Riesling Grand Cru 1989	Q:	1	2	3	4	5	6	7	8	**9**	10
	P:	1	2	3	4	5	6	**7**	8	9	10
	V:	1	2	3	4	5	6	7	8	**9**	**10**

Good Years 1989, 1988, 1985, 1983, 1981

Taste Notes The most famous Alsace wines are the Gewürztraminers with their intense spicy fruit. Muscat is very grapy and fragrant, and Pinot Gris or Tokay is honeyed and soft – yet all these wines, while smelling sweet, are *dry* to the taste. Riesling can be very steely and stern, while Pinot Blanc and Sylvaner are softer and lighter; good 'wine bar' wines.

FRENCH COUNTRY WINES

THE GENERAL PICTURE

It's a wonderfully evocative phrase – 'country wines'. Picnic wines, lazy summer meadow wines, seaside and riverbank wines, café table and sunshade wines. Well, country wines can be all these things, but they're a lot more besides. In fact, the title embraces all those wines, heavy with long and distinct traditions, which do not fit in to any of the famous units like Rhône, Burgundy, Bordeaux, and Loire. And even within those units, it embraces the oddballs which haven't swum with the tide and have consequently become beached and isolated. This means that some of France's most distinctive wines – Jurançon, Ardèche, Fronton, Thouarsais, Baux en Provence, Cahors – are country wines. But although we use the term 'country wines' to cover all these wines, the French term 'Vin de Pays' has a more specific legal meaning. Since 1968, the French government has issued numerous decrees delimiting Vins de Pays, according to grape types, yields and styles of wine-making, in an effort to raise the standard of basic table wine production in France. In terms of classification, therefore, the wines we shall be dealing with in this section will cover wines in the AC and VDQS categories, as well as legally designated Vins de Pays.

The grape varieties cover every conceivable flavour and type, although many of the country wine grape varieties in regions like the south-west, the Jura and the Alps, or the Loire, only exist in little pockets, and never appear in the major appellations.

The co-operatives are tremendously important in country wines, especially in Vins de Pays. Yet many of the finest wines are still from single growers, and in the small, traditional Appellations Contrôlées, the grower's influence is crucial in determining and establishing a wine's reputation.

In general, these country wines are to be drunk as young as possible, yet there are some, in particular the various appellations of the south-west, where vintages are all important, and aging is crucial.

As a rule, the price-quality ratio is very good. Although a few wines like Rosé des Riceys and Mas de Daumas Gassac are very expensive by any standards, the general price level is very low and offers good value.

General availability of country wines as a type is good, unless otherwise stated. Yet, by their very nature, most are local wines, often consumed locally, and – particularly in the case of small Appellations Contrôlées – may be very difficult to sniff out elsewhere.

EAST AND NORTH-EAST

The northern part of this swathe of France, running south from Champagne to the Rhône valley, isn't really country-wine country. There are wines like Côtes de Toul (VDQS) or Vin de Moselle (VDQS) in Lorraine and there is a Vin de Pays de la Meuse, but even on the spot they're difficult to find and are uninspiring. The majority of the north is taken up with the great wine regions of Champagne, Alsace and Burgundy, stretching from Chablis, through the Côte d'Or, down to Beaujolais. These regions are full of famous names which we talk about elsewhere.

However, away to the mountainous east, where the Jura and the Alps make a jumbled splendour of France's frontier, there are out-of-the-way, but individual, wines. And south of the Beaujolais capital of Lyons, as the Rhône throws its influence wider to the east and west, there are various wines which haven't yet got the flavours or the political

know-how, or even simply the geographical luck to belong to the mainstream. They can frequently rival the AC Rhône wines in flavour and price. They're increasingly available, so let's take a serious look at them.

BURGUNDY

Burgundy has three country wines. **Rosé des Riceys** (AC), made from Pinot Noir, is a rare and extremely expensive rosé which is made inside the borders of Champagne; it is dark and fruity, and costs more than a very decent bottle of champagne *or* burgundy.

Sauvignon de St-Bris (VDQS) is one of the most distinctive Sauvignon wines in France. It is not Appellation Contrôlée because the authorities don't like the idea of the Sauvignon growing in Chablis, which they see as Chardonnay territory. That lets us, the consumers, in to take advantage of the low price asked for a first class tangy white.

The reds are usually uncharmingly heavy, and, though Pinot Noir is grown, the local Trousseau variety rules the roost in a hefty uncompromising manner. Similarly, with whites, although Chardonnay is grown, it pales before the fierce raw flavours of the native Savagnin variety. Rosé, sometimes called *vin gris*, from the local Poulsard grape, can be big but good, but the most successful wines are sparkling, with some very good champagne-method Chardonnay. And then there's the inimitable *vin jaune*. It's the kind of wine of which more than a small glass makes you quite grateful it is as rare as it is. It grows a *flor* fungus like dry sherry, yet, unlike dry sherry, which is best drunk young, this intense, startlingly concentrated dry wine demands aging. No-one seems to know for how long, because the wine is virtually indestructible, and as long as the cork is healthy, should live as long as any man.

The commonest appellations are **Arbois** and **Côtes du Jura**, with **l'Etoile**, in particular, being good for sparklers and the home of the very rare *vin de paille*. *Vin jaune*, rare and expensive, can be Arbois, Côtes du Jura, or at best, **Château-Chalon**. The others are medium-priced and more available but a little too rugged to recommend whole-heartedly.

SAVOIE

A mountain district with an array of special grape varieties like Roussette, Jacquere and Mondeuse and a titillating diversity of character in the wines to show for the multiplicity of vine types. Savoie wines are mostly white and very 'mountain valley' light – sharp, tartly fresh, sometimes very slightly *pétillant*. Since the area embraces much of France's best skiing, much of it is knocked off after a hard day on the piste. This is a pity, because these mountain-meadow flavours do have the ability far from their source to bring back memories of the holiday atmosphere and the stunning scenery. There used to be a wonderful feather-light, spring snow-fresh sparkling wine from Seyssel. This disappeared for a while into a coarse commercial blend, but is now thankfully re-emerging under its own colours. The best wine is **Roussette de Savoie** (AC), the most common is **Vin de Savoie** (AC). Drink them on the spot with the local fish or when you're in holiday mood off their home patch.

Way down by Lyons, south even of Beaujolais, the **Coteaux du Lyonnais** (AC) produces lovely sharp but cherry-fresh light reds often more Beaujolais than Beaujolais in everything except price.

Burgundy Vins de Pays: Vin de Pays de l'Yonne can be very good and very cheap because its chief source is from Chardonnay vines in Chablis vineyards which are still too young to be called Chablis.

JURA

Jura wines are outside the mainstream of French wine, and you only have to attempt a single mouthful of one of their strange, strong reds and whites to see why. Mountain wines often harbour curious indigenous grape varieties and wine-making styles out of sync with the fast-flowing world of lowland winemakers, and the Jura certainly follows this pattern. Reds, whites, rosés and sparkling wines are made, and a high strength *vin jaune*, or 'yellow wine'. All have an uncompromising flavour and few reach export markets.

FRENCH COUNTRY WINES
East and North-East

Above *In the high Alpine uplands of Savoie, vineyards are rather less important than grazing meadows, but some of the gentle slopes do produce light, simple mountain wines.*
Right *The Ardèche spreads over a wide part of the hilly hinterland to the west of the Rhône. It has recently become the centre of attention and expansion for its excellent Vins de Pays.*

THE RHÔNE VALLEY

The Rhône valley area is large and fairly well defined, but it *does* have a few extra areas that are not quite in the mainstream.

Côtes du Vivarais (VDQS) are pleasant wines, mostly red, and mostly light, from the unspoilt rugged Ardèche region to the west of the Rhône. The grapes are generally Grenache, Cinsault and Carignan. These are, frankly, best knocked back in the region itself, but the few that leave the region are cheap, and resemble a pale Rhône in style. There is a little rosé and white, which is less than exciting.

The **Coteaux du Tricastin** (AC) area begins the southern Rhône vineyards, and was virtually 'invented' to cope with the influx of North African winegrowers in the 1950s and 1960s. It's parched, scrubby land, relentlessly buffeted by sun and wind, yet the wines can be extremely good – and cheap. They are almost all red, from the usual Rhône grapes, but frequently surpass ordinary Côtes du Rhône in fruit and flavour, while usually being cheaper. Virtually starting from scratch, the wines have to try harder. Frequently they succeed, and as simple full-bodied Rhône reds they can be excellent value.

There is so much Ventoux wine being pumped out at a very low price, that one could be forgiven for thinking of it as yet another Côtes du Rhône. Yet the **Côtes du Ventoux** (AC) is a distinct vineyard area, spread out across the wide southern slopes of Mount Ventoux to the east of the Rhône, and the wines are much more like Beaujolais Nouveau in style than the beefy Côtes du Rhône. That's to say, they are very light and fruity, pale red rather than purple, and, at their best, reeking of fresh strawberry fruit, backed up by a slight peppery bite. There are one or two private growers such as Domaine des Anges in particular, who make a sturdier wine, but, for once, it is usually less attractive, and the local co-ops are the most reliable producers of this simple, glugging red. There is a little white and rosé. Despite recent price rises, the reds are still cheap and good value.

Rhône Valley Vins de Pays: The most promising are from the **Ardèche**.

The Ardèche, a brusque but beautiful haven from the hurry of late twentieth-century life, makes some of the finest of all France's Vins de Pays, under the name Ardèche or **Coteaux de l'Ardèche**. The Ardèche wines are marked by tremendous fruit. This is the result of some inspired innovation which has not only produced some of the best Syrah red wine outside the top Rhône vineyards, but has also brought about whopping successes from Beaujolais's Gamay and Bordeaux's Cabernet Sauvignon and Merlot in the reds, as well as Burgundy's Chardonnay in whites and the Rhône's Grenache in rosés. They've also planted such grapes as Pinot Noir and Sauvignon Blanc, and judging by their achievements so far these will probably be brilliant too.

Prices are low for reds and medium for Chardonnay white. The local co-ops are the chief producers, and are very good.

Other Vins de Pays basically make lighter versions of mainstream Rhône wines, and the vast majority are red, although the **Collines Rhodaniennes** to the north, and the **Coteaux de Baronnies** to the south-east both make respectable whites. However, the commonest wines are red, and they are usually light, peppery but fruity too. So long as modern wine-making techniques are employed, **Vaucluse** is simple and attractive, while both Coteaux de Baronnies and **Principauté d'Orange** have a bit more stuffing.

For an area fairly far to the south-east, the **Côtes du Lubéron** (AC) is remarkably successful at producing decent white wine, almost appley-fresh if one can catch it young enough. The rosé is also fresh and reasonably fruity – again, if you catch it young enough, which means less than a year old. The reds have a similar light, fast-drinking style to the Ventoux wines, though as yet with slightly less fruit. They are cheap and reliable. Val Joanis, the leading estate, is far superior in all colours to the modern co-operatives.

Châtillon en Diois (AC) are the still wines made in the wonderfully out-of-the-way valleys round Die, where the excellent sparkling **Clairette de Die Tradition** (AC) is produced. The reds are mostly Gamay, with some Syrah and Pinot Noir, and the whites mostly Aligoté with some Chardonnay. As yet the reds are a bit harsh, and the whites a bit biting, but this far south these are faults in the right direction, so when Chardonnay and Syrah get more involved, the results could be very interesting.

CONSUMER CHECKLIST		
Vin de Pays/ Syrah de l'Ardèche	Q: 1 2 3 4 **5** 6 7 8 9 10 P: **1** 2 3 4 5 6 7 8 9 10 V: 1 2 3 4 5 6 7 8 **9 10**	
Sauvignon de St-Bris VDQS	Q: 1 2 3 4 **5** 6 7 8 9 10 P: 1 2 3 4 **5** 6 7 8 9 10 V: 1 2 3 4 **5** 6 7 8 9 10	

Good Years The Vins de Pays should be drunk as young as possible as should the lighter reds from near the Rhône. Only Jura wines may benefit from some aging.

Taste Notes Jura wines have strong, unusual flavours, and Savoie wines very frail fleeting flavours. Otherwise, most of these wines have fresh tastes for immediate enjoyment.

FRENCH COUNTRY WINES

LOIRE

APPELLATIONS CONTRÔLÉES

VDQS

Vins de Pays *Maine et Loire*

If you look at a map of France and pick out the River Loire, snaking its way to the Atlantic from its source near the Rhône and almost in sight of the Alps, it looks as though it should be fertile 'country-wine country' sprinkled with numerous local wines. Yet, although there is a profusion of wine names strung out along its length, most of them have been absorbed into the main appellations of Anjou and Touraine, and some of the odd pockets are of such quality or renown that they merit their own separate headings in the Loire section. But if one digs below the surface there are quite a few little appellations and a fair number of Vins de Pays. Some, like **Châteaumeillant** (VDQS) or **Coteaux du Giennois** (VDQS), have tiny production and are drunk up in the locality, while others – and in particular various Vins de Pays like **Retz, Urfé** or **Nièvre** – are only available locally. So we have picked out the wines which either have particular character or for which there is a reasonable availability other than in the backroom of the local post office or village store.

Côte Roannaise, along with **Côtes d'Auvergne** and **Côtes de Forez**, provides the Loire's best rebuke to Beaujolais. The wine is usually red, from the Gamay grape of Beaujolais, and the vineyards, particularly of **Roannaise** (VDQS) and **Forez** (VDQS), are close to the Beaujolais capital, Lyons. In fact, quite a lot of the wine is drunk there – as well as the **Coteaux du Lyonnais** (AC) and all that Beaujolais. They must have enormous thirsts in Lyons – but good taste too, because the wine is often delicious to drink very young.

Miles from anywhere – except Vichy, where they are drunk in considerable quantity as an antidote to the spa waters – the wines from **St-Pourçain-sur-Sioule** (VDQS) are lighter, slightly sharp, but often possessed of a fairly unnerving personality. The whites from the local Tressallier grape are decidedly rustic – farmyard rustic, damp hayrick rustic – though they are sometimes improved by mixing in some Chardonnay. The rosé is OK, while the reds only just deserve the name, being lighter, almost as sharp as the white, a few saved by a dry smoky plum fruit.

Orleans is chiefly famous for its vinegar, and tasting a **Vin de l'Orléanais** (VDQS) wine from a cool year one can see why. Yet the rosé from the Pinot Meunier grape of Champagne fame is often delicious, light, slightly smoky and soft, while the Chardonnay, here masquerading under the local name of Auvernat, can be first rate. **Clos St-Fiacre** is one of the best Orleans wines.

Cheverny (VDQS) is little further downriver than Orleans, similarly obscure, and making similarly acid wines. One important similarity is its excellent Chardonnay; light, slightly green, but with a lovely, sure, nutty fruit. But it also possesses the Romorantin grape. Nowhere else grows it, and to taste this fiercely acid farmyardy white wine, one can see why. The other reds, whites and rosés are rarely exciting, but they do make some excellent champagne-method fizz.

Right out in the hinterland, the little, but expanding area of **Haut Poitou** (AC) huddles round its large and modern co-op, which has single-handedly created an impressive reputation for its wines. Good red Gamay, fine sharp-scented Sauvignon and remarkable tangy Chardonnay are now augmented by a really ritzy champagne-method sparkler.

Thouarsais (VDQS) is one of France's forgotten wine areas, and most undeservedly so, because the wines are excellent. The white from Chenin is full of fruit, and manages to integrate the high acidity in an exciting way, while the red from the Cabernet Franc is delicious, combining an uncompromising earthy, green pepper flavour with startling sweet fruit. These are *very* rare but the wine of Monsieur Gigon in particular is worth finding – and it's *not* expensive.

Now we come to **Coteaux d'Ancenis** (VDQS). Ancenis is really a Muscadet town, but has a quite deserved, if rarefied, reputation for producing a gentle, sweet white wine from the Malvoisie or Pinot Gris grape. From its leading exponent, Monsieur Guindon, it is the kind of soft, easy wine which performs happily as an apéritif. The other whites from Chenin, and the reds and rosés mostly from Gamay are fair, but too dry to be much fun.

Gros Plant du Pays Nantais (VDQS) is the most seaward of the Loire's wines. By itself it is difficult to see the virtue in this tart, harsh white, but put it with rock-fresh seafood and it transforms into a good thirst-quencher. Not pretty, but it does the trick.

Loire Vins de Pays: These are less important than you might expect, the reason being simply that the Loire is such a traditional quality wine area that even quirky little backwater vineyards were usually of an established reputation leading to their being granted full AC status. Indeed, the 'Vin de Pays' title is frequently used by progressive growers who

are unhappy with the traditional permitted grape varieties and wish to experiment. This is particularly the case with the white Chardonnay and Sauvignon. However, the overall, and beautifully aptly titled, **Vin de Pays du Jardin de la France** – 'The Country wine of the Garden of France' – is highly successful especially when the label states Sauvignon or Chardonnay, and is widely available. But it can also produce reasonable Chenin, and some rather pleasant light reds, usually from Gamay, sometimes from Cabernet. Other Vins de Pays you may come across and which are worth a try are **Loir-et-Cher** and **Indre-et-Loire** from Touraine, **Maine-et-Loire** which fronts several good Anjou wines, and the fairly sharp seaside wines of **Loire-Atlantique** and **Marches de Bretagne**.

CONSUMER CHECKLIST											
Chardonnay de	Q:	1 2 3 4 **5 6** 7 8 9 10									
Haut Poitou	P:	1 2 3 **4** 5 6 7 8 9 10									
	V:	1 2 3 4 5 6 **6 7 8** 9 10									
Vin de Pays du	Q:	1 2 3 **3 4** 5 6 7 8 9 10									
Jardin de la	P:	1 **1 2** 3 4 5 6 7 8 9 10									
France	V:	1 2 3 4 **5 6** 7 8 9 10									

Good Years Nearly all of these wines are to be drunk young, and because the majority are light and white, they should be enjoyable, if sharp, even in cool years.

Taste Notes Tangy, tart, very fresh, rather green, these are the flavours to expect in the whites; the reds are quite sharp and earthy, but even so, fruity enough to enjoy.

The hinterland of the Loire is full of half-forgotten vineyards, divided up into little plots.

FRENCH COUNTRY WINES

PROVENCE, THE MIDI AND THE SOUTH

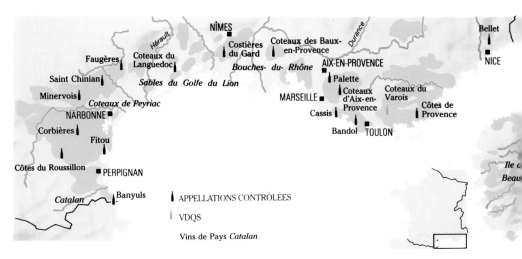

This is where it's all happening. This is where France's wine revolution is sweeping away generations of suspicion, prejudice and inefficiency, as though some wizard were indiscriminately flashing a laser beam to and fro across these parched southern lands, and every time the beam settled for a moment the cobwebs, the dirt and the laziness disappeared in a flash to be replaced by enthusiasm, initiative and innovation.

There's never been any doubt that Provence can affect the heart and soul like a magic drug, nor that its wine can affect the mouth and the stomach like paintstripper. All change! There's been no doubt that the Midi was one of France's most scrubby, bedraggled, exhausted looking regions, and that any over-indulgence in its wines produced a decidedly scrubby, bedraggled and exhausted drinker. All change! Nor any doubt that as the Pyrenees rose on the southern horizon and the sun and wind scorched the arid land, that a long draught of light, cool, refreshing wine would ease the pain. And that was precisely what the local wines would fail to provide. All change again! The whole of the South of France is at last waking up to the fact that no-one wants her filthy, fourth-rate plonk – but that she is brilliantly suited to providing large amounts of simple, cheap, wholesome wine, and even some special stuff too.

'The New California', the Midi has been called. What a *volte face*! One of Europe's oldest vineyard areas having to turn meekly to the new iconoclasts of the West to see how she should be setting about things. Luckily, it was humility or bankruptcy: the growers sacrificed the haughty pride of centuries and replaced it with a new pride – in achievement, in quality, in satisfying a need. Sure, there's still plenty of downright frightful wine in the Midi, and much overpriced tourist mouthwash in Provence, but we don't have to drink it and we shouldn't, because the tide has turned, and one of the world's most natural wine regions is heading back to doing what comes naturally – making good wine, and lots of it, cheaply. Let's start with Provence and then head west for the Pyrenees.

PROVENCE

The **Côtes de Provence** (AC) is a massive sprawling appellation, which has spent much of its life spewing out uninspiring rosé for a heat-stricken and undemanding clientele, who were, in any case, usually near horizontal, near comatose when they drank it, and so were unlikely to complain – except about the price, which was always too high for the quality. Well, things are on the up. There are an increasing number of growers who are trying to make wine worthy of the high price. However, the rosés are still inclined to be just too 'stone-dry', and the whites, though improving, are still inclined to be flabby. The reds, traditionally rather tough and empty, are still tough, but at least there is now a lot more fruit, due to increased use of Mourvèdre and Syrah grapes. With a few single domaine exceptions such as Domaine des Féraud, Château de Pampelonne and Château St-Maurs, don't seek them out – though they do go well enough with sea water and sun-tan oil.

Côtes de Provence is the largest appellation but there are several smaller ones of some importance.

Bellet is a tiny appellation behind Nice. Although there's a rather unusual, nutty white, the wines are overpriced and not exciting. The good people of Nice seem undeterred, so I suggest we leave them to it.

Bandol is Provence's most revered appellation and therefore, by definition, in general overpriced. Yet there is no doubt that the reds in particular are very good, having a sweet spicy fruit to match the tough herby edge. This special flavour is largely due to the Mourvèdre grape. The wines can age well, but are delicious young. Both the dry white and the rosé can be the best in the region, the rosé keeping the soft spicy style of the red, and the white having a fascinating aniseed and apples freshness. There are many good properties, including Domaine Tempier, and Moulin des Costes, but, as usual down on the French Riviera, whatever the sensation you want, you'll be paying over the odds for it.

Cassis, not to be confused with the blackcurrant drink of the same name, is chiefly white wine from a small, but dauntingly beautiful, vineyard, tucked into the bluffs by the Mediterranean. The grapes are the usual

Top *The vines have to battle with rock and mountain in much of Provence, and while the vineyards are ruggedly beautiful, the wines are often merely rugged.*
Above *Little wine is grown round towns like St-Paul de Vence behind Nice, though further west above St-Tropez the hills are full of vines.*

FRENCH COUNTRY WINES

PROVENCE, THE MIDI AND THE SOUTH

southern blend of Clairette and Marsanne, with sometimes a little Sauvignon Blanc. The wine is certainly good, having a cool freshness and fruit which is rare on this coast and the rosés also have a remarkable fruit and style. But it is wildly overpriced and only worth paying for if the company's just right, and you are about to tuck into a locally prepared cauldron full of *bouillabaisse* with the full moon coming up over his or her shoulder.

The Aix region provides some of Provence's most drinkable wines in **Coteaux d'Aix-en-Provence** (AC) such as Pigoudet and Château de Beaulieu, and some of its most demanding and esoteric in Palette, of which Château Simone is virtually the only producer. **Palette** is a tiny appellation hidden in the pine forest, and the wine is mercilessly hard and resiny for most of its life. Coteaux d'Aix has an increasing number of good properties, which produce all colours, but particularly reds, ranging from very light, strawberry-fruited wines to drink at a great rate and without fuss, to such properties as Château Vignelaure, a Cabernet-based wine which achieves a kind of 'Provençal Bordeaux' style. The wines aren't expensive and are worth watching.

If anything, the wines of **Coteaux d'Aix en Provence les Baux** (AC) are even better than those of Coteaux d'Aix. I have *never* had a bad wine from Coteaux les Baux – not one – and I regard the area as one of my greatest discoveries of the last few years. Again, all colours, but the reds really are something special, often mixing Cabernet and Syrah, an amazingly rich, succulent, bramble and smoky blackcurrant blend of flavours. Remarkable. Seek out fast-movers like Mas du Cellier and Domaine de Trévallon before they become superstars.

Provence Vins de Pays: The general category of **Bouches du Rhône** has some fair reds and rosés, and the vast **Coteaux Varois**

(now VDQS), although covering a multitude of mediocrities, does have some good single estates. **Sables du Golfe du Lion** is probably the most interesting, since it takes in much experimental produce, as does the gigantic Listel operation out in the sandy marshes near the Camargue. These wines are amazingly light, helped no doubt by the Camargue's tendency to fog up and block out the sun, and they do interesting things with grapes like the white Chardonnay and Sauvignon and the red Syrah and Cabernet. **Mont Caume** is another interesting demarcation, since it often represents the lesser efforts of Bandol growers, and there is one particularly good Cabernet from the Bandol family of Bunan.

GARD
The Gard is the cushion between the Rhône proper and the Midi proper. If anything, the wines are a little closer to the Rhône in style, but rarely achieve their blend of fruit and super-ripeness. The white **Clairette de Bellegarde** (AC) is usually fairly dull, but the reds of **Costières de Nîmes** (AC) can be pretty good, often having a vaguely meaty, tarry taste, which isn't as bad as it sounds.

Gard Vins de Pays: Vin de Pays du Gard is usually fairly good and cheap, as are **Coteaux du Salavès** and **Uzège**.

HERAULT
With the Hérault, we're into the heart of the Midi with a bang. It's ugly country, this, with the sullen flat plains and care-worn hillocks sporting an endless parade of stubby, gnarled vines, which even in full high-summer bloom fail to look as optimistic and appetizing as a mid-season vineyard should. Till recently the wines reflected this unconcern but there are now pockets of achievement popping up at an increasing rate. In general all the best wines are red and fairly big on flavour. The top villages are now covered by the **Coteaux du**

Languedoc (AC) with their own name added, as, for example, in 'Coteaux du Languedoc La Clape'.

The two most original whites are **Clairette du Languedoc** (AC) and **Picpoul de Pinet** (one of the 'Crus' in the Coteaux du Languedoc AC), but neither is that stunning. The best reds are the faddish **Faugères** (AC) , and **St-Chinian** (AC) big, beefy wines, but soft and spicy with it. **La Clape** and **St-Georges-d'Orques** (both Coteaux du Languedoc 'Crus'), if a bit solid, can be good.

Hérault Vins de Pays: Hérault produces more Vins de Pays than any other region. There are 29 possible names, and the crucial factor is the winemaker, not the area. Some private estates, and the modern co-ops, are making light, fresh, rather dusty reds, and fairly decent clean whites and rosés, at very low prices. Estates like Cante-Cigale on the coast near Cap d'Agde, are leading the way to very exciting reds and whites. The dominant grape is the red Carignan, backed up by Cinsault, Grenache and some Syrah or Mourvèdre – if you're lucky.

AUDE

The Aude embraces less of the mindless, featureless prairie vineyards, and many more of the hills and crags. So we are immediately in an area with a much more self-confident wine tradition. Historically this has been based round cockle-warming reds ready to take on all comers and remain unbowed, but the Aude's most exciting revelation is in fact a sparkling wine – **Blanquette de Limoux** (AC). This is usually made by the champagne method (see p. 100), though occasionally by an even older and similar method called *méthode rurale* (see p. 26) – sounds wonderful, all cowsheds and sugar beet! The locals swear they invented the champagne method a century before the Champenois. Maybe, but the modern Blanquette is very fresh and clean, with the dominant Mauzac grape giving an almost apple-skin tang to it. It can be France's best sparkler outside Champagne. The classiest red is **Fitou** (AC), a big, strapping plum-flavoured red based on Carignan grapes. The most famous red is **Corbières** (AC), a peppery, aggressive but ripe-fruited wine from the welter of mountains stretching from Narbonne towards Spain. The most forward-looking red is **Minervois**

(see p. 116)

VIN DOUX NATUREL

'Naturally Sweet Wine' is what this title means. In fact the wines are fortified with the addition of strong alcohol spirit when about half the natural sweetness of the grape has been converted to alcohol during fermentation. They call this process 'muting', i.e. damping down the fermentation, and certainly the general effect of these wines is rather mute, since you do expect a strong aroma from sweet wines, and very few of these do have a decent smell. In particular the wines from Languedoc-Roussillon based on the red Grenache grape from such villages as Maury and Banyuls are big, raisiny, but somewhat lifeless. The Muscat-based wines are far better, particularly from Rivesaltes, Lunel and Frontignan, yet, despite their sweet grapy fruit, they still lack perfume and just don't quite fire the senses. The only one which does is **Muscat de Beaumes de Venise** (see p. 116), a few hundred kilometres away up the Rhône valley.

(AC), from the northern hillsides between Narbonne and Carcassonne. Usually lighter than Corbières, but with lots of raspberry fruit and pepper from the Carignan grape.

Aude Vins de Pays: There are 21, including France's biggest, the **Coteaux de Peyriac**, churning out 35 million bottles a year. Merchants like Chantovent and Nicolas, as well as a progressive co-operative movement and some enlightened individual growers are making an increasing number of exciting wines in the Aude.

THE EASTERN PYRENEES

You can taste the heat, the wind, the dry dusty soil in these reds from the base of the Pyrenees. But it's a good taste, especially when, as in the startling, intense red wine of **Collioure** (AC), or the big, strawberry and dust wines of **Côtes du Roussillon Villages** (AC), it's tempered by a sweet ripeness too. **Roussillon** can be red, rosé or white, and the 'Villages' wines are usually better, coming from communes higher up in the foothills, and away from the searing heat round Perpignan. The Carignan is the dominant red grape mix-

FRENCH COUNTRY WINES

PROVENCE, THE MIDI AND THE SOUTH

ed with Cinsault, Grenache and Mourvèdre, and the whites are from the Maccabeu. The Beaujolais method of *macération carbonique* (see p. 20), is increasingly used for reds to draw out a really juicy fruit. The rosés are big and good, while the best whites, although a little neutral, are clean and fresh.

Eastern Pyrenees Vins de Pays: There are six, the best being **Catalan, Côtes Catalanes** and **Pyrénées-Orientales.** The co-ops are of enormous importance, particularly the grouping of Vignerons Catalans. There are some good growers such as Cazes and Puig. Prices in general are low.

CORSICA

Much of Corsica's vineyard land is owned by determined, innovative refugees from France's colonial withdrawal in North Africa and their presence is felt in some very good fresh, light, rather piny reds and rosés, some clean, liquorice-tinted white, and by some daring experiments with the international grapes of Cabernet, Merlot, Syrah, Chardonnay and Sauvignon.

Corsica has seven Appellations Contrôlées, but the most exciting wines are the **Vin de Pays l'Île de Beauté.** Co-op groups such as Sica Uval are producing remarkable imaginative Cabernets. Chardonnays and Syrahs, at prices as low as any in France.

CONSUMER CHECKLIST		
Coteaux d'Aix	Q:	1 2 3 4 5 **6** 7 8 9 10
en Provence	P:	1 2 3 **4** 5 6 7 8 9 10
les Baux	V:	1 2 3 4 5 6 7 **8** 9 10
Vin de Pays de	Q:	1 2 **3** 4 5 6 7 8 9 10
l'Hérault white	P:	**1 2** 3 4 5 6 7 8 9 10
(single domaine)	V:	1 2 3 4 **5 6** 7 8 9 10

Good Years Some of the heaviest reds do need a few years' aging; the Vins de Pays, whites and rosés, should be drunk young.

Taste Notes The reds are dominated by the chewy dusty flavour of the south, inreasingly matched by a full raspberry fruit which makes for excellent drinking. Rosés can be very good but must be drunk young.

THE SOUTH-WEST

We talk a lot about 'discovering' new areas of France all the time, and frequently that is exactly what we do – finding new, modern wines, trying to make their mark on the world. The south-west is different; she is crying out to be 're-discovered'. Her wines are hardly known, yet 700 years ago they were better known and more highly thought of than the greatest wines that Bordeaux could produce. Indeed, their historical superiority to Bordeaux wines is shown by the fact that they were frequently used to beef up and add body to the pale, insipid efforts of the claret-makers in Bordeaux. Well, Bordeaux is now enjoying a well-deserved heyday and is not only the greatest wine area of the south-west, but possibly the greatest in the world. The other wines of the south-west have long been languishing in an ill-deserved obscurity. Yet they are some of the most individual, memorable wines in France, and though many of their wine traditions have only survived by the skin of their teeth, there is now a resurgence of activity, in which we should participate – for our own good!

THE WESTERN PYRENEES

Right under the lee of the Pyrenees, there is a fair amount of wine, and there is a lot of tradition, but this is not, as yet, reproducing its old glories in any great quantity.

The Basque mountain wine of **Irouléguy** (AC) is a must if you're in the locality, but not if you aren't. **Béarn** (AC), too, is unlikely to arouse great passionate discourse out of sight of the Pyrenean foothills. **Jurançon** (AC), however, *is* still capable of great things. Although most of the production is now dry, and from the major co-operative, usually over-sulphured and nuttily dull, a few dedicated growers *do* still make the great sweet wine of Jurançon. From a grower like Barrère or Guirouilh using shrivelled, late-harvested, grapes, Jurançon reeks of the great 'noble rot' wines of Barsac yet keeps a tremendous fresh acidity to tease the honey out of the wine. Rare, expensive, worth it.

MADIRAN AND PACHERENC DU VIC BIHL

These two daunting names are the red and white, respectively, which hug into the south-

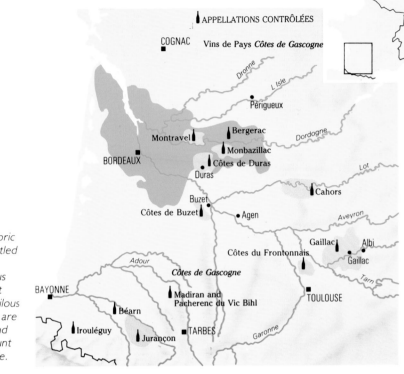

APPELLATIONS CONTRÔLÉES

COGNAC Vins de Pays *Côtes de Gascogne*

Dronne
L'Isle
Périgueux
Montravel Bergerac Dordogne
Monbazillac
BORDEAUX Côtes de Duras
Duras
Lot
Buzet Cahors
Côtes de Buzet Agen
Aveyron
Gaillac Albi
Côtes du Frontonnais Gaillac
Adour Côtes de Gascogne Tarn
BAYONNE TOULOUSE
Madiran and
Pacherenc du Vic Bihl
Béarn TARBES
Irouléguy Garonne
Jurançon

Jurançon is one of France's most historic vineyard areas nestled in the Pyrenean foothills and famous primarily for sweet wines. After a perilous survival, vineyards are being expanded and an increasing amount of good wine made.

western frontiers of the large Armagnac brandy-producing area. They received last gasp mouth-to-mouth resuscitation after World War Two, when there was hardly a vine left, and now look healthy, if a little 'recherché'.

Madiran (AC) has been described as the best red of the south-west outside Bordeaux. I would disagree. In general it has a strangely ill-defined flavour. The balance is usually excellent, yet the fruit is dominated by a slightly 'green apples' sharpness from the mixture of Tannat, Cabernet Franc and Cabernet Sauvignon. Certainly they improve with age, but only wines like Château Montus, matured in fairly new oak barrels, seem to improve into anything exciting.

The white **Pacherenc du Vic Bihl** (AC), made from an array of local grapes such as Ruffiac and Courbu, is rare but worth seeking out, since this full, very dry white has a remarkable pear-skin fruit which is unique.

The nearby VDQS **Côtes de St-Mont** makes very good fruity reds and whites.

CÔTES DU FRONTONNAIS (AC)

This is one of those 'local' wines which is so delicious it travels to the four corners of the world with consummate ease. Except that there's not that much to do the travelling, and the nearby city of Toulouse wisely drinks it at a great rate. There is some rosé, but the joy is the red, based on the Negrette grape. From a good property like Flotis, Montauriol or La Palme, the wine is silky smooth, bursting with remarkable liquorice and strawberry fruits, and tremendous value for money. Drink it young, and drink it often.

FRENCH COUNTRY WINES

THE SOUTH-WEST

GAILLAC

Gaillac (AC) is one of the best known of the south-west wines, but far too much of her wine is too mediocre to deserve such renown. However, this is one of France's most ancient vineyards and a new director at the main co-op is revitalizing the basic wines, while some growers such as Cros and Albert are bent on preserving the traditional qualities. The whites, which can be sweet or dry, are a little terse and could usually do with softening a bit, though they can have a quite big apple and liquorice fruit if you're lucky. The reds should have a most intensely peppery, dry flavour, as strong and as effective as the fiery, tangy perfume of fresh ground pepper. The wines are not deep or rich, but the fruit is ripe and this 'pepper-grinder' taste is surprisingly more-ish. There are various semi-sparkling wines, but the best from the *méthode gaillaçoise* – a 'nearly' champagne method like the *méthode rurale* sometimes used for Blanquette de Limoux (see p. 26) are absolutely superb: peppery, honeyed, apricoty, appley, all at the same time. From producers like Cros or Boissel-Rhodes, they're very good, and not expensive.

BUZET, CÔTES DE DURAS

Though separated by 50 km (30 miles), these are two dynamic mini-regions dedicated to making claret look-alikes. **Buzet** (AC) is as yet the more exciting. Her reds, from the Bordeaux grapes, are quite astonishingly

Above *Winter in Cahors can be bleak and bitterly cold. However, snow on the vines is a good sign because it protects them against the extremes of frost.* **Right** *The Château de Monbazillac is an imposing castle looking out over the Dordogne valley surrounded by its vines.*

good, combining a rich blackcurrant sweetness with an arresting grassy greenness. The **Duras** (AC) reds are less sweet, but just as grassy. However, Duras does make an excellent Sauvignon-based white, as fresh as the best Bordeaux Blanc, but just a little chubbier. Good co-ops dominate both appellations but a few single domaines like Château Sauvanères in Buzet are appearing. Duras is cheaper, but both are good value.

CAHORS

Cahors (AC) is a one-wine town, and that wine is red. It *can* be so good that you don't mind a bit about the shortage of white or fizz, because good Cahors has the remarkable ability to combine a tough, sturdy style with a fruit so gentle, so warm, that it is very difficult to persuade yourself to mature it for a while. What Cahors is *not* is the legendary 'black' wine, the very smell of which would reduce a hardened drinker to tea and sympathy at 50 paces. What it *sometimes* is, particularly from the co-op, is a dull, tired, dry wine of no great personality. However, from a single domaine, from a grower who is prepared to struggle, Cahors is fine wine.

Some growers make the wine to drink young, when it is marked by a wonderful, plummy richness, kept fresh by a distinct appley acidity. More generally the growers intend it to age, and the flavours it develops are often almost honeyed, but kept straight-faced

by that plummy fruit going deeper, spicier, darker, often resembling tobacco and prunes – what a combination! But *that* is the modern-day 'darkness', a darkness of big ripe flavours, and it is unlike any other red wine. Vintages are mostly good, with 1988 and 1985 being special recently. The chief grape is the Auxerrois (Bordeaux's Malbec). They don't think much of it in Bordeaux, but, with the flavours it can produce in Cahors, I doubt if the Cahors growers worry too much about what Bordeaux thinks.

BERGERAC

There are nine different appellations inside **Bergerac** (AC), yet they do little to dispel the feeling that the modern Bergerac is keener on sliding in to the market on Bordeaux's coat-tails than emphasizing her traditional flavours and styles. This is understandable, since Bergerac is, in effect, the eastward extension of the St-Emilion vineyards, and in reds at least has a similar reliance on the Merlot grape, with help from Cabernet Sauvignon and Cabernet Franc. However, the reds which Bergerac makes best are a good deal less substantial than St-Emilion's. One winemaker suggested that Bergerac was ideally suited to making fresh, bright 'Nouveau' reds after the Beaujolais style, and there is a lot of truth in that, but the tiny area of **Pécharmant** (AC) is an exception, making very fine full dry reds requiring considerable

aging. Most Bergerac reds made in a big, serious way are rather tough and meaty and charmless, while the light-style reds are often first class. Interestingly, Bergerac can make first class rosé – quite deep in colour, and dry but full of fruit.

The whites run the gamut from sweet to dry. **Bergerac Sec** (AC) is the driest, made in a Bordeaux Sauvignon style, although, as in Bordeaux, the majority grape is Sémillon. It is usually good, quite full, and grassy dry. The medium sweet wines have a variety of appellations of which **Côtes de Montravel** (AC) and **Côtes de Bergerac Moelleux** (AC) are the most important. The appellation of **Monbazillac** (AC) is one of the most famous names in the world of sweet wine. As with Sauternes the general standard has been debased to an over-sulphured, artificially sweet mediocrity, yet unlike Sauternes there are very few quality-conscious single properties prepared to make the real thing. Most Monbazillac is simply pleasant and fairly sweet. The occasional true Monbazillac is fine wine, yet not of the standard of a top Sauternes.

South-West Vins de Pays: There are a fair number but few of any particular interest or general availability. Two are worth noting. **Charentais** is the table wine from the Cognac region, often a very good, sharply fruity white. **Côtes de Gascogne** is the Armagnac table wine and is even better; it can also offer a fairly decent tart but tasty red.

CONSUMER CHECKLIST		
Fronton Ch. de	Q:	1 2 3 4 5 6 **7** 8 9 10
Flotis 1988	P:	1 2 3 **4** 5 6 7 8 9 10
	V:	1 2 3 4 5 6 7 8 **9** 10
Vin de Pays des	Q:	1 2 3 4 **5** 6 7 8 9 10
Côtes de	P:	1 **2** 3 4 5 6 7 8 9 10
Gascogne	V:	1 2 3 4 5 6 7 **8** 9 10

Good Years The reds often need several years to develop, though wines like Fronton and Buzet are immediately delicious. Rosés and white Vins de Pays are best very young, though some whites like Jurançon and Pacherenc du Vic Bihl need time.

Taste Notes Many of the old-fashioned wines have flavours as original and memorable as can be found throughout France. The newer wines and the Vins de Pays are mostly of a very high quality, to be drunk young.

GERMANY

It is joyous to relate that the world is drinking ever-increasing amounts of German wine, with the English-speaking markets in particular developing an unquenchable appetite. It is, therefore, that much more distressing to relate that this buoyant export market is based almost entirely upon the flattest, dullest, most forgettable wines that Germany can produce – simple Tafelwein, Bereich Nierstein, Bernkastel and, most famous of all, Liebfraumilch. Particularly so since, while the export market has been consuming increasing quantities of these innocuous low price blends, the top estates of one of the world's greatest wine nations have been fighting for survival.

To create the best German wines requires real dedication. They are usually produced on steep, tricky, cost-intensive slopes, in regions where the full ripeness of the grapes is by no means assured. Indeed, you would be forgiven for questioning whether the grape will ripen at all so far north. But in that uncertainty of climate lies the greatness of German wine.

With a long, slow ripening season which can often drag on perilously into the uncertain autumn gloom, the level of acidity remains piercingly high in the classic German grape – the Riesling. And German winemakers since Roman times have developed ways of matching this high, cool-climate acidity with a fragrant, perfumed orchard fresh fruit which makes German wines often seem closer to the essence of the grape than almost any other wines. And through their techniques of developing new grape varieties which will ripen early to a spicy sweetness even as far north as the River Rhine, and by the perfection of a system called 'Süssreserve', or 'sweet reserve' (which involves blending back fresh unfermented grape juice into the fermented wine, thus catching all the summer freshness of the fruit while retaining the high natural acidity), they have set a standard of fruit flavours in wine for the rest of the world's winemakers to strive for.

They are experts at producing light, fruity, not quite dry, low alcohol and low price wines, ideal for people just starting to drink wine, or for uncritical summer quaffing and their methods are taught to winemakers of every warm climate country in the world, in particular their secrets of fermenting the wine at a cool temperature. This is natural in chilly Germany, but is the source of inspiration for winemakers intent upon making simple popular whites in the USA, Australia, South Africa, New Zealand, and, increasingly, in the Mediterranean countries too. They are also experts at using the presence of 'noble rot' which shrivels and sweetens the wine grapes when it occurs, to produce what are quite possibly the world's sweetest wines from its coolest major wine region. Again, the formula of acid and fruit is preserved.

The following sections try to set out the differing regions and styles Germany has to offer, and to persuade you that these wines are indeed worth sampling.

CLASSIFICATION

German quality criteria are not, as in France, based on a hierarchical ranking of vineyards, but on the level of ripeness (i.e. sugar content) of the grape when it is picked. Minimum requirements are laid down for each category in each wine region.

Sugar levels are measured in degrees Oechsle – one degree Oechsle is each gram by which a litre of grape juice is heavier than a litre of water. Thus, a reading of 95°Oechsle means that a litre of the grape juice in question is 95 g heavier than a litre of water. Since this extra weight is sugar ripeness, the higher the reading the greater the potential alcohol.

There are three main classifications. Starting from the best, these are:

Qualitätswein mit Prädikat (QmP)
The top quality designation, it is literally translated as Quality Wine with Special Attributes. 'Special Attributes' means simply that the grapes were harvested at one of the following levels of ripeness and then made into wine without any further addition of sugar.

Kabinett Ordinary ripe grapes from a normal harvest.

Spätlese Late picked (and therefore riper) grapes.

Auslese selected bunches of 'specially ripe' late picked grapes.

WINE REGIONS

1 Ahr
2 Mittelrhein
3 Mosel-Saar-Ruwer
4 Rheingau
5 Nahe
6 Rheinhessen
7 Rheinpfalz
8 Hessische-Bergstrasse
9 Franken
10 Württemberg
11 Baden

Beerenauslese Specially selected single grapes, picked at the peak of over-ripeness.

Trockenbeerenauslese Shrivelled, specially selected single grapes. (These 'noble-rotted' grapes are picked one by one and make some of the greatest sweet wine in the world).

Qualitätswein bestimmter Anbaugebiete (QbA)

'Quality Wine from a Designated Region' The 'Region' can be a *Bereich*, as in Bereich Nierstein, which is a grouping of villages using the village's name, a *Grosslage*, or grouping of vineyards of supposedly similar style, or, best of all, *Einzellage* – a single vineyard of proven personality. All are made with added sugar.

Tafelwein

Ordinary table wine – usually a low-quality blend, which must be artificially sugared to achieve a semblance of ripeness. 'Deutscher Tafelwein' must be German. 'EEC' or no qualification at all means a rock-bottom blend from another European country (probably Italy) and should be avoided.

Landwein

A German equivalent of the French Vin de Pays, made only in dry and semi-dry styles.

There is one further category which is separate because of the way it is made:

Eiswein

Made by crushing grapes that have frozen on the vine. By pressing the grapes before they have thawed, the water stays as a chunk of ice, and the sugar (which has a lower freezing point) can easily be squeezed out in supremely concentrated form.

MOSEL

THE GENERAL PICTURE

The Mosel wine region is almost too beautiful to bear. Nature has created such a brilliant combination of gentle twisting river valley, and soaring, broad-shouldered swathes of vines that it would be callous and cruel if these vineyards, coating the steepling valley sides with greens and gold through half the year, did not produce something altogether exceptional in the way of wine. And, luckily, they do. The white wines of the Mosel are unlike any other in the world – when they are based on the Riesling grape, and when they come from one of the numerous steep-slanted, slaty, south-facing sites nestled into the folds of the river, or strung out for mile upon mile in its golden heart between Bernkastel and Erden and, less breathtakingly, but just as importantly, between Bernkastel and Piesport. These can achieve a thrilling, orchard fresh, 'spring flowers as well as autumn apples' flavour, allied to an alcohol level so low that it leaves your head clear enough, glass after glass, to revel in the flavours of the fruit. This is the joy of Mosel wine at its best, and no-one has succeeded in duplicating this taste. Only Luxembourg, which is on the Mosel anyway, and, occasionally, England, have got anywhere near it.

The great majority of Mosel wine comes from the river valley itself, but there are two small tributaries which have been incorporated into the general designation: the Saar and the Ruwer. The overall designation is thus Mosel-Saar-Ruwer. With the Ahr and the Mittelrhein, the Mosel is the most northerly vineyard area in Germany, but is nonetheless an important producer, having 12.8 per cent of the vineyard acreage, and, despite her finest wines coming from the acute-angled vineyards towering over the river, there is also a fair amount of wine of a fairly un-Mosel type grown away from the immediate river banks.

GRAPE VARIETIES AND WINE STYLES

Every single one of the greatest Mosel wines is made from the Riesling grape. One could almost say that *only* the Riesling grape is capable of producing true Mosel-style wine. Yet this grape is in decline. Whereas in 1910 it occupied 88 per cent of the vineyards, and all the best sites, and as late as 1964 still accounted for a proud 80 per cent, by 1988 it was little over 55 per cent.

Even the prime slate based and south-west slanting sites are being invaded, primarily by the easy, adaptable Müller-Thurgau grape. The reason is higher yields and earlier ripening, and a reflection of modern taste which supposedly does not like the stark, steely flavours of a cool-ripened Mosel Riesling. That 'coolness' is a crucial part of Mosel quality. The biggest, hottest years, like 1976 and 1959, which bring juicy, succulent flavours flooding out from the rather more raunchy River Rhine, are likely to put a Mosel out of balance.

The Mosel does make wines right up to the very sweet **Eiswein** and **Trockenbeerenauslese** level, but they are definitely not as sweet as equivalents from the Rhine, and the fundamental delicacy of the Mosel fruit can be rather swamped by overripe richness. **Auslese** wines are quite often made, but, unless infected by the sugar-concentrating 'noble rot', they are likely to be simply sweetish and bland. The true genius of Mosel wine is usually found in **Rieslings** of **Kabinett** and **Spätlese** quality, which, since they're cheaper than the sweeter types,' is rather good news for us enthusiasts.

THE IMPORTANT DETAILS

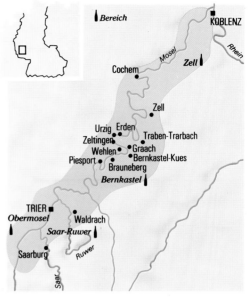

Left *Almost every Mosel village has its castle. At Beilstein the vines cover all available ground below the Burg Metternich.*
Below *Zell is situated on a loop of the Mosel. The central section, between Cochem and Trier, is one long spectacular wall of vines.*

CLASSIFICATION

The same classification system is used for Mosel wines as in the rest of Germany, but with one important difference – all the minimum ripeness levels for the various quality categories are lower. This reflects the fact that it is more difficult to ripen grapes on the steep slaty valley vineyards of the Mosel, and also that the basic Mosel style, with its fresh lemony fruit and high natural tartaric acid level, is traditionally lighter, fresher, and lower in alcohol than an equivalent Rhine wine. Along with the Ahr and Mittelrhein, these are the lowest levels in German wine production. The figures are as follows:

Basic Tafelwein 44° Oechsle sugar in the grape, yielding 5° potential alcohol. This could have at least 3° of potential alcohol added by additional dollops of sugar.

Qualitätswein 57° Oechsle sugar in the grape, yielding 7° potential alcohol. This could also be beefed by by a couple of degrees.

Kabinett 70° Oechsle producing 9.1° potential alcohol. A good natural low alcohol level for a Mosel, many of which are Kabinetts.

Spätlese 76° Oechsle producing 10° potential alcohol. A slight rise in ripeness, hardly noticeable in the main Mosel vineyard sites.

Auslese 83° Oechsle producing 11.1° potential alcohol. By now we have dropped a whole category behind the Rhine, where you need 85° Oechsle to make a Spätlese. Auslese wines are rare on the Mosel, and are often disappointing, not having the succulent ripeness of the Rhine, but having lost freshness and bite too.

MOSEL

THE IMPORTANT DETAILS

Beerenauslese 110° Oechsle, producing 15.3° potential alcohol. This is *very* ripe. Only astonishingly hot years like 1989 are likely to produce any Beerenauslese. Despite this ripeness, which will be concentrated by the occurrence of late autumn 'noble rot' sucking the water out of the grapes, and leaving greatly enhanced sweetness, a Mosel Beerenauslese will retain that sharp smack of acidity which may be lost in many of the Rhine vineyards. The remarkable, frozen-fingered 'harvest to end all harvests' of Eiswein must also reach this sugar level.

Trockenbeerenauslese 150° Oechsle producing 21.5° potential alcohol. This is so rare that all the German areas have the same virtually unattainable ripeness level. Maybe one year in ten will they squeeze out any of this from the November mists in the Mosel valley.

ORGANIZATION/S
It is difficult to produce cheap Mosel, and few companies do it successfully, since the exotic aromatic grape varieties which can mask a multitude of sins on the Rhine just don't grow on the Mosel, and if they were thrown in to any blend they certainly wouldn't taste like Mosel. Even so, every major wine company offers a basic Bereich Bernkastel and a basic Piesporter. The standard of all but a few is diabolical. The only companies who regularly produce good Mosels are those which actually own vineyards such as Müller and Deinhard. The Mosel has never been a co-operative stronghold, but about 20 per cent of the crop

Left *On the steeper parts of the Mosel, terracing has to be used to climb up the valley slopes. A special single stake goblet training system is needed in such hillside vineyards.*

Above *As autumn comes, the grapes ripen and the leaves turn to a sea of gold, which seem to mirror the optimism and hopes of the growers for a ripe, golden wine.*

is now made by co-ops, and four-fifths of this amount is handled by the huge Zentral Kellerei, or 'Central Cellars', at Bernkastel, which, luckily, sets a high standard at all levels. However, for the true taste of Mosel, one must go to the numerous single growers such as Lauerburg, J. J. Prüm, Staatlichen Weinbaüdomänen, von Schubert or Friedrich Wilhelm Gymnasium, since it's remarkably hard work making great Mosel wine, and owning your own piece of land is a great incentive to quality.

READING THE LABEL
There was a time when you did not expect to see 'Riesling' on a Mosel wine label, since it was automatically assumed that all the wine would be Riesling. Sadly, this isn't so any

more. Most cheap Mosel is made from the Müller-Thurgau grape or even the Elbling. A Riesling wine nowadays will state the fact proudly on the label. As a rule, avoid the general brand names like Moselblümchen – an evocative name likely to be hiding a fairly hideous concoction – Zeller SchwarzeKatz and Kröver Nacktarsch – the Black Cat and Bare Bum wine beloved of the tourists – and Bereich Bernkastel. Look for the daunting words Erzeugerabfüllung or Originalabfüllung, which shows the wine is estate-bottled.

WHAT DOES IT TASTE LIKE?
Good Mosel is a thrilling taste. There's nothing caressing, gentle, seductive about it, but it simply bursts with the happy, blossoming tastes of spring and early summer. As the

MOSEL

THE IMPORTANT DETAILS

first spring buds appear, everyone should whip out a bottle of the last year's Mosel, a Kabinett or a Spätlese, to remind themselves of the freshness and beauty of a world waking up again after the long dead haul of winter. What is remarkable about good Mosel wines is that as they age they can still hold on to this freshness in a steely, tautly acid way. A good Mosel should always have a high acid level, though the wines of the central villages of Piesport, Brauneberg, Graach, Zelting and Erden are likely to give wines with a softer honeyed feel to them. The wines from the side valleys of the Saar and Ruwer are certainly lighter. They used to be renowned for a wonderful steely bite, which went deliciously, dangerously petrolly as they got older. Obviously Public Opinion couldn't take their remarkably individual flavours, since only the finest estates still make this type of wine.

THE GOOD YEARS

Vintage matters enormously in the Mosel, since it is by no means possible to ripen the grape properly every year. And even when the ripening is achieved, the large cropping which all of Germany pursues can mean the light, delicate flavours are too diluted to have much to say for themselves. However, the finest estates can still make wonderful steely dry wines in years like 1984 or 1987 when a poor ripening season demands great wine-making skills, but the best recent vintages are the exquisitely balanced 1988s and the super-ripe 1989s. 1985 and 1983 produced lovely balanced wines, and these are still drinking well. Good Mosels keep well, cheap ones don't.

ENJOYING THE WINES

There's nothing quite so refreshing as a light, well-made Kabinett from the Mosel, Saar or Ruwer to drink absolutely by itself, for the simple pleasure of the taste that it gives. The flowery, apple freshness, the low alcohol, the tangy acidity all make Mosels marvellous any-time refreshment wines. They are less good with food, since, even up to Auslese level, the flavours are basically delicate. The new style 'Trocken' wines are being promoted as good accompaniments to food, but most Mosels were naturally fairly dry anyway, without having every last ounce of sugar squeezed out of them, and they are generally too light and acid to be much fun, with or without something to nibble on.

CONSUMER INFORMATION

WHAT DO I GET FOR MY MONEY?
Mosel wines *can* be very good value for money, but not right at the bottom end of the scale. The Mosel is a high cost wine-producing area, and so is unlikely to churn out vast quantities of decent plonk. Even so, the prices of good German wines have risen remarkably little in recent years, and at **Kabinett** and **Spätlese** level they are reasonably priced given the quality. **Saar** and **Ruwer** will be a little more expensive.

AVAILABILITY
You can get Mosel wine everywhere. However, much of it will be commercial brands or blends. These are not often worth buying. The production of estate wines is limited, and outside Germany the distribution is not good. However, all good merchants will stock one or two. You are unlikely to be able to find Beerenauslese or Eiswein with any frequency.

CONSUMER CHECKLIST

Piesporter	Q:	**1** 2 3 4 5 6 7 8 9 10
Michelsberg	P:	1 2 **3** 4 5 6 7 8 9 10
QbA	V:	**1** 2 3 4 5 6 7 8 9 10

Ayler Kupp	Q:	1 2 3 4 5 6 **7** 8 9 10
Riesling Spätlese	P:	1 2 3 4 **5 6** 7 8 9 10
(estate-bottled)	V:	1 2 3 4 5 6 7 **8** 9 10

Good Years For basic wine, less sunny years can produce some tart but reasonably fruity wine. For high quality 'prädikat' wines, really good years only come about twice a decade – i.e., 1971, 1975/76, 1983, 1985 and 1988/89. But good estates can make fine steely wines in poor years. Delicious young, good Mosel wines *can* age.

Taste Notes The impression should be of cool, tingling freshness, sharp as a lime, sweet as an apple, sometimes with a splash of honey. The Kabinett and Spätlese quality levels are usually the best.

THE RHINE VALLEY

WINE REGIONS

- Nahe
- Rheingau
- Rheinpfalz
- Rheinhessen
- ▮ Bereich

The Rhine valley is the heart of German wine-growing. The three main regions are the Rheingau; a concentrated wall of vines situated where the Rhine turns briefly west between Wiesbaden and Assmanshausen; the Rheinhessen, with its finest sites round Nierstein on the 'Rhein-front', but encompassing a very large and prolific area away from the river itself to the east; and the Rheinpfalz or Rhine Palatinate, the most southerly region on the slopes of the Haardt mountains just north of French Alsace. The Nahe is a northern tributary running through Bad Kreuznach to the Rhine at Bingen, and, since it just about resembles the Rhine more than the Mosel, we include it with the Rhine. Let's take a more detailed look at these regions.

A perfect Rhine landscape – steep, slaty slopes, vines and the river.

THE RHINE VALLEY/Rheingau

THE GENERAL PICTURE

Left *The evening sun slants across the famous vineyards of Schloss Johannisberg.*
Right *Schloss Vollrads, nestled in the hills above the village of Winkel, is one of the great wine estates of Germany. It produces brilliant sweet wines as well as an unusually high proportion of dry wines.*
Far right *Rüdesheim is the last of the great white wine villages of the Rheingau before the Rhine turns north.*

Of all the great vineyard areas of Germany, this is the smallest, with only 3 per cent of the total national acreage of vines, but into this small area are packed many of the greatest names in German wine. At Wiesbaden the Rhine's rather stately progress north is met by the implacable wall of the Taunus mountains, and the river sullenly veers westwards beneath the high barrier of hills until Rüdesheim. Rüdesheim to Wiesbaden is not much over 30 km (20 miles), yet between the two towns there is a parade of vineyards of concentrated brilliance on the south-facing riverside slopes, glittering names each promising to scale the heights with the Riesling grape as their standard bearer. The most famous village names are Rüdesheim, Johannisberg, Winkel, Erbach and Rauenthal, but there are other villages producing equally fine wine, and even several vineyards so renowned that they are given leave to omit their village names from the label. Great wines are made at Geisenheim, Oestrich, Hallgarten, Hattenheim, Kiedrich, Eltville, Martinsthal, and the enclave of Hochheim on the Main tributary 24 km (15 miles) to the east. Among vineyards sufficiently famous not to have to use their village name are Schloss Vollrads at Winkel, and Steinberg at Hattenheim.

GRAPE VARIETIES AND WINE STYLES

The Riesling dominates this carpet of vineyard slopes. It has 82 per cent of the acreage and virtually every great Rheingau is a **Riesling** wine. There is a little **Müller-Thurgau** – where is there not? – about 7 per cent, and about 5 per cent **Spätburgunder** (or Pinot Noir). This red Burgundy grape is centred on the village of Assmanshausen, which, alone of the Rheingau villages, is famous for red wine. And the wine institute at Geisenheim is the centre of German wine research, which has created many of the new vine hybrids, so grape names like **Ehrenfelser**, **Scheurebe** and **Kerner** may turn up on the label. You may also see **Weissburgunder**, which is the Pinot Blanc, and Erbach's Rheinhell vineyard even has some **Chardonnay**.

Although the Rheingau's fame rests on her astonishing sweet wines of **Beerenauslese** (see p. 177) standard and higher – which manage to combine an intensity of honeyed sweetness with an acidity which is so strong and clean it is as fresh as a squirt of lime or blood orange into the grape juice – yet her true worth is measured lower down the scale, with her **Kabinetts** and **Spätleses**. These wines give the Riesling the chance to show off not only its flowery tastes, but also the remarkable grapiness it can produce, and in the Rheingau the soil adds a bite, a steely, minerally, even smoky toughness which is exhilarating and delicious, and, as the wines get sweeter, the honeyed ripeness takes on a musky beeswax aroma which is quite unique in the world of wine. The dry, 'Trocken' wines can be good, but are usually just too tart to give much pleasure without food, and the red wines are pleasant but light and pretty one-dimensional.

THE IMPORTANT DETAILS

CLASSIFICATION

The Rheingau's classification is topped by the estates which do not have to use the village name – a kind of historic 'Great Growth' status. At present, however, these are not always producing the greatest wines. Otherwise, the German system of judging quality through ripeness remains in force. As with all great vineyard areas, the Rheingau teeters on the edge of the heat requirements for ripening its grapes; too often the climate is dangerously cool. Only in great years like 1989, when 65 per cent of the crop reached the 'Prädikat' level, will the majority of the grapes be fully ripe. In the more usual lesser years, the majority will be Qualitätswein, requiring the addition of sugar to make the wine. However, the Rheingau is very quality-conscious and many growers will declassify Kabinett wine despite a minimum legal ripeness, if they consider it not up to par.

ORGANIZATION/S

There are co-operatives in the Rheingau, and their standard, as, for instance, at the Hallgarten co-op, can be good, but they do not have much influence on the wine trade. Every merchant will make up blends of such wines as Bereich Johannisberg, and will probably offer village wines from the larger and less-defined vineyard sites. However, all the finest wines come from individual growers, although barely a fifth bottle their own wine. For fine Rheingau it is always worth buying estate-bottled wine.

READING THE LABEL

Rheingau labels are frequently very ornate, and there is a lot of Gothic script in evidence, but if you can read the letters, they are perfectly logical. Look for 'Riesling' to be marked, and also check whether the wine is 'Trocken' or 'Halb-trocken' – ('Dry' or 'Half-dry') – since many growers are trying out the new dry styles. Some growers make use of differing cork capsule colours to try to indicate the relative sweetness of the wines, or their superiority in a given category. In general, the more gold on the capsule, the sweeter and classier the wine.

THE RHINE VALLEY/Rheingau

THE IMPORTANT DETAILS

It is only in the warmest years that vintage time is a shirt-sleeves and sun-tan lotion affair. More often, as here at the famous Steinberg vineyard, it is a chilly time, with barely ripe grapes being gathered under sullen skies.

WHAT DO THEY TASTE LIKE?

Usually, Rheingau wines are marked by an astonishing balance between grapiness and slatiness, between perfume and smoke, between luscious honey and austere acidity. They often have the most lingering, endlessly shifting flavours the Riesling is capable of producing, and even the Kabinetts have body and ripeness. The new 'Trocken' style wines in general seem to miss this balance.

THE GOOD YEARS

The Rheingau is susceptible to poor weather, since its chief grape, the Riesling, needs decent warmth to ripen. There weren't many decent wines made in cool years like 1987, 1986 and 1984. However 1983 and 1985 both produced very attractive florally fragrant wines, while 1988 and 1989 produced a wide range of superb flavours. Of older years both 1976 and 1971 can still be outstanding – in fact many 1971s took years to reach their best.

ENJOYING THE WINES

Although Rheingaus have more body than Mosels or Nahes, they are not at their best with food. You can partner some of the traditional salmon, trout, pike and eel dishes with a Spätlese, but in general, food is best accompanied by the all-purpose Qualitätswein or the increasing number of 'Trocken' wines. These need food and seem to go as well with a white radish salad as with a fatty chunk of pork knuckle in a sweet sauce.

CONSUMER INFORMATION

Although stainless steel modernity is increasingly in evidence on the Rheingau, big old barrels are still used for the best ones. This venerable decorated example, however, is more ornamental than practical.

through good merchants, but aren't difficult to find if you look.

CONSUMER CHECKLIST		
Bereich	Q: 1 2 **3 4** 5 6 7 8 9 10	
Johannisberger	P: 1 **2 3** 4 5 6 7 8 9 10	
Riesling QbA	V: 1 2 **3 4** 5 6 7 8 9 10	
1989		
Oestricher	Q: 1 2 3 4 5 6 7 8 **9** 10	
Doosberg	P: 1 2 3 4 5 6 **7 8** 9 10	
Auslese 1989	V: 1 2 3 4 5 6 7 8 **9** 10	

Good Years The Rheingau, with the Mosel, is the most susceptible of Germany's great wine areas to weather variations. Consequently, years are important and 1989, 1988, 1983, 1976, 1975 and 1971 are fine years, all of which need or have needed 3 to 5 years to reach any maturity. The top sweet wines age best of all German wines. Cheap Rheingau wines should be drunk young.

Taste Notes There is a wonderful balance to Rheingau wines. Even at the basic level, they have a delicious, quite dry grapiness, balanced by a slaty dry edge, and the sweet wines, maintain this wonderful refreshing edge.

WHAT DO I GET FOR MY MONEY?

In general, remarkable value. Rheingau wines are never Germany's cheapest, but they are frequently the most reliable. Even Bereich Johannisberg maintains a fairly solid quality level. The sweetest estate wines will be fiendishly expensive, though worth it, but the **Kabinett** and **Spätlese** are often cheaper than those from other regions.

AVAILABILITY

Not brilliant. Even the basic wines are not produced on an enormous scale and many are quickly consumed in Germany itself. The estate wines will generally only be available

THE RHINE VALLEY/Rheinhessen

THE GENERAL PICTURE

The Rhein-front is a group of four villages comprising Bodenheim and Nachenheim in the north and Nierstein and Oppenheim in the south. All the greatest Rheinhessen wines comes from vineyards such as these, overlooking the town of Nierstein.

The Rheinhessen is the largest of the Rhine's wine-producing areas – as far as vineyard acreage and volume go – but if you look on the map you will see that this does not tell the whole story. The Rhine flows north from Worms to Mainz, then angles west to Bingen before forcing its way north again at Bingen, leaving an enormous hinterland resembling the shoulder, chest and neck of a man. All this is Rheinhessen and some 165 villages nestle there in a bland anonymity. But between Mainz and Worms, like a small vein on the arm, the names Oppenheim, Nierstein, Nackenheim and Bodenheim appear, and, way round the bend of the shoulder, Bingen. Five villages, on whose fame and limited output rest the reputation of the entire region. These are villages which have their vineyards on the river, the first four sharing a sweep of land called the Rhein-front ('Rhine Front' or 'Rhine Terrace'), and they can make some of Germany's finest wine.

Of the other 160 villages, there are literally half a dozen whose names occasionally turn up on the label. Nearly all their produce goes into the faceless blends of hock and Liebfraumilch with which Germany floods an ever-increasing market. Indeed, the general names of Bereich Bingen and Bereich Nierstein cover the output of about two-thirds of the whole area, with Bereich Wonnegau mopping up the remainder. No wonder the growers of Nierstein in particular feel that their own fame and excellence is being seriously eroded by all the other villages, many of whom offer their own wines as Nierstein at half the price and half the quality. The very low priced Niersteiner Gutes Domtal is one of the most commonly met wine names in the world, yet the vineyard is a relatively small 34 hectares (85 acres) in Nierstein. How? Fifteen other villages inland over the hill have the right to use the name of this one small vineyard!! However, the growers at Nierstein really do seem to have had enough, and may refute the other villages' right to use their name, returning Nierstein to what it should be – a high quality, and relatively high cost, wine village.

Liebfraumilch initially began as a trade name, but has become a catch-all designation for Rhine wine made from most grape types and of a pleasant character. The great majority of this pretty basic wine comes from the Rheinhessen and the Rheinpfalz.

THE RHINE VALLEY/Rheinhessen

THE GENERAL PICTURE

GRAPE VARIETIES AND WINE STYLES

Name me a grape, and they're sure to grow it somewhere in the Rheinhessen, because this is the great experimental area of Germany. Indeed, it is to try to add a little floweriness and excitement to the generally dull tastes of the hinterland Hessen wines that many of the new varieties have been developed. There is not a lot of **Riesling**, and most of that is in the Rhein-front villages and Bingen. It can be wonderful wine. The Bingen wines have a dry, steely, sometimes positively smoky, quality close to Rheingau in style – well, it *is* just over the river. The Rhein-front wines, particularly

of Bodenheim and Nierstein, can be wonderfully scented, rising to some of the richest sweetest wines in Germany, yet still retaining their acid edge. The **Müller-Thurgau** is the main grape, especially for the **Liebfraumilch** blends, and is usually fairly mild and pleasant in a grapy way, while the **Silvaner** has a more earthy style. Names like **Scheurebe, Gewürztraminer, Ortega, Kerner** and **Optima** all pop up, and all have a 'spicier' style. Since much of the hinterland wine tends to mirror the flat, uninteresting meadows and fields it comes from, any little bit of extra personality helps.

THE IMPORTANT DETAILS

CLASSIFICATION

The majority of Rheinhessen wine at any one time is likely to be of the fairly basic Qualitätswein standard – indeed, most of it is likely to appear under the all-embracing name Liebfraumilch. However, true Nierstein is a particularly ripe wine and in most years the village will produce a large amount of Qualitätswein mit Prädikat, or 'Special Quality' wine. There is an increasing amount of Kabinett and Spätlese wine, especially from new vine crossings which ripen early, and these should be marked on the label.

ORGANIZATION/S

Given the predominance of branded Liebfraumilch and branded Bereich Nierstein on the market, obviously merchants' commercial blends play a large role. It is a role which does not cover them with glory since the wines concerned are traded with as much concern for quality and personalities as pork bellies in Chicago or cocoa futures in London. The co-operatives handle a lot of produce and can turn out reasonable wine. However, the serious growers of Nierstein and Oppenheim,

like Senfter, Balbach, Heyl or G.A. Schmidt and Villa Sachsen in Bingen, produce some of Germany's finest wines at all levels up to Trockenbeerenauslese.

READING THE LABEL

If you want to try a genuine Rheinhessen wine of style and personality, you should avoid Bereich Nierstein and Bereich Bingen, even though these are now being marketed at up to Spätlese level, since these two names account for about 16,000 hectares (40,000 acres) between them. Avoid Liebfraumilch unless you're looking for something simple, cheap and cheerful. If you *do* buy it, check the label for the date. You want it as young as possible. Check the label for dust, too. Since it doesn't improve with age, you don't want one which has been lying around on the shop shelf.

WHAT DO THEY TASTE LIKE?

Rheinhessen wines can have a delicious, scented floweriness to them, nearly always gentle, sometimes slightly grapy, but with the fragrant whiff of a rose garden in bloom.

Single-estate wines should often show this. Branded Niersteins and Liebfraumilchs might still be flowery, but they'll resemble a squirt of air freshener rather than a good lungful of a gardener's pride and joy.

THE GOOD YEARS

Some good wine is made in the Rheinhessen every year. Nierstein, in particular, has various sites which always seem to ripen whatever the weather. The new early-ripening grape types also mean that ripe wine can be produced annually. For the top wines, 1989, 1988, 1985, 1983, 1976 and 1971 were particularly good. For the branded wines and blends, drink the youngest available.

ENJOYING THE WINES

The Liebfraumilch blends have established themselves as wines of no great complexity which can be drunk at any time – simple, light, grapy. The better estate wines are often marvellous by themselves because of their flowery perfume, but they also have enough flavour to go with the various river fish and innumerable sausages of the area. The very sweet wines are some of the few in Germany which are really rich and luscious enough to go with heavy puddings and other weight-watcher's delights.

The Rheinhessen boasts few top class steep sloping sites, but Nierstein has a string of brilliant slopes, of which Oelberg is one of the best.

CONSUMER INFORMATION

WHAT DO I GET FOR MY MONEY?

What you pay for, that's what you get. Cheap **Liebfraumilch** and **Bereich Nierstein** blends, if they're fresh, are fairly decent cheap wines. However, basic **Kabinetts** don't cost much more and can be good value. The top wines are fairly expensive, particularly from Bingen and Nierstein, but are normally of very high quality.

AVAILABILITY

For the basics – total. Liebfraumilch is one of the most easily available wines in the world – outside Germany, that is. The Germans are more likely to demand some kind of pro-venance for their wines. High-quality Rheinhessen wines are not easy to find, since few importers will pay the deserved high price for wines tarnished with the Lieb-fraumilch brush.

CONSUMER CHECKLIST

Bereich Nierstein QbA	Q:	**1** **2** 3 4 5 6 7 8 9 10
	P:	**1** **2** 3 4 5 6 7 8 9 10
	V:	**1** **2** 3 4 5 6 7 8 9 10
Niersteiner Orbel Riesling Spätlese 1988 (estate-bottled)	Q:	1 2 3 4 5 6 **7** **8** 9 10
	P:	1 2 3 4 5 **6** 7 8 9 10
	V:	1 2 3 4 5 6 7 **8** 9 10

Good Years Most vintages are reasonable to good in the Rheinhessen. The best single vineyard wines of Nierstein, Oppenheim and Bingen age almost as well as Rheingau wines.

Taste Notes These basic and light fruity wines are to be drunk young. 'Prädikat' wines have a fresh lusciousness and honeyed sweetness. Bingen wines resemble the steelier Rheingau wines.

THE RHINE VALLEY/Rheinpfalz

THE GENERAL PICTURE

The Rheinpfalz falls just behind Rhein-hessen in vineyard acreage, her 22,618 hectares (56,550 acres) comprising 23.1 per cent of the total German vineyards, as against Rheinhessen's 25.4 per cent. However, due to a less fragmented, more highly mechanized and co-operative dominated wine trade, her actual volume of wine produced is often the highest of any German region. The Rhine valley is at its widest here, and you have to strain your eyes to see the river at all from the gentle sloping vineyards which amble quietly up the east-facing edge of the Haardt mountains, from the southern tip of the Rheinhessen just above Mannheim, to the French border at Schweigen. The whole feel of the place is immensely easy-going, the ancient villages rather chubby and contented, and the vineyards joining imperceptibly with the wide, flat agricultural plain. Much of the wine follows the same pattern, broad, soft, rather smugly fruity, memorable for the ripeness of the fruit but not the bite, nor for the racy flash of acidity. Certainly this is true of the southern section – the Südliche Wein-strasse which links up with the Rheinhessen is simply a large-scale producer of lightish, fruity wines often used in Liebfraumilch. In the centre of the Rheinpfalz, however, round the wines often used in Liebfraumilch. In the centre of the Rheinpfalz, however, round the villages of Bad Dürkheim, Wachenheim, Forst and Deidesheim, are some wonderful vineyards, and some tremendously quality-conscious producers of great wine, often from the Riesling grape.

The gentle slope of the vineyards above Forst – particularly those of Ungeheuer and Jesuitengarten – give extra ripeness and spice to the wines.

GRAPE VARIETIES AND WINE STYLES

With the exception of the central group of villages round Bad Dürkheim, this is not **Riesling** country, chiefly because it is relatively flat, and the majority of the area has no tradition of excellence, merely one of competent production of large amounts of pleasant plonk. Even so, this is Germany's sunniest wine region (though Baden's average temperature is higher), and so the Riesling, which covers 14.1 per cent of this gently rolling, fertile land, can do some astonishing things. The great central estates regularly achieve 'Prädikat' ripeness levels for the majority of their wines, and the Riesling maintains its characteristic acidity, yet throws in flavours so exotic and spicy that words like lychee, mango, passion fruit and peach are all bandied about to try to describe the luscious ripeness of the wines. The next most exciting grape is the **Scheurebe,** with rather less than 5 per cent, but capable of producing remarkable pepper-and-sweet-grapefruit flavours, and the **Kerner,** a new Riesling look-alike, with 10.4 per cent at the last count, which gives out a whole range of exotic, oriental flavours. As expected, the **Müller-Thurgau** at 23.9 per cent is the commonest grape, and even it adds a little oriental mystery to its habitual simple fruity taste.

THE IMPORTANT DETAILS

CLASSIFICATION

The two 'Bereich' areas are enormous, and the northern one is less reliable for good basic wine than the southerly 'Südliche' one, since all the best wine there uses a vineyard name. All the different classifications of wine – Qualitätswein, Kabinett, Spätlese, Auslese, Beerenauslese, Trockenbeerenauslese, etc. – are likely to taste bigger, and sweeter, than their equivalents from further north. For this reason, the dry 'Trocken' wines can be reasonably good, having enough ripe body to keep their fruit even when fully dry.

ORGANIZATION/S

This is an area where the co-operatives are not only enormously important, but their general effect on quality is very good. Indeed, the Südliche Weinstrasse has been transformed from a quality backwater into a dynamic, hard-selling, export-orientated region entirely due to co-op efforts. The Deutsches Weintor co-op is one of the biggest in Europe. In the central Mittelhaardt, the co-ops of Forst, Bad Dürkheim and Niederkirchen, amongst others, maintain a high quality. Much of the Rheinpfalz crop is processed into merchants' blends, including Liebfraumilch, and these are generally fairly good, if a bit hefty. However, the central villages, with their top estates such as Bürklin-Wolf, von Buhl, Bassermann-Jordan, Deinhard, Schaefer, and Stumpf-Fitz, have a good concentration of growers bottling their own, and producing great wine in the process.

READING THE LABEL

Watch out for the grape variety on the label, since this is the best indication of the flavour of the wine, especially if one is unfamiliar with the village or Bereich name. In Südliche Weinstrasse village names are infrequently used, a label usually simply stating the Bereich, the grape variety and the quality level. There are many 'Trockens' and 'Halb-trockens'. They can be good, so don't shun them. For quality, look in particular for Riesling and Scheurebe, and the word Winzerverein or Winzergenossenschaft (co-operative) often indicates good quality in the Rheinpfalz.

THE RHINE VALLEY/Rheinpfalz

THE IMPORTANT DETAILS

WHAT DO THEY TASTE LIKE?

Even at the most basic level, the tastes are big, strong and ripe. It's not a joke to say the wines remind you of oriental fruits, because many winetasters use such memory traces as a means of identifying Rheinpfalz wines. However, there is usually a decent balance going with the near-blowsy fruit. In good Rieslings, the sheer concentration of flavour can be startling, while Kabinetts from growers like Bürklin-Wolf and von Buhl can match their ripe fruit with a delicacy the Rheingau would be proud of.

The vineyards of Deidesheim mark the end of the best Pfalz vineyards. As the land becomes flatter the wines become less exciting.

THE GOOD YEARS

There is hardly such a thing as a bad year in the Rheinpfalz as far as quality goes, because even in the coolest, wettest years, a reasonable amount of wine reaches 'Prädikat' level. In any case, many of the growers and co-operatives, supplying bulk blends to the market, are not attempting to make Prädikat wines. On the good estates, years like 1989, 1988, 1985, 1983 and 1976 have produced large amounts of Spätlese and Auslese wines, and some Beerenauslese and Trockenbeerenauslese. Lesser years like 1986 and 1981 produced lovely wines, particularly Kabinetts and Spätleses. Rheinpfalz wines keep well but can be drunk immediately.

ENJOYING THE WINES

Well chilled down, the Kabinetts and Spätleses, with their full spicy flavour, are delicious by themselves, but it is also their body and extra fruit which make them excellent picnic or 'summer lunch' wines, when the mixture of pâtés, meats, salads and cheeses could scare away a light Mosel, but would blend happily with a Rheinpfalz wine. The 'Trocken' wines can go very well with fish and fowl, and, from a good vineyard and a ripe year, they even go fairly well with game and strong cheese. The luscious sweet wines, big enough to go with the local cream and fruit concoctions, are best by themselves.

CONSUMER INFORMATION

WHAT DO I GET FOR MY MONEY?

Pretty good value, on the whole. The Südliche Weinstrasse wines resemble those of Baden further south, but in general offer better value. The Prädikat wines from unpopular vintages like 1987 and 1986 and the high-quality co-op wines are particularly good value. Top estate wines are of a very high quality, and the prices asked high, but fair.

AVAILABILITY

Germany drinks a large amount of the Rheinpfalz wines, but the general availability is fair. All merchants will have some of the basics, and many should also have some Prädikat wine because the price-quality ratio is good. Top estate wines are difficult to find, but worth the search.

CONSUMER CHECKLIST

Wachenheimer	Q:	1 2 3 **4** 5 6 7 8 9 10
Gerümpel	P:	1 2 3 **4** 5 6 7 8 9 10
Riesling QbA 1987	V:	1 2 3 4 **5** 6 7 8 9 10
Forster	Q:	1 2 3 4 5 6 7 **8** 9 10
Jesuitengarten	P:	1 2 3 4 5 **6** 7 8 9 10
Riesling	V:	1 2 3 4 5 6 7 8 **9** 10
Auslese 1983		

Good Years The best villages produce 'Prädikat' wines almost every year, and these will be drinkable early but age well. The great estates produce wine of tremendous power in years like 1989, 1988, 1983, which last well. *Taste Notes* Rheinpfalz wines have an exotic, pungent character, very ripe and musky.

THE RHINE VALLEY/Nahe

THE GENERAL PICTURE

The best wine of the Nahe does have an uncanny ability to unsettle the winetaster by being similar to a Mosel in lightness and freshness, yet even more similar to a Rheingau in the intensity of fruit and power of bouquet. One might also detect some Rheinhessen floweriness there. The Nahe region has 4.8 per cent of Germany's vineyards, with its 4,450 hectares (11,125 acres) making it appreciably bigger than the Rheingau. Yet the majority of this is in the flatter lower part of the river where the well-known Rüdesheimer Rosengarten produces a large amount of pleasant fruity wine hardly distinguishable from Rheinhessen. But the real fame of the region lies in a far smaller thin line of vineyards stretching upriver from the Spa-town of Bad Kreuznach. The vineyards of Kreuznach, Traisen, Niederhausen and Schloss Böckelheim produce small amounts of outstanding Riesling wine.

GRAPE VARIETIES AND WINE STYLES
In terms of reputation, the Riesling is by far the most important grape, since the great upriver sites are almost exclusively planted with Riesling. But only 23 per cent of the total acreage is Riesling. As usual, the Müller-Thurgau has the highest share with 26 per cent, concentrated in the flatter downriver sites. Silvaner is also important with 12 per cent – nearly twice the national average – and can make very good, and underrated, wines in good sites. The Nahe, like the Rheinhessen, also has a large number of experimental grape varieties. The entire range of wines from basic **Qualitätswein** to great **Trockenbeerenauslese** and **Eiswein,** is made here. The most typical and exciting are the **Spätleses** and **Ausleses** (see p. 177), where an astonishing grapiness blends with a wonderful, minerally chill vein of flavour to produce full, but superbly balanced, wines.

THE IMPORTANT DETAILS

CLASSIFICATION
The Nahe occupies a middle position between the Rhine and Mosel as regards the required minimum ripeness for the different categories. Up to Kabinett level, the Nahe and the Mosel are the same. For Spätlese and Auslese the Nahe creeps ahead, though only by 2 Oechsle degrees. By Beerenauslese the requirement is 10° Oechsle more than for the Mosel. Wines simply labelled Bereich Schlossböckelheim or Rüdesheimer Rosengarten should at best be light, fruity wines, but in no way resembling the good single vineyard wines.

ORGANIZATION/S
A great deal of Nahe wine is sold 'at the farm gate' – as much as 40 per cent. Another sizable amount is sold by the door-to-door salesmen based in the Nahe. Otherwise, the wines from the co-ops are normally fairly good, while the commercial blends usually stick to the basics, although at a higher standard than in the Rheinhessen. Although growers are fragmented, some of the nation's finest are in the Nahe valley, and the Niederhausen Staatlichen Weinbaudomäne is likely to produce wines breathtaking in their flavour and class.

All the best Nahe vineyards are steep and rocky. Round Bad Münster and Ebernburg, castles and woodland squeeze the tiny vineyards right down to the riverbank.

THE RHINE VALLEY/Nahe

THE IMPORTANT DETAILS

READING THE LABEL
The best wines on the Nahe, Rieslings, from upriver, frequently number among the best German wines in a vintage. Producers' names to get excited about are Staatliche Weinbaudomänen, August Anheuser and Crusius. Their wines will be from the top villages named above, with, perhaps, Winzenheim, Münster and Norheim. Other village names will probably yield pleasant, but unexceptional wines.

WHAT DO THEY TASTE LIKE?
Caught between the acid freshness of the Mosel and the cool, grapy brilliance of the Rheingau, Nahe wines have a freshness which is almost sweet, and yet this steely, mineral edge keeps them startlingly fresh. Of all German wines they accentuate the grapy side of the Riesling's character.

THE GOOD YEARS
In classic years, all the Nahe can produce great wines, burning with the flavour of the soil and the grape. In lesser years, the flatter downstream vineyards will still produce pleasant wine, but only the best upstream properties, and in particular the Staatlichen Weinbaudomänen, will bring out the best from underripe grapes. Best years are 1989, 1988, 1985, 1983, 1976, 1975, 1971.

ENJOYING THE WINES
I have always eaten particularly massive meals in the Nahe, with which the wines went well enough, but the best combinations were between quite full Kabinett Rieslings and early season white asparagus. Because of their slight grapy sweetness, allied to just a hint of metallic bite, they make marvellous wines to drink by themselves.

CONSUMER INFORMATION

WHAT DO I GET FOR MY MONEY?
In general, excellent value for money. Not only are the top wines fairly priced because their names are less well known than the nearby Rheingau wines, but also the basic cheap and cheerful Nahe wines are almost always of a pleasant, fruity and nicely acid-balanced style. Again, up the Nahe side valley, they're not so famous – or notorious – and are good value.

AVAILABILITY
Not brilliant. Remember that at least 40 per cent of the wine is bought direct, and that there are relatively few top estates – even Rüdesheimer Rosengarten, the Nahe's equivalent of Niersteiner Gutes Domtal, is not widely seen. You may find that merchants with a normally good German selection will nevertheless be short on Nahe wines, but lobby for them, they're worth it.

CONSUMER CHECKLIST

Rudesheimer	Q:	1 **2 3** 4 5 6 7 8 9 10
Rosengarten	P:	1 **2 3** 4 5 6 7 8 9 10
QbA	V:	1 2 **3** 4 5 6 7 8 9 10
Winzenheimer	Q:	1 2 3 4 5 6 **7** 8 9 10
Berg Silvaner	P:	1 2 3 4 **5** 6 7 8 9 10
Spätlese 1988	V:	1 2 3 4 5 6 **7** 8 9 10

Good Years The Nahe can produce pleasant wines in most vintages, but her top wines need a year like 1989 or 1988. In general, the wines from a top grower age very well, but the wines are drinkable almost immediately.

Taste Notes There is a lovely fruity freshness about Nahe wines, with more acid balance than the Rheinhesse, more fruit than the Mosel, and less weight than the Rheingau.

FRANCONIA/FRANKEN

THE GENERAL PICTURE

Franconia is the area which everyone points to when the cry goes up that Germany 'cannot make dry wines, and no wonder the Germans prefer to drink beer with their meals'. Well, paradoxically, Franconia nestles in the top north-west corner of Bavaria, Germany's greatest, most utterly beer-devoted, state. This, in part, explains both Franconia's isolation from the mainstream of German wine styles and also her historical determination to produce a wine to go with food, while the rest of Germany was more likely to produce wine to knock back gaily before a meal, or to linger over cooingly after the feast. Franconia only has 7 per cent of Germany's vineyards, but that is greater than the more famous areas of the Rheingau and Nahe. And her relative lack of international fame is not due to a lack of quality. It's just that, until the recent advent of 'Trocken' or 'Dry' wines in the Rhine and Mosel regions, Franconia, way out on a limb on the river Main, was the only part of Germany to produce naturally dry, 'foody' wines.

GRAPE VARIETIES AND WINE STYLES

The style *is* dry. The grape *could* be anything. Only ten years ago one might blithely generalize and say that the **Silvaner** grape was Franconia's finest, and produced great wines only here. Well, it is still the finest grape, in its strong, earthy way, yet it is no longer the dominant grape. That role has been taken over, as in so many parts of Germany, by the **Müller-Thurgau**. Luckily, it does make good wine in Franconia, and seems to adapt to the rather dry, rooty Franconian style while giving just a little of its grapy freshness to 'brighten things up'. **Riesling** is grown and is exciting — dry, yet full bodied from a good vineyard. There are also a fair number of the modern 'white coat' laboratory varieties. Some make pretty weird wine, and one wonders why on earth the grower planted them. There are some sweet, aromatic wines, including Trockenbeerenauslese, but Franconia is best at producing full, dry, yet soft white wines, most of which put the average 'Trocken' to shame.

Franconia is situated to the east of the Rhine, on the River Main. The scattered river bank sites, like this one at Klingenberg, are most famous for their dry Silvaner and Müller-Thurgau wines.

FRANCONIA/FRANKEN

THE IMPORTANT DETAILS

CLASSIFICATION
Franconia follows the same rules as the rest of Germany, yet the wines up to Auslese level are always likely to be drier. Their fullness shows how rich they could be if their natural ripe sugar was left in the wine. The words 'Trocken' and 'Halb-trocken' are not much used, as these wines are known to be traditionally dry.

ORGANIZATION/S
A good 50 per cent of the crop is dealt with by the co-operatives whose produce is usually of a pretty good standard. Since there is no memorably brilliant name, the merchants have been unable to create a 'Franconian brand'. The individual estates are the real quality producers, and many are experimenting with new grape varieties and wine styles; successfully, certainly, but suddenly I find myself yearning for simple, old style, high-quality Silvaner – and at a reasonable price.

READING THE LABEL
The best wine is easiest to recognize by the squat green flask in which it comes. The best

villages are usually **Escherndorf**, **Randersacker**, **Iphofen** and the capital **Würzburg**. Particularly good producers are Juliusspital, the Bürgerspital and the Staatlicher Hofkeller. Look for 'Silvaner' or 'Riesling' on the label.

WHAT DO THEY TASTE LIKE?
Franconian wines often taste honeyed and slightly earthy – but that is no bad thing, since most of Germany's wines are markedly aromatic. The earthiness adds a savoury edge to wines which are by nature fuller and drier than a typical hock from the Rhine.

THE GOOD YEARS
Good years *do* matter in Franconia, because the whole region suffers badly from very harsh winters and late frosts. This cuts down the ripening period, and certainly the Riesling only ripens in hot years. The increasing use of modern grape varieties is an attempt to get a ripe crop every year.

ENJOYING THE WINE
Franconian wine is Germany's most successful dry wine style and goes very well with the fairly gutsy local cuisine. When served very young from the barrel, its dryness and almost fizzy freshness make it as effective with the local ham and sausages as any draught of Bavarian beer. Even when bottled, it can certainly be as good as a moderate white burgundy with most food. The occasional sweet wines are as big, yet not quite so luscious, as the ultra-sweet Rhine wines.

CONSUMER INFORMATION

WHAT DO I GET FOR MY MONEY?
You don't necessarily get value for money, because Franconian wines are some of the most expensive in Germany. Until the recent 'Trocken' explosion, they were Germany's only 'French-style' dry whites, and commanded high prices, particularly in the north. However, quality is high, and the flavours are interesting, so don't pass them by.

AVAILABILITY
Not very good. In Bavaria and northern Germany they are easily obtainable, but elsewhere only a specialist merchant is likely to stock one.

Here, at Aschaffenburg, close to Frankfurt, vines and history create a scene unchanged for centuries.

BADEN-WURTTEMBERG

Here we are in the world of the German trencherman – who is a formidable pro-position. Until recently, these two areas have been largely overlooked on the international market mainly because the Baden growers tended to be fairly fragmented and were such keen drinkers of their own stuff that they consumed double the national wine-drinker's average. Since Baden produces about 13 per cent of all German wine, they probably need to have pretty big thirsts to keep pace with each new vintage. Württemberg doesn't produce so much wine, but her citizens are nearly as keen on drinking: in the central town of Stuttgart the wine consumption is 80 per cent greater than the national average. They even have vineyards well inside the city boundaries, presumably patronized by the less patient of the local drinkers. And both these areas are renowned for hearty eating, which is reflected in a high planting of red wine grapes.

Baden is the only German wine area classified by the EEC as Zone B – i.e., vaguely warm like Alsace or the Loire in France. (The rest of Germany is in Zone A, the coolest zone, along with England and points north.) So the wines have a natural fat ripeness. This has meant that in the current fashion for 'Trocken', or 'Totally Dry', wines, the Baden whites can easily achieve the flavour of ripe fruit and the relatively low acidity necessary to make good dry wine. No other German wine area does it so well. The warm climate also means that tremendous big, spicy wines can be produced and the Ruländer (or Pinot

These vineyards, facing the Vosges mountains, are on the Kaiserstuhl, a volcanic outcrop into the Rhine valley; they give Baden's best wines.

Gris) and Gewürztraminer grapes can produce wonderful wines here. Even the reds can be fairly big and tasty. Württemberg is famous for reds, in particular Trollinger, and, though light, they do give off quite recognizable flavours of each different grape variety. Even so, the best Württemberg wines are her Rieslings, big and spicy, but beautifully balanced.

Baden wines are becoming increasingly available due to the heroic efforts of the massive central co-op at Breisach which is the largest co-op in Europe and has a remarkable quality record, considering its size. There are also some very traditional and good-quality private estates, and the whole area looks poised to go from strength to strength, with the 'Baden Dry' style leading the way. Württemberg is a much less centralized operation, though even here over 80 per cent of the wine is co-op produced. But we are once more in the land of numerous tiny, part-time producers. However, there is no great need for export markets while the local consumption keeps up. The few bottles, mostly red, which do find their way on to the export market are generally overpriced, and never as good as an equivalent bottle of red from further south in Europe. Even so, drunk young and fresh enough, they are a *must* if you visit Stuttgart.

AHR, MITTELRHEIN AND HESSISCHE BERGSTRASSE

THE GENERAL PICTURE

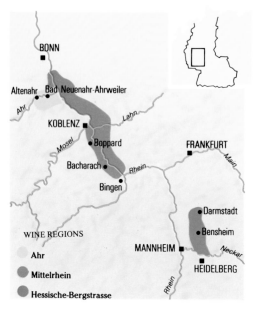

WINE REGIONS

Ahr

Mittelrhein

Hessische-Bergstrasse

These are the least known of the German wine areas – only partially explained by the fact that they are the three smallest regions. The Hessische Bergstrasse is the tiniest, with only 0.35 per cent of Germany's vineyard area. Next comes the Ahr with 0.45 per cent, and even the Mittelrhein can only manage 0.8 per cent. However, there are other reasons for the relative unavailability of their wines outside Germany. The Ahr valley, despite being the most northerly of Germany's wine areas, actually makes red wine of a very pale and gentle sort which may be appreciated in Germany, but would find few takers in markets with a good supply of riper, stronger reds. The Mittelrhein is a white wine area, and uses the great Riesling for the majority of its wines. However, this long stretch of the Rhine valley is one of the most stunning, dramatic and romantic parts of Germany. Great scenery and a good dose of history draw the tourists like bees to honey and leave a chap with a formidable thirst, and the wine is almost all drunk on the spot. The Hessische Bergstrasse is indeed very small, and its wine not quite special enough to have established any reputation other than with the local inhabitants and visitors.

GRAPE VARIETIES AND WINE STYLES

The Ahr valley is only renowned for red wines. Two-thirds of the plantation is in the Spätburgunder (Pinot Noir) grape, and the rather less exciting Portugieser. The wines are very light, but the Spätburgunder can be fairly good in a slightly sweet way. The Mittelrhein is, with the Rheingau, Germany's main supporter of the Riesling grape, totalling 76 per cent of plantings. Since the vineyards are uniformly steep and daunting, it only makes sense to plant good grape varieties. The wines are often splendidly racy, full of acid *and* fruit, but they almost always have a slightly earthy finish to the flavour.

The Hessische Bergstrasse is also a major Riesling area, and the wines have a lovely fruity quality, catching something of the floweriness of the Rheinhesse as well as the tangy acid freshness of the Rheingau.

THE IMPORTANT DETAILS

Far left *The Ahr valley is Germany's most northerly wine area, yet specializes in light red wines.* **Left** *The fruit trees blossom ahead of the vines as spring arrives in Germany's smallest wine area, the Hessische Bergstrasse.* **Above** *Bacharach is typical of the beautiful river-side tourist towns which make up the Mittelrhein. The steep vineyards are almost entirely Riesling, producing lean, steely wines for summertime.*

CLASSIFICATION

Despite the Ahr producing primarily red wine, the label classifications are no different from white wines. In both the Ahr and the Mittelrhein, one finds a fair amount of QbA, or Qualitätswein. This means the grape musts were helped by sugar addition – a process which is often surprisingly successful in these northern regions.

ORGANIZATION/S

As is often the case in small vineyard areas, and in particular ones where the average size of an individual holding is tiny, the co-operatives are of considerable importance. This is further put into relief when one sees that many of the vineyard owners are in effect only growing grapes as a hobby, or weekend occupation, since most vineyard owners also have another job. In the Hessische Bergstrasse over 90 per cent of the wine is made by the co-operative movement, although there is also an excellent state domaine there. In the Ahr, the situation is similar, though not quite so extreme, with over half the wine coming from the co-ops. The Mittelrhein is more likely to yield single estate growers' wines.

AHR, MITTELRHEIN AND HESSISCHE BERGSTRASSE

THE IMPORTANT DETAILS

READING THE LABEL

Look out for the words 'Trocken' or 'Halbtrocken' on the Ahr red wines, since these will denote very dry, or fairly dry styles. Also buy 'Spätburgunder' in preference to Portugieser. In Mittelrhein check for 'Riesling' on the label. In Hessische Bergstrasse good wines are made from Müller-Thurgau and other modern grapes as well as Riesling. Kabinett styles are particularly good.

WHAT DO THEY TASTE LIKE?

None of these areas produces absolutely top-quality wine. Though the Ahr is famous for reds, the actual flavour is pretty light. The Mittelrhein wines rarely quite match up to the scenery, but are even so rather good, slightly sharp wines, with both an earthy background and a good slaty acid edge. Hessische Bergstrasse wines can reach the luscious dessert wine heights, but are best light, very fruity, and drunk young.

THE GOOD YEARS

Most of these wines should be drunk without too much fuss pretty young. However, when the sun does really get to work, the Ahr reds can even achieve a decent amount of colour, and the Mittelrhein Rieslings can become quite honeyed. 1989 and 1983 are such years. The Hessische Bergstrasse has a fairly equable climate, and produces decent wines almost every year.

ENJOYING THE WINES

The gentle fruit of the Hessische Bergstrasse wines makes them ideal café wines, to be drunk out of doors as the evening sun turns amber in the summer sky. However, this is probably how most Mittelrhein wines are drunk, at a thousand café tables above and below the Lorelei rock. They do have the bite, however, to go well with fish. Ahr reds should be drunk with food, but any spiciness may overwhelm their rather slight flavours.

CONSUMER INFORMATION

WHAT DO I GET FOR MY MONEY?

If anything, these wines are slightly expensive, scarcity fuelling demand. Some of the finer Mittelrhein Rieslings are worth seeking out, but in general enjoy them on the spot and drink other wines when you get back home.

AVAILABILITY

Poor. They are almost unavailable outside Germany, and not widely distributed inside Germany.

In the Ahr Valley, at Schloss Marienthal, the steep narrow valley forms a bowl which ripens the grapes just enough to give a light pinkish wine of low strength.

SWEET WINES

THE GENERAL PICTURE

If a wine is to be sweet – really mouth-warming, heart-gladdening sweet – surely the grapes must be super-ripe and packed with hot-summer sugar, which should mean that we'd start looking down the Rhône valley, and chase our suntans southwards, finding wines ever richer and more succulent. But it doesn't quite work out like that. If we're looking for some of the greatest sweet wines in the world, we should head north from the chilly Channel ports, put the sun at our backs, and head away from the heat, to Europe's most northerly major vineyard areas – in the Rhine and Mosel valleys.

When we think that Germany's weather isn't much of an improvement on anywhere else in northern Europe, where it's difficult enough to ripen the apple crop, let alone fill grapes with a positively sub-tropical strength of sugar sweetness, there must be more to it than meets the eye – and, of course, there is.

It's best summed up in the following folk tale. During the eighteenth century, the Church was a most powerful vineyard owner on the Rhine, and no grape picking could start until the Bishop or Abbot in question gave the nod. In 1775 the Bishop of Fulda obviously had other things on his mind, since the vintagers at Schloss Johannisberg waited in vain for the messenger to gallop over the horizon waving the episcopal authority to start picking. And as they waited they watched the grapes turn from ripe to over-ripe to rotten in the late summer sun. The messenger did finally turn up, full of apologies, and they set to, without much hope, on the soggy, rotten-looking bunches. Expecting a meagre, mildew-tasting crop, they were 'astonished' when the resultant Johannisberger 1775 outshone every other wine on the river, because, as they hung about for their marching orders, a very particular fungus had been at work in the vineyards shrivelling away those grapes – the 'noble rot'.

Although closely related to the horrid 'grey rot' which does make wines taste mildewy, and can turn a vineyard into a squidgy disaster area in a wet autumn, the 'noble rot', encouraged by warm sun alternating with humidity (morning fogs coming off the river are good for this), eats into the skins of the grapes, causing the water in the grapes to be sucked out, and the increasingly concentrated sugar levels to climb higher and higher. If the

It's the horrible ugly grapes rather than the bright, ripe green ones which will make great wine from this bunch, since they have had their sweetness and flavour concentrated by 'noble rot'.

autumn rains hold off, the grapes go brown and ugly and raisin-like, and may lose 80–90 per cent of their liquid volume. But what remains is so intensely sweet, yet still possessed of a high, northern European acidity, brought on by a long, cool ripening period, that it makes one of the world's great wine styles.

The word 'acidity' is the key to the pleasures these wines give. As a fruit ripens – be it a pear, a mango, or a grape – the sugar level increases, and the acidity reduces. Think what it's like to bite into an apple a couple of weeks before it's ripe – the acidity is green and high, the sugar is undeveloped and low. Not nice. But then go back to your apple tree or pear tree too late, when an Indian summer has been heating up the fruit and it is looking pudgy and tired. You pick off the soft fruit, bite into the unresistant soft flesh, and you find you've missed it – the flesh is all sweet and fluffy and unfresh, and that green acidity which was so tart a few weeks before is now exactly what you're missing. Sweetness *and* acidity – now we're talking! The one by itself is either sour or flabby and dull. Germany's greatest wine-making skill is to preserve the acidity while building up the sugar.

SWEET WINES

THE GENERAL PICTURE

Very hot climates over-ripen fruit and kill acidity. Cool countries struggle to ripen their fruit at all, and the long struggle is rewarded by a streak of limy, green-apple acidity which makes your lips smack and your mouth water. That's the acidity which is still present when the 'noble rot' fungus is busy building up the sugar levels. As the water is removed, the acid stays in the grape, building up along with the sweetness. There is a saying that the best fruit is grown at the coolest limit in which it can still just ripen. So it is with the great German sweet wines – the lightness and acidity remain, however ripe the grapes get.

Germany's Rhine valley is particularly susceptible to 'noble rot', and most other parts of Germany get a certain amount. Of course, it doesn't strike every grape on the bunch in the same way, any more than a truss of tomatoes in the greenhouse ripens at a uniform speed. So a grower has several choices, and the way in which he picks his grapes forms the basis of the classification of all German sweet wines (see below).

GRAPE VARIETIES AND WINE STYLES

Though there are a few super-sweet red wines, black grapes don't really react that well to 'noble rot', and the wines are overwhelmingly white. Or, they are gold, since any true sweet wine has a fairly rich golden colour.

The greatest wines are without question from the Riesling grape, from vineyards on the Mosel or Rhine rivers. The Scheurebe grape is also important for sweet wines and, to some extent, the Silvaner in the Franconia area, and the Ruländer in Baden. The Germans lead the world in 'inventing' new grape varieties. Most of these are rather perfumed and flowery, and a main objective is to get them to ripen very early, thus duplicating hot-country conditions, with all the consequent loss of crucial acid balance. New grapes like Huxelrebe can ripen so fast that they are picked to make Beerenauslese before the Riesling is ripe enough to make the dry, light, rather tart Kabinett level. The long, dangerous ripening period of the Riesling always produces a far more exciting wine than the fat, musky sweetness of a Huxelrebe or a Bacchus or a Morio Muskat – recent inventions all.

If your grapes aren't affected by 'noble rot', you can still concentrate the juice by picking them frozen.

THE IMPORTANT DETAILS

CLASSIFICATION

This is everything in German sweet wines. Indeed, the whole German wine law is based on classifying wines according to what level of sugar the grapes can naturally build up, to convert by fermentation into alcohol. The greatest German wines will have built up a formidable level of sugar ripeness in the vineyard, but will leave a large amount of that sugar unconverted, making the wines very low in alcohol, but very high in sweetness. A detailed description of German wine classifications is given on page 150. But it's worth taking a look at some of the key classifications again to be clear what kind of ripeness gives what category of wine, in ascending order of sweetness.

Kabinett From normally ripe grapes. The driest, lightest, German quality wine.

Spätlese From late-picked grapes. Rarely very intense, but often having an attractive sweetish taste.

Auslese From selected bunches of grapes, to some extent affected by over-ripeness. By definition these bunches will be late-picked, but the title also means that some effort will have been made to pick only the very ripest bunches. Sometimes, in years like the very hot 1976, these wines are affected by noble rot, and can develop rich, oily, honeyed

tastes. In recent years, however, the Ausleses have rarely been more than medium-sweet.

Beerenauslese Made from selected *single* grapes. This is when the going gets really sweet, and the pickers go painstakingly through the vineyards, very late in the year, plucking off single over-ripe grapes. These are always luscious, rich wines.

Trockenbeerenauslese Made from selected, shrivelled single grapes. Weirder and weirder – and just as convoluted as it sounds. The poor old pickers have to go out in the early winter weather and look for the nastiest, squidgiest grapes left on the vine and endeavour to pick them off, one by one, without the slimy little rotters just coming to bits between the fingers. That's the 'noble rot' at work again, wrecking the grapes' complexion, but concentrating the sugar and acid to an astonishing degree.

Any German Trockenbeerenauslese is going to be an astonishing experience; memorable, and fiendishly expensive. Well, think about it. To make a single bottle of Trockenbeerenauslese may take six to eight vines. If you just wanted to make a cheap, commercial hock, you could have made 15 to 20 bottles from those vines, and have had the grapes picked, the wine made and probably sold by the time your pickers are making their last painful trip

Harvesting 'noble rot' grapes. Often the most affected and therefore the sweetest grapes have to be individually picked from the bunch.

SWEET WINES

THE IMPORTANT DETAILS

through the vineyard to snip off the last few shrivelled grapes – which will then take at least a couple of years to be ready for sale.

Eiswein This is the final sublime absurdity. The long-suffering pickers for this are sent out to harvest only when the grapes have frozen with pre-dawn frost. It could be November, it could be December, it has been January. Either way they have to get the grapes picked and crushed before the temperature rises above zero, because water freezes at zero, but sugar doesn't. The sugar is a sticky, ice-cold, but still just liquid, gunge. Separate it from the frozen crystals of water by crushing the grapes at below zero and you've got some of the most concentrated grape juice nature can possibly offer. Not surprising that it can be more expensive and even more sought after than Trockenbeerenauslese.

ORGANIZATION/S
All the best examples come from single growers. It takes dedication and considerable financial risk to make these wines. One late autumn storm could wash the grapes – and your annual income – into the river. A good one may surface under a merchant's or shipper's label, but the best alternative to a grower's wine is likely to be from one of the top co-operatives, such as the Zentralkellerei on the Mosel, Hallgarten in the Rheingau, or Niederkirch in the Palatinate.

READING THE LABEL
German wine labels are supremely logical, yet daunting for anyone who can't read Gothic script and pass pretty fair muster in the language. Above are several wine labels for a range of wines.

WHAT DO THEY TASTE LIKE?
The tastes of the best of these are some of the most memorable in the whole world of wine. They represent the peak of a German wine-grower's achievement.

These rarities have a higher acidity than any other sweet wine, often like the stab of fresh lime in a fruit salad, and this, combined with a deep, honeyed richness and a very low alcohol content, makes it impossible to resist a second glass, and difficult to avoid finishing the bottle. The finest of all are made from the Riesling grape, and the only slight warning is not to expect this brilliant complexity of flavours from wines of unfamiliar grape varieties from southern Germany. The grape names are marked on the label, and names like Huxelrebe, Ortega, Bacchus and Ribalonga will be the product of fiendishly clever scientists' crossings and clonings. Sweet they will certainly be, but also a little dull.

THE GOOD YEARS
German sweet wines last a very long time. Wines from 1959, 1945 and 1921 will still be in fairly fine fettle, slowly getting less sweet, but developing an almost overpowering depth of flavour. The best, indeed the only reasonably available, recent years are: 1985 – famous for its Eiswein; 1976 – big, fat and ripe, though surprisingly already at their peak since they lack a little of that crucial fruity acidity; and 1971, better balanced, fragrant, full of fresh, fruity flavours as well as sweetness; 1989 – shows signs of being the most classic sweet wine year since 1959.

ENJOYING THE WINES
Cherish them! Don't waste them! These wines are expensive and rare, and their flavours are so satisfying that they don't need any food at all. At best, perhaps a soft, juicy fruit like a peach or a pear, but, rather than try to match food with them, I'd try to match surroundings and good friends, preferring the friends old and close, and the surroundings leafy, lazy and flecked with evening sun.

CONSUMER INFORMATION

WHAT DO I GET FOR MY MONEY?
You'll get top quality and pay top prices for **Beerenauslese, Trockenbeerenauslese** and *Eiswein*. However, to get some idea of the wine styles, you'll find that many **Ausleses** 1976 and 1983 are absurdly cheap for such quality wines, and well worth trying.

The universally available flow of basic bargain-price fruity, slightly sweet wine from Germany has made the entire range of German wines become déclassé – which is a crying shame, as the finest wines of the Rhine and Mosel represent excellent value despite their cost. The big sweet southern wines from grapes other than Riesling, Ruländer or Scheurebe don't have that exquisite taste, however, and are a less good buy. It is *always* worth seeking out single growers' wines.

AVAILABILITY
The quantities made are so limited – a grower may sometimes make as few as 100-200 bottles – that availability is not good, and is almost entirely limited to specialist merchants and top wine bars and restaurants. But of what other wine can it be said that, if you gaily knocked back a couple of bottles, you might have consumed a whole percentage point of a grower's production?

CONSUMER CHECKLIST

Alsheimer	Q:	1 2 3 4 5 6 **7** 8 9 10
Goldberg	P:	1 2 3 4 5 6 **7** 8 9 10
Müller-Thurgau	V:	1 2 3 4 5 6 **7** 8 9 10
Beerenauslese 1988		
Erbacher	Q:	1 2 3 4 5 6 7 8 9 **10**
Marcobrunn	P:	1 2 3 4 5 6 7 8 9 **10**
Riesling	V:	1 2 3 4 5 6 7 8 9 **10**
Trockenbeeren-		
auslese 1971		

Good Years On the Mosel and northern Rhine only years like 1989, 1976, 1971, and 1959 produced great sweet wines. Further south, most vintages produce Auslese wines, and top years like 1989, 1988, 1983, 1976 and 1971 produce real stunners.

Taste Notes The taste is astonishing, deep, honeyed, intense, and yet filled out with a wonderful, shocking, limey acidity which is as thrilling a flavour as the wine world possesses.

SEKT/SPARKLING WINES

We wouldn't mention these if it weren't for the fact that Germany does produce about 480 million bottles of 'Sekt', as it is called, per year. That's a lot of wine. And most of it is knocked back in Germany itself. The original fizz industry in Germany was based on the indisputable fact that the grapes don't always ripen so far north – in the Saar and Ruwer valleys they hardly *ever* ripen – and so there is a lot of rather sharp, acid wine hanging round that is unloved and unsaleable. But worldwide the best sparkling wines are made from a strangely acid base, so the actual grape juice, from the notoriously late, if at all, ripening Riesling in the Saar, Ruwer or even Mosel valley does provide a splendid base for making high-quality sparkling wine. Some is still made by the champagne method, but, since the Riesling has a strong, green character when raw, industrial mass production methods, though usually inferior, can produce some pretty good wines. However, to get a decent 'Deutscher Sekt', or 'German Sparkling Wine' nowadays you must look on the label for evidence of a German 'quality' number and the letters QbA or QmP (see p. 150). Even so, there is literally a handful of brands which genuinely reflect the German origin of the grapes. Sadly, the simple words 'Deutscher Sekt' only mean that the wine's second fermentation has taken place in Germany – not that the actual grapes are German. Very few German sparkling wines are the 'real thing', and the majority which aren't are concocted with good Mosel or Rhine addresses on the label, but from grapes which wouldn't know the Rhine or Mosel if it were staring them in the face.

ITALY

Not only is it true that there is a great deal of Italian wine, it's also true that there are a great many different wines. Not only do we have all the wines which are included in the Denominazione di Origine Controllata (DOC) regulations (the equivalent of the French Appellation Contrôlée), which already account for more than 500 wines from 200 different zones, but we also have the relatively recent DOCG or DOC 'Garantita' wines. And on top of the great sea of ordinary table wines – Vini da Tavola – which are not entitled to DOC status we now have a wave of new wines carrying the Vino da Tavola designation not because they don't live up to DOC standards but because they don't qualify because their growers think they are better for *breaking* the rules. All this means that there may be as many as 3,000 more individual wines which certainly have personality (for better or worse), but no legal standing.

Italy is the world's biggest producer of wine, yet less than a quarter is exported and much of that is base blending wine sent off to beef up the efforts of winemakers further north. Of the wines with actual titles, how many do we know? Soave, Valpolicella, Bardolino, Chianti? Orvieto, Verdicchio, Frascati? Barolo and Barbaresco? We're beginning to run out of names already. And what of their tastes? Can we genuinely say what a Chianti, a Soave, a Valpolicella should taste like? Well, sadly, if we've learnt about Italian wine outside Italy, the chances are that we have no idea what these famous names *should* taste like, because most of the export market is not interested in the quality or the flavour, simply the name on the label and the price – as low as possible. The result is that, although the American and German markets are now taking some of the top estates seriously, the rest of us have become accustomed to Italian wine being by definition cheap, and not of necessity all that cheerful.

The Italians may cry foul, and complain that the whole world is too dominated by French ideas, yet they largely have themselves to blame. No attempt has been made to persuade the rest of the world to accept the very peculiar and remarkable tastes which constitute great Italian wine. Any evangelists there *have* been have set out with a truckful of rot gut, and a sackful of interchangeable famous name labels and a sliding scale of prices, rather than a sense of commitment, shining eyes and a zealous belief in quality and style. Consequently, on those few, treasured occasions when we are faced with the real thing, we are rocked back on our heels by the weird, wild flavours which mark out the finest wines. And it is these flavours, properly husbanded, which the world should be getting, instead of a parade of famous names made to the lowest legally acceptable standards and, frequently, even lower.

With that in mind the sections which follow may often be critical of Italian wines, but only because so often in this great country, the true potential is not being realized, the astonishing flavours which are possible are being cast aside for neutrality or wasted through idle malpractice. Traditional methods have much in their favour, yet are frequently abused to produce tired fruitless wines, and ultramodern methods are often over-employed to produce clean, neutral wines of no personality whatsoever. Between these two extremes there are great wines to be discovered and in the following pages we intend to sift through the dross and pluck out the gems when and where they occur.

CLASSIFICATION

The Italian wine classification, put into motion in 1963 under the general title Denominazione di Origine Controllata (DOC) has *not* been an unqualified success. It has so far managed to delimit and define around 14 per cent of the annual wine production, and although most of the famous names are included, their quality is by no means guaranteed by the system. At the same time, many wines which seem to have no particular features whether well or badly made have been squeezed into the register by fair means or foul. The DOC bases its regulations on geographical delimitations of vineyard land;

yields of fruit; and wine-making and maturation practice. Although some wines have benefited, too many quality loopholes have been left at the insistence of local pressure groups, and frequently the finest wine of the area sports the most basic title of all – Vino da Tavola, or Table Wine – often signifying that a good winemaker may have a contemptuous disregard for any consensus decisions which restrict his right to do as he pleases. Very Italian, and one of the reasons why both much fine wine is proudly displayed without legally accepted pedigree, and also why much stale, tasteless wine is flaunted under a title its quality patently does not deserve. The latest attempt to improve matters is the DOCG – where the origin is controlled and guaranteed. With supposedly more restrictive and quality conscious regulations one can only say that first sightings seem to show only sporadic signs of a quality improvement. In Italian wine, one must not follow the regulations and classifications; one must follow the particular winemaker and his skills, whatever title he uses on the label.

Here are the three main designatons:

Denominazione di Origine Controllata (DOC)

This follows lines similar to France's Appellation Contrôlée laws and comprises a legally binding stipulation as to geographical origin, permissible grape types, permitted yields, pruning methods, alcoholic strength, and aging requirements of a wine or group of wines. Although many wines have improved since the 1960s through application of DOC regulations, many others have found themselves caught in a time warp at precisely the time when innovation and technical know-how are flooding through the world's wineries at an unprecedented rate.

In the Consumer Checklists
Q = Quality   P = Price   V = Value

Denominazione di Origine Controllata e Garantita (DOCG)

This 'Guaranteed' DOC is supposed to apply to the greatest of Italy's wines, and, as well as demanding lower yields and elimination of less good grape varieties, all DOCG wines are supposed to undergo stringent panel-tastings to ensure quality.

Vino da Tavola

Table wine; the most basic category, but frequently the designation used of necessity by imaginative winemakers whose methods and preferred grape varieties do not conform with the dictates of their local DOC.

NORTH-WEST ITALY

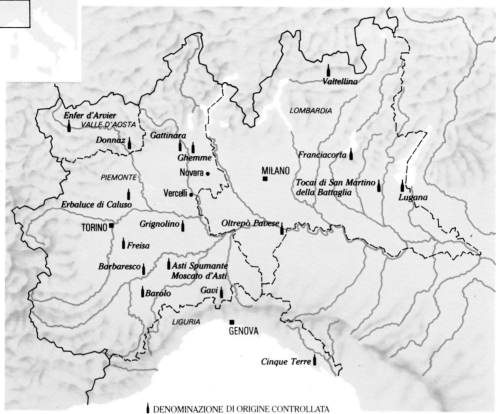

DENOMINAZIONE DI ORIGINE CONTROLLATA

The north-west of Italy is dominated by the haughty mass of Piedmont and its world-famous wines, but there are three other provinces making wines of some quality and a good deal of tradition. Most romantic of these – and least obtainable on the export market – is the mountain valley DOC of Valle d'Aosta; most generally exploited is Liguria, spread meagrely along the thirsty Italian Riviera coastline; and most unjustly overlooked in the north-western Hall of Fame is the very good, reasonably productive Lombardy.

Valtellina's vineyards stretch up into the mountain passes on the Swiss border. Though not widely known, they produce more wines from the Nebbiolo grape than any other region – including Barolo.

NORTH-WEST ITALY/Piedmont

THE GENERAL PICTURE

Piedmont has the dubious distinction of harbouring within her borders the sternest-faced 'worthies' of Italian wines as well as the giggling ne'er-do-wells. Barolo and Barbaresco, with the other big, tough, terrifying reds from the Nebbiolo grape, are these giants of propriety, while the lightly dismissed but disarmingly charming sparkling wines of Asti Spumante are the scallywags everybody can't quite admit to liking, but can't quite resist either. Indeed, the reds of Piedmont can be so massive and unyielding to taste that a slug of Asti Spumante is well and truly earned. And, if you don't go for the sweet grapy fizz of Asti as a refresher, most of the great vermouth companies are near Turin.

Although Piedmont only ranks seventh in the Italian production league, that is because the majority of her wine-making is committed to quality in a self-denying manner that is generally uncommon in Italian viticulture. Many of the hill vineyards are high and bare, the climate is harsh and the grapes, in particular the Nebbiolo, need to hang on late into the misty autumn to bring their dense black skins to full ripeness. Asti Spumante, often derided as kindergarten happy-juice, is in fact made with great care under DOC regulations from the Muscat grape – one of the most expensive varieties in Italy.

GRAPE VARIETIES AND WINE STYLES

The Nebbiolo grape dominates the consciousness of Piedmont – although the Barbera dominates the thirst – since it accounts for over half of the region's reds and is certainly the automatic choice for most of the meals one is likely to enjoy there. However, Nebbiolo, like Syrah and Cabernet Sauvignon in France, is a surly fierce variety, producing wines which are dark, chewy and exhausting for the first few years of their life, yet which can blossom out into a remarkable shower of flavours. Dark wild flavours, unyielding, but behind the almost inevitable cold tea tannin and acidity there is a richness full of chocolate, raisins, prunes, and an austere perfume of tobacco and pine and herbs. These flavours all intermingle in **Barolo** (DOCG) and **Barbaresco** (DOCG) at their best but, sadly, the fruit and sweetness are often leached out of the wines by careless fermentation and excessive aging in big old wooden barrels. However, the movement against over-aging is

Carema is positively mountainous and the rocky terrain requires the Nebbiolo vines to be trained high on orchard trellises.

growing and these two famous wines are likely to become increasingly exciting in the next few years. The Nebbiolo grape can be found in a softer, plummier form as **Nebbiolo d'Alba** (DOC) and **Nebbiolo del Piemonte**, when the fruit often has a remarkable apple or melon freshness to tone down the toughness. **Nebbiolo delle Langhe** is a table wine. Further north, in the Novara and Vercelli hills, **Gattinara**, **Ghemme** and **Carema** (all DOCs) give a much softer Nebbiolo style, while the unclassified **Spanna** can be easily the most enjoyable of all Nebbiolo wines.

Barbera wines are widespread in Piedmont and are remarkably consistent. They usually have a fairly high acidity, a slightly resiny edge and yet a very 'sweet/sour' raisins taste or even a brown sugar sweetness. They have lots of Piedmont bite but don't make the gums suffer such a full frontal assault as Nebbiolo.

THE GENERAL PICTURE

The **Dolcetto** grape is also good. It makes brash purple wine, full, yet soft, slightly chocolaty, wonderfully refreshing when young – and it *should* be drunk young, preferably only a year or so old. **Grignolino** is an attractive, curiously citrous red, while **Freisa** also pursues the Piedmont 'sweet/sour' trail and is often fizzy as well.

The still, white wines of Piedmont are only now finding their feet. **Gavi**, from the Cortese grape, has become wildly fashionable and wildly expensive. The wine is very clean, fresh and appley. **Erbaluce di Caluso** (DOC) offers better value for sharp, lemony, nutty wine, and **Arneis dei Roeri** is a fascinating, slightly bitter white, mixing liquorice and peach fruit with an unnerving perfume of fresh hops.

The Muscat grape is at its most brilliant in **Moscato d'Asti Naturale** (DOC and Vino da tavola), which is very sweet, slightly fizzy, and captures all the crunchy green freshness of a fistful of ripe table grapes while adding spiciness and richness too. **Asti Spumante** (DOC) is, after champagne, the world's most popular sparkling wine, and, drunk young, it can also have a magical grapy freshness.

THE IMPORTANT DETAILS

CLASSIFICATION
Piedmont is more carefully organized into DOC zones than any other region of Italy. It has 37 different DOC and DOCG zones, and for once, most of them *do* have a particular personality worth defining. Even so, some of the finest wines can be found outside the DOC umbrella, in particular Spanna and Moscato Naturale. The arrival of the DOCG category for Barolo and Barbaresco has not made much difference as yet to standards – a far more interesting development is the increasing use of vineyard names by producers of wines such as Gaja and Ceretto, which may eventually lead to a French-Style *cru* or 'growth' classification according to inherent vineyard quality.

ORGANIZATION/S
A great deal of Barolo and Barbaresco is sold under merchants' or co-ops' commercial labels, and it is largely these which have diminished the wines' considerable reputations. However, the number of growers bottling their own wine – such as Altare, Mascarello and Ratti – is increasing, and with it, a chance for us to see what all the fuss over these wines is about. In Asti, the co-operatives are of a high standard and well equipped to produce good *spumanti*, or 'sparkling wine', as are the big merchants. However, Moscato Naturale is always best from an individual producer such as Ascheri.

READING THE LABEL
In Barbaresco and Barolo, it's important to look for a label showing domaine-bottling, which will be indicated by the words 'Imbottigliato dal produttore all'origine'. A vineyard name like Gaja's Sorì Tildin, or Ceretto's Bricco Asili, on the label marks a wine of definite superior quality. Riserva guarantees at least four years aging for Barbaresco and five for Barolo. The term Riserva Speciale is no longer seen on the label. After DOCG was introduced the aging requirements were adjusted downwards, benefitting fruitiness in the wines.

WHAT DO THEY TASTE LIKE?
The Nebbiolo grape certainly gives memorable tastes, but not necessarily en-

joyable ones. Toughness and tannin are the hallmarks of Barolo and Barbaresco and they often overshadow the finer points. Yet great Barolos and Barbarescos, Spannas and sometimes Gattinaras, can produce that bewildering mixture of unexpected fruits and perfumes which are the sign of great wine. The non-Nebbiolo reds of Piedmont try to make up for this unfriendliness by having strong, gushing, highly drinkable tastes, and the whites – both the dry Arneis and Gavi, and the sweet Moscato – have simple, direct flavours which again make you feel Nature compensates for the Nebbiolo's intransigence.

THE GOOD YEARS
Great vintages are infrequently proclaimed, but much revered for Barolo, Barbaresco and Spanna, 1988, 1985, 1983, 1982, 1978, 1974 are all famous vintages, yet I have often had more enjoyable wines from lesser years like 1983 and 1980, simply because the fruit wasn't strangled by the toughness. In wines like Nebbiolo d'Alba and Barbera, two or three years' aging is quite enough, and drink Dolcetto, Grignolino and Freisa *very* young.

Interestingly, the Barbaresco producers are trying to catch on to this 'drink young' market, and Gaja's Vinòt shows how delicious Nebbiolo can be at less than a year old if made with modern methods. All the whites should be drunk young.

ENJOYING THE WINE
If ever red wines needed big, brawny foods to stand up to them, Barolo and Barbaresco do. Dark, heavily spiced stews, jugged hare, fondues, beef casseroles and *bollito misto* are all

The Nebbiolo vines ripen slowly into the misty autumn amongst the Langhe hills where Barolo and Barbaresco are grown.

THE IMPORTANT DETAILS

prepared locally with such relish, and, if you're lucky, accompanied by a sharing of the local white truffles, that the contest seems to be a fairly even one. Away from the region, Piedmont reds are very suitable for casseroles, ragoûts and game, and they can also handle most cheeses, which many red wines can't. The sweet whites and Muscat *spumantis* have such a delicious fresh richness they will go with virtually anything. However, they are probably best slightly cool, and sipped reflectively by themselves.

CONSUMER INFORMATION

WHAT DO I GET FOR MY MONEY?

The great Piedmont reds are very tricky to buy. They are always offered for sale far too young, and you can by no means be sure that the wine inside the bottle will correspond with your expectations without lengthy trial-and-error experience. There *is* cheap **Barolo** around, but it's usually filthy. Straight **Nebbiolo** is often the best value, along with the underrated **Spanna**. **Barbera** is cheap and very good, while **Dolcetto** is less cheap, but can be even better. **Gavi** and **Arneis** are expensive and it is questionable whether Gavi is worth the price. **Asti Spumante,** which used to be a cheap drink, is now moderately dear and **Moscato Naturale** costs even more, but, since it will probably blow your mind, the expense is worth it.

AVAILABILITY

Good Barolo and Barbaresco are difficult to find. Even highly recommended wines can turn out to be just too harsh and acidic to gain pleasure from. The other Piedmont reds are not very widely distributed either, which is a pity because they're highly drinkable. The dry whites are rare outside the region, but Asti Spumante is universally available, and the only important thing is to make sure the stock is fresh. Moscato Naturale is very rare, but worth a two-day hike to find.

CONSUMER CHECKLIST		
Barbaresco	Q:	1 2 3 4 5 6 7 8 **9** 10
Bruno Giacosa	P:	1 2 3 4 5 6 7 **8** 9 10
1982	V:	1 2 3 4 5 6 7 **8** 9 10
Moscato	Q:	1 2 3 4 5 6 7 **8** 9 10
Naturale	P:	1 2 3 4 **5** 6 7 8 9 10
Ascheri	V:	1 2 3 4 5 6 7 8 **9** 10

Good Years The north-west has not had a great run of recent vintages. Moscato Naturale should be drunk as young as possible. Good red years are 1988, 1985, 1983, 1982, 1978, 1974.

Taste Notes Most of the wines of the region are marked by strong unmistakable flavours, whether they're the dark, tough plummy reds from the Nebbiolo grape like Barolo and Barbaresco or the strong, grape-scented Muscats, sparkling or still.

VALLE D'AOSTA

Lost in the steep Alpine valleys which twine up towards Mont Blanc or the St Bernard pass, Valle d'Aosta is Italy's tiniest region, producing the smallest quantity of wine, yet her inhabitants defy the present Italian domestic slump in wine-drinking by being easily her thirstiest drinkers, putting back two-and-a-half times what the parched southerners of Sicily can achieve. I always feel it's unfair when mountain people, with their savage climate and a food style built on burly, heroic lines can only produce such fleeting, delicate wines, but Valle d'Aosta, while hardly hitting the jackpot for weight and blubber in her wines, does at least produce tasty stuff. The best are grouped under Valle d'Aosta DOC. They're never exported, but, on the spot, white **Blanc de Morgex** and **Blanc de la Salle** from the Blanc de Valdigne grape, are delicious, while the red **Donnaz**, from the Nebbiolo, and **Torrette**, from the Petit Rouge, can pack a perceptible punch – in the flyweight division – and the rarities of **Malvoisie de Nus, Vin du Conseil** and **Enfer d'Arvier** are worth a detour. And if you're wondering about the language – you're right. French! That's what they speak up there on the border.

NORTH-WEST ITALY

LIGURIA

Liguria is a long thin sliver of land curving gracefully round the Genoese coastline from France to Tuscany. On a map it looks almost too tight to squeeze in many vines, and, indeed, it is one of Italy's least productive wine regions. Yet Genoa, its capital, is a great gastronomic centre, working wonders with fish, seafood and some of Italy's most original pasta creations. So what Liguria primarily produces is a fair amount of immediate drinking wine from the hills behind the coast. The good stuff goes to the Genoese, the mediocre

stuff goes down the uncomplaining and uncritical throats of the hordes of holiday-makers on the Italian Riviera.

In whites, one should look for wines from the **Pigato** and **Vermentino** grapes – not classified, but often good. In reds, **Rossese di Dolceacqua** (DOC) is the best, going from strangely fragrant to jammy-strong. The most famous, and most abused, wine is **Cinqueterre** (DOC). It's some years since I talked to anyone who reckoned he'd drunk an honest bottle.

Cinqueterre, where vines and olives are grown together in the traditional manner along the spectacular coastline near La Spezia. Today's wine, unfortunately, does not live up to its historical reputation.

LOMBARDY

If Liguria is only of passing interest, Lombardy, with Milan as its capital, is a serious wine area, but an underrated one, primarily because Piedmont carries all the partisan colours for this part of Italy, and produces twice as much wine. And, remarkably, Milan doesn't seem to realize her good fortune. Fine wines from all over Italy are readily available in Milan – except from her own backyard of Lombardy.

Although the Nebbiolo doesn't excel here, and its chief manifestation, **Valtellina**, always seems a little stringy, nonetheless other black grapes can do very well, often under the umbrella DOC of **Oltrepò Pavese**, with the

Bonarda making plummy, liquoricy wine, and the **Barbera** giving high-acid chewy reds. In **Franciacorta Rosso** (DOC), Nebbiolo blends with Cabernet and Merlot to give a raw but tasty blackcurrany wine. **Franciacorta** (DOC) is best known for its sparkling wines, and Ca' del Bosco makes one of Italy's best champagne-method wines here. Oltrepò Pavese white grapes, including Riesling and Pinot Bianco, are largely used in Piedmont as the base for sparkling wines. The few whites which don't get processed, like **Lugana** (DOC) and **Tocai di San Martino della Battaglia** (DOC), are pleasant but unexciting.

NORTH-EAST ITALY

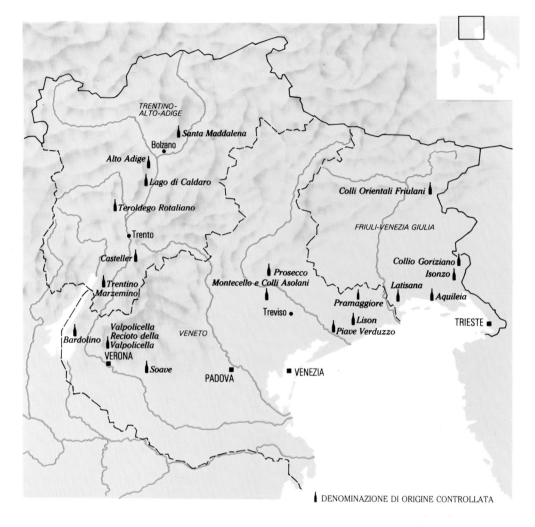

TRENTINO-ALTO-ADIGE

Santa Maddalena
Bolzano
Alto Adige
Lago di Caldaro
Teroldego Rotaliano
Trento
Casteller
Trentino
Marzemino
Bardolino
Valpolicella
Recioto della
Valpolicella
VERONA
Soave
PADOVA

Montecello e Colli Asolani
Prosecco
Treviso
VENETO
VENEZIA

Colli Orientali Friulani
FRIULI-VENEZIA GIULIA
Collio Goriziano
Isonzo
Latisana
Pramaggiore
Lison
Piave Verduzzo
Aquileia
TRIESTE

DENOMINAZIONE DI ORIGINE CONTROLLATA

The north-east of Italy is where the most exciting advances in wine-making are being made and where a wide variety of grapes produce wines of marked fruit and freshness. The Alto Adige–Trentino area north of Verona and the Friuli–Giulia area up towards the Yugoslav border, use many 'international' grape types with notable success. The large Veneto area produces a gigantic amount of wine, but of very variable quality. Three of Italy's most famous wines – Soave, Valpolicella and Bardolino – are produced in the Veneto.

The Alto Adige vineyards smother the steeply angled slopes of the Dolomites, where the burning southern sun is always tempered by the crisp mountain air: many are at over 900 metres (3,000 feet).

NORTH-EAST ITALY/Alto Adige

THE GENERAL PICTURE

Although the Alto Adige is politically joined to Trentino in the Province of Trentino–Alto Adige, this conjunction is purely for political convenience to avoid the embarassment of having one province – Alto Adige – with a German-speaking majority and separatist inclinations. The wine-making traditions and styles of both regions differ dramatically, and although the Trentino was first in the field in trying to upgrade her quality levels, with isolated exceptions, the general standard is not as high as the Alto Adige's, and the wines are usually flatter and broader, rarely having the incisive, mouth-watering bite of the Alto Adige reds and whites. The most exciting developments are taking place in the Alto Adige, so let's look at that in detail first.

The **Alto Adige,** or **Südtirol,** is one of the most fascinating of Italy's wine areas, and without question one of the most beautiful. It comprises a long, narrow valley, stretching up north from Verona, flat as prairie land on its floor, but bounded by magnificent peaks, dwarfing the towns and villages. The valley floor is largely given over to apple-growing but every square metre of dizzily steep mountainside is planted with vines. It looks impossibly difficult to tend vines at such angles, and if one were in the mainstream of Italian wine tradition, that would be correct. But the majority of these winemakers are Germanic – and have been for 2,000 years. For Germans, steep river valley slopes are accepted as the norm in wine-growing.

The Alto Adige wine region is frequently referred to as Südtirol, or South Tyrol. The name Alto Adige implies that the vineyards of the Adige are at the northern tip of Italy, reaching high into the frontier mountains of the Dolomites. Südtirol implies that this is the southernmost finger of Austrian soil, sneaking down from the mountainous Austrian Tyrol to aggravate Italy's national pride on her northern flank. Well, both are true.

The Alto Adige *is* in Italy – politically. Yet emotionally it is in Austria. Most of its inhabitants would like to be thought of as Austrian, and from 1363 to 1920 this long, steep-sided valley *was* part of Austria, until it was forfeited to Italy after Austria's defeat in World War One. There is a very Tyrolean feel to the buildings, cuisine and customs of the area, and outside the main town of Bolzano, most people speak German as their first language.

Certainly it is the oldest wine region of all the German-speaking nations, and as such it is one of Europe's oldest too. When the Romans took it over in 15 BC the Tirolers not only taught their new masters how to train vines on wooden frames in the modern manner, as against up the sides of trees, but they also showed them how to use wooden barrels for storing and transporting wines – and wood, even in this present age of plastic and stainless steel, is still on the whole regarded as the perfect material for making and maturing fine wines.

NORTH-EAST ITALY/Alto Adige

THE GENERAL PICTURE

GRAPE VARIETIES AND WINE STYLES
The Alto Adige makes every conceivable kind of table wine with considerable success, and some of her wines are unique in style.

Eighty per cent of the vineyards are red, and they are chiefly given over to the Vernatsch or Schiava (*Schiava* means 'slave-girl', suggesting that this grape does what it's told under virtually any circumstances). It is often derided as feeble and tasteless. Not true. It makes wonderfully quaffable light reds and is at its best in the wines of Kalterersee Auslese and Santa Maddalena.

Lagrein is another local red grape variety, the Lagrein Dunkel ('dark Lagrein') making dark, intense reds. Pinot Noir, the Burgundy grape, and Cabernet Sauvignon, the Bordeaux grape, are increasingly planted.

Although the minority planting, much of the current excitement about Alto Adige wines centres on the whites. The grapes are divided between the French and Germanic styles. On the French side there is some Sauvignon, but primarily two grapes which have a lot in common: Pinot Bianco and Chardonnay.

On the German side are Sylvaner, Müller-Thurgau, Gewürztraminer and different varieties of Muscat.

The Alto Adige excels even with rosé, produced from the Lagrein Kretzer grape which makes a marvellously fruity, totally dry wine.

The sparkling is only just getting going, and a lot of the Pinot Bianco and Chardonnay grapes are still shipped southwards to the fizz factories. But the new champagne-method production promises to be mouthwatering.

THE IMPORTANT DETAILS

CLASSIFICATION
Over three-quarters of the wines are now inside the Italian DOC system, and represent by far the highest proportion of such 'quality controlled' wines of any region in Italy. But until 1985, DOC regulations meant that Chardonnay, potentially the most sought-after wine style, could only be labelled 'Vino da Tavola', the most basic designation (see p. 181). An oft-repeated state of affairs in Italy.

ORGANIZATION/S
Most of the best wines are made by growers, but not necessarily only from their own grapes. There are various microclimates which suit such high quality vines as Pinot Noir, Cabernet, Lagrein and Chardonnay, and grower-winemakers will bid high prices for batches of these 'special quality' grapes to mix with their own. Otherwise, there are various big commercial concerns, some of whom control vineyards, and most of whom have one or two specialities – often Pinot Bianco, Lagrein, or Santa Maddalena. The co-operative system is extensive, but so far, despite some undeniably good wines, the results are patchy.

Old and new are successfully combined here at Schloss Schwanburg, where wooden barrels rub shoulders with the first stainless steel tanks introduced to the area (now used region-wide for whites).

READING THE LABEL

These, sadly, can be rather confusing. They may be in Italian, German, or even French. While something like Cabernet is the same in any language, there can be confusions with place names appearing in Italian and German, and grape varieties appearing in French, Italian or German! Pinot Noir can also end up as Pinot Nero or Blauburgunder, Pinot Bianco can be Pinot Blanc or Weissburgunder and Riesling can be either Rheinriesling or Riesling Renano. However, the important thing to understand is that Lago di Caldaro Scelto is the same as Kalterersee Auslese.

WHAT DOES IT TASTE LIKE?

The basic wine style is light and intensely fresh. Few of the whites *need* any age at all, though some can mature surprisingly well if they have to and most are marked by a delicious lemony streak of acidity, and some refreshing 'spritz', a gentle prickly effervescence which is lost within two years.

Pinot Bianco and Chardonnay These two grapes here give some of their purest, snow-fresh flavours, but always flecked with honey.

Müller-Thurgau, Sylvaner and Riesling The first two are workhorse grapes in Germany, pressed into uncomplaining service to provide the endless flow of Liebfraumilch and Niersteiner the world seems to demand. Nothing could be more different from their shockingly sharp, biting-fresh flavours in the Alto Adige, where the tastes are as close to the cold shiver of a high mountain stream in spring as a wine will ever get. The Rheinriesling is the true German Riesling, and produces marvellously steely dry wines sharp, green and wonderfully refreshing – as good as most Mosel or Rhine Kabinetts in Germany.

Gewürztraminer Although this grape is supposed to have originated in the Adige village of Tramin, most plantations are now of the 'red' Traminer, rather than the spicier, more memorable 'Gewürztraminer' of Alsace fame. They're OK but are often made a little too soft to be satisfying.

Muscat The different varieties of Muscat make dry wines to rival Alsace, and light, fragrant sweet wines unrivalled elsewhere in Europe.

The vineyards of Terlano, famous for Pinot Bianco wine, are on the slopes, while the valley floor is Italy's leading apple-growing area.

NORTH-EAST ITALY/Alto Adige

THE IMPORTANT DETAILS

The Goldmuskateller can be sweet, but is more often a delicious off-dry, grapy white.

The Rosenmuskateller is one of the world's most remarkable flavours. Sweet or dry, it tastes exactly of roses!

Kalterersee Auslese Good light red, soft with an unbelievable flavour of home-made strawberry jam. Delicious and unique, it is best as a young gulper.

Santa Maddalena A fuller version of the above, the strawberry fruit enhanced by a woodsmoke savouriness; it makes an even better young gulper!

Cabernet or Pinot Noir These need warm years, but their style is unique. The Cabernet has a fresh, earthy, grassy feel, but also a marvellous, pure blackcurrant fruit. The Pinot Noir, though often too light, can produce a mini-version of the luscious plums and cherries flavour of good red Burgundy.

Lagrein Dunkel A dark, chewy wine, with a remarkable amount of depth and flavour for the product of a high mountain valley, where one expects things to be light and cool. These intense reds have a tarry roughness jostling with a chocolate-smooth ripe fruit. The flavour is a very successful mix between the strong, chunky style of many Italian reds, and the fresher, brighter tastes of France. Like an Italian Nebbiolo it needs aging.

THE GOOD YEARS

Most Alto Adige wines should be drunk very young yet they can age for a surprisingly long time. The pale red Vernatsch wines are often at their best within six to nine months of vintage. All the whites are drinkable at six months, but their excellent acid levels mean they are better at about one year old, and some Pinot Biancos, Chardonnays and Gewürztraminers need at least three years to show their best. Cabernet and Pinot Noir (Blauburgunder) grow well here and usually need three years to show their best with the finest examples capable of another dozen years aging. Only the deep, dark local grape Lagrein needs a lot of time, perhaps five years to blossom out. Of recent years 1989 was pretty good all round, 1988 was excellent if smaller in quantity, the coolness of 1987 was good for whites not reds. 1985 is the best recent year for reds.

ENJOYING THE WINES

Alto Adige wines are so adaptable they will fit any bill, from light apéritif white, or big sturdy red, to sweet dessert wine. However, the most reliable wines as yet are the whites, and these are ideal as apéritif wines or accompaniments to simple, light dishes. Their delicate flavour would be swamped by too many big, creamy sauces. The Lagrein Kretzer is marvellous picnic rosé, and the reds can be matched to virtually any dish.

Any of the whites would be good with fresh mountain trout, while Lagrein Kretzer or Kalterersee in great long draughts are just the thirst-quenchers one needs with the local noodles or sauerkraut, and Cabernet, Pinot Noir or Lagrein Dunkel would be best for the spicy game and beef dishes which the combined Italian and Austrian cultures provide.

Kaltern, in the Alto Adige where architecture, ambience and dress demonstrate a pervasive Austrian influence.

CONSUMER INFORMATION

WHAT DO I GET FOR MY MONEY?

Since these wines come from hillside vineyards, they are not as cheap as many better-known Italian wines. But their very high overall quality actually makes them more of a bargain than most other Italian wine and the Pinot Bianco or Chardonnay, for example, is far cheaper than an equivalent French Chardonnay from Burgundy. Such a position will continue until the wines achieve the fame their flavours deserve. The whites in particular are certain to become a major force in the top quality market within the next decade.

AVAILABILITY

These wines are not yet as widely distributed as they should be, since over half of their annual production goes straight to the established export markets of Austria, Germany, Switzerland and the Low Countries. But now that the growers' associations are promoting the wines they are beginning to find a place in the large chains and supermarkets in northern Europe too. As yet they are not common in Italian delicatessens and restaurants outside Italy, but keep asking for them because they are worth the search.

CONSUMER CHECKLIST

Chardonnay 1989		
Q:	1 2 3 4 5 **6** 7 8 9 10
P:	1 2 3 **4** 5 6 7 8 9 10
V:	1 2 3 4 5 6 **7** 8 9 10

Trentino Casteller		
Q:	1 2 3 **4** 5 6 7 8 9 10
P:	1 **2** 3 4 5 6 7 8 9 10
V:	1 2 3 4 5 **6** 7 8 9 10

Good Years Most Alto Adige wines should be drunk very young, yet can age for a long time. The pale red Vernatsch wines are often at their best within 6-9 months of vintage. All the whites are drinkable at 6 months, but are better at 1 year old. Some Pinot Biancos, Chardonnays and Gewürztraminers need at least 3 years. Cabernet and Pinot Noir (Blauburgunder) usually need 3 years, with the finest example capable of another dozen years aging. Only the deep dark local grape Lagrein needs a lot of time, perhaps 5 years, to blossom out. Of recent years, 1988 is the best overall, though good producers made attractive 1989s and 1987s.

Taste Notes The whites are very fresh, with almost sharply defined fruit. The reds are light yet remarkably intense in flavour.

TRENTINO

The Trentino vineyards are to the south of Alto Adige and far less influenced by the geological structure and climate of the mountain valleys. Most of the same grapes are grown, and, in the case of the Schiava or Vernatsch grape, the name Lago di Caldaro or Kalterersee is often borrowed without great justification. The reds are a mixture of international grapes like Cabernet, Merlot and Pinot Noir, along with local varieties like Lagrein and Marzemino. They usually have a fair amount of flavour without any great definition, but often an attractive smoky dryness. **Casteller** (DOC) is a pleasant, very light red, while the **Marzemino di Isera** (DOC) can be highly individual, big and rubbery with a eucalyptus fragrance to lift it out of its boots. **Teroldego Rotaliano** (DOC) is a more famous but less approachable red.

In the whites, there are some interesting wines from Germanic varieties like Riesling and Müller-Thurgau, but the genuinely exciting wines are from Pinot Bianco and Chardonnay. Especially when grown to the north of the town of Trento, they match the austere freshness of the Alto Adige with an extra dimension of creamy depth which can make them some of Italy's finest whites, from producers like Pojer & Sandri, Barone de Cles and Istituto di San Michele all'Adige. Such quality of still dry white wines is a new departure, because the Trentino has up till recently preferred to use Pinot Bianco and Chardonnay for sparkling wine – often champagne method, and often very good, if horrifyingly expensive. Two of the best are Equipe 5 and Ferrari – both with strong Grand Prix connotations, but the Càvit co-operative group, which controls nearly 75 per cent of Trentino's production, also produces a deliciously dry Chardonnay Spumante – quite unnervingly like champagne in style – and very much cheaper.

NORTH-EAST ITALY/Veneto

THE GENERAL PICTURE

The Veneto almost matches Sicily and Emilia–Romagna in the massive quantities she produces, coming in a close third. However, in terms of quality wines – those with DOC status – the Veneto produces more than any other region, totalling nearly 20 per cent of the national total. Moscato d'Asti comes behind Tuscany's Chianti as the second biggest DOC in Italy, and in terms of white DOCs is easily the largest; in the USA, Soave is the most consumed white DOC. As if this weren't enough for one region, the red Valpolicella and Bardolino make up an Unholy Alliance of recognizably affordable Italian wine which, with Chianti, have come to represent the mainstream of Italian wine abroad.

I wish I could be more enthusiastic about these flagbearers but, sadly, the quality of what at best are only supposed to be light, simple, local wines, has largely fallen below what even their low prices can make accept- able. The flatlands stretching between Padua, Venice and Treviso, without the same famous names, but with a history of providing fresh, bright wines for the hearty Venetian cooking, are now producing much better and even cheaper reds and whites. As always, there are also some fine 'rogue' wines which fail to qualify for DOC despite their qualities.

GRAPE VARIETIES AND WINE STYLES
The Veneto uses a mixture of indigenous grapes and international varieties, and the most famous wines are basically from the local types. Up till World War Two, **Soave** (DOC), based on the local Garganega grape, with a little hindrance from Trebbiano, was simply the light local wine of Verona. It was dry, slightly nutty, inoffensive. (Maybe it was this very neutrality which rocketed it to such stardom that Bolla, Soave's biggest producer, shipped precisely 3,360 bottles to America in 1948, and now sends off more than 10 million a year.) Until recently dramatic vineyard expansion and increased yields were wrecking quality, but there has now been a revival, both by the main co-op, and by leading growers such as Pieropan and Anselmi. Also good, fresher and fruitier in a green apple way, is the unsung white **Bianco di Custoza** (DOC).

Further over to the east, **Piave** (DOC) pro- duces a lot of low-priced white, the **Verduzzo** being very soft and nutty, the **Tocai** being quite full and slightly aromatic and the **Prosec- co,** either still or sparkling, giving a lovely, fresh bouncy light white.

The reds of **Valpolicella** (DOC) and **Bar- dolino** (DOC) suffer from the twin ills of over- popularity and over-exploitation much as Soave did. Made from a variety of local grapes, in particular Corvina Veronese, Rondinella and Molinara, Bardolino can be the palest of pale reds, with a wispy cherry fruit to it and a slight bitter snap to finish. Valpolicella, from the same grapes, should be all this but just a little bit fuller and deep- er. Right now, Bardolino is delivering the goods far more often than Valpolicella. Producers who might oblige are Anselmi, Guerrieri-Rizzardi, Masi and Tedeschi. Val- policella partly atones by making some very good non-DOC table wines – big, strong and full of a strange, intense fruit, the best being **Campo Fiorin** and **Capitel San Rocco**. And, best of all, Valpolicella produces small amounts of one of Italy's most exciting and unusual red wines – **Recioto della Valpolicella Amarone**. *Amaro* means 'bitter', and this remarkable wine, made from half-shrivelled Valpolicella grapes, *is* bitter, but it also has a quite brilliant array of flavours – sweet grape skins, chocolate, plums, woodsmoke, all bound up in a wine which is positively sour at the same time. With that description try it.

Elsewhere in the Veneto there is good red. **Venegazzù** makes an excellent Bordeaux- style red, smoky and blackcurrant all at once. Above Venice, in Piave, Cabernet Franc and Merlot can provide pleasant reds, while **Raboso** (DOC) can be excellent, tannic, acid, bursting with raw fruit.

THE IMPORTANT DETAILS

Valpolicella comes from gently sloping hills to the north of Verona. Here, Rondinella grapes are picked into baskets suspended on wires as the vines are trained high.

CLASSIFICATION

Although Superiore appears on various labels, in the case of Valpolicella, Bardolino and Soave, it doesn't mean better, merely older. So avoid it. Because the quality of these wines had deteriorated so much, the best producers have begun labelling their top wines with a *cru* or single vineyard name. These are all based in the original central Classico areas, and might well help improve quality. Much of Veneto is not covered by the DOC designation, yet still uses geographical descriptions. These may apply to high-quality yet individualistic products like Montericco, Campo Fiorin or Capitel San Rocco in Valpolicella, Venegazzù in the Montello hills, or the simple, uncontrolled production of wines such as Raboso and Verduzzo from the wide plains above Venice.

ORGANIZATION/S

The co-operatives are tremendously important. They are large, usually modern, and in areas like Soave dominate the whole production. Particularly in the north-eastern areas of Piave, Lison and Paramaggiore, the standard of co-op wine is very high. Most Veneto wines are marketed as merchants' commercial blends, but the grapes will normally be from co-ops. There are individual growers in all the areas, whose wines are much more likely to reflect the true nature of the local flavours than commercial blends.

READING THE LABEL

It is worth looking for 'Classico on Soave, Valpolicella and Bardolino labels, because the chances of some decent wine are much higher. Superiore denotes a minimum aging requirement of one year, but, since you want to drink these wines as young as possible – avoid Superiore. Some wines are sold non vintage: buy from a high turnover store.

WHAT DO THEY TASTE LIKE?

Veneto wines should be some of the most enjoyable in Italy, since they are nearly all by tradition light, refreshing, and undemanding. The cherry kernel nip of good Valpolicella or Bardolino is absolutely delicious, yet usually the wines are tart and fruitless. Soave can have a lovely nutty taste with just a flick of liquorice; it rarely does. However, the great Amarones will rarely let you down, nor will the thick-flavoured 'special' Vini da Tavola from people such as Masi Tedeschi. Wines simply labelled with a grape name and 'del Piave' or 'del Veneto' should be light and easy-going anytime, anyfood, anybody wines.

THE GOOD YEARS

The rule in the Veneto is mostly to drink as young as possible. With a ripe vintage like 1989, or 1988, there may be some excuse in holding the bottle for a year or so. Special Vini da Tavola and Amarone do need some time to open out; the early 1980's are now good, though the Amarones in particular age well, and years like 1974 and 1971 should still be excellent.

ENJOYING THE WINE

The Venetian cuisine is almost too rough-and-tumble to called a cuisine, and the great mishmash of soups and rice, pastas and beans are ideally accompanied by large jugfuls of fresh light Veneto wine.

On the whole the wines are light in taste, therefore strongly flavoured foods will swamp them. Which in some cases is no bad thing. Bardolino should be served chilled, and proper Valpolicella and light Veneto Merlots can also be cool. Amarones are such a remarkable flavour, sweet and bitter and sour, that I can't think of any food which would really go well with them, and I'd drink them after a meal or just possibly with a nibble of cheese.

CONSUMER INFORMATION

WHAT DO I GET FOR MY MONEY?

Soave, **Valpolicella** and **Bardolino** are almost always traded entirely on price considerations. Consequently, even when cheap, they are unlikely to be good value. The growing numbers of single estate wines are probably 50 per cent more expensive, but still worth it. **Amarone** is usually about twice the price of ordinary Valpolicella, which makes it good value for a remarkable wine. The Vini da Tavola of **Venegazzù** are fairly priced for the quality, while the basic **Veneto** and **Piave** wines are very cheap and often good buys.

AVAILABILITY

Basic Veneto and Piave wines and Soave, Valpolicella and Bardolino are some of Italy's most widely available wines. However, estate-bottled versions are not easy to find and Amarone is also rarely sighted anywhere. Bianco di Custoza is beginning to appear but it is a relative newcomer on the export market. Wines such as Raboso, Verduzzo, Prosecco and Tocai are not often seen but are cheap and worth seeking out.

CONSUMER CHECKLIST

		1	2	3	4	5	6	7	8	9	10
Bardolino Classico	Q:	1	2	3	**4**	5	6	7	8	9	10
	P:	1	2	**3**	4	5	6	7	8	9	10
	V:	1	2	3	4	**5**	6	7	8	9	10
Friuli Cabernet Franc	Q:	1	2	3	4	5	**6**	7	8	9	10
	P:	1	2	3	4	**5**	6	7	8	9	10
	V:	1	2	3	4	5	**6**	7	8	9	10

Good Years These wines are to be drunk as young as possible, because the light fresh styles rarely improve over more than a couple of years.

Taste Notes The north-east is a fascinating area of Italy and its tastes are some of the lightest, freshest, brightest in the whole country. Although some names like Soave and Valpolicella have become overworked and taste like it, this area is in general Italy's best for clean, fruity reds and whites.

NORTH-EAST ITALY/Friuli

Friuli spreads from the flatlands of the Adriatic as it curves round at the top of Italy, to the wild jumble of hills which crowd the somewhat arbitrary border with Yugoslavia just above Trieste. It's been a tug-of-war part of Europe through the ages, and it wasn't until 1954 that Trieste, its capital, was returned to Italy after the war. Consequently, there were very few preconceptions about what kind of wine should be made, where, and by whom. The land seemed good, the climate, particularly in the Collio Goriziano hills squeezed up against the border, seemed ideal; what was needed was a sense of direction. This came in the 1960s when Friuli set up what is Italy's least complicated, most logical DOC system. The authorities set up six different zones – Collio Goriziano, Colli Orientali del Friuli and Grave del Friuli (the best three) as well as the flatter Latisana, Aquilea and Isonzo. The wines are simply labelled with their grape variety and the area, except for the DOC 'Collio' wine from Collio Goriziano which is a blend of the three local grapes of Ribolla, Malvasia and Tocai.

The range of grapes and styles is incredibly wide, but, right through the range, the wines are characterized by something rare in Italian wines – fruit! In particular the 'international' grapes of Cabernet Franc, Merlot, Pinot Bianco, Chardonnay and even Sauvignon and Müller-Thurgau all have a juicy direct stab of flavour which is absolutely delicious. The Pinot Bianco, so often dull in Italy, manages a lemony bite to go with its smoky fruit, and the brilliant, nutty white **Tocai,** along with the tough, tarry **Refosco,** are also exciting.

Most famous of all Friuli wines is **Picolit.** This should be sweet and luscious and has been called Italy's Château d'Yquem, a pointless comparison presumably based on sugar content and rarity value. Nowadays it is certainly decidedly sweet but just slightly insubstantial. Which couldn't be said about the sensational **Ramandolo di Verduzzo** which packs so many flavours of smoke and apple skins and apricot and mint, all wrapped in a lanolin smoothness that it takes your breath away. From a producer like Giovanni Dri or Comelli this is much more likely to stand comparison – with any sweet wine in the world.

Friuili wines are best from independent producers, like Attems, Schiopetto, Plozner, Jermann and EnoFriulia but, particularly in Grave del Friuli, the big companies on the whole make good wines. These wines are best drunk young. Their availability is increasing, but having discovered the styles through those wines, it really does pay to find a grower's wine, because the wine-making here seems to improve with every vintage. Apart from wines like Picolit and Ramandolo, the prices are in the middle to lower range.

Refosco wine should be drunk as fresh and pink as it is here, straight from the bucket!

CENTRAL ITALY

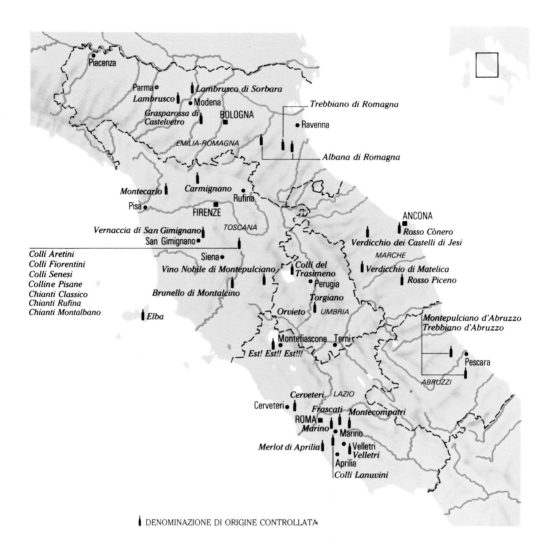

Piacenza
Parma
Lambrusco
Lambrusco di Sorbara
Modena
Grasparossa di Castelvetro
BOLOGNA
Trebbiano di Romagna
EMILIA-ROMAGNA
Ravenna
Albana di Romagna
Montecarlo
Carmignano
Rufina
Pisa
FIRENZE
Vernaccia di San Gimignano
San Gimignano
TOSCANA
ANCONA
Rosso Cònero
Verdicchio dei Castelli di Jesi
MARCHE

Colli Aretini
Colli Fiorentini
Colli Senesi
Colline Pisane
Chianti Classico
Chianti Rufina
Chianti Montalbano

Siena
Vino Nobile di Montepulciano
Colli del Trasimeno
Verdicchio di Matelica
Rosso Piceno
Perugia
Brunello di Montalcino
Torgiano
Orvieto
UMBRIA
Elba
Montepulciano d'Abruzzo
Trebbiano d'Abruzzo
Montefiascone
Terni
Est! Est!! Est!!!
ABRUZZI
Pescara
Cerveteri
LAZIO
Cerveteri
Frascati
Montecompatri
ROMA
Marino
Marino
Merlot di Aprilia
Velletri
Velletri
Aprilia
Colli Lanuvini

❚ DENOMINAZIONE DI ORIGINE CONTROLLATA

Central Italy has a remarkable diversity of famous wine names. Tuscany's Chianti and Brunello, Emilia-Romagna's Lambrusco, Latium's Frascati, Umbria's Orvieto and the Verdicchio of the Marches are all household names. Only the Abruzzi has no famous wine. Yet these traditional centres of excellence are struggling to adjust themselves to the changing tastes of the market with greater or lesser success, and many of the best wines are appearing in areas like Abruzzi where there is no tradition to hinder the winemaker, or in Tuscany, where many winemakers are discarding historical precedent and sticking out for quality on their own.

Ripe bunches of dark purple Sangiovese grapes, the heart of good Chianti, glinting in the bright autumn sun.

CENTRAL ITALY/Tuscany

THE GENERAL PICTURE

A farm, its vines, its olive and cypress trees – and a whiff of woodsmoke: the heart of Chianti Classico near Greve.

Tuscany should be the most glittering of all Italy's wine regions. After all, Florence and Siena, of all Italy's cities, have a history which positively shines with achievements in art, philosophy and science, and luckily the astonishing beauty of these two main towns is largely unaffected by twentieth-century ugliness. And between them, as the road rises and dips and twists past San Casciano, Greve and Castellina, as every turn in the lane seems to offer a picnic spot even more perfect than the last, flanked by olives, vines, the rough rock of the hills, and the occasional copse of cypresses hiding another country villa from intimidating eyes, it is easy to sink back and contentedly feel one is slap in the heart of everything Italian wine, Italian life even, should stand for. Sadly, reality won't quite let you get away with the dream. Tuscany is a region at the crossroads, where crisis and salvation beckon to wine-growers in about equal measure. So let's look at the wine a little more closely to try to separate the great from the gruesome and understand what makes the area tick.

Tuscany possesses more vineyard land of potentially brilliant quality than any other province. She possesses in Chianti (DOCG) the most famous of Italian wine names virtually synonymous with all things Italian, from the glittering candlelight in the dingiest trattoria to the majestic flights of Michelangelo. She also possesses in Brunello di Montalcino (DOCG)

CENTRAL ITALY/Tuscany

THE GENERAL PICTURE

the wine which has as its prime objective the title of 'most expensive Italian wine'. Along with that there is the majestically named Vino Nobile di Montepulciano (DOCG) whose flavour rarely rings with the self-confident timbre of its title, and Vernaccia di San Gimignano (DOC) which can often do justice to the elegant multi-turreted hill town near Siena which lends its name to the wine.

And there are the iconoclasts – chiefly those who have watched in dismay as Chianti set itself on a course of ritual dismemberment and vowed that they would go their own way to draw out the potential for greatness which quite patently lies in the soil of the Tuscan Hills. Such wines as Tignanello, Vinattieri, and even the fabled Sassicaia from the coastal flatland, along with Carmignano (DOC), are the leaders here. We are only now seeing a revival after a period of infighting, greed and stupidity which threatened to tear the region apart. At last the various stony-headed antagonists have begun to pull together, at last realizing that this is the only sane course of action they can possibly take if they're going to survive!

Tuscany is still in a state of crisis, and often seems to take two steps backward and one step forward, but it now looks as though the disastrous 1984 vintage did finally reverse the decline by the simple expedient of saying 'There's the abyss. Deep and dark, isn't it? Right, this is your last chance. Shut your eyes and jump, or swallow your pride and clamber back to safety.' Some shut their eyes and jumped, by which I mean that they continued to produce too much wine from their grapes; they blended, vinified and aged it unsuitably and far too long in old retirement-age wood. We should hear no more of them. The ones who, at the last gasp, grabbed the straws proffered by increasing their proportion of black grapes in the blend, reducing vineyard yields, introducing Cabernet Sauvignon to improve flavour and only aging wine which would genuinely benefit by it – these have the chance to return themselves and Tuscany to the centre of the stage.

GRAPE VARIETIES AND WINE STYLES
Above all, Tuscany is red wine country, and the wild but fundamentally good-natured Sangiovese grape is by far the most important influence, being the mainstay of all **Chianti**.In

a way, too much is often asked of this grape which is extremely good at providing purple-fresh, slightly rasping, herby wines, full of thirst-quenching acid fruit, to be drunk young. All over Italy it fulfils this role, and when Baron Ricasoli virtually invented modern Chianti over 100 years ago, it was precisely this quality he wanted to harness, to provide young, tangy reds to be consumed within the year in the cafés and bars of nearby Florence. But Chianti got high fallutin' ideas and began increasingly to adopt a policy of aging the wines for years at a time in big old wooden barrels.

The Sangiovese by itself might have been able to cope, but this is where Tuscany's second most important grape comes in – and it is *white* – the dull, prolific and rampant Trebbiano. This grape is the weed of Italy and nowhere has distressing influence been more strongly felt than in Tuscany. Initially introduced, along with the vastly superior Malvasia, to soften the red Chianti wines, it quickly achieved such a following amongst farmers more concerned with quantity than quality, that it was allowed to make up 30 per cent of a red Chianti blend. Thank goodness the DOCG regulations grasped this nettle and reduced the permitted amount in red Chianti to between 2 and 5%. Some producers now use none at all. This has radically reduced the amount of thin, orange, fruitless – and cheap – Chianti we had been used to enduring, which was rightly blamed on an excess of Trebbiano, and on laws which insist on aging wines much better released young.

The most exciting development in the Chianti region has been the gradual emergence of the Cabernet Sauvignon grape as a component part of red wines. Although not really permissible for more than 10 per cent of the total, the variety is so brilliantly suited to Tuscany that even 5 per cent can transform a blend. There is an increasing number of growers who are including Cabernet Sauvignon in their Riserva wines to good effect. Wines like **Carmignano** and **Tignanello** use 10 to 15 per cent Cabernet and its juicy, gentle, sweet fruit blends excitingly with the tougher texture of the Sangiovese. Those who also use small oak barrels, like Tignanello, are taking a path away from Chianti, but the restrained influence of Cabernet and smaller barrels, which produce wines which lose less fruit and oxidise slowly, can only be good.

The Sangiovese Grosso grape is a relation of the ordinary Sangiovese of Chianti, but makes a far deeper, plummier and more provocatively perfumed wine. Provocatively priced too, since it is the grape which produces **Brunello di Montalcino,** Italy's most effective drain on a wine-lover's bank balance, and it is the chief grape in **Vino Nobile di Montepulciano,** which is no slouch when it comes to emptying wallets of their loose change.

The white Trebbiano is at last being utilized to produce light whites like **Bianco della Lega** and the rather better **Galestro,** usually in tandem with Malvasia.

The **Vernaccia** grape makes Tuscany's most interesting white at San Gimignano; dry, but nutty and slightly honeyed with a fair amount of fruit. And there's one more grape, until recently dismissed as unimportant – the Muscat. **Moscadello di Montalcino** (DOC) is the base for the latest stage in Villa Banfi's plans to take over the world. Villa Banfi are owners of the most widely sold European brands in America – in particular their Riunite Lambrusco – and have invested $36 million in a gigantic vineyard holding in Montalcino.

Over half their vineyards are planted with Moscadello to produce a cheap, mass market wine and, remarkably, it's grown vine for vine alongside those very same Brunello grapes in Montalcino which at present produce Italy's priciest reds. With this biggest upheaval ever to hit Montalcino, maybe the price won't stay sky-high for that much longer.

Today the vintage is mechanized to some extent (as at Vicchiomaggio **above***) and the once ubiquitous Tuscan ox-carts are seldom seen.* **Below** *The turreted town of San Gimignano is the centre of Tuscany's best white wine.*

CENTRAL ITALY/Tuscany

THE IMPORTANT DETAILS

CLASSIFICATION

Tuscany is bang in the middle, not only of all the fuss which the new DOCG regulations are creating, but also the furore created by many forward-looking growers who have been most active in discrediting their local DOC by making high-quality Vino da Tavola according to their beliefs, and selling it for a higher price than the equivalent DOC. Chianti is the biggest DOCG zone in Italy. Chianti Classico is the central and most famous region, situated between Florence and Siena. The quality is more effectively controlled by the Consorzio di Chianti Classico, with its black rooster emblem, than by the fledgling DOCG laws. There are six other Chianti regions, grouped under the collective title of Chianti Putto, which are Colli Aretini, Colli Fiorentini, Colli Senesi, Colline Pisane, Montalbano and Rufina. Some basic wine is simply called Chianti, without further definition. The DOCG laws will require all Chianti samples to be submitted to tasting panels, and if the wines do not pass, then they demote straight to the Vino da Tavola category. An intermediate, less demanding DOC is there for those who do not wish to risk possible demotion. First estimates in 1984 were that up to 30 per cent of Chianti Classico and up to 70 per cent of other Chiantis would be declassified, and, having regularly put myself through the hoop

of comprehensive Chianti tastings, I must say I wasn't surprised.

There are some very good Vini da Tavola in Tuscany, notably Tignanello, Sassicaia, Ghiaie della Furba and Vinattieri which work outside the laws of DOC in the name of quality. Carmignano is a DOCG area allowed to use Cabernet inside the Chianti region, but only because they could prove they'd been classifying and controlling their wines since 1716! The two other DOCGs are Brunello di Montalcino – which produces a frequently excellent big red which, again, does not meet traditional Brunello requirements, under the name Rosso di Montalcino and Vino Nobile di Montepulciano. There are various other reds and whites, the best of which are the DOCs Vernaccia di San Gimignano and Montecarlo.

ORGANIZATION/S

Tuscan wines are produced under very haphazard conditions, but all the finest wines, without exception, come from the single domaines of committed growers and winemakers. Some, like Antinori, manage to combine high standards as growers with quality-orientated merchants' businesses. In general, though, the merchants' commercial blends are one of the reasons why the standards of Tuscan wines have fallen so low.

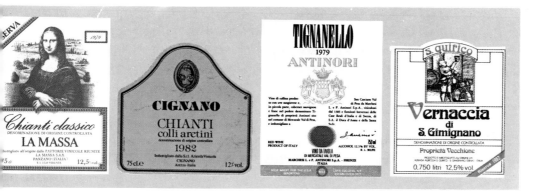

They have wittingly created and offered their brands solely based on price criteria, buying in and blending wines arbitrarily from throughout the region. They are now reaping the whirlwind, with reduced sales and bulging cellars of mediocre wine, though it is the many small peasant-properties which will suffer most. The co-operatives, to which many such small growers also belong, have not been notable for any pre-occupation with quality. In Montalcino, the American Villa Banfi organization have turned the local balance upside down by a massive investment in nearly 3,000 hectares (7,500 acres) and people are cautiously optimistic about the result.

READING THE LABEL

The labels of Chianti, Brunello and Vino Nobile are still in a state of flux as DOCG regulations come into effect yet older wines are still available. The improvement in quality is, so far, patchy. 'Classico' denotes the central and most tightly controlled Chianti areas. 'Riserva' is supposed to mean superior and more mature since it demands a minimum of three years' aging before bottling. In practice it usually means the wine is drying out and losing its fruit. 'Riserva' as a term is only a reliable quality indicator from the best Chianti estates or wines such as Carmignano. The

words 'Vino da Tavola' on a red from a single estate are often a sign of extra quality from grapes not conforming to DOCG regulations.

WHAT DOES IT TASTE LIKE?

The gap between the ideal and actual is wider in Tuscany than in most areas, simply because so many wines of mediocre quality are allowed to sport famous names, or because many fundamentally healthy wines are spoilt by the procedures they are subjected to. There are two basic styles of Chianti. The first is the type of sharp young red which used to come in wicker flasks, and just occasionally still does. This starts out quite purple-red, but within 18 months has taken on a slight orange tinge and is sometimes very slightly prickly, with a rather attractive taste, slightly sour, but backed up by a good, slightly raisiny sweet fruit, a rather stark peppery bite and a tobacco-y spice. This style is traditionally made by the *governo* method, which involves adding in a little concentrated Tuscan grape juice to the wine before bottling. This causes the slight sweetness and prickle. It makes very good food wine, and I'm sorry this method is used less and less.

The second type is traditionally several years old, light red fading to orange in colour. The taste is tannic, with an almost lemony searing acidity. Yet the increasing number of

CENTRAL ITALY/Tuscany

THE IMPORTANT DETAILS

good examples do show with this toughness a range of strawberry, raspberry or blackcurrant flavours – slightly raw, but backed up by a herby, tobacco-y spice – which makes the wine demanding but exciting. Most Chiantis of more than four years old have all the acidity and tannin, but the only fruit on show is likely to be a fistful of sour raisins and a curious and unwelcome whiff of tomatoes. The Cabernet-based Vini da Tavola like Tignanello and the DOC Carmignano are notable for the pure sweet fragrance of blackcurrant fruit and a certain toughness which inspires confidence in the wine's aging potential rather than merely concern about the enamel on the teeth. Vino Nobile di Montepulciano has the Chianti characteristics, but magnified. Usually this means more pepper, acid and tannin but occasionally a fine Vino Nobile surfaces and it can have a marvellous dry fragrance almost reminiscent of sandalwood, backed up by good Sangiovese spice.

Brunello, also, is more often than not a disappointment, due to having lost its fruit during the interminable four years' wood aging requirement, but when the fruit has held out against the oxidation it can achieve a remarkable combination of flavours. Raisins, pepper, acidity, tannin are all there, but that

Castello di Cacchiano, to the north-east of Siena, **above,** *and Castell' in Villa, at the southern limit of the Chianti Classico area,* **below,** *are good examples of the sort of single property that produces most of the finest Chiantis.*

haunting sandalwood perfume can appear again, and the whole thing is bound together by an austere richness resembling liquorice and fierce black chocolate. As such, I'll admit, it can be great wine. The whites are less exciting, though the honey of the Vernaccia di San Gimignano and the rather lanolin nuttiness of Montecarlo can be good. The Galestro usually tastes of greengages!

THE GOOD YEARS

Quality and consistency in Tuscan vintage years look increasingly to divide down a pre-DOCG, post-DOCG line. Among the post-DOCG vintages those of 1988 and 1985 are two fine examples which at last allow us to see what Tuscany can do. Both 1988 and 1985 are gorgeously rich and ripe – even at the lower levels – a remark I couldn't have made two or three years ago. The 1986 vintage was good if lean in structure and 1983 and 1982 are two more excellent vintages. Both are bedevilled by slap-dash wine-making, but the good examples are exciting, and show what we can expect for the even better 1985s and 1988s as they mature. In all these vintages some of the finest wines are non-classified, barrel-aged superior Vini di Tavola, often with Cabernet adding fruit to the Sangiovese. Brunello and Vino Nobile also had fine vintages in 1988/5/3/2 but they are a thoroughly difficult style to appreciate and the first DOCG wines showed little improvement. 1977 and 1979 are worth looking at, though the highly-praised 1987s are disappointing.

ENJOYING THE WINES

Tuscan wines have to be used with food. The Vernaccia and Montecarlo are wines with a fair amount of body which would go well with the local strongly herbed salads and bean dishes. With most of the simple Tuscan meat dishes, liberally coated in the wonderful local olive oil and herbs, I would drink very young Tuscan Vino Rosso or unclassified Sangiovese Vino da Tavola and, with the bigger, stronger-tasting dishes, either Rosso di Montalcino or one of the Cabernet-influenced reds.

The dry Chiantis or the big, burly Brunellos or Vino Nobiles I would drink with the big roasts of game and beef if they had fruit, and drink them with the local pasta, *ribollita* soup or Pecorino cheese if they didn't. The curious Vin Santo, though almost never exported in its honest and traditional state, can make quite a decent, leisurely after-food relaxer.

CONSUMER INFORMATION

WHAT DO I GET FOR MY MONEY?
Tuscan wines veer from some of Italy's cheapest to her most expensive, yet at neither end is the value particularly good. At the top, the flavours of **Brunello** have yet to justify the price to me, and all the most enjoyable ones I have tasted have been from serious producers outside the ring of 'leading estates'. The same could be said for **Vino Nobile**. In **Chianti**, there is good, cheap wine available locally; indeed, drunk in the year of the vintage, it can be delicious, refreshing red, but again, too much of the exported Chianti is neither good, nor value for money. Estates worth watching would include Antinori, Fonterutoli, Riecine, Badia a Coltibuono. Podere il Palazzino, Volpaia, Monte Vertine, San Polo in Rosso and Isole e Olena. **Carmignano,** particularly from Capezzana, is very good and not expensive. **Sassicaia** and **Tignanello,** with an increasing number of other 'mavericks', are expensive and excellent. The whites are usually of a fair quality.

AVAILABILITY
Chianti *per se* is possibly the world's most famous wine, and as such is available almost everywhere. However, good Chianti is rare, because most importers believe they can only sell Chianti on price at the bottom of the market. Unless we begin to take an interest in the finer estates, this unfortunate situation won't change. The other Tuscan wines are not widely available. Brunello and Vino Nobile are rare and seldom worth the risk, though Rosso di Montalcino is. However, Carmignano, Sassicaia, Tignanello etc., are also rare, but well worth the asking price.

CONSUMER CHECKLIST		
Brunello di Montalcino 1985	Q: 1 2 3 4 5 6 **7 8** 9 10	
	P: 1 2 3 4 5 6 7 **8 9** 10	
	V: 1 2 3 4 **5** 6 7 8 9 10	
Chianti Classico 1985	Q: 1 2 3 4 5 6 **7 8** 9 10	
	P: 1 2 3 4 5 **6** 7 8 9 10	
	V: 1 2 3 4 5 6 **7 8** 9 10	

Good Years Traditionally most Tuscan reds have undergone a good deal of wood-aging, the best wines are increasingly being released for drinking young and fruity, if sometimes a little tough. Recent successes: 1988, 1986, 1985, 1983, 1982, 1979.

Taste Notes Chianti veers from the delicious to the very basic, but at its herby, rather aggressive best is one of the best accompaniments to spicy Italian food.

CENTRAL ITALY

ABRUZZI

The Abruzzi is very much a one-vine vineyard, and that vine is the excellent Montepulciano vine, which is the basis for all its red and rosé wines, and constitutes the only red DOC – **Montepulciano d'Abruzzo**. Montepulciano is one of Italy's most underrated grapes, because, while it has the characteristic toughness of Italian red varieties, it also has fruit – masses of it. A good Montepulciano d'Abruzzo manages to be citrus fresh, and plummily rich, the fruit sweet yet biting. Great wines are made by producers such as Mezzanotte and Pepe while the standard of co-ops such as Casal Thaulero and Tollo is remarkably high. Prices are *not* high, and this rather forgotten red from the Adriatic seaboard is one of Italy's most consistent wines. I have never had a bad bottle or an overpriced one – an almost unheard-of statement concerning Italian wine! The rosé is called **Cerasuolo** or 'cherry' and is good, though not making the best of the Montepulciano fruit. The white DOC **Trebbiano d'Abruzzo** is less exciting but adequate.

UMBRIA

It must be all too easy to feel overshadowed when you are nestled next to Italy's most famous and loudest-mouthed wine region. Even Umbria's most famous wine, **Orvieto** (DOC), has seemed to go into decline. Yet, as Tuscany's fortunes have become ever more mixed, Umbria has got its act together. The prime mover in this resurrection was Dr Lungarotti, who, during the 1960s, virtually created the DOC of Torgiano single-handed. At the same time, Orvieto shook off its old semi-sweet, yellow-gold image, and emerged, less dowdy and, if anything, rather too slick, but just right to benefit from the boom in light white wine.

Orvieto used to have a rich, smoky honey flavour, which was chiefly from the Grechetto and Malvasia grapes and historically made in the slightly sweet, *abboccato* style. Its modern pale, very dry style owes more to the feckless Trebbiano. **Torgiano** is best known for Lungarotti's **Rubesco** – a full, plummy red, but unless you like a disconcerting amount of fizz and a slight sour yeast flavour in your reds, this is no longer the wine it was. Much better are the experiments with Cabernet Sauvignon, showing once again how suited central Italy is to this grape and the excellent Rubesco Riserva from the single Monticchio vineyard. The Torgiano whites, however, show a freshness and straightforward fruit not often found in central Italy, and can be excellent. Lungarotti's dry, refreshing **Torre di Giano** and **Chardonnay di Miralduolo** show what can be done.

There are a variety of less well known wines in Umbria. The best red is from the Sagrantino grape and as **Sagrantino di Montefalco** (DOC) can have a tremendous, shocking, sweet-and-sour richness. The best whites are based on the Grechetto grape. Two recent DOCs, **Colli Altotiberini** and **Colli de Trasimeno**, whose most famous producer is Lamborghini, are fairly unexciting.

Good vintages are important for the Torgiano wines and for Sagrantino reds, but the rest should be drunk young. The finer reds are excellent companions for the surprisingly common truffle dishes. Torgiano wines are not cheap, though other Umbrian wines are usually fairly priced. Orvieto is widely available, and **Rubesco di Torgiano** is not too difficult to find, but other Umbrian wines are not much seen.

The town of Orvieto remains unchanged while the wine, once an old-style, honey and nuts type, could now be any one of a dozen ultra-modern, high-tech whites.

EMILIA-ROMAGNA

Emilia-Romagna is centred round Bologna, frequently described as the 'belly of Italy'. So it makes sense that the region annually has a battle royal with Sicily to see who will be the nation's top producer. Sicily usually wins by the odd litre in a million. And the wine which swamps the region is the thought-free thirst-quencher *par excellence* – **Lambrusco**. In America, led by the Riunite brand, Lambrusco accounts for about half of all Italian imports, and with the advent of a very successful white version to match the red, Britain looks ready to fall before the fizzy tide.

Good Lambrusco should be lightly fizzy, low in alcohol, red or white, ranging from dry to vaguely sweet – but it should *always* have a sharp, almost rasping acid bite to it. Most Lambrusco is not DOC and is softened for fear of offending consumers, which is a pity, because this type of 'baby-juice' is often right-ly derided as feeble stuff. Real Lambrusco, with a DOC, from Modena, Sorbara or Castelvetro is anything but feeble. However, the region isn't all Lambrusco; **Colli Piacentini**, **Gutturnio** and **Bonarda** reds are strong and excellent accompaniments to Bologna's big blowouts. The rather vapid **Albana di Romagna** (DOCG) achieved brief notoriety when political pressure finally got it accepted as Italy's first white DOCG. Drunk very young and red **Sangiovese** (DOC) and white **Trebbiano di Romagna** (DOC) are also good all-dinner-long drinks, and there is a remarkable array of 'foreign' wines, from such grapes as Chardonnay, Cabernet, Sauvignon and even Müller-Thurgau, which are clean, light, and very drinkable. The Cabernet and Chardonnay wines of Vallania, and the Barbarossa and Pagadebit wine of Pezzi show the region's quality potential.

CENTRAL ITALY

MARCHES

Verdicchio vineyards near Ancona. After Soave, Verdicchio is probably Italy's most famous white.

This long hilly sea coast region to the south of Emilia has one world-famous wine – Verdicchio. Only Soave of Italy's dry whites produces more wine, and only Soave exports more to the United States. Yet the general standard of Verdicchio is far higher than that of Soave. It is made from the Verdicchio grape, with a little Trebbiano and Malvasia.

There are two leading styles – **Verdicchio dei Castelli di Jesi** (DOC) – famous for its amphora-shaped green bottle which was actually only invented in the 1950s as a good sales gambit! – and **Verdicchio di Matelica** (DOC). Verdicchio is a very reliable light, dry white, fairly neutral, but above all clean, and justly appreciated even by the French for its suitability with fish and seafood. The Matelica wines are rare but do have more flavour. Also rare is sparkling Verdicchio, which can be excellent from a producer like Garofoli or Colonnara. However, the majority of Marches wine is red, and can be very good because the chief grape is the excellent Montepulciano. **Rosso Cònero** (DOC) and to a lesser extent, **Rosso Piceno** (DOC) are sturdy reds, mixing herbs and fruit with a frequent slight prickle, because, as in Chianti, the *governo* method (see p. 203) is much practised here. Some people, like Mecvini, even use new oak barrels with excellent results. Marches wines are never Italy's cheapest, but are usually worth the slightly higher price.

LATIUM

Latium is the very attractive hill-studded region which surrounds Rome. Romans have always been particularly thirsty people and the chief objective of most of Latium's viticulture seems to be to keep the tumbrils laden with gulping wine trundling up the Appian Way to the city. Nearly all of Latium's famous wine is white, yet it is unlikely that any of us will ever taste her best wine unless we head into the hills of Frascati, Marino or Montecompatri, because these frothy, gurgling white wines have always been useless at travelling, often even at being bottled, and the 30-km (18-mile) journey in from the vineyards to the sidewalk cafés is too much for most of them. So true **Frascati** (DOC) remains a mirage for almost everybody, since nowadays most of it is spoilt by pasteurization before sale. It is made from Malvasia and Trebbiano, and it should have a lovely white, fresh feel, nutty, and with an unusual but very attractive tang of rather sour cream about it. That sort of knife-edge flavour is never achieved on the export market where, at least, it is often decent, reliable white. **Marino** (DOC), from the next-door village

south of Rome is becoming increasingly popular with the Romans, and although in bottle it doesn't have much 'sour cream' softness either, it is usually fresher than Frascati, as is the somewhat peppery, appley **Montecompatri** (DOC) from the neighbouring village on the other side. Don't have high expectations of these, don't age them, don't pay too much for them, but, when in Rome . . . Other 'Roma' whites worth taking a slug of are the soft and slightly *frizzante* **Colli Lanuvini Bianco** (DOC) and the very good, fruity white of **Cerveteri** (DOC), north-west of Rome. North of this, at Montefiascone, is a wine which is indeed usually an overpriced fiasco – **Est! Est!! Est!!!** (DOC). This ridiculous name is supposed to reflect the hysterically repetitive enthusiasm of a visiting bishop's butler in the twelfth century. Rarely the real thing, it should have a gentle angelica and almond paste sort of fruit when it is. However, the Romans don't only drink whites. **Aprilia** (DOC) has some good Merlot, the **Cerveteri** (DOC) reds are tough but tasty and **Velletri** (DOC) make some rather dusty but ripe and soft reds.

SOUTHERN ITALY

Setting out from Rome with the compass set due south-east, you are heading into the most concentrated and productive vineyard land in the world. But try to think of a single famous name, and you will draw an almost total blank. Lacryma Christi we've all heard of but probably never drunk a bottle which was halfway decent. Marsala we've heard of but never tried a mouthful except in the frothy golden confines of a *zabaglione*. Aglianico del Vulture? If I said it's one of Italy's greatest red wines, would we be any the wiser? Probably not, because, great though it may be, Naples and Rome have taken care of its fate up till now. So this sweep through the south is of necessity going to sound a little un-

familiar. But be patient, because as wine-making modernizes and the demand for base blending wines drops, there may be some future classics huddled into the nooks and crannies of these parched and daunting hillsides which will one day have us excitedly waving our cheques and feverishly consulting our reference books.

MOLISE

It would be easier to simply ascribe a little footnote saying – oh, yes, there is a province called Molise which has no DOC wines at all, and so we can't really comment. But things are changing. Molise does at last have a pair of bouncy young DOCs, to grace this rather at-

SOUTHERN ITALY

tractive forgotten chunk of Italy stretching from the Apennines to the Adriatic. The DOCs are **Biferno** and **Pentro,** for both red and white. Although the Trebbiano-based whites don't promise a lot, the reds, with a liberal portion of the excellent sturdy Montepulciano grape, should be fairly beefy and decent once the area settles down.

CAMPANIA

Campania is the most infuriating of provinces. The Greeks and the Romans were infatuated with the wines of this lovely region based round Naples, Sorrento and Mount Vesuvius. Many of their greatest, most fabled wines come from within a day's hike of Naples or Sorrento, and the Falernian draught which Cicero, Horace and the boys grew maudlin and lyrical about in turn, came from the coast north of Naples on the road to Rome.

Nowadays, the authorities reckon that only 0.4 per cent of the wine produced appears under a DOC label. Of these DOC **Capri** is a farce, since the grapes don't even need to be grown on the island of Capri to make the wine. There is a DOC on offer to Campania's most famous wine – **Lacryma Christi del Vesuvio** – but the measure of disregard for even the most fundamental quality control in the region is shown by the fact that the growers' consortium still can't get its act together and enforce the DOC.

However, large amounts of volcanic soil, cooling sea breezes and mountain ranges of various shapes and sizes do show that there *is* an innate quality in the land and the climate, and one has to go inland behind Vesuvius to find any evidence of the potential glories of Campania. Centred on the town of Avellino, the chewy, liquoricy white **Greco di Tufo** (DOC) and the more fragrant **Fiano di Avellino** (DOC) as well as the remarkable plummy but strangely austere **Taurasi** (DOC) from the Aglianico grape show what can be done. Mastroberardino is the most famous producer; his wines are fine but not cheap.

APULIA

Talk to any North Italian winemaker about the South, and it will mean only one thing to him – Apulia. Experienced tasters can frequently be seen spitting out a sample with sour conviction and muttering one of two words – 'Concentrato' or 'Apulia', because

Apulia is the most famous of all the providers of dark strong cutting wines, and concentrated grape juice used to add guts to many frail, pale wines in the north. Her output is massive and she is the fourth member of the 'Big Four' of wine production – Sicily, Emilia-Romagna and Veneto being the other three. However, as the consumption of basic, nameless red and white jug wine declines in Italy, and the demand of the vermouth houses in particular for their neutral but alcoholic whites declines in the face of determined opposition from Sicily, the winds of change are beginning to tease the winemakers into maximizing their resources.

So far, most of the experimental work has been done on whites and rosés. Certainly, the whites are light and clean, and the advent of grapes like Sauvignon, Chardonnay and Pinot Blanc shows the direction things are going. The rosés are mostly still a little hefty and grape-skinny, though new cool fermentation installations will improve things. There have been moves to plant Sangiovese from Tuscany and Merlot, Pinot Noir and Cabernet from France, but Apulia has two forceful, fascinating grapes already: the Negroamaro and the Primitivo. The Negroamaro (meaning 'bitter. black') makes good rich reds; the Primitivo is even better. It ripens incredibly early, often by mid-August, and as such has always, in the past, been the darling of the northern blenders. But now it's emerging under its own flag as a big, peppery, briar-sweet red. Some people say it's the same grape as the Californian Zinfandel. A glass or two of some of these big bruisers from Brindisi nearly convinces you that they just might be on to something.

BASILICATA

It comes as a bit of a shock to find that Potenza, the capital of Basilicata, the southernmost Italian province above Calabria, regularly records lower temperatures than Bolzano, the capital of the Alto Adige within spitting distance of the Dolomites and Austria in the far north. This, combined with a barren rock-strewn landscape which, one feels, had all the goodness sucked out of it generations ago, combines to form what is probably Italy's poorest province even in the chronically poor far south. And it doesn't even have much of a wine industry to sustain it; only the Valle

The south of Italy has long laboured under a reputation of being simply a provider of heavy, dull blending wine to ship off to the the rest of Europe. Although the old style is very much in evidence, this is changing fast.

d'Aosta in the Italian Alps produces less than Basilicata. But one wine makes it almost worthwhile – the rare, elusive and ominously named **Aglianico del Vulture** (DOC). More than 600 m (2,000 ft) up the side of the gaunt Mount Vulture, on wretched, arid land with hardly a scratch of good soil in sight, the Aglianico grapes grow great wine. Not only is it cold up there, but the Aglianico is a very late-ripening grape, of Greek origin. The harvest is late but this big thick-flavoured red wine can be superb. The colour isn't that deep but the tremendous almond paste and chocolate fruit, matched by a tough dusty feel and quite high acidity make for a remarkable wine, which is *not* very expensive. Producers are erratic and only Fratelli d'Angelo can be recommended without reservation.

CALABRIA

One could almost include Calabria as another of the islands, since it seems so far removed from the babble and fuss of Italian life. But this wonderfully distant mountain province occupies the entire 'toe' of Italy in a splendid isolation. Geographically a part of mainland Italy, the mood of the land is wild and untrained. But if we look for this same splendour in her wines, there's not much evidence of it now. Even so, the Greeks called this part of Italy 'Enotria', or the 'land of wine', so it must have been able to deliver the goods at one time. But then, if we delve into Greek preferences in wine 2,500 years ago, their habits of mixing spices and honey, seawater, pitch and goodness knows what don't exactly speak volumes for the basic flavours of the

SOUTHERN ITALY

wines. Because it is so mountainous, Calabria isn't really a big blending wine producer, and her wines are virtually never seen outside the region. **Cirò** (DOC) is her most famous, available in all three colours, but the most exciting Calabrian wine is the **Greco di Gerace** or **Greco di Bianco** (DOC), big, sweet and fairly agricultural in its grape-skinny way, but full of exotic, orange peel fruit.

SARDINIA

If Sicily has rushed into the modern wine world with gay abandon, Sardinia has been more circumspect. But then, the character of this isolated island, and the strong, brash flavours of her wines, have always been out on a limb, away from the headlong currents of mainland Italy. Even so, the Sella & Mosca winery in Alghero, on the north-west side of the island, along with some, though not all, of the co-ops, have begun to drag Sardinia, kicking, into a world where export sales are crucial and the domestic market for high alcohol monsters is on the wane. As elsewhere, do not feel you have to see DOC on the label – you won't find *any* DOC Sella & Mosca wines – but out of several Sardinian wines with a fairly beefy character, the following are worth a try: **Cannonau** (DOC and Vino da tavola) – this can be virtually any colour or strength but is best red and can be exciting sweet and fortified. **Vernaccia** (DOC) – if you like a big, dry sherry taste, this remarkable wine has it a-plenty. **Torbato** – rather good dry whites. These wines are not wildly cheap, but pack a fair punch.

SICILY

This mountainous, aggressively self-assertive island hunched at the southern toe of Italy produces more wine than any other region of Italy. Not only that, but she has seen the trend away from the production of vast amounts of undistinguished blending wine rather earlier than her neighbours and is already producing a good deal of high-quality table wine, as well as her historically famous sweet Marsala and Moscato di Pantelleria.

Marsala (DOC) at its best has a delicious deep, brown sugar sweetness allied to a cutting lip-tingling acidity which makes it surprisingly refreshing for a fortified dessert wine, and also particularly effective in cooking, where the brown richness is kept in check by the acidity. There are several Moscatos about but the **Pantelleria** (DOC) from an island closer to Tunisia than Italy is the most famous.

The dry whites show just what can be done with a determined approach, and a bit of investment in modern machinery and forward-looking winemakers. Most of the best wines do not use a DOC, for the same reasons as elsewhere – restrictions on wine-making initiative and innovation, but the wines can be tart and apple-fresh, while, at the same time, retaining a decent splash of hot southern body. The reds will bring a smile to the face of anyone who regrets the passing of the big, fat, chunky wines which used to pass for Nuits St-Georges and Châteauneuf-du-Pape in the Bad Old Bad Old Days. The thing is, the good bits in a bad burgundy would probably come from Sicily in any case. Well, there's no need to pay burgundy prices for that taste any more: it's alive and well and pouring out of Sicily at a great rate. These reds have that lovely, big, old-fashioned flavour of herbs, chocolate and jammy fruit and they *don't* have the hard, sour taste of over-pressed grape skins which is the problem with most southern reds. Again, don't look for DOC wines; they'll usually be less good, but the produce of concerns like Regaleali, Settesoli, Steri and Libecchio, without DOC, offers very good wine at a very low price.

CONSUMER CHECKLIST

Regaleali (Sicily)		
	Q: 1 2 3 4 **5 6** 7 8 9 10	
	P: 1 2 3 **4** 5 6 7 8 9 10	
	V: 1 2 3 4 5 **6** 7 8 9 10	

Aglianico del Vulture (Basilicata) 1981		
	Q: 1 2 3 4 5 **6 7** 8 9 10	
	P: 1 2 3 4 **5** 6 7 8 9 10	
	V: 1 2 3 4 5 6 **7** 8 9 10	

Good Years In general these are not wines to age, and most vintages are fairly similar. Aglianico del Vulture is particularly good in 1985, 1981, 1978, 1975, and 1973 and needs 6 to 10 years aging. Taurasi is fine and deep from Campania and can age for 20 years.

Taste Notes The south used to be regarded simply as an enormous grape bowl supplying vast amounts of blending wines. Things are now much improved and there is some increasingly good, if simple, wine, coming from these mass producing regions.

SPAIN

Santander •
Bilbao •
Valdeorras
Ribeiro
Navarra
Ampurdan-Costa Brava
Rioja
Ebro ZARAGOZA
Penedés Alella
VALLODOLID
Campo de Borja
Priorato
BARCELONA
Duero
Ribera del Duero
Cariñena
Tarragona
Rueda
Salamanca
MADRID
Utiel-Requena
Mentrida
Valencia
Tajo
La Mancha
VALENCIA
Valdepeñas
Almansa
Valdepenas
Jumilla
Alicante
Alicante
Córdoba
Yecla
Guadalquivir
Montilla-Moriles
Sevilla
Granada
Condado de Huelva
Málaga
Jerez-Sherry
MÁLAGA
Cádiz

DEMARCATED WINE REGIONS

Spain has the largest vineyard area of any country in the world. So she should be choca-bloc with famous names, exciting, individual wines and historical excellence. Then let's name a few of her star turns. Sherry. Certainly. Rioja, yes. Umm . . . Penedès? Cava? Or what about Navarra, Cariñena, Jumilla, Alella or Malaga? It's difficult, isn't it? However, it does reflect what has been Spain's role in wine up till very recently.

Sherry was created by international trade as an international wine. Well, it was actually used as ballast for Dutch and British merchant ships to start with, but they discovered to their surprise that the heavy, coarse wine they set out with from Cadiz to keep the ship upright in the Bay of Biscay could turn out to be a very pleasant mouthful in the chilly dank watering-holes of London and the Low Countries. It is still an international wine, and it's still extremely difficult to find a decent glass of sherry in Spain outside Andalusia, where it is made.

Rioja is the next famous wine. However, it has only been famous abroad for ten years. The Bordeaux and burgundy price spiral of the early 1970s led merchants south over the Pyrenees looking for quality at a price. In Rioja, they found it. But in Spain, Rioja had always been regarded as the one national quality wine. Every hotel wine list would carry some highly priced Riojas – and then carafe wine. No other region had developed a quality reputation for table wine, so the majority of them simply concentrated on producing barrels full of heavy anonymous reds and whites, laden with alcohol and devoid of any recognizable taste. This is further illustrated by the fact that the Defined Quality Control System, called the Denominación de Origen (DO), only has 32 different regions, most of them unheard-of outside their own locality, yet they cover over half the entire vineyard area. So obviously the DO is not so much an assurance of quality as simply a vague geographical convenience. But things are changing. In the face of declining domestic consumption and membership of the European Economic Community, the Spanish government is investing money and expertise in maximizing the evidently vast potential of her vineyards, and in persuading the winemakers that individuality and flavour will sell while Samsonian strength and inky anonymity will lead straight to the poorhouse. With modern wine-making techniques and an overdue awareness of what the consumer wants to drink, we're seeing the beginning of a movement which can bring Spain to the forefront of European table wine production.

NORTHERN SPAIN

The north of Spain is completely dominated by a relatively small region – Rioja. For many years this was regarded as virtually the only quality table-wine region of Spain. This is no longer true, but Rioja still does have a pre-eminent position on the quality table-wine scene in Spain. The other areas of the north are mostly in a state of evolution. Navarra is beginning to produce large amounts of good red, and Rueda and Ribera del Duero, which indeed contain Vega Sicilia, Spain's most expensive wine, are reviving interest in their wines. The other areas of Aragon, Leon and Galicia produce a mixture of blending wines and local jug wine which hasn't quite got its act together yet except on a purely local scale.

There are three regions in the DO Rioja: Rioja Alta (the area round the town of Briones is shown **below**); *Rioja Alavesa,* **right**; *and Rioja Baja, which supplies blending wine to nearly all the Rioja bodegas.*

NORTHERN SPAIN/Rioja

THE GENERAL PICTURE

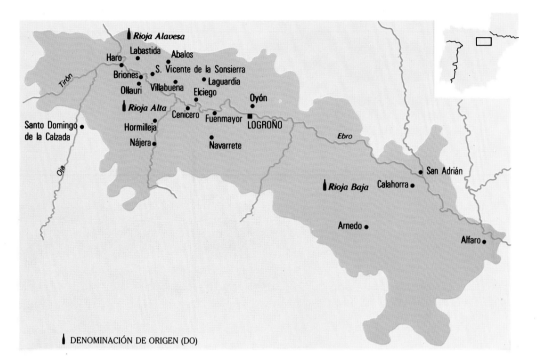

DENOMINACIÓN DE ORIGEN (DO)

The red wine of the Rioja region is the most famous of all Spanish table wines. For many of us it may be the only specific Spanish wine name that comes to mind, even if we've never tasted it. That is our loss. For too long the export markets have looked on Spain simply as the bulk supplier of large amounts of cheap, hefty plonk. Only 15 years ago, with the exception of a few dedicated specialist outlets, no-one outside the Spanish-speaking world sold Rioja, and very few people knew what it was.

But this isn't some kind of *parvenu* wine area we're taking about – these are vineyards which may even pre-date the Romans, and which were certainly thriving before Bordeaux had ever pruned a vine or trodden a grape. Some beady-eyed historians twist the knife further in Bordeaux's side by claiming that the glory of Bordeaux, the Cabernet Sauvignon grape, was actually found in Rioja and transported north by the Romans.

That's quite possible, because, as the crow flies, Bordeaux isn't all that far from Rioja. Rioja is almost due south of Bordeaux, about 300 kilometres (186 miles) up over the Pyrenees, snuggling in the high, thin-aired mountain valley of the River Oja. But wherever the Cabernet came from, the next moves came from Bordeaux. As Bordeaux

began to shine in the eighteenth century, her influence was quickly carried south. And the idea from Bordeaux which was to change Rioja's entire future first appeared in 1787 – that of using small oak barrels to mature the good wines, because of the delicious sweet vanilla flavours the wood could impart. It didn't really catch on till the 1860s, but Bordeaux was soon to have good cause to be glad that it had passed on some of its secrets. The Phylloxera vine louse was devastating Bordeaux, destroying vineyards and livelihoods like an avenging flood, but Rioja was as yet unaffected. The Bordelais poured south, bringing their knowhow, their money and their dreams, building a Bordeaux look-alike south of the Pyrenees.

That boom didn't last long. Phylloxera was defeated, and the Frenchmen upped sticks and went home, but they left behind their methods and their skills. And while Bordeaux became one of the centres of modern wine-making techniques, testing, evolving and improving their wines, Rioja slumbered on, simply duplicating the good old original Bordeaux methods.

Throughout Spain and South America, Rioja's unique smooth, buttery style did establish itself as the finest Spain could produce, but it took events in Bordeaux to drag

NORTHERN SPAIN/Rioja

THE GENERAL PICTURE

Rioja into the international limelight. In the early 1970s Bordeaux and its wines became the object of the ragtag band of international financiers and speculators, who saw the great Château wines as an ideal hedge against inflation in that time of global economic turmoil, thinking that such a finite quantity of supreme quality wine would always increase in value faster than inflation. The Bordelais responded with enthusiasm, doubling, tripling prices, and flooding the market in their lust for cash.

Merchants who actually dealt in wine to drink, not to re-sell endlessly like share certificates, could not and would not any longer pay the prices for these glossy-eyed clarets and looked southwards for a replacement. After nearly a century of obscurity, Rioja achieved its place in the sun. With its old-style Bordeaux barrel-aging methods, it provided the cheap alternative to the mature Bordeaux and burgundy wines which were out of the reach of ordinary wine lovers.

It is to Rioja's great credit that this time she took her chance, and established her name internationally for producing at a fair price silky-soft, oaky reds. There are now pressures to reduce the oak influence, and, consequently, the silky softness. If Rioja wants to lose friends and stop influencing people in a rush, she's going about it the right way.

GRAPE VARIETIES AND WINE STYLES

Rioja is red, white and rosé – and there is even a tiny amount of sparkling. However, its fame rests squarely on its red wines, largely because reds in general take much more successfully to oak-aging methods than whites.

There are three main regions in Rioja, the most important being the Rioja Alta, or High Rioja. About 30 important wine companies, or 'bodegas', are based in the Rioja Alta, and although most bodegas blend their wines from all three regions, the Alta-based red wines tend to be firmer and leaner in style. The Alta-based rosés are Rioja's best. Rioja Alavesa is a small area, neighbouring the Alta, and it produces the most delicate, perfumed reds. The Rioja Baja, or Low Rioja, is big, hot and fairly flat, and the wines are similarly stolid. They are needed to give weight to the lighter wines from the other two regions, but they are usually a bit lumpish by themselves. There are now some new vineyard plantings which may improve quality.

The Red Grapes
Tempranillo The best Rioja variety, not intensely coloured, but giving the strawberry-sweet fruit which marks out the best wines, and blending brilliantly with oak.

Garnacha This is the big, solid, alcoholic Grenache found all over southern France. It can be peppery and slightly empty, and is much improved by blending with Tempranillo. Yet it makes a brilliant rosé, especially in the Rioja Alta.

Graciano and **Mazuelo** are two lesser grapes, and there are still patches of Cabernet Sauvignon from those 'Bordeaux days'.

The White Grapes
Viura This is the chief grape. Made in the ultra-modern, cool and slow way, it develops a remarkable sharp grapefruit taste. However, it also takes well to oak and can develop a lovely big, creamy flavour.

Malvasia and **Garnacho Blanco** are the other white grapes.

THE IMPORTANT DETAILS

CLASSIFICATION

This is most important for red Rioja, and is a more useful guide to the style of wine than is the name of the producing company. Here are the main categories of wine, starting from the youngest.

Sin Crianza (literally, 'without nursery') Very young wine, often only a year or so old, probably without oak, and likely to be raw and uninteresting, with the exception of the successful attempt at a Beaujolais style – Viña Faustina.

Con Crianza (literally, 'with nursery') The 'nursery' refers to a statutory period of maturation in oak barrels. The wines must be two years old, and have at least one year in barrel. These are not the best wines but can often have a pleasant light fruit and enough oak sweetness to make a good drink.

Reserva These wines must be at least three years old, with a minimum of one year in barrel; however, in Rioja, a Reserva will usually be at least five years old on release, after at least two years in barrel. These are often the

most enjoyable of all Riojas, having taken on a lot of the sweet vanilla from the oak barrels, without losing their fruit through too many years in oak before bottling.

Gran Reserva These *must* be at least five years old and have at least two years in barrel. In Rioja they are more likely to be at least seven years old, after three to four years in barrel. Though these *can* be the greatest, too frequently all those years in barrel have done for the fruit and one is left with a browning wine, sweet and acid at the same time, and just a little empty, silently bemoaning all the fruit it left behind at the bottom of the barrel.

White and rosé Riojas are not much troubled by classifications, though some whites get wood-aging. These are likely to be deeper in colour, and bottled in clear glass. Green glass is increasingly used for young dry whites.

ORGANIZATION/S

In Rioja, the bodega rules supreme. Although there are some groupings of growers, they almost always sell their grapes or their young wines to the bodegas for use in their blends. The chief reason for this is the expense of making Rioja in the traditional way. Many thousands of expensive oak barrels must be bought for maturing the wine, and a lot of stock must be financed, the amount of wine held by quite an average-sized company running into millions of litres, much of it in oak barrels. So vineyard names and growers' names rarely appear on the labels. There are about 30 co-operatives; some sell wine under their own name, but most sell to the bodegas. Their quality is average.

Left *Laguardia, in the heart of Rioja Alavesa.*
Above *Marqués de Murrieta wines are still made by traditional methods – here a powerful blend of foot treading and a modern 19th-century press!*

THE IMPORTANT DETAILS

READING THE LABEL

Reading a Rioja label correctly also requires looking at the back label since this is where the wine's classification will be recorded, be it Crianza or Reserva, etc. Although in Spain, a wine can simply be labelled '3rd year', '5th year', and so on, stating at what age it was bottled, but not the particular vintage, all EC countries now demand vintage dating.

The label will have:

1. 'Rioja', plus 'Denominación de Origen' (see p. 213).

2. The 'name' or title of the wine, which may be either a registered brand name, or simply the name of the bodega.

3. The vintage. Nowadays this is pretty reliable, though in previous times, if a winemaker thought a vintage particularly good, he'd just go on stamping it on his wines, year after year, until he had a better year.

4. The bodega name. The address, in small letters under the name, may give a clue to the style of the wine (see above, under Grape varieties and wine styles).

WHAT DO THEY TASTE LIKE?

Above all, red Riojas should taste of oak. I'm not suggesting that you dash off and sink your teeth into the nearest dining table, just to check, but try to remember the smells which waft out of a carpenter's shop – they are incredibly sweet and aromatic. Of all the woods used in wine-making, oak has the sweetest sap, and American oak the sweetest of all, so that's what they use. It is full of vanilla, and when a wine has spent a year or two in an oak barrel, it will have caused that vanillin to leach out, giving it a tremendously buttery taste. Butter, vanilla, toffee – these are the sorts of tastes you should get off a good Rioja. The actual fruit content is usually rather light, sometimes peppery, but more often likely to be matching the buttery richness with a kind of strawberry jam sweetness. Add a couple of pieces of toast and you could have it for afternoon tea! Of course, these tastes are not quite as sweet as they sound, but red Rioja is nevertheless one of the softest, most succulent of red wines.

White Riojas *can* also be tremendously golden and buttery, but this style is now on the wane, and the 'New Wave' white Rioja is spanking fresh, zipping full of sharp, breath-catching raw fruit. If anything, it has that acid attack of unsugared grapefruit! A real Space Age gulper.

There are still some wines which catch neither style, not being oaked, nor being fighting fresh. These are just plain dull.

The rosés, or *rosados,* are unfairly over-looked. They are dry, but full of soft fruit, and are some of Europe's best. Pity no-one wants them.

THE GOOD YEARS
Don't be tempted to buy anything too young or too old. A very young wine, that is one or two years old, will have had no chance what-soever to develop any personality, and these basic, unoaked reds are fairly uninteresting and can be positively harsh and fruitless. A wine of 15 to 20 years age may look a bargain, but remember that all the time spent

in oak barrels speeds up the aging of a wine, with the intention of making it taste mature when it is still young. By the time it really is old, it may well be past it. Only the very finest Gran Reservas will hold up this long. A Reserva or Gran Reserva of six to ten years age is most likely to give pleasure, retaining sweetness and fruit and giving a very stylish drink for a low price.

1981 and 1978 are both good years now fading. 1982, 1983, 1985 and 1986 should be better. Whites and rosés should be drunk as young as possible, even the oaky whites not wanting too much age.

ENJOYING THE WINES
Rioja made its international reputation by of-fering in both red and white sumptuous flavours which had previously been associated only with the best wines of Bordeaux and Burgundy – at a fraction of the price. They can still do this – a Reserva red or oaked white is good enough for the finest of cuisines – and go particularly well with the more solid meat and fish dishes of northern Europe – Rioja's cuisine is nothing if not solid! The place is a trencherman's delight, with some of Europe's best asparagus, an ever-present array of spicy sausages and cured ham, stews full of virtually anything, but especially arti-chokes, beans and good doses of garlic. The young whites are sharp and fresh and are ideal wines for seafood and the local speciality of tiny freshwater eels, quick-fried in olive oil, but are a little too dry for apéritif drinking. Only the sweet course wine is missing. There are some sweetish Riojas, but they're not very special.

Far left *An oak barrel 'nursery' for Rioja con crianza.* **Left** *Traditional celebrations after a successful harvest in Rioja include a feast cooked over wood cut from last year's vines.*

CONSUMER INFORMATION

*Rioja's characteristic taste comes from its aging in oak barrels, **left**. Note the light bulb held up to the wine so that sediment can be detected the instant it appears.*

WHAT DO I GET FOR MY MONEY?

Riojas rarely achieve the great heights of complex lingering flavours. The grapes used are just not capable of that kind of fruit, and the wines are a little two-dimensional for the highest class. Even so, they can offer a soft ripeness at almost all price levels, and the buttery influence of those oak barrels is one of wine's great pleasures.

Constant steep prices year after year mean that most Rioja is no longer good value. However, if you like the taste of old wine, it can be unbeatable value. And at the straight Reserva level, the reliable bodegas can offer you a fair glimpse of the good life without burning a hole in your pocket.

AVAILABILITY

Excellent. Only ten years ago one would have said that availability was very poor. Now, however, Rioja has become a household word in many countries, since it managed brilliantly to fill a quality gap when Bordeaux and Burgundy wine prices went loony in the 1970s. Gran Reservas will be difficult to find, but most shops will stock Crianza and Reserva wines.

CONSUMER CHECKLIST

Rioja Gran Reserva 1982	Q:	1	2	3	4	5	**6**	**7**	8	9	10	
	P:	1	2	3	4	5	**6**	7	8	9	10	
	V:	1	2	3	4	**5**	**6**	7	8	9	10	
Rioja Blanco 1989	Q:	1	2	3	**4**	5	6	7	8	9	10	
	P:	1	2	3	**4**	5	6	7	8	9	10	
	V:	1	2	3	**4**	5	6	7	8	9	10	

Good Years Whites and rosés should in general be drunk as soon as they are released on to the market. Reds may well differ according to vintage conditions. 1988, 1986, 1985, 1983 and 1982 are good recent years. Crianza wines are best at 3 to 4 years old, Reservas at 6 to 8 and Gran Reservas at 8 to 12.

Taste Notes Rioja has long been Spain's leading quality area. It is usually associated with soft, vanilla-flavoured red wines of a very traditional style. However, the rosé wines are good, though underappreciated, and the white wines can either be some of Spain's most traditional, with years of oak aging giving rich, yellow wines, or some of Spain's most modern, with almost aggressively sharp, grapefruit-fresh flavours.

ARAGON

Catalonia and Rioja occupy such dominant positions in Spanish table wine production that any region caught in their crossfire is likely to wither under the assault. Aragon, wedged between Catalonia and Rioja, patently suffers by comparison, and though she has three DOs and one of them, **Cariñena**, is relatively well-known, the vast majority of her wine is drunk without name or fame in the local bars and restaurants, or as part of faceless blends.

NAVARRA

Navarra, like Aragon, is in the shadow of Rioja – in fact, some of the lower end Rioja Baja is actually inside Navarra, but the government and winemakers of Navarra have organized themselves to make the best use they can of their 'Rioja Country Cousin' position. They are helped by only having a single DO – that of 'Navarra', and a virtually identical set of grapes to Rioja. The Garnacha is the chief red grape, which means that the wines lack a little of the elegant strawberry perfume of Rioja, but they are much cheaper too, and the Reservas, with a couple of years' aging in oak casks, have a fairly pale colour and a great deal of soft buttery vanilla sweetness. At half the price of a Rioja Reserva they can be extremely good value, from companies like **Chivite, Irache** and **Monte Ory** and **Señorio de Sarria**. Experiments with younger styles are particularly successful, with firms like Monte Ory producing intense strawberry and liquorice flavours in the reds, and good sharp green apple flavours in the whites. Navarra is one to watch.

OLD CASTILE–LEON

This whole area, spreading from the high valleys of Rioja, right across Spain to the Portuguese border, is by no means as important a wine producer as she used to be. However, change is in the air here, too, and several wine regions are undergoing a renaissance. Most important of these is **Rueda,** to the west of Valladolid, one of only two DOs. Rueda is famous, or, rather notorious, for its heavy, oxydized sherry-type wines, high in alcohol, low on fruit and freshness. However, the major Rioja producer, Marqués de Riscal, after a nationwide study, decided Rueda could grow high-quality modern light white wine. The local Verdejo grape is neutral but flexible and the white made by Marqués de Riscal, while certainly not memorable, is clean, simple and balanced in a dry nutty way. They also make a white Reserva Limousin, aged in Limousin oak barrels from France, which is softer and more interesting, and they have planted a big chunk of Sauvignon Blanc, which should be fun. A slightly fruitier, new-style Rueda is Marqués de Griñon, and there are sure to be others.

RIBERA DEL DUERO

This DO is situated north-east of Valladolid, on the River Duero, which, called Douro in Portugal, is the artery of the port-producing region. It contains Spain's most fabled red – the headstrong, fascinating, turbulent wine of Vega Sicilia. Production is limited and prices are sky-high, but you ought

not to miss the chance of trying Vega Sicilia at least once. Aged ten years in oak, the wines, based on a mixture of Bordeaux and local grape varieties, are intensely dark, stinking of sweet oak, and taste quite unique. The tannin seems to remain remorselessly high and the vinegary volatile acidity defies modern definitions of hygiene, yet the fruit is so rich, like Muscovado brown sugar, chocolate and bruised plums all churned together, that it achieves the kind of 'beauty breaking all the rules' that Italy's unwielding giant Barolo often promises, but rarely manages. The lighter, more down-to-earth Valbuena and the newly fashionable Pesquera and Pedrosa are beginning to show the considerable potential of the region.

LEON

The Province of León has no DO, and the wines, while achieving a fair amount of chunky fruit, are not that exciting. The most interesting are the *aguja,* or 'needle', wines, in which bunches of ripe grapes are added to the fermented wine thus starting a small second fermentation, which gives a tiny prickly fizz to the finished wine. It is similar to the *governo* method in Italy (see p. 26).

GALICIA

Galicia, jutting out into the Atlantic, is a wet humid land, draped in lush greenery quite unlike the rest of Spain, and it has the unlikely total of six DOs. Of these, only **Valdeorras,** with its smoky red and sharp dry white, is seen abroad. However, the best wines are the tangy, prickly *vinos verdes* – 'green wines' similar to Portugal's Vinho Verde which grows just to the south. The whites, from Albariño and Treixadura, can be bitingly sharp, full of raw green fruit, and wonderful with *caldeiradas* and numerous seafood dishes of the region, and with the marvellous local concoctions based mostly on tripe and *chorizo*.

NORTH-EAST SPAIN/Catalonia
THE GENERAL PICTURE

It is the north-east which is leading the march towards modernization in Spanish wine, and doing so in uncompromising style. The large Catalonian region is making the biggest splash and, using a mixture of indigenous Spanish grapes and international stars like Cabernet and Chardonnay, some remarkable wines are being produced. Alella to the north of Barcelona, Ampurdán to the north-east and Raimàt to the west are also taking up the challenge of the modern export market, while only Tarragona, producer of big, strong wines, sweet or dry according to whim, is still trundling along in its old-fashioned way.

Catalonia, Spain's north-eastern province, is now rivalling Rioja as Spain's most important wine region. She is doing so by a combination of diverse vineyard locations and Catalan-commercial nous. Miguel Torres at Penedès began it all with a string of increasingly exciting and totally innovative wines at the 1979 French-based Gault-Millau Wine Olympics, where, amidst a potent mixture of disbelief and unfettered enthusiasm, a panel of 27 Frenchmen and just 2 Spaniards voted the Torres Gran Coronas Black Label 1970 top of the prestigious Cabernet class against the best that Bordeaux had to offer. Torres had arrived with a bang, dragging all of Catalonia and the rest of Spain in his wake. Since then the areas of Alella, north of Barcelona, and Raimàt, to the west near Lérida, have leapt on the bandwagon, while Penedès – previously best known for *cava* sparkling wines – is no longer a one-man band as others follow the Torres lead.

GRAPE VARIETIES AND WINE STYLES

Despite Torres's trailblazing with new grape types, most Catalan vineyards are still planted with traditional Spanish varieties. For red wines, these are primarily the Cariñena, the Garnacha, the Monastrell and the Ull de Llebre (known as the Tempranillo in Rioja). Whites are based on Parellada, Xarel-lo and the Macabeo (which is the same as Rioja's Viura). None of these grape types is renowned for perfume and fruit. Tarragona is the biggest Catalan region, producing rather heavy wines, both dry and sweet, while the champagne-method *cava* wines centred on Penedès are the single most important wine style – indeed, the Codorníu company is the largest producer of champagne-method wines in the world. These *cava* wines are good, but always rather full, sometimes a bit peppery or earthy, and could usually do with a bit more fruit.

The still reds and whites of Penedès from traditional producers are fairly big and satisfying without having any great fruit, but the new-style wines from such producers as Viñedos Torres, Jean León, and René Barbier, based on Cabernet Sauvignon, Merlot and Pinot Noir in the reds, and Chardonnay, Chenin Blanc, Sauvignon Blanc and Gewürztraminer in the whites, have an intense fruitness and perfume which is startlingly attractive by any standards.

The Raimàt wines of Lerida are red and white, and the reds in particular, based on Cabernet and Ull de Llebre, are delicious. Alella is another area reviving its fortunes, and the white from Marqués de Alella is nutty, apricoty, off-dry and very good. Elsewhere, the historical Priorato, high in the hills, remains strange, dark, unmoved by the passage of time, while Ampurdán in the north has finally latched on to having the Costa Brava holiday haunt on its doorstep, and has begun to produce a pretty decent Vi Novell after the fresh, fruity style of Beaujolais Nouveau.

THE IMPORTANT DETAILS

CLASSIFICATION

Catalonia has the most varied wine production in Spain, possessing eight DOs, including one for sparkling wine (Cava) and a variety of wines not sold under the DO designation. Many of the most interesting wines, like León's Chardonnay, Torres's Viña Esmeralda, which mixes Muscat and Gewürztraminer, and Raimat Abadia, do not qualify as DOs.

ORGANIZATION/S

The co-operatives are the most important producers in much of Catalonia. In Tarragona one merchant, Bertran, sells nearly 40 per cent of the total production, with ten local co-ops dominating the rest. In Alella the co-op dominates, though the quality comes from the small Marqués de Alella outfit, and in Ampurdán it is the co-ops which are leading the modernization drive. The co-ops are also important in Penedès, but increasingly the top merchants are using their influence to put grape-growers under a contract which includes control of their yields and quality levels.

READING THE LABEL

Since several of the best Catalan wines are not DO, you should check the label to see if it gives a grape type (e.g. Cabernet Sauvignon) or wine style (e.g. Joven, meaning 'young'), or Reserva, which indicates a minimum aging requirement (three years for red, and two years for white and rosé). Sparkling wines must have Cava on the label if they are made by the champagne method, and will be marked according to sweetness from Brut Nature or Brut at the dry end, through Seco, Semiseco, and Semidulce to the pretty rich Dulce. Wines from Sitges and Tarragona may well be sweet, and Tarragona and Priorato make a heavy oxydized type called Rancio – check the label if this adventure into Catalan wine history is not for you.

Old habits live on in Spain; the last basketfuls of grapes are loaded on to the cart after a long day's harvesting in the hot sun.

WHAT DOES IT TASTE LIKE?

The taste of Catalan wine varies enormously, from some of the tangiest, freshest whites and impressive oak-aged reds to the sweet Moscatel flavours of old Sitges and Tarragona, and the blackstrap mouth-fillers of Priorato. What you rarely get in Catalonia is anything bland or anonymous. Memorable, maybe, forgettable, maybe, innocuous, hardly ever.

THE GOOD YEARS

There isn't a great deal of variation in climate to affect vintage, though occasional years like 1984 and 1972 are reckoned to be less than exciting. The vintage will affect red producers more than white, in particular those who are planting high and cool to try to improve grape quality. The reds age well, while the whites are best drunk young.

ENJOYING THE WINE

Catalan whites made by forward-looking winemakers like Torres or Marqués de Alella can be some of Spain's best apéritif wines because of their fresh fruit. The cuisine in Catalonia is more exciting than in most parts of Spain, and her reds in particular are big and tasty enough to go with the local variety of raw hams, *butifarra* sausage, stews based mostly on poultry and game, and herb-perfumed grills. With the seafood and fish *zarzuela,* most reds or whites will do, but a light Ampurdán red or rosé often goes better.

NORTH-EAST SPAIN/Catalonia

CONSUMER INFORMATION

WHAT DO I GET FOR MY MONEY?

The *cava* sparkling wines are much cheaper than champagne and can be fair. Wines from areas like **Tarragona** and **Terra Alta** are cheap, but usually disappear in blends. **Alella** and Raimàt are excellent value. **Penedès** is not cheap from the best producers, but the quality is as high as anywhere in Spain.

AVAILABILITY

Cava wines, from Codorníu and Freixenet in particular, are easily available, and the Torres range of wine is fairly easy to find. Otherwise, the wines are not very widely exported, although there has certainly been an improvement, particularly from Raimàt, Alella, and some Penedès producers, in the last few years.

<table>
<tr><td colspan="5">CONSUMER CHECKLIST</td></tr>
<tr><td>*Cava* champagne</td><td>Q:</td><td>1 2 3 4 **5** 6 7 8 9 10</td></tr>
<tr><td>method</td><td>P:</td><td>1 2 3 **4 5** 6 7 8 9 10</td></tr>
<tr><td></td><td>V:</td><td>1 2 3 4 **5** 6 7 8 9 10</td></tr>
<tr><td>Raimat Abadia</td><td>Q:</td><td>1 2 3 4 5 6 **7** 8 9 10</td></tr>
<tr><td>(red from</td><td>P:</td><td>1 2 3 **4** 5 6 7 8 9 10</td></tr>
<tr><td>Lerida)</td><td>V:</td><td>1 2 3 4 5 6 7 8 **9** 10</td></tr>
<tr><td>Torres</td><td>Q:</td><td>1 2 3 4 5 **6** 7 8 9 10</td></tr>
<tr><td>Esmeralda white</td><td>P:</td><td>1 2 3 **4** 5 6 7 8 9 10</td></tr>
<tr><td></td><td>V:</td><td>1 2 3 4 5 6 7 **8** 9 10</td></tr>
</table>

Good Years In general, the vintage quality is remarkably consistent, and most variations will be due to changes of policy in a winery, rather than particular climatic extremes.

Taste Notes Catalonia offers an increasing variety of wine styles, and is certainly the most imaginative and exciting of Spanish wine areas. Her reds are usually richly fruity, big wines, often with some vanilla taste from oak aging, while the whites range from dry sharp new styles, to big Chardonnays and aromatic Muscats and Gewürztraminers. Sparkling *Cava* wines are unsubtle but good.

CENTRAL SPAIN

With the lowest production costs of any major wine-growing country in Western Europe, the great central swathe of vines which blankets the land from south-west of Madrid right across to Valencia and Alicante in the east has always been able to trade so effectively on price that there has been little incentive to create any individual image for the wines concerned.

Yet at a time when wine surpluses choke much of southern Europe and entry to the EC has brought in regulations which traditional practitioners would find it difficult to comply with, the regions, in any case each possessing a DO, have begun to modernize their wine-making and promote their particular personalities. Not a lot is seen of **Tierra de Barros** and **Mentrida** though both are DOs and sizable areas. Yet these pale into insignificance beside the massive plains of La Mancha, with 5 million hectares (12 million acres) of vines. For long dismissed as the most mediocre kind of base wine producer, **La Mancha** is now bringing in cold fermentation methods (see p. 26) for the whites, and sterile vinification for the reds which are already drawing out quite unexpected fresh flavours from both – and still at rock-bottom price.

Valdepeñas, till now home of soft unmemorable reds, is on the same trail. So far, **Manchuela** and **Almansa** are not following, but the eastern area of the Levante *does* produce wines of considerable character – possibly too much, because the pitch-black palate-scrapers of **Utiel-Requena** are shipped off to less full-blooded climes with the minimum of fuss. Further south, **Alicante, Yecla** and **Jumilla** are just beginning to emerge from a lifetime of aspiring to other people's blending vats, and **Valencia** is already making decent red and whites, and some of the best dry rosés and sweet Muscats in Spain. The wheels are moving, but there's still a lot of rust to loosen.

SOUTHERN SPAIN

The south of Spain is overwhelmingly a fortified wine area, with Montilla, Malaga and sherry from Jerez as its top names. Table wine is produced, mostly at a basic level, but some of sherry's present problems are highlighted by the introduction in Jerez of white table wines made from the over-production of Palomino – the chief grape variety used in sherry.

Montilla, in the fiercely hot hill country near Cordoba, originally shared much of sherry's glory, and shipped much of her wine to help out in Jerez. Even the name 'Amontillado' means 'in the style of Montilla'. However, the region was demarcated in 1945 and has since then suffered mixed fortunes. It makes the same styles of wine as Jerez (though they are fermented in Ali-Baba type earthenware jars known as *tinajas*), but is not allowed to use terms like Fino, Amontillado(!) etc., so the wines are labelled Dry, Medium, etc. They can be good value, but mostly the **Pedro Ximénez** grape is used rather than the Palomino, and the wines rarely achieve the definition of flavour of a good sherry.

Malaga in the far south was hit by Phylloxera very early in 1876 and has struggled since. A pity, because the wines from Pedro Ximénez and Moscatel grapes, which range from nutty and medium dry to big, luscious, smoky, raisiny and very sweet, are good value. They are rarely seen but the Scholtz Hermanos Solera 1885 which in fact contains wine from a 1787 *solera* (see p. 227), is sometimes available and shows what Malaga is capable of.

Map key:
- Barros or Arenas
- Albarizas

Map labels: Trebujena, Sanlúcar de Barrameda, Chipiona, Añina, Macharnudo, JEREZ DE LA FRONTERA, Guadalete, Balbaina, Los Tercios, Puerto de Santa Maria, CÁDIZ, ATLANTIC OCEAN, Chiclana de la Frontera

A Gonzalez Byass property near Jerez de la Frontera. One of the largest and most important sherry firms, Gonzalez Byass, founded in 1835, owns almost 15 per cent of the area's vineyards and is still under family control.

SOUTHERN SPAIN/Sherry

THE GENERAL PICTURE

It is sometimes difficult to remember that sherry comes from Spain. A recent generic advertising campaign in Britain went out of its way to emphasize that sherry does indeed come from Spain, stating that 'True Sherry comes only from the ancient vineyards of Jerez' and suggesting that for further information about authentic sherry, we should write to The Sherry Institute *of Spain*.

What all this means is that the title 'sherry' has come to describe a *type* of wine, not an actual wine. However, although *true sherry* does only come from Spain, the wine style which developed during the eighteenth and nineteenth centuries became so popular that it spawned imitations throughout the world. In particular wherever entirely new vineyard areas were being developed, one of the first things the pioneers would do was to create a 'sherry'. Cyprus, South Africa and Australia all made early reputations doing just that.

The name 'sherry' is an anglicization of the word 'Jerez', pronounced 'hereth' by Spaniards but more likely 'sherezh' by the slightly tipsy sailors whose job it was to haul this rough, crass wine back to northern Europe. Jerez de la Frontera is the central town of the sherry-producing region, about 16 kilometres (10 miles) from the Bay of Cadiz in the south-west corner of Spain. As with port and madeira in the south of Europe, and champagne in the north, the basic wine style wasn't very nice – in this case dull and flaccid – but at least it was strong in alcohol and therefore found a ready market in the cold north. As with port and madeira, much of the business was created by Irish and English businessmen funding companies in and around Jerez, and as tastes became more sophisticated, they learned how to create a remarkable array of tastes out of this strong local wine.

What gives sherry its remarkable flavours is, firstly, the incidence of a swathe of chalky soil, or *albariza*, which sweeps right across the central growing area. Chalk always produces particularly light, fresh-tasting wines. This means that, with modern techniques, wines of considerable delicacy can be produced, even in such a torrid region as this. Secondly, there is the remarkable phenomenon of the *flor*. After fermentation, the wines are put into barrels of 500 litres called butts, but only four-fifths full. The finest wines rapidly develop a gungey, creamy film on their surface. This film is the *flor* and is in fact a protec-

Modern methods enable today's sherry producer to exercise much greater control of the wine than was possible in the past. To produce sweeter grapes the fruit may be left to dry out in the sun, as it is at Gonzalez Byass, **left.**

tive layer of yeast which sits on the top of the liquid, and, while imparting a rather pungent, almost sour herbiness, to the wine, also stops it oxydizing. The wines which develop this *flor* are the ones that will become dry Fino sherries.

If the *flor* looks unlikely to grow, the wine is fortified with brandy to stop any further fermentation activity and these wines then undergo the opposite treatment to the light Finos. They are put in barrels with the whole objective of the air's oxydizing them. It is at this moment in a young sherry's life that the path divides for good between the more favoured, light Fino wines, and the more lumpish, browning Oloroso types. I always used to feel a bit sad for the Oloroso fatties who failed to make the cut, but good Olorosos can finally achieve even greater heights than Finos.

GRAPE VARIETIES AND WINE STYLES

The dominant grape is the Palomino, but whereas for a dry Fino the wine will probably be 100 per cent Palomino, for the sweeter and darker sherry styles, the Pedro Ximénez and the Moscatel – both fermented separately for sweetness, and sometimes boiled down to 20 per cent of their original volume, to make them intensely dark and sweet – will be added in small quantities to adjust both colour and sweetness of a blend.

There are two basic styles of sherry – Fino and Oloroso – each with certain further subdivisions (see also Classification). **Fino** is pale and dry, with a quite unnerving austere woodiness to it. It is usually drunk cool and young. **Manzanilla** is a form of Fino matured by the sea at Sanlúcar de Barrameda. It can be almost savoury dry and have a definite whiff of sea salt – if you're lucky to catch it young enough.

The most widely used name for sherry is **Amontillado**. Usually this simply means a downmarket, bland, vaguely sweetened medium drink of no great style or interest. However, it *should* be a term applied only to aged Fino which has deepened and darkened in cask to a tantalizing nutty dryness. Very occasionally this is still true.

Olorosos in their natural state are deep, dark, packed with violent burnt flavours – yet totally dry. In that state drinking them would be a Lenten penance rather than a pleasure, and so they surface, sweetened to various

levels with Pedro Ximénez and Moscatel. Though some are labelled Oloroso, they will usually be titled Milk, Cream, Amoroso or Brown. Pale Creams, interestingly, are not Olorosos, but sweetened Finos.

Finally, **Palo Cortado** is a 'half-breed' sherry which got confused and developed both Fino and Oloroso characteristics. It is rare and should be superb with a pungent acid bite.

Oloroso sherries which are naturally dry are sweetened and darkened by the addition of concentrated treacly wines called arrope.

THE SOLERA SYSTEM

All sherry is blended, from different vineyards, wine styles and vintages. The objective is to achieve consistency in a blend year-in year-out. To this end a *solera*, or group of butts of sherry of a particular style, is begun. Each year wines of a similar character are put into another series of butts in the same group. As the older wine matures, it is partially drawn off, and topped up with the next oldest wine in its group, which is then topped up by the next oldest, right back to the *criadera* or 'nursery' where the youngest wine is waiting. The younger wine quickly takes on the character of the older wine it is topping up. There are some *soleras,* for famous wines like San Patricio or Tio Pepe, which were begun a century ago. These fine old 'staircases' of blends gain enormous depth of flavour, and the commercial blends of any substance all rely on a proportion of old *solera* wine for their quality.

SOUTHERN SPAIN/Sherry

THE IMPORTANT DETAILS

CLASSIFICATION

The vineyards of Jerez are divided into three classes. *Albariza* is white chalky clay and is termed Superior. All bodegas must use a proportion of Superior wine, but, since 70 per cent of all vineyard land is now Superior, as inferior vines are grubbed up, this doesn't present a problem. *Barro,* the second vineyard class, is heavier clay, producing heavier wine. *Arena,* the third class, is sand and is in fact being returned to tomatoes and grain which it's much better at.

The wine is also classified in the cellars. Initially, wines with a strong *flor* growth are classified as Finos, those without as Olorosos. Fino wines are then further classified by *palmas* – 'palms' chalked on the barrels – the more *palmas* the better. Olorosos are marked with *rayas* or single strokes of chalk, and the less *rayas* the better! Later these classifications are further broken down as character becomes evident so that, for instance, a Palma Cortada will be a full Fino beginning to incline towards Amontillado, while a Palo Cortado will be an initially delicate wine which failed to develop *flor.* Once the potential style of the wine becomes apparent – usually during the first year – it will be assigned to a *solera,* and taken to the *criadera* or 'nursery' to begin its life in the *solera* system (see page 227).

ORGANIZATION/S

Since the production of sherry is a continual process involving a number of years aging, the shippers who process the wine are very much the dominant feature of Jerez life. Many of them own large vineyards. There are, even so, large numbers of smallholders who will usually be under contract to a shipper, or belong to a co-operative, of which there are seven. These are quite important, controlling about 20 per cent of the vineyards. One co-op at Sanlúcar even markets its own wines under the C.A.Y.D. brand.

READING THE LABEL

The first thing is to check that the wine really is Spanish since other countries' wines labelled as sherry are still circulating widely, and likely to do so for some years yet. In general terms, a sherry label will either show the wine's official style – Fino, Manzanilla, Amontillado, etc. – or else it will describe it in more or less fanciful terms. Occasionally, a special term will be included and this will virtually guarantee high quality. Examples are Palo Cortado, Dos Cortados, Fino Viejo or Manzanilla Pasada. The first two are delicate but well-flavoured Oloroso styles, the last two intensely flavoured old Fino styles. Most sherry is now bottled in Spain, and this can be checked from the label, or from the official seal over the cork.

WHAT DOES IT TASTE LIKE?

Good sherry, dry or sweet, has a bite to it. After all, it is fairly high in alcohol, a lightly fortified Fino being 15 to 18 per cent in strength, while a big Oloroso may be up to 24 per cent. Also, even the youngest Fino should be four to five years old, and the wine will have been gaining flavour all this time. Old sherries have a positively painful intensity of flavour mixing sweet and sour, rich and dry all at once. However, most brands nowadays are aiming for mass acceptance and are bland and forgettable. This is a particular problem in the 'medium' sector which embraces many leading brand names.

THE GOOD YEARS

Certainly some harvests are better than others, but the *solera* system is designed to even this out. Very occasionally the starting date of a *solera* will be named on a Special brand, like Gonzalez Byass's 'Solera 1847'. Occasionally wines are marked with their bottling date. Since good Olorosos improve in bottle, these can be very exciting.

ENJOYING THE WINE

Sherry got itself rather stuck in a dowdy, compromise 'when you couldn't think of anything else to order' situation, which rather limited its usefulness, but it is in fact a fairly versatile drink. Fino or Manzanilla sherry, fresh and frigidaire-cool, is a wonderful anytime drink, strong enough to brighten you up, fresh and biting enough to refresh you, and as an appetite-whetter before dinner it is difficult to beat. Not only that, but chilled down or kept cool with a lump of ice, you can easily drink it *through* a meal. Finos and Manzanillas must be drunk as young as possible, and will deteriorate quickly after opening.

Medium sherries are still often makeweights, but these too can be improved by chilling, and there are now brands specifically created to go with soda, or lemonade or tonic water – which ends up tasting, of all things, like a rather refreshing vermouth! Sweet sherries are usually not quite sweet enough to accompany puddings, but their acid bite can nevertheless make them very welcome after a meal.

CONSUMER INFORMATION

WHAT DO I GET FOR MY MONEY?

Sadly, there is a lot of very second-rate sherry on the market, at an impossibly low price. Sherry is an expensive wine to produce and requires care and skill to make well. Much of the sherry at present on sale does no credit to the region. Much of this can be traced to the collapse of the giant RUMASA company which controlled many bodegas. The government and the shippers have both stated their intention of returning to a quality-first approach. The top Finos, like Garvey's **San Patricio**, La Riva's **Tres Palmas**, Gonzalez Byass's **Tio Pepe** or Domecq's **La Ina** have kept their standard but most of the medium and sweet brands are dull indeed. However, the rare, specially bottled sherries, and in particular ones from a single small stockholder or *almacenista* are often superlative wines and very cheap for what they represent.

AVAILABILITY

The International Brands are widely available, especially in the USA, Great Britain, the Netherlands, Belgium and Germany. However, to buy a good Fino at peak freshness, or an interesting Oloroso or sweet sherry is not easy. Rare specialist sherries and *almacenistas'* individual wines are some of the most difficult of any great wine style to obtain. But to get to the heart of sherry as a great yet underrated drink, you should try to locate an example.

```
┌─────────────────────────────────────────────┐
│            CONSUMER CHECKLIST                 │
│                                               │
│ Fino La Ina     Q: 1 2 3 4 5 6 7 8 9 10       │
│                 P: 1 2 3 4 5 6 7 8 9 10       │
│                 V: 1 2 3 4 5 6 7 8 9 10       │
│                                               │
│ Palo Cortado    Q: 1 2 3 4 5 6 7 8 9 10       │
│ Lustau          P: 1 2 3 4 5 6 7 8 9 10       │
│                 V: 1 2 3 4 5 6 7 8 9 10       │
└─────────────────────────────────────────────┘
```

CONSUMER CHECKLIST

Fino La Ina	Q:	1 2 3 4 5 6 **7** 8 9 10
	P:	1 2 3 4 **5** 6 7 8 9 10
	V:	1 2 3 4 5 6 7 **8** 9 10
Palo Cortado	Q:	1 2 3 4 5 6 7 **8** 9 10
Lustau	P:	1 2 3 4 5 **6** 7 8 9 10
	V:	1 2 3 4 5 6 7 8 **9** 10

Good Years There are no vintage years as such in sherry. Obviously there are some vintage variations, but virtually all sherries are blends of several years.

Taste Notes Sherry is only the real thing when it comes from the south-west corner of Spain centred on the Andalusian town of Jerez de la Frontera. Many other countries have copied the style, but none have quite got it right. However, true sherry does come in a wide range of styles, and a wide range of qualities, ranging from cheap, forgettable medium sweet blends to fine, handcrafted wines of quite inimitable, penetrating character.

PORTUGAL

I DEMARCATED WINE REGIONS

The wine most enthusiastically glugged at home is Vinho Verde – wonderful with oily local dishes but a complete non-starter abroad. Mateus Rosé, on the other hand, is now one of the most successful brands on earth yet the conservative Portuguese drinker hardly drinks a bottle himself.

If this makes Portugal sound a little offbeat, that's not far from the truth, and, indeed, apart from her famous fortified wines of port and madeira and her rosés, Portuguese wines *are* little known abroad. She is nevertheless a formidable producer, usually occupying seventh position in the world league. She is an even more formidable consumer. At a time when historically important wine-producing nations are suffering a decline in consumption, Portugal is knocking it back in large quantities.

Portugal was the first European country to begin to classify and demarcate her vineyards. The Douro valley was classified for port pro-duction as early as 1756, and the Dão area was keen to protect its reputation by law way back in the thirteenth century. By 1908, eight separate types of wine/areas of production had been officially demarcated, with three more being added in 1979. Today there are 14, with further additions in the pipeline. The most important of all the demarcated areas is Vinho Verde, covering the northern part of the country. The centre has two im-portant wines, Dão and the new Bairrada, while the south is a mixture of historically revered yet declining production – Colares, Carcavelos, Setúbal and Bucelas – along with the mass production lands of the Alentejo and Ribatejo and the Algarve.

There can't be many wine-producing countries whose finest wines are often blends cloaked in anonymity with no hint as to where they came from or what grapes made them. There can't be many countries whose most eagerly drunk wine at home has totally failed to make the least impression on the ex-port market, or whose wildly successful wine export is not even noticed by her own drinkers. Yet these paradoxes, and many others, are true of Portugal, one of the most roguishly wilful and independent of Europe's wine producers. Many of her best wines are simply called 'Garrafeira' or 'Merchants' specially matured selection' – the label giving no idea, apart from a brand name, as to what actually constitutes the wine. Membership of the European Economic Community is chang-ing attitudes and there is already a move to give regional and varietal identity to the wines.

THE NORTH

The Minho region, from Oporto up to the northern Spanish border, is disorganized, hilly and lush, with torrential downpours and blin-ding sun trading places throughout the sum-mer and vines literally sprawling all over the landscape, since most vinegrowers are smallholders.

This is the land of **Vinho Verde** – literally, Green Wine. Seventy per cent of it is, surpris-ingly, red, made from four different native grapes, of which the Vinhão is the best. The wine is wonderfully sharp, harsh even, and is the perfect accompaniment to the numerous varieties of *bacalhao* or dried cod which would murder any wine of less stark flavours. The white wines are considered more suitable for export. They are naturally low in alcohol and high in acidity, but with a brilliant, haunting, peachy peppery taste blending with the tart lemon sharpness. The Loureiro and Trajadura grapes are the most important, with an occasional, bigger style being made from the Alvarinho in the far north. These wines are usually slightly sweetened for export, which is a great pity, since the delicate fragrant fruit is usually lost. Even so, the low alcohol, high acidity, and slight induced sparkle make them good, and cheap, summer wines. The great majority come from co-ops or are sold under merchants' brand names, but there is an increasing tendency for the good growers to bottle their own, and names to look out for are Grinaldi, Quinta da Aveleda, Solar das Bouças and the Palacio de Brejoeira. Two of the best reds, surprisingly, are from the co-operatives of Ponte de Lima and Ponte de Barca. There is no point at all in aging the wines, red or white, but, young and fresh, the whites can make lovely apéritif wines and the reds can cope with just about any dish you might throw at them, from cod to kippers to curry and *chili con carne*.

The Douro valley is primarily concerned with port production. However, only a certain amount of the crop – usually about 40 per cent – is made into port, the rest being sold as table wine. Although the white is a little oily, the reds can be extremely good, and keep their fruit while aging to a gentle, liquoricy mellowness after ten years or so. Traditionally, the grapes for the famous rosé blends came from the wild land above the Douro round Vila Real. Because of their phenomenal success, however, the wines are now drawn from all over Portugal. Mateus and Lancers are remarkable for the consistent, vaguely fizzy drinkability of their product. However, the true rosés do not usually sparkle, are quite a deep pink, and have a fairly strong strawberry flavour.

Top *Vinho Verde vines are trained high to allow other crops to flourish beside them.* **Above** *Portugal is the traditional supplier of top quality corks.*

THE CENTRE

Between Oporto and Lisbon lie Portugal's two greatest red wine areas: Dão, famous for over 700 years, and Bairrada – only recognized in its own right in 1979. **Dão** is an upland eyrie, ringed by mountains, reached by steep, exotic forest-choked river gorges, while **Bairrada** is situated in the flat scrubland towards the sea, where the placid vineyards mingle easily with wheat fields, olive trees and meadows. Portugal differentiates between Vinho Verde, or young wine to be drunk immediately without aging, and Vinho Maduro, or wine for maturing. Dão and Bairrada are Vinho Maduro areas. The maturing usually takes place in a mixture of concrete and large wooden barrels.

PORTUGAL

Dão reds are Portugal's most famous reds, and are reputed to go velvet-smooth with age. My experience is that they rarely achieve this and could do with less aging in wood and more in bottle, to preserve their rather sinewy fruit. The reds are made from a mixture of six grapes, of which Touriga Nacional is the most important, and develop a strong, dry herby taste, almost with a pine resin bite. However, companies like Grão Vasco are making highly successful experiments of aging the reds in smaller, newer oak barrels, and the inherent gentle strawberry fruit is immediately more evident. Dão reds are good, all-purpose food wines, and are not expensive. Exciting wines are rare, but the best names to look for are Grão Vasco, São João and Aliança. The whites, which comprise only 3 per cent of production, are pleasant and dry without being special. The Dão has a curious production system. Only one private estate – Conde de Santar – sells estate-bottled wine. All the other wine is made by co-ops or a couple of tiny wineries, who will then sell the wine to merchants to blend and mature. This is not good for quality, and merchants like Grão Vasco have now entered into associations with single co-ops to try to improve standards.

Bairrada's wines are red and white. Most of Portugal's best champagne-method sparkling wine is based on white Bairrada grapes, in particular the Maria Gomes. However, the red wines are more exciting and frequently overshadow the more famous Dão wines. The chief grape is the Baga, which gives tough tannic red wine, but, though long wooden barrel aging is used as in Dão, the Baga gives a sturdier fruit to the wine, and at ten years' old the resiny bite is apparent, but a delicious dry fruit, is there too. These wines can age 20 to 30 years, and have a great future on the export market. They are becoming easier to find and the Portuguese government is actively promoting them. Interestingly, the best Portuguese merchants will tell you that their own 'Garrafeira' blends are usually based on Bairrada. If Bairrada is as successful under its own colours as it deserves to be, they'll have to look elsewhere for their source of supply.

THE SOUTH

Around Lisbon there are four ancient wine regions, now of decreasing importance.

Carcavelos has almost disappeared under housing re-development but produces a strong, nutty fortified wine which it is sad to see dying out. **Colares** is a blackstrap red wine grown in the sand dunes on the Atlantic from the doughty but scented Ramisco grape. **Bucelas** is a rather fruitless though pleasant white. **Setúbal** is chiefly famous for its fortified Moscatel wine, which, though good, is always a little spirity and never quite as perfume-sweet as one would like. However, Setúbal also grows good red wine, and J.M. da Fonseca of Azeitão is probably Portugal's most innovative wine company. They make Lancers Rosé but also such excellent local styles as Periquita, a juicy red, Tinto da Anfora, herby and dry, and Pasmados, a chunky, chewy red – all without official demarcation – as well as Quinta da Bacalhoa, a highly successful experiment with Cabernet Sauvignon. The wines of the Algarve in the far south are really not very special, but the flatlands of the **Alentejo** are increasingly producing interesting reds, while the less well thought of regions of the **Oeste**, with its enormous Torres Vedras Co-op, and the **Ribatejo**, with its impressive wine company Carvalho, Ribeiro & Ferreira, can also produce a mixture of good juicy wines, and excellent old 'Garrafeira' blends as well.

CONSUMER CHECKLIST

Bairrada	Q:	1 2 3 4 5 **6** 7 8 9 10
Reserva Red	P:	1 2 3 **4** 5 6 7 8 9 10
1985	V:	1 2 3 4 5 6 **7** 8 9 10
Vinho Verde	Q:	1 2 3 4 **5** 6 7 8 9 10
Quinta da	P:	1 2 3 **4** 5 6 7 8 9 10
Aveleda	V:	1 2 3 4 5 **6** 7 8 9 10

Good Years Many of the best wines are still blends of several vintages, though vintage dating for wines like Dão and Bairrada is increasingly important. Vinho Verde is rarely vintage-dated and should be drunk as young as possible.

Taste Notes The whites of the Vinho Verde or 'green wine' style, in particular, can seem rasping and sharp until you get used to them, when they are particularly refreshing, and the dry, though rather resinous, reds also take some getting to know, but, again, it's worth it, because they are original flavours.

PORTUGAL/Port

THE GENERAL PICTURE

The Douro valley is so far removed from the grimy, crazy activity of the city of Oporto at the river's mouth that a child's cry will hang in the still, warm air for a good distance up the hillside terraces above the river banks, whispered conversation seems inevitably indiscreet as the smallest sound fills the night air and the thunder of the mountain train which, for much of the valley, provides the only link with the outside world is so intrusive it physically pains you.

In a country like Portugal, where much of European so-called sophistication seems not yet to have showered its doubtful benefits, the Douro valley is even older, more stuck still in time than any other area, with a remote beauty to its cruelly angled vineyards stumbling down to the idly lapping river's edge that makes a town-tired traveller catch his breath in relief. And from these lovely hills comes port wine, a wine whose worldwide fame was built in the languid smoking-rooms of London's St James's Clubs and the raucous chaos of a thousand urban taverns across Great Britain.

Port is very much a British invention. It came about because of increasing friction between England and France in the late seventeenth century. This meant the usual supply of French table wines dried up, so England looked to Portugal, her oldest ally, for an alternative source of supply. The red wines were the opposite of the light, easy-going French wines, being harsh and lumpish, but as British merchants pushed up the Douro valley away from Oporto, into what was then a completely untamed wilderness, they began experimenting with the local Douro reds and found that if you threw in a bucket or two of brandy, the wine seemed to cope with the sea journey back to England fairly well. It still didn't taste very good, however, until they began adding brandy when the fermentation of the wine hadn't quite finished. Since yeasts suffocate and cease working if the alcohol level is raised sharply, an addition of about one-fifth total volume of strong brandy when the wine is half-fermented will stop the fermentation with a jolt and leave a great deal of natural grape sweetness in the wine. This strong, rich drink proved immensely popular in northern Europe and to this day the principles of making port wine remain the same. The Douro valley didn't do much to give

Sharply terraced vineyards rise from the River Douro as you work your way inland from Oporto on the coast.

Englishmen a claret substitute while the bickering with France continued. Instead, it provided the base material for a totally different, unique fortified wine, which has since been copied throughout the world.

GRAPE VARIETIES AND WINE STYLES

Grape varieties are tremendously important to the eventual quality of the wine, but their names never appear on the label. There are 18 different grapes used to make red and white ports and of these the most important in terms of quality – i.e., giving only a fair yield, and of concentrated flavour – are the Roriz, Tinta Francisca and Touriga amongst the reds, and the Malvasia Dorada and Malvasia Fina in the whites.

White ports are basically made in two styles, dry and sweet. In general, the flavour is a bit thick and alcoholic, with the sweet ones even tasting slightly of rough grape skins. There are, however, a few good dry ones. When someone said that the first duty of a port is to be red, he wasn't far wrong because all the most exciting wines are indeed red, going from angry, impenetrable purple to a pale, frail tawny brown, depending on their age and style. (For more information on styles, see Classification.)

PORTUGAL/Port

THE IMPORTANT DETAILS

CLASSIFICATION

Port is one of the most rigidly controlled and classified of all wines, and the production area in the Douro valley was demarcated in 1756, a whole century before Bordeaux's famous 1855 Classification. The present port vineyard regulations are the most comprehensive in the world. Every single one of the 85,000 vineyards, some producing as little as 200 litres in total, is marked on productivity (the lower the yield, the higher the mark), altitude, soil, geographical position, variety and quality of grapes, gradient, shelter, age of vines and distance from root to root. Even upkeep of the vineyard is tested! Then the marks are totted up and the vineyard is given a rating from A (the top) to F (the bottom). The crucial thing is that the government only allows a certain amount of the Douro red wine to be made into port in any one year, the rest being sold as much less profitable 'red table wine'. 'A' vineyards can make up to 600 litres of port per 1,000 vines', 'F' vineyards only 260.

The wine itself is classified by the shippers into several categories, depending primarily on methods and length of aging. The main classifications are as follows.

Wood Ports The term given to port wines whose character has been framed by aging in wood. There are two main types: Ruby and Tawny. **Ruby** port is the simplest and least expensive port, usually blended up from the unexceptional grapes of unexceptional vineyards to create a tangy, tough but warmingly sweet wine to knock back uncritically. It can be good, but it should have a spirity rasp with the sweetness to make it more than just sugary. **Tawny** port is much paler and gentler than Ruby, the colour being a rather faded russet brown with a slight red blush on the younger versions. Proper Tawny is produced on a kind of *solera* system (see p.227) to en-

sure a consistent product. The wine is kept in wooden barrels for at least five to ten years, to let the colour leach out. Cheap Tawny, often offered at the same price as Ruby, is simply a mindless mixture of Ruby and white, and is almost never as good as the Ruby would have been, left to itself. A Tawny should have an age on the label – 10 years old, 20 years old, etc. This means that the youngest component wine in the blend has spent that length of time maturing, largely in wooden barrels. Few ports can possibly improve with more than 20 years in a barrel, so don't pay inflated prices for 30- and 40-year-old Tawnies.

Vintage Ports The opposite to the paler port wines, since the objective here is to make a big, impressive, concentrated mouthful rather than the gently fragrant Tawny style. Vintage years are 'declared' by port shippers when the quality seems particularly good – usually about three times a decade – and the best wines are matured separately in wooden barrels for two years or so and then bottled with long corks in black glass bottles. They should then be left to mature for at least a dozen years and sometimes twice that. The final effect should have far more weight and richness than a similarly aged Tawny, since the maturation has taken place in the almost airless and neutral confines of the glass bottle which ages the wines far more slowly.

Between Tawny and Vintage there are several compromise styles as follows:

Single Quinta/Single Farm Port When the overall vintage quality is not quite good enough to be 'declared', many shippers will make a special wine from their best 'farm' and treat it like a Vintage port. It will be mature at 10 to 15 years old, but will show much of the gutsy intensity of vintage wine.

Crusted/Crusting Ports These are bottled slightly later than Vintage, but still retain the peppery attack of the top wines. They are called 'crusted' because of the crust of sediment which will form after two or three years in bottle. They are rare, but excellent value. The term is often used wrongly to describe Vintage Character Port.

Vintage Character/Vintage Reserve (shipper's descriptions of a wine he thinks approximate to a mature Vintage style) and **Late Bottled Vintage Ports.** These are bottled four to six years after vintage. The vintage date refers to the year the wine was harvested, but the date of bottling should also be on the label. Ideally, this extra time maturing in wood should bring about an effect similar to a dozen years of bottle-aging. Bottled at four years and not too heavily filtered or artificially frozen to remove all the sediment, it still can, but most Vintage Character and Late Bottled ports are, sadly, too browbeaten into early maturity and, accordingly, lose much of their personality.

ORGANIZATION/S
Port is very much a two-place operation, since the basic red wine has to be radically altered to produce the final produce. The grapes are mostly grown by smallholders, though all major shippers own some land. The shippers then try to buy the grapes uncrushed to ferment at their own vinification centres, though growers may still crush the grapes themselves. After fermentation and fortification with brandy, the wine is then removed to Vila Nova de Gaia, opposite Oporto, to mature in the shippers' cellars or lodges. There is a co-operative presence, though, since co-ops were originally set up only to deal with surplus wine, their influence is not yet that marked.

READING THE LABEL
The most important thing on a label is to check that the wine is Portuguese at all, since most wine-producing countries create a style of wine which they describe as port! Moves are afoot to protect the name of 'port' as applying only to Portuguese wine, but nothing has been achieved yet. Wines labelled Tawny will always be lighter and often slightly less sweet. The best will have a minimum age marked. True Vintage port will be clearly marked with a vintage date – when the grapes were picked – and a bottling date, preferably two years later. Late Bottled Vintage port will usually be fairly full and sweet, but will usually offer nothing in terms of the richer more exciting flavours of Vintage style, since these are created by long aging in bottle, not in wood. There are various leading 'brand names' in the port market, and if they don't specify what they are, they can be assumed to be of 'Vintage Character', and likely to offer the same half-and-half style as Late Bottled. Older ports may show that they were not bottled in Portugal. This is quite all right, since the habit of bottling in Portugal is recent. Crusted, or Crusting port, a good style, can in fact only be bottled abroad, as the name is not recognized in Portugal. The word Colheita followed by a date implies a wood-aged port, not a true vintage wine.

WHAT DOES IT TASTE LIKE?
Except for the very rare dry white ports, the taste will be of varying degrees of sweetness and fieriness.

The fieriness is important because although the techniques of aging port are designed to reduce its bite, all but the finest old Tawnies, which have a gentle, brown sugar softness to them, need some bite to balance the sweetness. The best ports have a peppery background to a rich fruit which is both plummy and raisiny, getting a slight chocolate sweetness as they become older, and managing to mix perfumes as unlikely and incompatible as fresh mountain flowers, fierce Dickensian cough mixture and hard-ridden old leather. Port is a remarkable wine – these are only a few of the tastes you can find.

THE GOOD YEARS
Most port sold is a blend of various years. Rubies are young blends, and good Tawnies

PORTUGAL/Port

THE IMPORTANT DETAILS

will be older blends. However, the greatest glories of port are in the single-vintage dated wines. The finest years are 'declared' vintages some 18 months after they have been picked. This should only happen every few years, and in any case will apply to only a tiny proportion of their best wine. However, the reputation of the house is often created by the quality of the vintage wine. From a good shipper, a Vintage port should take 15 to 20 years to mellow and mature. This applies to good years like 1985, 1980, 1970, 1966 and 1960. Lighter years like 1975, and perhaps 1982, may be ready in ten years. The greatest years like 1983, 1977, 1963, 1955, while ready in 20 years, should continue to blossom for a decade or so longer and can be excellent at 50 years old. Lesser vintages, from 'undeclared' years, are best under 'single *quinta*' labels and are ready at ten years old,

though certainly able to last twice that time. Late Bottled Vintage will be made any year it suits the shipper.

ENJOYING THE WINE

The French drink their port primarily as an apéritif, the British primarily after meals, the Portuguese before and after meals. White port is best as an apéritif, cooled down and served with pre-dinner nibbles. If it tastes too strong you can add mineral water, lemonade or tonic water without ill-effect. Tawny is also best slightly chilled, before or after a meal. The big red ports are best either as a 'pick-me-up' in fierce winters, or, ideally, at the end of a meal. Vintage port is one of the few wines which can go with blue cheese, but is best with nuts and fruit, good conversation and the occasional wisp of cigar smoke trailing through the candle light.

CONSUMER INFORMATION

WHAT DO I GET FOR MY MONEY?

Port used to be a cheap drink. With drastically mounting production costs and very high domestic inflation and interest rates, it isn't any more. Yet good port is nonetheless excellent value for money. Basic Tawny is the only one to avoid. Otherwise the top dozen or so shippers, often with Anglo-Saxon names, offer quality at a price. Names to look for are **Taylor, Fonseca, Dow, Graham, Warre, Churchill, Ferreira, Quinta do Noval, Cálem** and **Poças Junior**. The price is worth paying, because the wine is unique. With Late Bottled Vintage ports, do not feel you are getting vintage wine at a cut price, because you're not. Only **Warre** and **Smith Woodhouse** offer a good approximation. Otherwise you're getting a clever marketing device. Nice wine, maybe, just not the real thing. Crusting is a rare style in which Smith Woodhouse specializes, but good wine merchants may offer it under their own labels.

AVAILABILITY

For basic ports, very good. Old Tawnies are more difficult to find and Vintage port is not easy. Until recently it has been a northern European phenomenon, but the USA is now the biggest growth market, so availability will spread there too.

CONSUMER CHECKLIST		
Ruby	Q:	1 2 3 **4** 5 6 7 8 9 10
	P:	1 2 3 **4 5** 6 7 8 9 10
	V:	1 2 **3** 4 5 6 7 8 9 10
10-Year-Old	Q:	1 2 3 4 5 **6 7** 8 9 10
Tawny	P:	1 2 3 4 5 6 **7 8** 9 10
	V:	1 2 3 4 5 6 **7 8** 9 10
1980 Vintage	Q:	1 2 3 4 5 6 7 **8 9** 10
	P:	1 2 3 4 5 6 7 **8 9** 10
	V:	1 2 3 4 5 6 7 8 **9** 10

Good Years All cheap port is a blend of vintages, and all Tawnies of whatever quality consist of the wine of various years. The great 'Vintage' ports are the produce of a single year and usually need between 15 and 20 years aging to reach their best. Best recent years are 1985, 1983, 1982, 1980, 1977, 1970, 1966, 1963.

Taste Notes Port wine is much imitated round the world but should only apply to the fortified wines of the Upper Douro valley in Portugal. The vast majority of the wines are sweet and red though a few are white and even dry. The range of styles is wide for cheap rough red Ruby to pale delicate browning Tawny, from medium-bodied Vintage Character to massive, rich Vintage ports.

PORTUGAL/Madeira

THE GENERAL PICTURE

Madeira is one of the great forgotten wines of the world. Even amongst enthusiastic wine-drinkers, few people have drunk this remarkable fortified wine from a lonely island about 600 kilometres (373 miles) off the Moroccan coast and shaped like a giant cake of rock rearing steep-sided through the fog from the Atlantic waves. The output is certainly small, since the island of Madeira measures a mere 56 km by 24 km (35 miles by 15 miles). No easy vineyards here, every metre of ground, steep, terraced, and exhausting, which means that it is only through making a greatly appreciated, expensive wine that there is a reasonable chance of any of the islanders making a decent living. Madeira's unique properties were discovered in the seventeenth century, when it was found that long sea voyages actually improved the wine. By the nineteenth century, it was as highly prized as any port or sherry, and indeed in the USA, and particularly in the southern states, it was well-aged high-quality madeira wine more than any other which connoisseurs would gather to discuss and appraise, long into the muggy, warm hours of the night. However, the island was fiercely hit by the twin vine scourges of Oidium and Phylloxera in the nineteenth century, and for most of the present century, great madeira has been little more than a memory. But since 1979, after a drastic government initiative to improve the quality of the wines, things are once more on the move, and we should see madeira gradually easing itself back into its seat at the High Table of the world's finest wines.

GRAPE VARIETIES AND WINE STYLES

Each madeira style is supposedly based on a particular grape. **Malmsey** is the sweetest, from the Malvasia grape which seems to have originated in Monemvasia in the Peloponnese.

In fact, there are now several types of Malvasia grape on the island. Malmsey wine is startlingly sweet, reeking sometimes of the finest Muscovado sugar, dark, rich, brown but with a smoky bite and a surprisingly high acidity which make it almost refreshing after a long meal. The Bual grape produces **Bual madeira**, again rich and strong, but not quite so concentrated as Malmsey, sometimes with a faintly rubbery whiff to it and with a slightly higher acidity. The **Verdelho** grape may well be the same as the Pedro Ximénez grape which makes the sweetest sherries. Here it makes a pungent, smoky, medium sweet wine, with a more obvious gentle fruit. The **Sercial** grape seems to be related to Germany's Riesling, and it makes a most dramatic dry wine, savoury, spirity, tangy, and with a steely, piercing acidity. There is a fifth grape, the Tinta Negra Mole, which is used to make imitations of these four main styles. It does it quite well, and at a much lower price, so any suspiciously cheap bottles of madeira are likely to be based on this grape. However, from now on the insertion of the grape name on the label means that at least 85 per cent of the wine must be of the variety stated.

Since these four noble varieties represent only 9 per cent of the vineyard acreage, there is still a long way to go before the integrity of madeira wine is re-established.

THE IMPORTANT DETAILS

CLASSIFICATION
There are two main classifications in Madeira. The first is a bleak official rating system which is simply: Class Three – for wines of five years' minimum age; Class Two – for wines of seven years' minimum age, and Class One – for wines of ten years' minimum age. Most quality madeira needs at least seven years' aging.

These classifications translate on the label as Reserve – a blend with the youngest component 5 years old; Special Reserve – a blend at least 10 years old; and Extra Reserve – for wines at least 15 years old.

The second classification is used by shippers to describe the wine styles and is based primarily on grape types – from sweet to dry,

PORTUGAL/Madeira

THE IMPORTANT DETAILS

Top Vineyard at Achado do Gramacho on relatively tractable terrain; most madeira vines are grown on steep terraces clinging to the edge of this dramatically rocky island. **Above** The best madeiras are not released until they have gained considerable maturity.

Malmsey, Bual, Verdelho and Sercial. New regulations insist that the wine is at least 85 per cent from the grape mentioned.

'Rainwater' is a pale Verdelho style very popular in the USA and got its name, literally, through casks of wine being mistakenly diluted by rainwater during shipment and appreciated the more because of it. Madeira, indeed, used to be called after the ships in whose holds it had matured, and, more recently, with the shortage of classic grapes, firms used various brand names, often with regal or 'City of London' connotations to describe their wines. With these one must look for such words as Fine Dry, Fine Rich, Dark, Delicate Choice, etc., in order to get the right style.

ORGANIZATION/S

The whole production of madeira wine is in the hands of the shippers. In Madeira's heyday there were more than 80 of them. Now there are under twenty. The grapes are mostly grown by smallholders who may belong to one of the co-operatives. Some of these press the grapes and sell the must to the shippers. However, nowadays grapes are usually sold uncrushed and direct to the shippers who will then take total charge of all the wine-making stages.

READING THE LABEL

At the moment, bottles labelled according to grape type, i.e. Bual, Verdelho, etc., may still be merely a wine 'in the style of' the grape described, though in fact based on Tinta Negra Mole. However, as new regulations take effect, the grape name used on the label will guarantee a content of at least 85 per cent of the variety named. If no grape is indicated, check for a descriptive title such as Rich, Dry, etc., to ensure you are getting the style you want. Some wines are now being released commercially with a minimum age stated, as in '10 years old'.

WHAT DOES IT TASTE LIKE?

Sweet or dry, madeira wine has a brilliant biting flavour, slightly resembling fine old sherry, and slightly resembling old Tawny port, but having an intensity, a startling acidity and a husky, brown, burnt flavour which is all its own. Madeiras have a fair amount of weight, and the flavours are likely to become more and more concentrated as they age.

THE GOOD YEARS

Vintage madeira wines are very rare, and, in any case, madeira vintages are only 'declared' or announced some 30 years after the wine has been made!! 1956 has only recently been released on to the market. A bottle of madeira bearing a vintage date is certain to be a remarkable wine. More frequent are 'Solera' wines. These may bear a date, as in 'Solera 1864', which means the wine is based on an original vintage, i.e. 1864, and that this particular 'batch' of wine has been topped up with younger wine to keep a style resembling the original vintage. Typically, madeira will simply have a general description, like 'old' (!) and sometimes a minimum age.

ENJOYING THE WINE

Although madeira is much used in cooking to make *sauce Madère*, madeira wines are usually best with little or no food accompaniments. Both Sercial and Rainwater can make excellent and unusual apéritifs, and are also sometimes served with soup, while Bual and Malmsey are less heady and more refreshing than port for long, slow after-dinner drinking. There's no getting away from the fact that sitting down with a bowl of nuts and a decanter of old madeira is a highly civilized way to end the day.

MADEIRA

Two things make madeira special, apart from her grape varieties and rich but rocky volcanic soils. Firstly, the wines are made by the *solera* system (see p 227). An initial 'batch' of good base wine is laid down to act as the foundation for a company's various blends, and it is 'refreshed' with younger wine whenever the *solera* is drawn upon. Secondly, madeira wine is 'cooked'. Originally it was sent to the East Indies or on some other long sea voyage to mature and bake in the holds of the ships as they sweltered through the equatorial waters. Nowadays the wine is heated at 45° C (113°F) for up to six months in an *estufa* or 'hot house'. This explains the smoky, deep brown taste in much madeira; this kind of 'semi-pasteurization' is also reckoned to contribute largely to madeira's incredible longevity. I have never tasted a madeira which was too old. I have tasted madeiras back to 1808, and have always been aghast at the undimmable brilliance of their flavours.

CONSUMER INFORMATION

WHAT DO I GET FOR MY MONEY?

With the new government quality regulations, madeira is returning to being a fairly expensive but highly dependable quality wine. But, before complaining about the price, remember madeira's costs of production are double those of port. When the label states a vintage, a *solera* date, or a minimum age of ten years, it can be bought with complete confidence.

AVAILABILITY

Exports were drastically cut back in 1979 to recover a stock of properly aged, quality wines. There is still a shortage of madeira on world markets, but there are signs that chain stores and supermarkets, as well as specialists, are becoming interested in the wine again, so availability is likely to widen gradually.

CONSUMER CHECKLIST

Sercial (no age stated)	Q:	1 2 **3** 4 5 6 7 8 9 10
	P:	1 2 3 4 **5** 6 7 8 9 10
	V:	1 2 3 **4** 5 6 7 8 9 10
10-Year-Old Malmsey	Q:	1 2 3 4 5 6 7 **8** 9 10
	P:	1 2 3 4 5 6 7 **8** 9 10
	V:	1 2 3 4 5 6 7 **8** 9 10

Good Years Madeira is hardly ever vintage dated, being a blend of different vintages. However, age is important and the best madeiras are at least 10 years old.

Taste Notes Madeira ranges from tangy and dry (Sercial) through the increasingly sweet Verdelho to the intensely rich Malmsey. The most recognizable characteristics in all these are a smokiness and an appetizing sharp acidity.

USA

There was a time, not so long ago, when French winemakers would look at American wine, sniff rather grandly, and pronounce that the wines, at best, were rather lacking in subtlety and complexity for their Bordeaux- and burgundy-trained palates. Bordeaux's greatest showman, the late Baron Philippe de Rothschild, was heard to grumble, 'Californian wines are like Coca Cola – they all taste the same.'

Well, when you've held sway over the world of wine for several hundred years, as France has, you're not likely to greet kindly the appearance of a challenger to your position, a confident, assertive, combative fistfighter, who slams down a track record of some single decade with all the confidence of a habitual winner, declaring it the equal of your own carefully created, centuries old reputation. But that's exactly what happened between the USA (or, more specifically California) and France in the 1970s and 1980s.

Wine-making in the 1970s seemed to epitomize everything which was most exciting and innovative about the Californian psyche. This tremendous, super-optimistic innovativeness was fed on, and fed by, two things. First, European models were used as targets to aim for. But not just any old European targets. No, the Californians went right to the top – to Le Montrachet and Románeé-Conti in Burgundy, to Latour and Pétrus in Bordeaux, and to the great rare sweet wines of Germany. With the ability to ripen grapes fully every year, it made sense to copy the richest, most impressive wines that Europe could offer – in other words, great vintages from great properties. That such a remarkable number of wines aimed so high and got so near in such a short time is due to the second factor – the presence of wine-making schools without rival anywhere in the world (except, perhaps, Roseworthy, in Australia) and, in particular, the Davis Campus of the University of California. Here, for the first time in history, the whole range of the fundamental principles of wine-making has been identified and analysed. The revolutionary work at Davis has produced and is still producing studies which plot the most perfect series of interactions which every grape variety can undergo in all conditions to produce

every type of wine. A modern Californian winemaker can actually design the wine he wishes to make, weeks before the grapes are ever picked. But while innovations have been avidly made use of by the winemakers intent on hand-crafted creations, the true global importance of Davis's contribution to wine is seen in the production of basic table wines.

In the 1970s, the popular tastes in the USA's drinking habits changed, from spirits and beer to wine, and from sweet fortified wines to lighter, smarter wines. The image of success was becoming younger, leaner, fitter and more sophisticated and wine increasingly fitted the bill as the preferred drink. What the scientists of Davis did was to transform the bulk wine industry in less than a decade by daring, far-reaching innovations which are now being copied throughout the world.

The most apocalyptic of these, which would make every torrid parched grape field in the world a potential supplier of good fresh wine, is cold fermentation. Large refrigerated tanks can simulate the cool conditions of Germany, where the world's lightest, most fragrant wines naturally occur. Thus, with the help of Davis technology, the Central Valley – accustomed to pumping out gallons of sweetish heavy wines from vineyards full of sun-baked grapes – has been able to produce gigantic quantities of light fresh wines from stainless steel refineries.

However, Davis's influence has been even more wide-reaching than this. Davis scientists have charted a five-stage grading system for every inch of Californian vineyard which is based on the number of degrees Fahrenheit above 50°F any area will receive during the grapes' growing season (50°F is regarded as the temperature above which the ripening process takes place). This is combined with an intensive study of microclimates to attempt to match ideal grape varieties to ideal vineyards. What took Europe centuries of trial and error, they are trying to achieve in a decade! Along with this they are refining the healthiest 'clones' of existing grape varieties, so that a vineyard owner can choose which vine cuttings to plant as though he were in a department store.

Davis has also made innovations in methods of actually growing the vines, introducing new

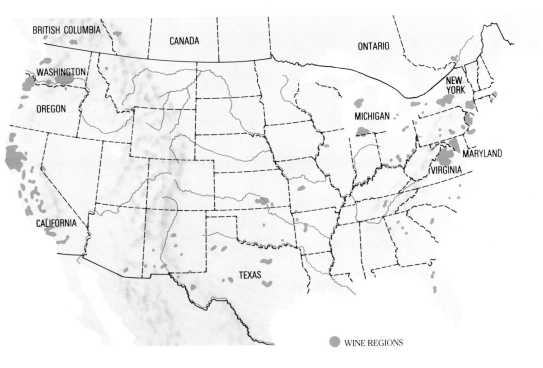

BRITISH COLUMBIA

CANADA

ONTARIO

WASHINGTON

NEW YORK

OREGON

MICHIGAN

MARYLAND

CALIFORNIA

VIRGINIA

TEXAS

● WINE REGIONS

trellis-systems of pruning the vine which keep it cool during the midday heat, as well as methods of irrigation and mist-irrigation which water and cool in the heat, and can protect against frost in the winter. And if you don't like the grapes you've planted, if your varieties are unfashionable, you can chop off the vine at ground level, and slip a single bud of a different variety into a T-shaped cut in the bark – and get all the advantages of another rootstock for your new variety. An entire red wine vineyard can be converted to white in a couple of seasons.

And it doesn't stop there. Under Davis's system, once the vines are growing, there are mechanical methods of pruning and harvesting which are dramatically cutting the costs of producing basic wine. It goes on and on.

Davis's efforts obviously had some effect, and by the 1980s France had enough wit to realize that the grit and determination, and the quality consciousness, matched with investment and the burning desire to excel which marks out the American winemaker, must be courted not counteracted. The 'Coca Cola quipper' Baron Philippe suddenly announced he was teaming up with Robert Mondavi of the Napa Valley. Christian Moueix, producer of what may be France's greatest red wine, Château Pétrus, bought into Napanook vineyards to create the provocative Dominus Cabernet. Other Bordeaux growers were found looking hungrily westwards for partnerships in vineyards, and the French champagne houses have gone into co-production ventures in the Napa and Sonoma to produce high-quality sparkling wines.

Having thrown that early knock-out punch, California is easing back into a skilful, gentler use of what must be the world's most plentiful supply of great wine grapes. But where California led, others are following. Oregon and Washington are well on the road with their light, fragrant wines. New York State, once dismissed as grape-jelly land, is producing wonderful wines. Maryland, Pennsylvania, Ohio, Idaho, Texas . . . the bug has bitten them all. American world-class wine-making has certainly come of age, and we look forward with trepidation and excitement to what can be achieved in the 1990s.

CALIFORNIA

California is the most important name in American wine, and, for that matter, in world wine too. Many of the technological advances which revolutionized wine-making were invented and pioneered in California, and it was California which had the courage and the talent to challenge European quality supremacy in the 1960s – a move which has opened up the path to recognition for the new generations of winemakers across the world. The Napa Valley is by far the most famous of the regions, but, increasingly, new cool-climate areas are being found and developed north and south of San Francisco in Sonoma, Mendocino, Monterey, San Luis Obispo and elsewhere. These are where the most exciting wines are from, but the great bulk continues to be created in the baking grape bowl of the Central Valley which probably rates as the world's most super-fertile and abundant grape-growing region.

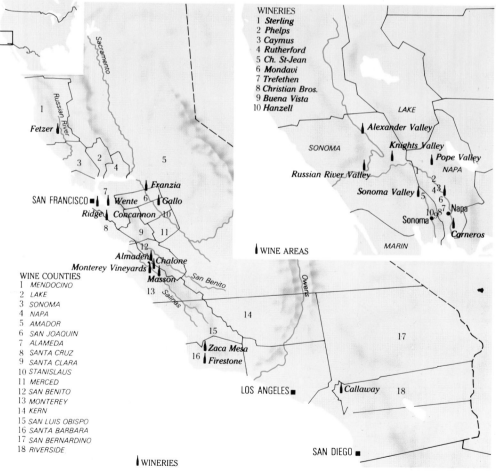

WINERIES
1 Sterling
2 Phelps
3 Caymus
4 Rutherford
5 Ch. St-Jean
6 Mondavi
7 Trefethen
8 Christian Bros.
9 Buena Vista
10 Hanzell

WINE COUNTIES
1 MENDOCINO
2 LAKE
3 SONOMA
4 NAPA
5 AMADOR
6 SAN JOAQUIN
7 ALAMEDA
8 SANTA CRUZ
9 SANTA CLARA
10 STANISLAUS
11 MERCED
12 SAN BENITO
13 MONTEREY
14 KERN
15 SAN LUIS OBISPO
16 SANTA BARBARA
17 SAN BERNARDINO
18 RIVERSIDE

CALIFORNIA/Napa Valley

THE GENERAL PICTURE

The floor of the Napa Valley, where conditions are ideal for grape-growing, is carpeted with vines, although it is the newer vineyards on the higher slopes that are producing the subtler, more interesting Napa Valley wines.

The Napa Valley stands arrogantly in the centre stage of California, just as France dominates the winelands of Europe. It was the Napa which forged the modern California wine industry, and which acted as the magnet drawing money, ambition and genius from other walks of life; and it set standards against which not only the rest of California but also the rest of the world have to measure up.

The old Indian name for the Napa was 'Valley of Plenty' and on reaching the mouth of the valley, less than two hours' drive north from San Francisco, that plenty is vividly illustrated. The valley is about 3 to 4 miles (5 kilometres) wide in the south, just above San Francisco Bay, and is a tight-meshed carpet of vines. It extends north for 30 miles (50 km), narrowing to a kilometre (just over half a mile) just north of the town of St Helena. And everywhere it is vines. More than 80 per cent of the Napa's workable land is under vine, and over 90 per cent of its agricultural income comes from grapes.

The Napa Valley was the obvious starting point for any fledgling winemaker, because its climate had long been considered ideal for grape-growing – free from frost dangers, with average rainfall, rich soil, and a very long, reliable ripening period of hot but not sweltering days. These conditions make for regular crops of perfect grapes, which allow the winemakers to exercise all their skills and passions on moulding the grapes into their own personal styles of wine.

The styles that were to rocket the Napa to stardom began to appear in the 1970s, following the rapid escalation of prices for Burgundy and Bordeaux wines. They were usually of a quite startling depth of flavour, both reds and whites having enormous, big, mouth-filling personalities, tremendously impressive, though not always greatly refreshing. You couldn't fail to notice them – but at the same time they called to mind the old European adage that to make the best wine, the vine must suffer. It must struggle to ripen. The vine must be forced to push its roots deep into unnutritious soil to find what nourishment it can. On the floor of the Napa Valley, which resembles a patchwork of vines from end to end, with rich soil and even temperatures, this struggle does not exist.

However, the Napa Valley is a freak flat valley in a very mountainous area. In the 1960s and 1970s, many winemakers *did* begin to find their wines a little too fat and ripe, and all the best recent vineyards have been established on plateaux and slopes in the heavily wooded mountains above the valley floor. It's cooler there and the soil isn't good – so vines *have* to struggle. Between these two extremes of hot valley floor and chilly mountain eyrie, the Napa produces an astonishing array of wines, covering the entire spectrum of red, white, rosé, sparkling and even fortified wines. The San Francisco end of the valley is one of California's coolest regions, while the top end around Calistoga is too hot for all but sturdy reds.

Sights such as the colourful but erratic husbandry above are becoming increasingly rare.

CALIFORNIA/Napa Valley

THE GENERAL PICTURE

GRAPE VARIETIES AND WINE STYLES

The two most famous styles are the **Cabernet Sauvignon** (the red Bordeaux grape), and the white **Chardonnay** (the white Burgundy grape). These are the two that the Californians put forward as world-beaters, and they delight in staging blind tastings against their French counterparts. Frequently the Californians win, because the succulent ripeness of their fruit simply overwhelms the more delicate pleasures of the French classics. Other grapes are successful too:

Pinot Noir Burgundy's red grape is increasingly successful in the Napa, and it provides excellent base material for sparkling wines.

Petite Syrah and **Zinfandel** These grapes make chunky, chewy red wines at the hot end of the valley above St Helena.

Sauvignon Blanc This Sancerre grape is often called Fumé Blanc. It is made either fat and oaky, or, in the cooler areas, as a sharp, gooseberryish thirst-quencher.

Johannisberg Riesling Only partly successful since the Napa is just a little too hot for it to keep its freshness. However, it has made some very good 'noble rot' sweet wines.

Various other, less important, grapes, such as Chenin and Gewürztraminer, are grown.

A typical Napa Valley vineyard. Spring frost on the vines can be a real hazard, and windmill-type fans like the one in the centre of the picture are often used to disperse the cold air.

THE IMPORTANT DETAILS

The Charles Krug Winery, shown here, is said by many to be the oldest in the Napa valley. Founded in 1861, it has an excellent reputation for whites.

CLASSIFICATION

This is still in a state of flux in the Napa Valley, and in general the name of the winemaker and his remarks on the label as to grape varieties, vineyards and wine-making style will tell you more than any particular classification. Napa Valley is the central classification, and a high proportion of Napa County wines are in fact entitled to this geographical appellation, whether the grapes are grown on the valley floor or up the slopes.

In the Napa Valley itself, there are already sub-divisions – small areas and villages with defined characteristics – and, in the French 'geographical' manner, these are being classified. A wine's grapes are often bought from several areas and trucked many miles to the winery for vinification. The back label should state where the grapes are from. Look out for Carneros, Stags Leap, Yountville, Mount Veeder, Rutherford and Oakville.

ORGANIZATION/S

California is the land of the self-made man, and it is the growers and winemakers who reign supreme, even though some operations are owned by large, multinational companies like Coca Cola and the giant distillers. The finest producers are the small-to-medium-sized wineries, although Mondavi, one of the top names, is a very large concern. Most will own some vineyard land, but there is a large group of farmers who concentrate purely on growing quality grapes, not making wine.

READING THE LABEL

Napa labels are informative and easy to understand. They show the vintage, the winery and, except in blended 'house' wines, the dominant grape variety. Other things to look for, on the main or back label, are:

Alcoholic strength Often rather high. While 12^{0} is an average French strength, Napa wines can be up to 14^{0}.

Sugar content Chardonnays and Fumé Blancs should be dry, but Gewürztraminer and Johannisberg Riesling probably won't be. Residual sugar (i.e. sugar that is not converted to alcohol) gives sweetness and is shown in percentage terms. Above 3 per cent certainly isn't dry. By 10 per cent the wine is approaching dessert wine levels.

Grape varieties The chief grape need only make up 75 per cent of the wine for it to be labelled as 'varietal', so look to see if any other varieties are included.

The area For an area to be named, 85 per cent of the grapes must come from there. Check to see where the possible other 15 per cent may have come from.

WHAT DOES IT TASTE LIKE?

It tastes Big. If one generalization were possible, it would have to revolve round the massive, ultra-ripe flavours produced from these bulging, sugar-filled grapes. For some years it seemed that the winemakers were straining to extract the maximum amount of flavours from their grapes, to ensure the maximum amount of alcohol, then slam the wines into highly perfumed, new oak casks to age. By the end, you almost needed a knife and fork to drink – if that's the word – the result. But wine is not just about massive flavours and tonsil-bashing strength. It's about balance, beauty of flavours, and refreshment! The message is getting through. Napa wines are now becoming subtler, fresher – and much more attractive.

Cabernet Sauvignon This red can still be marked by a somewhat raisiny fruit, but the wines are becoming increasingly drier and lighter. They're fairly hard and tannic when young, but the fat, ripe fruit is now more likely to be blackcurranty, with the perfume of cedar.

Pinot Noir This is working better and better, and the Napa winemakers will go on trying till they crack it. In Burgundy, this red grape veers between very light, fragrant and strawberry-tasting, to dark, plummy and chocolaty. Through the whole spectrum, however, it remains fruit-perfumed and gentle. Especially from Carneros to the south of Napa, we are now seeing examples of scented, cherry and plum fruited Pinot Noir of tremendously high quality which can increasingly rival the best wines of Burgundy.

Zinfandel A fascinating red grape, virtually unknown in Europe, but highly successful in California. It makes a whole gamut of styles, from pink (they call it 'white') through juicy and Beaujolais-like, to deep, strong and peppery, with a wonderful brambly, briar-sweet fruit. It's all things to all men.

CALIFORNIA/Napa Valley

THE IMPORTANT DETAILS

Petite Sirah Not the same as the great Syrah red grape of the Rhône in France, or the Shiraz of Australia. It produces big, stark, dry, almost tarry wines. Impressive, certainly, but usually lacking pizzazz.

Blends There is a move away from single-variety wines, and the above grapes are increasingly blended, as well as others such as the Merlot and Cabernet Franc. From a good winery, the basic blended 'house' red is now often a fine wine.

Chardonnay The white grape can achieve remarkable things. A few years ago the market was so thirsty for Chardonnay that standards did slump while prices rocketed, but Napa Chardonnay is now as fine as it has ever been, and it being made lighter and fresher than before. Sometimes you find a positive fruit salad of flavours, with such delights as figs, melons, peaches or lychees all fighting for prominence, with some buttery oak to round it out. But the best Napa Chardonnays are drier, steelier, with a slightly smoky, toasty taste from the partially charred oak barrels they mature in.

Sauvignon or Fumé Blanc Not as trendy as it used to be, it was brought to prominence by the Mondavi winery who make it full and oaky, and a bit Chardonnayish. New releases, however, confirm a trend towards lighter, drier wines, with a delicious side-swipe of tart blackcurrant and gooseberry fruit.

Johannisberg Riesling This white grape often has the grapiness of a German Riesling from the Rhine, but rarely the marvellous lime-juice

streak of fresh acidity which makes great 'hock' so exciting. The most interesting Napa Rieslings are from grapes infected by the 'noble rot', allowed to wither and concentrate in sugar, and then made in tiny quantities in the classic sweet German style.

Other white wines The Chenin Blanc occasionally makes grassy, appleskin-fresh wines after many flabby years. Some producers make Semillon in a full-bodied, barrel-fermented style, *and* there are one or two good sweet Muscats. The Gewürztraminer is usually still a little gross and chubby.

Sparkling The Napa is less important than some other parts of California, but does have several top-quality producers, including California's finest, Schramsberg, who make a wine that is as great as all but the rarest champagnes.

THE GOOD YEARS

There is a great deal more similarity between one Napa vintage and another than there is between different years in the classic wine areas of Europe.

The hot climate fruit mostly produces quick-maturing wines, despite their force of flavour and most Americans prefer to drink their wines younger than Europeans – Cabernets at less than 5 years old, whites at less than 2. With so many microclimates and different wine-making methods, generalization can be misleading. However, 1987, 1986 and 1985 reds are very good, with 1987 being the most forward. Both 1989 and 1988 produced first class whites.

ENJOYING THE WINE

Napa's 'big country' wines are best with big country food; the whites are excellent, with the clear flavours of fresh-grilled fish and chicken as well as being able to cope with the spicy or creamy flavours of more exotic dishes. Many Napa reds will overwhelm delicate cuisine. Rich red meat – roast, grilled, or stewed – would be my choice, or even some of the less violent cheeses. But remember that these wines – red and white – are rarely terribly refreshing. With a meal you might welcome alternating draughts of mineral water. The top sparkling wines *are*, however, good right through the meal.

The Napa Valley is California's most traditional wine area yet is also a front runner in the new technology. Here old-style wooden vats and ultra-modern stainless steel vats co-exist in the same winery.

CONSUMER INFORMATION

WHAT DO I GET FOR MY MONEY?

After a long period when the massive strength of the dollar meant that not only were Californian wines very expensive in Europe, but that European wines of every quality were almost absurdly cheap in the USA, things have now evened up and California wines have found a more natural price level.

It's impossible to generalize about the Napa wines in terms of value for money. Though many of the Cabernet Sauvignons have impressive flavours, the balance is not always there, and the price can reflect the vogue for a particular winery as much as its enduring quality. Interestingly, a good Pinot Noir is often underpriced for its quality. White Zinfandels are pretty cheap, but the reds offer more interesting flavours and better value. Petite Sirah makes rough-and-tumble wines, fairly priced. Merlot is a rising star and no longer cheap, and has obvious potential as a gentler, softer version of the Napa Cabernets.

Amongst the whites, Napa Chardonnays can be some of the greatest white wines in the world, but many are just a little too blunt – as can be the prices. Sauvignon/Fumé Blanc was a trendy grape, and therefore expensive, but the variety has lost vogue just as the wines have begun to shine.

Dry Johannisberg Riesling is rarely terribly interesting, being both too full and dull. The sweet Napa Rieslings are very expensive, but these luscious sweet wines are increasingly successful as a style.

AVAILABILITY

Outside the USA, this always depends on the strength of the dollar. At present the wines are represented in quality outlets in most countries but sales are small. Inside the USA all good liquor stores will have various examples, but they are still underrepresented on the East Coast because of the flood of cheap French and Italian wines. Either way, the wines must be tried, because they exhibit a remarkable and vital wine-making style at the forefront of the modern wine world.

CONSUMER CHECKLIST

Mondavi	Q:	1 2 3 4 5 6 **7** 8 9 10
Cabernet	P:	1 2 3 4 5 6 **7** 8 9 10
Sauvignon 1986	V:	1 2 3 4 5 6 **7** 8 9 10
Grgich Hills	Q:	1 2 3 4 5 6 7 **8** 9 10
Chardonnay	P:	1 2 3 4 5 6 7 8 **9** 10
1986	V:	1 2 3 4 5 6 7 **8** 9 10
Schramsberg	Q:	1 2 3 4 5 6 7 **8** 9 10
Blanc de Blancs	P:	1 2 3 4 5 6 7 8 **9** 10
	V:	1 2 3 4 5 6 7 **8** 9 10

Good Years 1989 is tricky for reds but good for whites. 1988 is rich and ripe – excellent when the balance is kept. 1987 is a lovely balanced year for reds and whites. 1986 reds are tough but good quality, 1985 ripe and classic. 1984 is extremely good in a strong, direct way. 1983 is the nearest Napa gets to a poor vintage.

strong-flavoured reds and whites. *1980* Excellent. The vintage was very ripe, but the wines are marked by an eagerness to accentuate fruit and balance, but not alcoholic strength.

Taste Notes In general Napa reds are marked by big ripe flavours; the whites used to be deep and almost too ripe, but nowadays demonstrate the natural acidity and freshness of the grape.

The Napa Valley seen from Spring Mountain, home of some of the highest Napa vineyards.

CALIFORNIA/North Coast

THE GENERAL PICTURE

The North Coast Wine Region of California stretches for 125 miles (200 km) north of San Francisco. The persistent fogs which cool the inland valleys are too prevalent here just north of the city for there to be much chance of successful wine-making – and anyway, everyone wants to build houses there, but Marin County does have a few vineyards. Things really begin to buzz when you cut across from Route 101 to the old town of Sonoma, the central town of the Sonoma Valley, and the site of Buena Vista Vineyards, where the Hungarian Agoston Haraszthy is generally reckoned to have first introduced to California the great European grape varieties of Cabernet, Pinot Noir, Chardonnay, Riesling, and several hundred others, which have since made Californian wine world-famous.

Buena Vista means 'Beautiful View' in Spanish, and the Sonoma Valley, with the Mayacamas mountains running like a spine up the eastern flank, is a very beautiful area. Only 2 miles (3 km) out of the town of Sonoma, Hanzell Winery, constructed to look like Clos de Vougeot in Burgundy, has a view of San Francisco which would make any property developer drool. Indeed, the beauty of the region and the proximity to San Francisco have already had an effect; property prices are sky-high, and it is difficult for many grape-growers to resist selling their land for urban development.

The Sonoma Valley is the cool southern end of Sonoma County, and contains many of the region's best wineries. The northern area is large and more diverse and its overall title is the Russian River. The Russians were the first people to plant vines in Sonoma, back in 1812! Much of the land here is valley floor, and the area has traditionally been a major supplier to the American brand leaders in the jug wine market – E. & J. Gallo, the biggest wine producers in the USA, still use Russian River wine to improve their blends. Yet, as always, the most interesting wines are being made on the hillside vineyards, or in the little side valleys. Korbel, who make one of California's original sparkling wines, are established amidst the redwood forests as the Russian River twines down to the Pacific Ocean; Iron Horse, producers of some of California's best sparklers, are in the foothills of the Green Valley; while Matanzas Creek are making delicious reds and whites in the Bennett Valley, east of Santa Rosa.

As the Russian River Valley runs north, there are several offshoots, all important as separate wine areas: Dry Creek to the west is particularly good for full whites and Zinfandel red; Alexander Valley, in the central part of the Russian River Valley, is producing big juicy Chardonnay and Cabernet, and Knight's Valley to the east is excellent for Cabernet.

Sonoma County adjoins Mendocino County to the north. Mendocino is, in general, hotter than northern Sonoma, but the Anderson Valley, which has a clutch of wineries only 12 miles (20 km) from the Pacific has frequent fogs and the coastal breezes actually lower the temperature as the sun rises higher in the sky. The northern top of the valley above the Ukiah produces high-quality, soft, fruity reds and whites.

GRAPE VARIETIES AND WINE STYLES

All the major wine grapes are grown in the North Coast area, and Sonoma has the state's biggest acreages of Pinot Noir, Zinfandel and Gewürztraminer. In general, the reds and whites both lack the intensity, the attack, the massive grandeur of the wines from the Napa Valley, which lies adjacent just over the Mayacamas mountains to the east. But that is no bad thing, because they make up for it with some of the most approachable, richly perfumed fruit in California. In the reds, the Cabernet Sauvignon of Bordeaux is usually delicious. Softer than the Napa equivalent, the most attractive, like **Clos du Bois, Dry Creek** and **Laurel Glen** in Sonoma, and **Fetzer** in Mendocino, have a gorgeous juicy flavour, mixing blackcurrant fruit with lovely minty and eucalyptus perfume and some soft buttery oak. **Iron Horse** is the driest and most Médocain in style, while **Jordan** is the most expensive; luckily the wine is deep, strong and very good. The Merlot grape (which dominates in Pomerol and St-Emilion in Bordeaux) is often blended in, but can be successful by itself from wineries like **Matanzas Creek** and Clos du Bois. The very difficult Pinot Noir is a problem, although wineries like **Buena Vista, Sea Ridge** and **Kistler** are having some success with a light, fragrant style, as **Kalin** with something fuller.

Zinfandel is highly successful on the North Coast, from the soft and gulpable **River Oaks** style through the beefy but rich Mendocino wines of **Parducci** and Fetzer to the massive brambles and pepper style of **Lytton Springs**. Fetzer also makes a white Zinfandel. It's creamy and delicous.

In the whites, Chardonnay is successful, sometimes wildly so, though its gentle fruit can be slightly overawed by oak. The rich yet balanced styles of **Simi**, Matanzas Creek, Kistler, **Saintsbury, Sonoma-Cutrer** and **Jordan** can be some of the best that California has to offer.

Sauvignon Blanc is encouraging, with Fetzer, River Oaks and Dry Creek all producing zingy, grassy styles. Even the rather ordinary Chenin is smartening up its act.

Gewürztraminer, despite the large acreage, is usually rather dull and lack-lustre, but Riesling can be good. Made dry it is often a little fat and dull. However, **Chateau St Jean** produce not only a good flowery dry wine, but some brilliant, intensely sweet, Late Harvest styles. Iron Horse sparkling wine is excellent, others are gradually improving.

THE IMPORTANT DETAILS

CLASSIFICATION
All the wines are covered by the 'North Coast' appellation; however, the new regional designations are much more specific, and most wineries attempt to produce wines which qualify for these more valuable appellations. Sonoma County includes Sonoma Valley, Russian River Valley, Dry Creek Valley, Alexander Valley and Knight's Valley. Mendocino is less organized but has recognizable areas in Anderson Valley, Ukiah Valley, McDowell, Redwood and Potter Valleys. Lake, to the east of Mendocino, is also an appellation with some potential.

ORGANIZATION/S
As in the Napa, many of the grapes are produced by independent growers who then sell to wineries. Many of the smaller outfits do largely use their own grapes, but most of the big wineries augment their own vineyard production with bought-in grapes. Many of the wineries are on a fairly small scale and owned by businessmen who pulled out of the rat race such as Davis Bynum in Sonoma County. The changing ownership pattern is shown by Suntory's purchase in 1985 of Chateau St Jean.

READING THE LABEL
There are still a fair number of 'old-style' wineries, and so names like Chianti, Burgundy, Chablis and the like will appear without the slightest chance that they will resemble the real thing. The front or back labels on the better wines will give vineyard names, as this new trend of pinning down the provenance of grapes is particularly marked on the North Coast. The label should also tell you whether grapes are locally grown, and whether they are blended with any other variety.

WHAT DO THEY TASTE LIKE?
North Coast wines don't have quite such dramatic flavours as Napa wines, but, as the present trend towards lighter, fresher wines continues, the Napa producers are finding it very difficult to tone down their flavours and retain personality, while the less intense tastes of North Coast wines need less lightening, and in any case the style is gentler. The move towards tangier, 'greener' white wines suits the area, and the Chenin and Sauvignon are beginning to provide bright, cheap whites.

CALIFORNIA/North Coast

THE IMPORTANT DETAILS

THE GOOD YEARS

With the exception of wineries such as Jordan and Iron Horse, North Coast red is drinkable at an early stage. Consequently there are some good 1987s already on the market as well as the delicious, ripe 1985s and the lighter but beautifully flavoured 1984s. The whites should be drunk young and fresh. 1989 is absolutely delicious for whites though many 1988s and 1987s are now at their peak.

ENJOYING THE WINES

Most North Coast wines have a freshness and a soft edge which makes them very suitable for drinking on their own. Even the reds are often made in a fruity, gulpable style. However, they have enough interest to partner strongly flavoured fish and meat dishes. The heftier, old-style 'Chiantis' and 'burgundies' positively demand the spicy, mouth-filling cuisine which San Francisco is past master of.

CONSUMER INFORMATION

WHAT DO I GET FOR MY MONEY?

On the whole, the wines are good value. Wineries like **Chateau St Jean, Sonoma-Cutrer** and **Jordan** do charge high prices but this is more than matched by the good quality and low price of **Parducci, Fetzer, River Oaks, Glen Ellen, Buena Vista** and others.

AVAILABILITY

This is fairly good on the West Coast, but less consistent elsewhere. On the export market only the larger wineries or some of the more ambitious 'boutiques' are likely to be seen much. Many wineries may only have a single outlet in any one foreign country.

CALIFORNIA/South of the Bay

South of San Francisco, the Central Coast Area spreads 300 miles (480 km) down to Santa Barbara. It consists of two totally different regions, which might be described as the traditional north, encompassing various vineyard areas clustered round the towns of Livermore, Fremont, San José and Santa Clara, and the trailblazing south, beginning round Monterey Bay and spreading through the Salinas Valley to San Luis Obispo and Santa Barbara.

The northern section is as old a wine-making centre as the Napa Valley and sports many of the USA's most historic names: **Paul Masson** from Saratoga, **Almadén** from Los Gatos, **Wente Bros.** and **Concannon** from Livermore and **Mirassou** from San José. Yet all these are situated in agricultural enclaves being eaten into by sprawling urban development, and so these early pioneers have taken up pioneering once again – by establishing wineries in the San Benito mountains and the Salinas Valley which some wine experts saw as being a major California wine region of the future. From a negligible vineyard acreage before Mirassou began planting in 1961, Monterey County, with over 40,000 acres (12,000 hectares) of vines, now has more vineyards than either Napa or Sonoma. What is otherwise left in the north is a mixture of the old-style farm wineries – often of Italian origin and seen to best advantage in the Hecker Pass area of Santa Clara County; and a collection of some of the state's most interesting and individual wineries: **Ridge**, above the clouds in the Santa Cruz mountains in a setting made even more serene by the industrial hurly-burly on the valley floor below; the nearby **Mount Eden** which frequently produces the area's most interesting Chardonnays, **David Bruce** and **Felton-Empire**, perched in the hills between San Francisco and Monterey Bay, producing remarkable heavily flavoured wines, **Bonny Doon**, the pioneer of the Rhône grape varieties in the state, and **Calera**, producing great Pinot Noir on the limestone ridges of the Gavilan mountains.

In the south the Salinas Valley has returned to its original occupation of being the salad bowl of America, but there are still good quality grapes being grown. Although there are some highly individual wineries such as **Chalone, Jekel** and **Morgan** in Monterey County, the real reason behind the plantings was to provide enormous volumes of cheaply

*Intensive cultivation
(Paul Masson, left)
modern equipment
(Firestone, above)
characterize the region.*

produced, cool climate grapes for the vast wine companies. The Salinas Valley acts as a funnel for the cold air of Monterey Bay which is sucked up every day by the heat of the interior. In the event, the chill breezes were more like typhoons and the grapes just didn't ripen properly. Which explains why you now see more lettuces and less grapes around the central town of Soledad.

Below Monterey is San Luis Obispo, an even newer area, which is producing good reds and whites. There are few famous wineries yet, although the county is more established than Monterey, but the quality is undoubtedly good, and Ridge make a special batch of **San Luis Obispo Zinfandel** frpm Paso Robles Vineyards, while **Edna Valley** is building a reputation for whites. However, the Santa Barbara region in the far south does have several famous wineries, chiefly because the cool, hazy conditions of the Santa Maria Valley and Santa Ynez Valley seemed to suit the Pinot Noir grape, which has so far defeated most Californian attempts to tame it. Wineries like **Sanford, Qupé,** and in particular, **Au Bon Climat,** have produced a range of exciting reds and whites.

In general, the wines have a less intense flavour than the wines of the Napa. Yet as always in California, there ,are exceptions. Ridge Vineyards make the greatest Zinfandels in the state as well as very fine Cabernet Sauvignon, and they are characterized by deep, peppery richness. **David Bruce** makes some of the heaviest Chardonnays going, while **Chalone** makes brilliantly balanced, savoury, toasty Chardonnays which any top-line Napa producer would be proud of.

Monterey wines could at one time be recognized by their overpowering smell of bell peppers or capsicum. However most of these vineyards, planted in unsuitably cool locations, have now been uprooted. The whites, in particular the tangy-fresh Sauvignon and lean Chardonnays are more successful, as are the nicely taut, aromatic Rieslings and floral Gewürztraminers.

Santa Ynez and **Santa Maria** have established themselves as front-line producers in less than ten years and their Pinot Noirs do have a richness, a smoky plum or strawberry fruit, and a slightly dangerous acidity which puts them close to the Burgundian model. Chardonnay is excellent, full of fruit and depth for aging. Cabernet and Merlot are good, and Riesling produces a gentle, honeyed fragrance.

CALIFORNIA/South of the Bay

The top single estates like Ridge and Chalone charge high prices for their wines, but they are of very special quality, and there is always a queue to buy. The Santa Ynez Valley wineries, on the other hand, offer high quality and individuality at very reasonable prices, and **Firestone** in particular is worth seeking out. Santa Barbara county in general and Santa Maria in particular are now providing some of the best cool climate fruit in California. Large Napa wineries like **Mondavi** and **Kendall Jackson** have made substantial investments in the region, and the French champagne house Deutz is there.

CALIFORNIA/Central Valley

California produces 90 per cent of all the wine made in the USA, and of that 72 per cent comes from just five companies! It's not difficult to guess where they will be located – in the Central Valley, a searingly hot sprawl of flat land running the length of the San Joaquin Valley from Sacramento County in the north to Bakersfield in the south which produces 80 per cent of all California's wine. It has rich alluvial-deposit soil which can and does produce enormous quantities of grapes, for both eating and wine-making. Until recently, these hot, overripe grapes were likely to be high in sugar and virtually devoid of acidity and aroma. However, as public taste in the USA has shifted away from fortified wines, and even from red wines, to tastes which are increasingly light and white, the giant Valley producers have reacted swiftly to meet demand. Aided by the University of California at Davis, the USA's leading wine school, many new grape varieties have been developed and planted, as well as methods of keeping wines refreshing and thirst-quenching despite the intense heat. **Gallo**, whose enormous capacity winery is the biggest in the world, has always paid great attention to modernizing and improving its operation, and others like **United Vintners, Guild** and **Franzia Brothers**, all with numerous different brand names, produce a tremendous range of good basic wines. There are not many pinnacles of quality in an area dedicated to jug wine, but at Madera, **Ficklin** have a reputation for fine 'port' wines. The Valley is primarily concerned with producing an endless flow of simple, tasty wine, and it achieves this end very well.

To the east of San Joaquin, there is one small outpost of very high quality grapes in Amador County up in the Sierra Nevada foothills. In particular the Shenandoah Valley has numerous plantations of old Zinfandel vines which give a wonderful peppery, blackberry-juice flavoured wine. And to the south, spread inland from Los Angeles in San Bernardino and Riverside Counties, there is a good deal of wine made. In general the Riverside County wines are better and the Temecula area is expanding, with wineries like **Callaway** drawing attention to it with some interesting wines.

CONSUMER CHECKLIST

Firestone	Q:	1	2	3	4	5	6	**7**	8	9	10
Riesling Late-	P:	1	2	3	4	5	**6**	7	8	9	10
Harvest 1986	V:	1	2	3	4	5	6	7	**8**	9	10
Au Bon Climat	Q:	1	2	3	4	5	6	7	8	**9**	10
Pinot Noir	P:	1	2	3	4	5	6	7	**8**	9	10
1988	V:	1	2	3	4	5	6	7	8	9	**10**
Fetzer	Q:	1	2	3	4	5	6	7	8	9	10
Zinfandel	P:	1	2	3	4	**5**	6	7	8	9	10
1988	V:	1	2	3	4	**5**	**6**	7	8	9	10

Good Years California produces almost every possible style of table wine and there is rarely a bad vintage, but there are considerable differences in style and quality which are worth noting. In general, most whites are at their best within 2 years, while some Chardonnays and sweet wines may need 3 to 5 years. Reds are usually at their best from 4 to 6 years and only the very best will improve to 10 years or more. For comments on Vintages see Napa Valley.

Taste Notes The Napa usually has the most concentrated California flavours, but it is impossible to generalize. As a rule the flavours of the wines are big and ripe by European or East Coast standards but increasingly freshness and fruit are taking over from brute strength and richness.

PACIFIC NORTH-WEST

THE GENERAL PICTURE

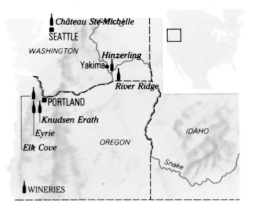

Having created an entirely new market, thirsty for the big brawny flavours of the Golden West, California was rather abruptly left in the cart at the end of the 1970s, when pressures towards fitness and healthfoods in society, and, paradoxically, an increasing desire to use wine as a refreshing, anytime social drink, led wine-drinkers to demand wines which were lighter, fruitier, more acid, more 'cool-climate' than California was used to producing. Although California has adapted her styles at breakneck speed, the one area which was always ideally suited to light, 'North European' style wines without any need to adapt, was the Pacific North-West region of Oregon and Washington, and, now, Idaho as well. In the quest for cool-climate vineyards, one had to look no further than a few hundred miles or so up the Pacific Coast from Mendocino to find the strong sun, tempered by fogs and cooling Pacific breezes which were already marking out Mendocino's Anderson Valley as California's coolest microclimate.

GRAPE VARIETIES AND WINE STYLES
Oregon shot to prominence in 1979 when a Pinot Noir from Eyrie Vineyards in the Wilamette Valley came second to a venerable 1959 Chambolle-Musigny at a blind tasting in Paris. Had the USA at last discovered its own 'Burgundy Côte d'Or'? Would the 'Holy Grail' of great Burgundy-type Pinot Noir wine miraculously appear in this warm but wet valley south-west of Portland? Yes and no. In fact, the Willamette Valley is on the latitude of Bordeaux rather than Burgundy, but the ripening season is slow and although the Bordelais Merlot grape does make delicious wine, the Pinot Noir's ripening pattern seems to match Willamette Valley's climate remarkably well. The light, but fragrant wines of **Eyrie Vineyards,** and the fuller, smokier, more lingering styles of **Knudsen Erath, Rex Hill** and **Cameron** definitely have a burgundian feel, but, hopefully, they will be allowed to develop their own individual character rather than ape burgundy.

Cabernet is not widely successful yet, though the warmer Umpqua Valley south of Willamette may deliver the goods. However, whites are good. Chardonnays are appearing both in a green, Chablis-fresh style, and a much fuller, fatter, vanilla-ey style.

Riesling and Gewürztraminer are much more successful here than they normally are in California – lighter, with a sharper fruit and a lot of grapy spice. Champagne-method sparkling wine is also looking very promising, and one of Australia's leading producers Brian Croser has set up plant in Oregon.

Washington wine-growing is based on the Yakima Valley, in the Columbia River Basin. The contrast with Oregon is stark, because this is a semi-desert in the rainshadow of the formidable Cascade mountains. It would be all sand and shrub were it not for an ambitious irrigation system which has produced vineyards with the unusual ability of matching enormous potential yields of grapes with considerable flavour definition. Both reds and whites are being grown here with great success and the desert climate has been turned to good effect since high daytime temperatures are matched by very cool nights, which means that the grapes ripen well during the day, but preserve their natural

Vines at Preston Wine Cellars, Washington's second-largest winery.

PACIFIC NORTH-WEST

THE GENERAL PICTURE

acidity – crucial in making a refreshing wine – during the chilly nights. That ripening is also affected by quality of light, since Washington boasts very long sunlight hours.

So far the white wines have been the most successful but Cabernet and Merlot are beginning to open out and make tasty wines too. **Columbia Winery** Merlot is soft and creamy, while the Cabernets of producers like **Hinzerling** and **Arbor Crest** show an excellent balance between tough tannin and strong direct blackcurrant and mint fruit. A wide range of white wines are produced and the Gewürztraminer and Riesling of **Columbia**

Winery are remarkably good, showing the dry balance of a French Alsace style, with a hint more perfume for pleasure. **Chateau Sainte Michelle** also makes excellent Riesling and Sauvignon as well as producing a Semillon which is bursting with the honey and green apples fruit that this grape often promises but rarely delivers. Whichever grapes are being used, the flavour intensity is considerable, and indeed many Oregon wineries buy Washington grapes to fatten out their own wines. Idaho's vineyards are very high up – nearly 3,000 ft (915 m) – close by Boise, and the wines are so far very flavourful.

THE IMPORTANT DETAILS

CLASSIFICATION

Oregon has very strict state wine laws. Misleading terms like Chablis, Sauternes, Burgundy, etc., are forbidden. The label must state where the grapes were grown, and a 'single varietal' wine must contain at least 90 per cent of the variety named. Cabernet Sauvignon, exceptionally, is allowed to blend in 25 per cent of the other Bordeaux varieties of Merlot, Cabernet Franc, etc. There are four designated areas: Willamette Valley, Umpqua Valley, Columbia River and Rogue Valley. Washington, dealing primarily with irrigated vineyards, and with less actual winemaking experience, is still in the process of working out how to classify her vineyards. David Lake, the winemaker at Columbia Winery, says 'All of us are involved in experimentation. The vineyards here are so young and inconsistent.' A Washington Wine Institute has been formed, and, with Washington already producing the second largest amount of Vinifera wine grapes after California, classification is sure to follow.

ORGANIZATION/S

Oregon has less than 4,500 acres (1,800 hectares) of vineyards, and these are mostly divided amongst small-holders. The biggest winery, Knudsen Erath, only has 125 acres (50 hectares). Thankfully, many small estates are bottling their own wine. Much wine is trucked across from Washington too for blending. Although Washington's main vineyards are east in the Yakima Valley, her traditional wineries have been in Seattle 150 miles (240

km) away to the west. The recent success of the Yakima wines, however, has caused the biggest companies to build new wineries close to the vineyards. Sagemoor Farms further east on the Columbia River is also a source of good grapes which many wineries buy.

READING THE LABEL

Oregon labels are very clear and direct, and are some of the most informative available. In both Oregon and Washington wines check the alcohol level, since the higher alcohol levels are likely to be drier and stronger. This is especially important with Riesling, since Late Harvest wines may be noticeably sweet, but usually have a low alcohol level marked.

Wine-growing is expanding wherever climatic conditions allow in the Pacific North-West.

WHAT DO THEY TASTE LIKE?

Balance is a key word in Pacific North-West whites. High natural acidity is matched by good natural sugar, giving wines with body, but also considerable fresh fruit and fragrance. Some of the reds are a little light, but the delicate fruit compensates for this.

THE GOOD YEARS

The vintage seems to break volume records every year in Washington. Even 1984's weather-reduced crop was the second biggest ever. But quality also improves; 1985 and 1988 produced some exceptional wine. In general, the whites should be drunk young, but will age, and the reds, even the Pinot Noirs, actually need time. The 1985s need six or seven years to peak.

ENJOYING THE WINES

The whites are marvellously refreshing and thirst-quenching, and the Sauvignons, Gewürztraminers and Rieslings can be drunk anytime. There are some good sweet Late Harvest Rieslings too. Chardonnays are usually delicate rather than massive and shouldn't be put with overpowering dishes, and the same goes for the reds.

CONSUMER INFORMATION

WHAT DO I GET FOR MY MONEY?

Since the Pacific North-West is still a rising star, you get excellent value for money, from Washington in particular. A varietal will normally cost about two-thirds the price of an equivalent Californian wine. As the area becomes more popular, prices will rise, so take advantage now. In particular, buy the light but exciting white wines since the reds can still be a little light.

AVAILABILITY

This is not terribly good so far, and outside the US is extremely poor. However, with the formation of Oregon and Washington Wine Institutes to promote and publicize the wines, distribution should improve, both at home and abroad.

CONSUMER CHECKLIST		
Columbia	Q: 1 2 3 4 5 **6** 7 8 9 10	
Winery Riesling	P: 1 2 3 4 **5** 6 7 8 9 10	
1988	V: 1 2 3 4 5 6 **7** 8 9 10	
Cameron	Q: 1 2 3 4 5 6 7 **8** 9 10	
Pinot Noir	P: 1 2 3 4 **5** 6 7 8 9 10	
1988	V: 1 2 3 4 5 6 7 8 **9** 10	

Good Years The whites are ready to drink as early as one to two years old but the reds, while drinkable young, often need time.

Taste Notes The whites are mostly light and delicate, and often some of the most perfectly balanced of the West Coast wines. Pinot Noir and Merlot are the best reds.

THE EAST COAST

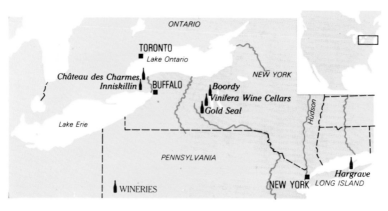

Taylor vineyards
(below, left and right),
bought by Coca-Cola
in the mid-1970s when
the US wine boom hit
the East Coast.

Suddenly vineyards are bursting out all over the country. I was brought up with a start to read that Arkansas had designated Altus on the Missouri-Oklahoma border as its first officially controlled wine region. Yet a look at the history books shows that Altus has been making good wine ever since it was settled and cultivated by Swiss immigrants in the 1870s. Indeed, before Prohibition, with the exception of Nevada and a half dozen Mid-Western States, every other state in the Union had some sort of wine industry. Prohibition killed a large number of these off, but as the interest in wine grows, and the *per capita* consumption heads enthusiastically higher, pioneers are once again establishing vineyards in numerous suitable microclimates right across the nation.

One area never lost its wine industry, and that is the East Coast, and in particular New York State. Indeed, New York has a unique wine-growing structure, because whereas

most wine areas only use the most effective grape species for wine – the Vitis Vinifera, to which family all the good wine grapes belong – New York bases its industry on the Vitis Labrusca, which is far better at making grape jelly and fruit juice than wine. And in between it uses hybrid grape types produced by crossing these two species.

Labrusca grapes can make good fortified wines, and good sparkling wines – New York makes more 'bottle-fermented' sparkling wine than California – but its insistent cherry-sweet perfume makes poor dry wines. The hybrids were developed to provide wine with a more neutral taste, and account for 25 per cent of plantings. The reds are particularly successful, with Marechal Foch, De Chaunac and Baco Noir grape names appearing on the better wines. Seyval Blanc produces attractive, if bland, whites.

The reason that Vinifera wines have only recently begun to make an impact is that for years it was thought that the freezing winters would kill the vines. Well, the arctic winters of 1980 and 1984 would kill just about anything, and yet Vinifera vines with carefully selected cold climate rootstocks survived. The best wines are light and white, and in the traditional Finger Lakes region, lovely scented Chardonnays and Rieslings are coming from producers such as **Wiemer, Heron Hill, Wagner, Gold Seal** and the **Vinifera Wine Cellars** of Constantin Frank, the man who proved such grapes could work in New York.

The most exciting developments are on Long Island where the more temperate climate is producing stunning crisp, delicate Sauvignons and Chardonnays and delicious dry Cabernets from **Hargrave Vineyard** on North Fork as well as hopeful signs from **Pindar** and **Bridgehampton. Long Island** wines could become some of the USA's finest.

No other East Coast state matches New York, but the quality potential is evident further south. Virginia has over 60 wineries trying Vinifera and hybrid grapes. The Italian company Zonin has planted 700 acres (280 hectares). So far both **Rapidan** and **Meredyth** look good for Riesling at least.

Pennsylvania with **Allegro Winery,** and Maryland with **Montbray and Byrd** have even managed to produce first-class dry Cabernet Sauvignon as well as delicate slightly steely Chardonnays and Rieslings.

Michigan, Ohio, Arkansas are all increasing vineyard acreage, and the Lubbock area in Texas looks particularly promising. Within the next few years we should all expect high-quality wines from all these states. It's an exciting prospect.

CANADA

Canada is rarely thought of as having a suitable climate for wine-growing, with its long icy winters, and short blasts of torrid summer. Yet the urge to grow grapes and make wine plods inexorably northwards, in Europe and in North America, and, as rootstocks which can cope with the extreme winters are developed, so wine-growing is gradually spreading in Canada.

There has been wine-growing in Ontario since 1811, but until recently the Ontario wine business has been entirely based on strong-tasting Labrusca grapes and dull hybrids. This meant that although Canada produced some extremely good 'ports' and some tasty 'sherries', the table wines mostly had a strong 'grape jelly' flavour. However, the last ten years have seen the Niagara peninsula sprout Riesling, Gewürztraminer, Aligoté and Chardonnay, and even an 'Ontario Superior' appellation. Names to look for are **Charal, Chateau des Charmes** and **Inniskillin.**

Chateau des Charmes in particular is making some remarkable wines from Chardonnay and, of all things, Gamay. At a blind tasting, I put down their Gamay as the best Beaujolais Villages I'd had all year and marked their top Chardonnay release higher than a Meursault Premier Cru.

Although Nova Scotia is also having a dip at wine grapes in the Annapolis valley, Canada's other main area is the Okanagan valley in British Columbia. The lake-filled valley with cool winters and a long ripening season has been growing grapes since the 1920s, but has mostly used Californian imported grapes and must as well as local grapes to make its wines. As legislation has enforced greater use of local grapes, quality has begun to improve, with wineries like **Claremont, Casabello,** and **Sumac Ridge Estate** beginning to make the best of the favourable conditions around Peachland and Summerland. What beautiful regional appellations those will make in time.

AUSTRALIA

Darwin

NORTHERN TERRITORY

Alice Springs   QUEENSLAND

WESTERN AUSTRALIA

Roma

SOUTH AUSTRALIA   Brisbane

Swan Valley   NEW SOUTH WALES
Perth
    SYDNEY
Margaret River   ADELAIDE   CANBERRA

VICTORIA
    MELBOURNE
WINE REGIONS
    TASMANIA
    Hobart

If we hear less about the amazing achievements of the Australians than of the Californians in pushing back the frontiers of winemaking knowledge and blasting the old-established classic areas of Europe with irresistible and original flavours, maybe it's because they spend less time talking about it, and more time drinking it. Australia has the highest annual *per capita* wine consumption of any English-speaking nation at over 20 litres, and the most solid annual rate of increase. And perhaps she doesn't feel she has a lot to prove, because international renown is nothing new for Australian winemakers. Over a century ago Australian wines were carrying

off top prizes at exhibitions in Europe, like the Vienna Exhibition in 1873, when a Hermitage grown in Victoria was adjudged so good that the French judges refused to believe it wasn't French and withdrew in protest.

Things looked set fair in 'John Bull's Vineyard', but it all fell apart in a rush. The Phylloxera louse managed to creep in during the 1870s and within 20 years had wrecked the nation's vineyards – with the exception of South Australia, protected by mountain and desert. Also, the great wines of the 1860s and 1870s had been made by first-generation immigrants from France, Germany and Switzerland who brought with them a love of

good table wine. Their children obviously didn't inherit it, for, with many of the finest vineyards killed by disease, the big, hot valley floor vineyards of South Australia began to pump out enormous quantities of brandy and thick sweet fortified wines. For 60 years, the fine wine tradition sank into the desert sands. But, just as the 1960s brought Californian wine to life, so improved communications, greater travel opportunities and greater wealth, bringing with them a new awareness of both European pleasures and the possibility of reproducing them at home, led to what must be one of the most remarkable explosions in the world of wine.

From seeing Australia as a tough arid land with the sun beating down and the throat eternally parched and croaking out for an ice cold beer, it is now possible to trace a thousand tiny dots across the five states of New South Wales, Victoria, South Australia, Western Australia and Tasmania, where enthusiasts have either sought out tiny microclimates to colonize and expand, or (particularly in the case of Victoria) have revitalized long dead acres.

The winemakers are characterized by a potent mixture of blind enthusiasm and high technical know-how. They are characterized on the one side by being fourth- or fifth-generation wine families, and on the other by being psychiatrists, lawyers and dentists who may not even have given up their practices, but for whom the lure of owning a vineyard and tilling the soil became irresistible. If you think that sounds schmaltzy and too story-bookish to believe, take a trip down to the Southern Seas, and you'll find that Australian winemakers are some of the most contented men in the world, producing some of the world's most individual wines. And, although from time to time a modern Australian wine has sauntered up to the opposition from Europe's classic areas and given the old-timer a roasting in open competition, nevertheless, whereas California has purposely headed out and challenged Europe with her best wines, Australia has pursued a policy of making her wines with rather less reference to European models. And when they therefore lack European 'class' or 'elegance', they're going hell for leather to add something definably and identifiably Australian in their place. Which the world of wine should be thankful for, because, in doing so, they offer us fascinating, original flavours which are already becoming a model many European winemakers would like to follow.

Above, the Yalumba winery, in the Barossa Valley, pictured in 1925; it looks substantially unchanged today yet houses one of Australia's most innovative wineries. **Left,** the Rosemount winery in the Upper Hunter Valley is a brand new operation which has swept the board in competitions from a standing start in 1969.

AUSTRALIA/New South Wales

THE GENERAL PICTURE

New South Wales is the home of the Hunter Valley, a small, thoroughly difficult area, which for years has been presumed to produce the archetypal Australian wine: the reds big, strong, tarry, sweaty – real 'man's stuff' – and the whites big, strong, oily, petrolly – 'man's stuff' again. Certainly, much Hunter wine is still of this thick, daunting style, but just as certainly, New South Wales is *not* just the Hunter Valley, and even within the ultra-conservative Hunter, the winds of change are beating against the battened windows of entrenched old-timers, and the finest wines are from winemakers who have the experience to deal with the Hunter's tricky conditions, as well as to innovate.

The Hunter Valley is inland from Newcastle, about 200 km (125 miles) north of Sydney, and the fact that 11 km (7 miles) of this on the main route are dirt road says something of the rugged individuality of the inhabitants. Rugged is an important qualification, because, as James Halliday, the scholar of the Hunter, says, 'The Hunter only makes 2 per cent of Australia's wine and is here because it makes great wine in spite of itself. In modern winemaking terms, you could never professionally allow anyone to plant here.'

The rainfall pattern is wrong – drought in the spring when you need moisture, downpours during the vintage period. The growing season is far too hot, and far too humid. Grapes get scorched, then go rotten. This could explain why the Hunter, which in the nineteenth century stood as Australia's first and finest vineyard, was almost extinct by the 1950s. It was just too much trouble. Luckily, the sweeping enthusiasm for wine which gripped California gripped Australia too. The Hunter was close to Sydney, Australia's most cosmopolitan city, and the stream of lawyers, accountants, surveyors and company executives, suddenly turned vineyard owners, which produced the re-birth of quality in California, did the same in Australia. This invasion by enthusiastic amateurs had another excellent side-effect. The large old companies which had let the Hunter decline were revitalized, and they, too, are now realizing that quality is the only way to make things pay.

The most historic part of the Hunter is the Lower Hunter, where the finest wines are produced. Here vineyards are mostly small and frequently eccentric. The Upper Hunter is flatter, drier, and the irrigated vineyards are mostly in the hands of large companies, intent upon producing high yields of pleasant wines rather than low yields of brilliant ones.

A little to the west is Mudgee. An unpromising name, but this high-altitude vineyard area specializing in Chardonnay and Cabernet is of high quality. Like Margaret River and Great Southern in Western Australia, it also has an appellation system, albeit voluntary!

Cowra is another slow-ripening area west of Sydney which seems so suited to Chardonnay that its grape prices are some of the highest in Australia, and the Chardonnay is trucked to both South Australia and Victoria.

On the Victoria border, Corowa makes fine 'sticky' dessert wines, but the grape basket of New South Wales, growing 70 per cent of the state's total is the Murrumbidgee Irrigation Area (MIA) based round Griffith. Absolutely anything grows here, and grapes are no exception, producing enormous quantities of light fresh wines, most of which end up in bag-in-boxes or wine casks; over 50 per cent of Australian wine is now drunk from these so-called 'bladder-packs', and their fresh, simple flavours make one wonder why European countries have such trouble in getting decent wine to flow from *their* wine boxes.

GRAPE VARIETIES AND WINE STYLES

There are over 60 different grape types grown in New South Wales, and the range of wines made is as wide as anywhere in Australia. Which means the world! The main red grape is the Shiraz or Syrah, here often called Hermitage. In the Lower Hunter and Mudgee it can make dark, glowering wines with the reek of cow-sheds and hard-ridden leather which has given the priceless description 'sweaty saddle' to the wine world. However, it can, as at **Rothbury,** develop a marvellous dry, peppery style. In the Upper Hunter it is often a little sweet and dull, and from Murrumbidgee it is usually soft and used in blending. Cabernet Sauvignon is the rising star, and is re-making the Hunter's reputation, yet 20 years ago it had died out in the Hunter till the great Max Lake met the complacent old-timers of the Valley head on, replanted Cabernet, and at **Lake's Folly,** in a burst of blackcurrant and mint perfume, allied to a dry dark Bordeaux-like superstructure, he produced one of Australia's greatest reds.

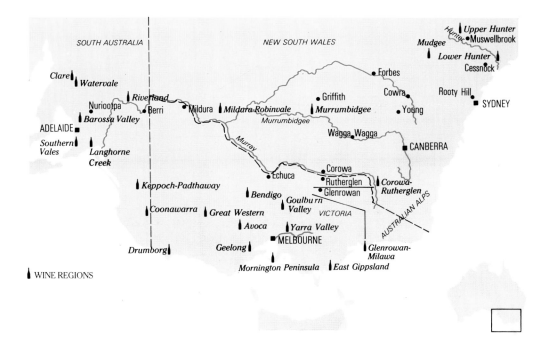

Brokenwood also is particularly successful in a deep, plummy way, while **Allandale**, and **Huntington Estate** and **Craigmoor** in Mudgee provide exciting fruity wines. Pinot Noir had an amazing boost when **Tyrrells** 1976 Pinot Noir beat all the French opposition hands down in Paris at the Gault-Millau Wine Olympics in 1981, but is rarely able to repeat this show-stopping act. In the whites, Semillon, often called Hunter Riesling, is the famous Hunter white, dry, tart and green when young, needing 10 to 20 years to blossom – if that's the word – into a strong-willed, tempestuous white, full of petrol and spice and, if you're lucky, some honey. A 'love it or loathe it' style.

Chardonnay is taking over as the most exciting white, both at wineries like Lindeman's and Lake's Folly in the Lower Hunter, at **Rosemount** and **Arrowfield** in the Upper Hunter, and at most wineries in Mudgee and Cowra. The flavours can be sensational. A full yellow green coloured wine gives out a rich buttery scent from the oak barrel maturing and a flavour of wonderfully honeyed softness, matched with fresh, thirst-quenching fruit. Very exciting. The aromatic grapes like Rhine Riesling and Traminer don't do much in the Lower Hunter, but are excellent in the Upper Hunter and the mainstay, with Semillon, Trebbiano and the wonderfully named Fruity Gordo, of the MIA.

The MIA is a bulk area selling good cheap wine, yet one winery, **De Bortoli**, makes a brilliant 'noble rot' sweet white as great as the best in Bordeaux! That's Australia for you!

THE IMPORTANT DETAILS

CLASSIFICATION

Mudgee has established its own appellation, otherwise there is no control in New South Wales, and, indeed, precise adherence to grape varietals and vintage are less common here than elsewhere, given a long history of blending and mixing. Serious new wineries, however, do follow the rules of varietal and vintage dating pretty closely.

ORGANIZATION/S

Until recently, the Hunter was made up of small and medium-sized family operations. In the 1960s big business interests took over many of the established vineyards and companies, while the 'amateur entrepreneurs' established the new small, high-quality vineyards. The MIA was largely established on 30-hectare (75-acre) land grants to soldiers

THE IMPORTANT DETAILS

after World War One, and moulded in wine style by a considerable influx of Italians in the 1920s. Many of these families still run vineyards, but the giant McWilliams group is the most important for quality and quantity.

READING THE LABEL
Australia is the land of the rogue label, and New South Wales is as bad as anywhere. Expect 'Claret' – a virtual guarantee there is no Cabernet in the wine; 'Burgundy' – certainly no Pinot Noir; 'Chablis' – little hope of Chardonnay here, and the like. Also, many companies launch wines under 'vat numbers' – Tyrrell's best Chardonnay, for example, is just 'Vat 47'. Big companies like Penfolds, McWilliams, and Lindeman's tag their best wine with 'bin numbers', but usually explain on the label what this entails.

WHAT DO THEY TASTE LIKE?
The overall impression of New South Wales is of characterful wines, plugging the personality of the soils and the winemakers. They are rarely the gentlest of Australia's styles. MIA wines vie with the Riverland for the title 'Best value everyday wines in the world'.

THE GOOD YEARS
Given Australia's climate, it is extremely difficult to generalize about vintages, and the skill of the winemaker in minimizing the sun's effects is often the most important factor. 1984 and 1985 were good but less exciting than elsewhere in Australia, while 1986 was outstanding and 1987 very good. 1988 and 1989 made good wine in difficult conditions, but vintage rains in 1989 spoiled the party.

ENJOYING THE WINES
The MIA reds and whites are delightful 'any time' wines – innocuous their flavours may be, but simple, clean, innocuous fresh fruit is OK by me. The great Chardonnays are fine enough to partner classic cuisine, while the Hunter Semillons are often better with meat than fish. Hunter reds are for red meats, winter stews and cheese.

CONSUMER INFORMATION

WHAT DO I GET FOR MY MONEY?
Lower Hunter wines are among Australia's most expensive, and are only good value from the top estates like **Lake's Folly, Peterson, Tyrrell** and **Rothbury Estate. Upper Hunter** wines and **Mudgee** wines can be cheap and good, while the **MIA** wines are dirt-cheap and fine value.

AVAILABILITY
This is better than it used to be, but the top estates are not big producers and can sell almost all they make locally. Lindeman's, McWilliams, Rothbury and Rosemount wines are more widely seen, and the MIA wines are slowly spreading outside the state.

Picnic areas frequently adjoin vineyards as at Lindeman's estate in the Hunter Valley.

AUSTRALIA/Victoria

THE GENERAL PICTURE

Victoria more than any other state suffered from the devastation of the Phylloxera louse and the shift in taste away from light table wine which occurred in Australia during the first half of this century, because, during the nineteenth century, Victoria was not only the biggest producer – her volume of wine in 1889, at over 7 million litres, was way ahead of South Australia at 2.3 million and New South Wales at 3.1 million – but the fame of her wines had spread worldwide, especially to Europe, and she won the great majority of awards both in domestic and international competitions. Geelong, Bendigo and the Yarra Valley were making delicate, balanced reds and whites which were building great renown for their areas.

Then came Phylloxera, which hit Bendigo and Geelong so hard that the government ordered the uprooting of every single vine. In 1881, just eight years after the wines had been trouncing European competitions at the 1873 Vienna Exhibition, the Phylloxera and the Victorian government had, between them, destroyed the entire area. It took 85 years before the next vine was planted in Geelong in 1966, 68 years before Bendigo saw another vine, and the Yarra Valley waited till 1968 for the re-establishment of her most famous vineyard, St Huberts. In the last 15 years, these three districts have shot to the fore of Australian wine-making once again, with the revived areas of Great Western, Pyrenees and Central Goulburn Valley also close behind.

If none of these names means much to us yet, it is because of the almost complete demise of wine-growing in Victoria during the first 60 years of this century while at least South Australia and New South Wales continued to release small amounts of their great wines. North-east Victoria, and in particular Rutherglen – already famous for brilliant sweet Muscats and fortified wines – was able to survive Phylloxera and the slump in demand for fine wine, and paradoxically is now the area which is struggling to find markets for wines whose greatness roars at you from the glass. Several other tiny wine areas are beginning to flower again, like Shepparton, Gippsland and Ballarat where the promising Yellowglen sparkling wine operation is based. And of course Victoria has her own grape basket irrigated area – this time round Swan

Baileys of Bundarra in N.E. Victoria the essential colours of an Australian vineyard: the deep green foliage of irrigated vines, the parched beige earth and the shimmering blue of vital water.

Hill and Mildura. In the last 15 years Victoria has begun to re-establish herself as a leading producer. Her wines are so fine, and so varied, that the next 15 years will see her fighting to regain her place as Australia's Number One quality producer.

GRAPE VARIETIES AND WINE STYLES
Victoria's great strength lies in the fact that so many of her best vineyards have been planted in the last 10 to 15 years, and so the grape varieties chosen are mostly modern, effective performers. However, with this narrower range of classic grape varieties, the variations in style are still greater than in any other state. Endless trial, not much error, and 'All Change' every vintage is the order of the day as Victoria's young winemakers probe further in the search for quality.

AUSTRALIA/Victoria

THE GENERAL PICTURE

Left, *Mitchelton Vineyards in Central Victoria are a new, futuristic operation situated along the banks of the Goulburn River.* **Right,** *the Brown Bros team graft new vines to Phylloxera-resistant rootstock; a shortage of popular varieties means go-ahead companies propagate their own grapes.*

Cabernet Sauvignon is as usual the leading red grape, but is often blended with the other Bordeaux varieties. In the Yarra Valley, from wineries like **Yarra Yering** and **St Huberts** or from **Delatite** and the **Mount Helen Vineyard,** the mixture of blackcurrant and mint is piercing, fragrant and unforgettable. The wines get fuller from **Chateau Tahbilk** in Central Goulburn and **Taltarni** in Pyrenees, adding a eucalyptus gum perfume to the blackcurrant, and are darkest and strongest in the northeast. **Brown Bros** make big fruity wines, while the Muscat specialists like **Baileys Vineyards** produce massive, black, 'drink me if you dare' wines to stain your lips purple.

Shiraz, too, is very successful. The lightest, most perfumed, yet peppery style is from the Ovens Valley where **Wynn** make a wonderful example. It can produce astonishing chocolate, plum and liquorice flavours in Great Western from **Cathcart Ridge,** and big plum pudding and leather wines too, from **Bests, Mount Langi-Ghiran** or Taltarni and Chateau Tahbilk, but if you're in any doubt about the mixture of sweat and hobnail boots and unwashed Old English sheepdogs which make up Shiraz at its most unashamed – get back to North-east Victoria for a Shiraz from Baileys. That'll really put hairs on your chest. Chest? It would put hairs on your teeth! Pinot Noir is looking tremendously optimistic in the Yarra Valley and the dry, fragrant flavours of **Coldstream Hills, Mount Mary** or **Yarra Yering** are full of excitement. **Delatite** is perfumed and original.

Chardonnay leads the whites, and Victoria Chardonnays are the softest, creamiest, most succulent examples. Wineries like **St. Huberts, Lillydale, St Leonard's, Coldstream Hills** and **Tisdall** lead the way.

Semillon is less planted but can be silky smooth from a winery like Brown Bros, while Sauvignon can be tart, tangy and nettle-green as at Taltarni or gooseberry-fruited and soft from oak barrels as at Tisdall.

Rhine Riesling is usually very dry, peppery, steely and quite spritzy when young, but is excellent at two to three years old, from wineries like **Knights Granite Hills,** and as an intensely sweet German-style 'Beerenauslese' wine from St Huberts and **Seville Estate** in the Yarra is quite superb.

Gewürztraminer is good too, often developing rich, Muscaty flavours, as at **Best's Great Western,** or being restrained, fruity and deliciously fresh as at **Delatite.**

And then there's Muscat. Brown Bros make a dry Muscat, but the glories of the north-east are the **Liqueur Muscats** of Glenrowan and Rutherglen. Fortified and aged in old oak barrels for years, they combine the body and guts of great madeira with a sweet beauty which is like the bottled essence of the ripest grapes on a late-summer hot-house vine. The Muscadelle grape makes the sweet raisiny **Tokay.** Sparkling wines are very good in Victoria. **Seppelt Great Western, Yellowglen** and **Domaine Chandon** are the leaders, but **Mildara** in the irrigated north-west can also make it very good and very cheap.

CLASSIFICATION
Victoria is still in a state of expansion, exploring how best to use her different vineyards and grape varieties, but they have tried a system of classification without much success.

ORGANIZATION/S
There is a lot of trucking of grapes in Victoria, often for considerable distances, as winemakers wait for their own vineyards to mature or decide how to influence the style their own grapes can produce. Many vineyards are small and run by owners with other professions.

READING THE LABEL
Victoria labels are less likely to be covered in jokes and nonsense than most other states' offerings, and there is a much higher incidence of accurate, informative varietal and vintage labelling. Some, like Yarra Yering, which labels its offerings 'Dry Red Wine numbers 1 and 2' or Bests, which keeps up the old 'claret' and 'hock' terminology, can be confusing, but they are in the minority.

WHAT DOES IT TASTE LIKE?
Victoria offers the lot, from the sharpest, freshest modern tastes to the ancient 'mountain man' chewiness of the last of the old timers. The wealth of styles in between makes Victoria Australia's most exciting state.

THE GOOD YEARS
Things are changing so continually in Victoria, that the vintage is often marked, not by weather conditions, but by how the winemaker adapted to the year's conditions and what he decided to have a go at that vintage. 1985 and 1986 were exceptional with 1987 a bit patchy but generally exciting. 1988 was excellent, 1989 more difficult, but 1990 exciting. Whites can be ready immediately; reds usually only need four to five years.

ENJOYING THE WINE
The peppery Rhine Rieslings are particularly good with seafood and grilled fish. The reds have a juicy fruit, best matched to simple meat dishes, but the biggest Shirazes could take on anything. Muscats and Beerenausleses deserve your undivided attention.

CONSUMER INFORMATION

WHAT DO I GET FOR MY MONEY?
Some of the small wineries, particularly in the Yarra Valley, charge rather high prices, but the larger wineries in Great Western, Central Goulburn and Pyrenees are very fairly priced. The north-west is good and cheap, while the great wines of the north-east are often grossly undervalued.

AVAILABILITY
The most fashionable small wineries are rarely available outside the state, but the bigger wineries are often available nationally. With a few exceptions, like Chateau Tahbilk, Taltarni and Brown Bros, export availability is not good, and the Rutherglen Muscats are distressingly difficult to find.

SOUTH AUSTRALIA

THE GENERAL PICTURE

South Australia towers over the other states in production terms – producing around 60 per cent of the national output in an average year, between two-and-a-half and three times as much as New South Wales, the nearest challenger. The Murrumbidgee Irrigation Area is New South Wales's grape basket, but the Riverland Irrigated Area of South Australia produces as much as the whole of New South Wales, and both the Barossa Valley and the McLaren Vale, closer to the capital city of Adelaide, are no slouchers when it comes to quantity.

Yet if this makes South Australia sound like a mere bulk producer of anonymous hooch, this is not being fair. South Australia took over the mantle of wine-supplier to the nation in the late nineteenth century when the rest of Australia was devastated by the vine louse Phylloxera, and South Australia, protected by desert and sea, was untouched. Consequently, she had to satisfy all of Australia's thirst for wine which was usually of the heavy, sweet, cheap sort, and her reputation has continued to be that of a supplier of big, flabby Barossa Valley Rieslings, and scorching McLaren Vale reds, rather than that of a quality producer of similar rank to the other states. There has been one notable exception to this – the Coonawarra district, tucked away in the parched, empty wilderness at the southern tip of the state. Out of nowhere, a thin slash of rich red soil cuts like a flame across the barren plain. This is the famous Terra Rossa, or red earth, which grows the grapes for Australia's most elegant, delicate reds. The Coonawarra was close to extinction after Phylloxera, with

plantings dwindling to 120 hectares (300 acres) before World War Two. But the 1960s were the turning point here, as in the Hunter Valley of New South Wales. The rush to fine wine caused people to realize how underused this great area was, and in the 1970s plantings in the region increased by over 700 per cent.

If Coonawarra is the most famous, South Australia also boasts other areas where fine wine is once more being made. Padthaway and Keppoch, just north of Coonawarra, are producing excellent whites, as is Langhorne Creek on the Murray River estuary. The Southern Vales and McLaren Vale have stopped simply producing blockbusting reds and are coming up with a remarkable line of grassy-fresh reds and whites.

The Barossa and Clare Valleys are still chiefly involved with bulk wine, but the Clare is now producing some cuttingly crisp whites as well as chunky reds, and the Barossa is using far more Riverland fruit to lighten the valley's rather solid style, as well as leading the way in turning hot-climate grapes into fresh, incisive whites.

The high-altitude areas of Pewsey Vale, Springton, and, in particular, the Eden Valley, have brought Rhine Riesling to its peak of achievement in Australia. Add to this the presence of Australia's most influential young winemaker – Brian Croser – and Roseworthy College, which, next to Davis in California, is the most influential wine school in the world, and you can see that South Australia has a lot more to offer than simply an endless supply of wine casks and 'sherry' flagons.

Far left, *The Petaluma vineyards above Adelaide are often wreathed in fog and drenched with rain. Here, Australia's messianic young wine-maker, Brian Croser is attempting to produce definitive cool-climate whites and sparkling wines.* Left, *irrigation in full flow at Wynns, Coonawarra, in spite of the fact that this is one of Australia's famous cool areas.*

GRAPE VARIETIES AND WINE STYLES

There is the usual vast array of grapes grown. However, Cabernet and Shiraz dominate the reds. Cabernet is at its finest in the Coonawarra. The climate is as remarkable as the soil here and it actually has a cooler ripening season than either Burgundy or Champagne – two of France's most northerly wine regions! The wine is often pale in colour but with a haunting blackcurrant and mint sweet perfume, and a delicate cedary dryness in the mouth which makes one realize why it is called 'The Médoc of Australia'. **Bowen Estate, Lindeman's Rouge Homme** and **Wynns** are three of the finest. Cabernet does well elsewhere – particularly in the Clare Valley where the minty fruit remains – but wines like **Taylor's Chateau Clare** add a tannic bite, as does the Cabernet-Malbec blend of **Stanley Leasingham,** and in the Southern Vales the

fruit is strong, as shown by Hardy's, Geoff Merrill, **Coriole, Chateau Reynella, Pirramimma** and **Maxwell** wines.

Up in the Riverland the standard of a cheap wine like **Berri–Renmano's Cabernet** is nothing short of astonishing. Shiraz, in the almost Nouveau-fresh style or the traditional buttery oaked style, is the top red Barossa variety. In Coonawarra, it produces a minty, gentle wine with a hint of peach and pepper far removed from its normal beefy reputation. **Wynns** and **Rosemount** give two particularly good examples.

One wine which doesn't quite fit into any category is **Penfolds Grange Hermitage,** Australia's most fabled red wine, with all the bull-necked power of old-fashioned blackstrap Shiraz, yet so piled with fruit and character, chocolate, blackcurrant and even that 'ole sweaty saddle, that you blithely agree with every accolade bestowed on it. Shiraz is often blended with Cabernet, and the soft, oaky **Wolf Blass Grey Label** from Langhorne Creek shows how successful this can be.

Rhine Riesling is the top white variety, and, though a little flabby in the Barossa, it can be superb, steely, lemony, almost hard, but wonderfully refreshing from a producer like **Enterprise,** or **Orlando's Eden Valley.** The fruitier styles of **Hill-Smith's Pewsey Vale,** or **Jim Barry's** fragrant apples and pears **Lodge Hill** wines show the grapes' versatility. Chardonnay is excellent from Padthaway, Clare Valley and Southern Vales. Riverland Chardonnay can be as shockingly good and cheap as the Cabernet. Various producers do a big 'port' style which is excitingly flavoured.

THE IMPORTANT DETAILS

CLASSIFICATION

South Australia's chief classification is that she will not allow one single grape across her borders for fear of Phylloxera. Inside her borders, a good deal of trucking of grapes and wine takes place, and in 1980 Krondorf Winery won the Jimmy Watson Trophy for best young red with a Cabernet from Coonawarra, Barossa and Southern Vales!

ORGANIZATION/S

Co-operatives are more important here than in any other part of Australia. The giant ir-

rigated vineyards of the Riverland region are dominated by four massive co-operatives, whose chief job it is to slake the thirst of the 'wine cask' or 'bag-in-box' market, but who also produce increasingly good bottled wine. Elsewhere, except in Southern Vales, large companies control most of the wineries.

READING THE LABEL

South Australia hides a lot of its best wine behind 'bin numbers'. Who but a vinous Sherlock Holmes would be able to decipher

SOUTH AUSTRALIA

THE IMPORTANT DETAILS

Orlando's 'Premium Burgundy Bin 732 ITI 1971'??? Yet those bin numbers all have a significance, as do the medal achievements at State and National Wine Fairs. Coonawarra labelling is usually by grape variety. In blends, the dominant grape will be placed first.

WHAT DO THEY TASTE LIKE?
South Australia creates a multitude of tastes, but in general the cool areas of Coonawarra, Padthaway, Eden Valley and Pewsey Vale will give particularly light, fragrant flavours, whereas the Southern Vales and Clare Valley will be well defined but stronger, and the Barossa can be a bit fat. The Riverland can astound with the true varietal tang of its wines.

THE GOOD YEARS
The Coonawarra is the most susceptible to vintage variation, yet bad years are rare. 1990 is tremendous, 1989 more problematical, 1987, 1986 good. 1985 and 1984 are good right across the state, and only 1983 provided a dicy Coonawarra vintage, though elsewhere it was good.

ENJOYING THE WINES
Lamb, simply roasted, is the ideal partner for Coonawarra reds. The steely Rhine Rieslings, on the other hand, are at their best with fish dishes. The Riverland wines are supremely multi-purpose.

CONSUMER INFORMATION

WHAT DO I GET FOR MY MONEY?
Riverland wines are brilliant value for money. Many of the modern winemakers like **Yalumba, Orlando, Hardy** and **Leo Buring** offer great value, particularly in whites. Coonawarra reds are rare, exquisitely flavoured, and rarely overpriced.

AVAILABILITY
Distribution for the big companies is fairly general throughout Australia, and is beginning to make itself felt abroad, particularly on the west coast of North America, and in Holland and Great Britain. Coonawarra reds are probably the most generally available.

WESTERN AUSTRALIA

Australian winemakers are an individualist bunch. They try to make wines with something of the stamp of their own personality on them. They often truck grapes hundreds of kilometres to satisfy a hunch they have as to what will make the best blend. And they don't take kindly to being told what to put on their labels and in their bottles. Not surprisingly, therefore, they don't take kindly to the idea of a government-regulated Appellation of Origin system. Yet it was some of the most rugged of all Australia's pioneer winegrowers, in some of the most inaccessible vineyards, who were the first to do just that. The Margaret River and Lower Great Southern Areas of Western Australia established Australia's first 'Appellation of Origin' system; others have followed, so we'll have to see! But then these are two extremely new regions, remote, cool and tricky to farm. As it is, these two fledgling areas clearly benefit from the notoriety of being first in with an appellation, but, as output grows, they won't need legal controls to succeed because the quality of wines is exciting. Names like **Leeuwin Estate, Vasse Felix** and **Moss Wood** in the Margaret River are producing delicious Cabernets, Chardonnays and

Pinot Noir, while Cape Mentelle has the audacity to grow Zinfandel – and successfully!

Lower Great Southern, on the far south-western tip of Australia, is even more remote and just as exciting; names to watch for here are **Chateau Barker, Conti Forest Hill** and **Plantagenet.** Closer to the capital city of Perth, and warmer too, is the less clearly defined area of the South West Coastal Plain. Vineyards here share the unlikely characteristic of being composed of light sand, not generally reckoned likely to produce good wine. Somehow it does here. **Capel Vale** produces lovely spicy Rhine Rieslings (true German Riesling is always called Rhine Riesling in Australia, to differentiate it from Clare Riesling, which is the obscure French grape Crouchen Blanc, and **Hunter Valley Riesling,** which is Semillon!!) as well as good rich Shiraz. This is the French Syrah of Hermitage fame, and the Australians also call it Hermitage.

Peel Estate is another Zinfandel outpost – this time the wine is pink-red and gushingly fruity – and produces a Shiraz which shows all the gentleness and none of the crassness of the grape.

These are the new directions for Western Australia. Its original vineyards, still thriving but less fashionable, are in the heat-bowl of the Swan Valley near Perth. Many of the wineries are tiny smallholdings, often with a strong Yugoslav presence, and a correspondingly solid approach to wine-making. Yet the big companies like Houghton and Sandalford are also here. Western Australian wines have been treated with scant respect in the east till recently, and the old adage of Jack Mann, Houghton's ex-winemaker, can still hold true here. 'Wines should be resplendent with generosity,' he said. 'Unless a wine can be diluted with an equal volume of water it wasn't worth making in the first place.' Yet even Houghton is changing, and the new releases of their white burgundy – traditionally made from Chenin and Muscadelle (not a whisper of Chardonnay) – now march to the pipes of the 'cool climate clone' brigade. Already a winery like Evans & Tate, where they pick weeks earlier than their neighbours and rigorously control fermentation and aging, produce fine wine with the right approach. Prices are high for the estate wines from the south, but lowish in the Swan. Availability is almost non-existent for the former, and poor outside the state even for the commercial Swan Valley wineries.

CONSUMER CHECKLIST				
Orlando	Q:	1 2 3 4 5 **6** 7 8 9 10	**Good Years** Only a few years ago Australia wines were likely to mature fast and age quickly. However, the gallop towards cool-climate vineyards and modern technology is creating reds and whites which are ready to drink quickly but will last well. Many whites now improve over 3 to 5 years and Semillons often need 10 years while reds are often enjoyable in 3 years but will last 7 to 10, 1989, 1987, 1986, 1985 and 1984 were in general cool years favouring reds and whites of great style; reds from these vintages can age, even though they are delicious young.
Riverland	P:	1 2 3 4 **5** 6 7 8 9 10	
Chardonnay	V:	1 2 3 4 5 6 **7** 8 9 10	
Taltarni Fumé	Q:	1 2 3 4 5 6 **7** 8 9 10	
Blanc	P:	1 2 3 4 5 **6** 7 8 9 10	
	V:	1 2 3 4 5 6 **7** 8 9 10	
Rosemount	Q:	1 2 3 4 **5** 6 7 8 9 10	
Traminer	P:	1 2 3 4 **5** 6 7 8 9 10	
Riesling	V:	1 2 3 4 **5** 6 7 8 9 10	
Hill-Smith	Q:	1 2 3 4 5 **6** 7 8 9 10	
Estate Shiraz	P:	1 2 3 **4** 5 6 7 8 9 10	
	V:	1 2 3 4 5 6 **7** 8 9 10	
Wynns	Q:	1 2 3 4 5 6 7 **8** 9 10	**Taste Notes** Australia is probably the most exciting and innovative wine country in the world, with an array of flavours and styles which are impossible to corral into any set format. The reds veer from heavy solid reds to some of the most clearly defined examples of their grape varieties, while the whites are usually outstanding in Chardonnay, Rhine Riesling and Semillon.
Coonawarra	P:	1 2 3 4 5 6 **7** 8 9 10	
Estate Cabernet	V:	1 2 3 4 5 6 7 8 **9** 10	
Sauvignon			
Coldstream Hills	Q:	1 2 3 4 5 6 7 **8** 9 10	
Pinot Noir	P:	1 2 3 4 5 6 7 **8** 9 10	
	V:	1 2 3 4 5 6 7 8 **9** 10	

AUSTRALIA/Tasmania

Tasmania's day as a leading wine state will come, but it hasn't come yet. What it has against it are the need to establish vineyards virtually from scratch, the relative lack of a wine-conscious local market as well as a generally recognized sense of isolation from the mainland. In its favour are climate and soil. All over Australia, winemakers are seeking out cooler and cooler regions to make fruitier, more elegant wines. Tasmania is a whole 5° of latitude further south than the mainland's most southerly vineyards. This puts it on a par with Bordeaux in the northern hemisphere. Also, the soil is good, and the Terra Rossa basalt soil which makes

Australia's Coonawarra wines so exceptional recurs in Tasmania. The best vineyards, in particular **Pipers Brook, Heemskerk** and **Moorilla,** are in the north near Launceston. Rhine Riesling is very exciting from Moorilla and Pipers Brook, flashing with strong, sharp dry, austere, 'French-style' Chardonnay. All these wineries make exciting Cabernet, the Heemskerk stark, herby, with a whiff of eucalyptus, while the Moorilla and Pipers Brook have all the juicy blackcurrant and mint of top-quality cool-climate Cabernet. The word's getting round, too. **Anakie Vineyards** in Victoria buys Tasmanian Cabernet grapes and ships them over to ferment on the mainland!

NEW ZEALAND

THE GENERAL PICTURE

New Zealand is such a newcomer to the production of great wines that it is easy to dismiss her efforts, saying that no-one could possibly have come so far so fast. That is, until you taste the wines, and then the piercing, memorable fruit flavours are more than enough to persuade anyone who hasn't got a lead palate that this little country marooned out in the seas south-east of Australia, is a new, rapidly rising star in the world of wine.

James Busby, the supposed father of the Australian wine industry, established New Zealand's vineyards in the nineteenth century, but it wasn't really until the 1960s that New Zealand was producing anything but heavy, sweet fortified wines and a little

cumbersome, rough, 'Dally plonk' for the local Yugoslav workers round Auckland. A visit by Dr Helmut Becker of the Geisenheim Wine School in Germany, during which he got very excited and said that New Zealand's climate was very similar to Germany's and so she should be concentrating on light, fragrant Germanic styles, spurred vineyard owners to plant Germanic grapes – in particular the Müller-Thurgau – and to use German methods to produce light, fruity, Liebfraumilch look-alikes. The 1970s saw the influence of California and Australia take hold, and with it the realization that simply to concentrate on Müller-Thurgau was absurd, because New Zealand had exactly the kind of long, cool ripening season the Californians and Australians craved for their great French grape varieties, to bring freshness and balance to their wines.

The change in direction has been more dramatic than in any other major wine-growing country. In 1960 there were less than 400 hectares (1,000 acres) of vines in the country, and most of these were dull, 'hybrid' grapes clustered round the hot and humid Auckland in the north. By 1988 there were nearly 6,000 hectares (15,000 acres) of vines, two-thirds planted in the areas of Gisborne and Hawkes Bay on the North Island, with the third biggest area being Marlborough in the South Island. 95 per cent of these grapes are now of the superior Vitis Vinifera species.

Cook's Te Kauwhata outfit on the North Island.

At the same time, New Zealand's drinking habits have been revolutionized. The country's first licensed resturant was only allowed in the early 1960s, and wine bars were not legal till 1979. In 1960, New Zealanders only drank 1.74 litres of wine *per capita* annually. Well over 1 litre of this tiny amount was fortified sherry-type wine. By 1984, consumption had roared up to 13.8 litres per head, with nearly 10 litres being light table wines. This burgeoning domestic demand for fine wine has been crucial in fuelling the now considerable drive into export markets, with countries like Australia discovering that the fresh light whites consumers were so keen on could be found on her own doorstep – in New Zealand. The creation of a tariff-free market with Australia has dramatically increased New Zealand's white wine exports.

GRAPE VARIETIES AND WINE STYLES

Almost all of New Zealand table wine consumption is white. There was a period in the 1970s when the majority of these were 'back blended', producing a soft, vaguely grapy, slightly sweet style. This style, unashamedly similar to German wines, is still used for the downmarket brands which are prevalent domestically, but it is increasingly rare in export wines. The dominant grape is still the Müller-Thurgau (here often titled the Riesling-Sylvaner after its probable parentage), which accounts for about 40 per cent of total plantings. When well made, as, for instance, by **Montana** in the South Island, it has an excellent, flowering currant green tang to a reasonably dry wine, or, from **Cooks** in the North Island, the same gentle grapiness as many Rheinhessen wines in Germany.

However, it is increasingly other grapes which are building New Zealand's reputation. The best of the Germanic grapes is the Gewürztraminer, which, in the right hands, as with Denis Irwin's **Matawhero** from Gisborne, produces a remarkably pungent wine, reeking of pepper and face cream and mangos(!), yet dry and refreshing too. New Zealand Gewürztraminer can be some of the world's finest. Rhine Riesling looks promising and, remarkably, some of the best wines are from **Selaks** and **Collards** in the warm north and **Redwood, Seifried** and **Giesen** in the cool south. Of French grapes, Chenin Blanc is at its most versatile in New Zealand, covering the

WINE REGIONS

1 *West Auckland*
2 *Kumeu/Huapai*
3 *South Auckland*
4 *Bay of Plenty*
5 *Waikato*
6 *Hawkes Bay*
7 *Gisborne*
8 *Southern North Island*
9 *Marlborough*
10 *Nelson*
11 *Canterbury*

entire gamut from stone-dry to rich. It is best with some sweetness left in. Semillon is steering away from the heavy, oily, Australian tradition, towards something much fresher, like the grassy **Vidal,** or the classic beeswax and sweet apples flavour of **Villa Maria.** Sauvignon Blanc is one of New Zealand's most exciting varieties. The best, like **Montana** Cloudy Bay and Hunters from the **Marlborough** South Island plantings, or **Esk Valley** from Hawkes Bay bring a depth of nettly, almost asparagus fruit to a style zinging with fresh, sharp balance. These are well up among the world's greatest Sauvignons.

Chardonnay has rapidly established itself, and every new release inspires confidence that great wines are on the way; the acidity is high, the fruit clear, lemony, with a whisper of honey, and then, depending on the oak treatment it gets, it can be either rich and buttery like Cooks, or, as with **Te Mata's Elston** so dry, so savoury, yet so lusciously ripe that it is one of the world's finest

NEW ZEALAND

THE GENERAL PICTURE

Chardonnays, in the tradition of great burgundy, not recent California.

Reds in general are less exciting, but each year the flavours improve. The curious Pinotage grape is quite common and makes a light, smoky marshmallow and raspberry wine – as usual. Pinot Noir is not generally successful so far although **Matua Valley** solves the problem by making an excellent creamy Pinot Noir White, but the Pinot palm has to go to **St Helena**, only founded in 1978 in the new South Island area of Canterbury, and **Martin-** borough in the even newer North Island area near Wellington. These vineyards are producing brilliant, dark plummy reds in the Côte de Nuits mould.

Cabernet Sauvignon, which initially seemed a little too weedy and green, has now developed into a very fresh, grassy, raw blackcurrants style, but there are some super-achievers, like **Cooks'** Hawkes Bay **Fernhill, Te Mata** and **Villa Maria,** where the freshness is matched by a tough, ripe, sweet blackcurrant fruit which is tremendously exciting.

THE IMPORTANT DETAILS

CLASSIFICATION

The concept of classification is recent in New Zealand. Nonetheless, there are obvious regional differences becoming very evident in the wines, and increasing emphasis is being placed on the provenance of the grapes. There are already numbers of areas taking shape varying from Gisborne, the biggest, to Bay of Plenty. Each year new vineyards and new wine regions come into operation particularly in the South Island, as more growers are bitten by the bug.

ORGANIZATION/S

The New Zealand wine industry has undergone several crises in recent years due to overenthusiastic expansion in its short history. At present, Montana is the biggest company, with a fair chunk of the table wine market, and improving annually. Four other companies control another third of production, and the rest is chiefly old-fashioned family firms specializing in fortified wines around Auckland, and the increasing numbers of 'boutique' wineries, who are set on producing top-quality wines. Grape growers who do not make wine have considerable influence in traditional areas, and in Gisborne, the biggest area, there is only one self-contained winery, Matawhero, though Montana also have a presence. Otherwise the grapes are sold though hard-nosed contract deals to wineries. At present Phylloxera has re-appeared in both islands, with Hawkes Bay particularly affected. Farmers have used this as an opportunity to replant higher quality vine varieties with the government bearing the financial brunt. Now that's what I call making the best of a bad job. The Hawkes Bay and Nelson growers have each formed themselves into units which will help to promote their regional wines.

READING THE LABEL

New Zealand is another enthusiastic bowdlerizer of European names, and even manages to label one wine Chablisse Chablis. Burgundy, Hock, Claret, Sauternes and Moselle are common, as well as Champagne, Sherry and Port. Since 1983, however, labelling has been tightened up. Varietal wines must now contain at least 75 per cent of the variety stated. When two grapes are used, the dominant partner will be the first named. (Indeed, it is only since 1983 that the wine has had to be made entirely from grapes!) Other

information now shown on the label is volume of bottle, alcohol content, producer's name and address, and, particularly in the case of blends, country of origin. 'Estate-bottled' is a term used, but since many wineries truck grapes large distances, lack of this term does *not* imply lack of authenticity. Medal awards are often cited, but one should check that the medal was given for the vintage actually in the bottle.

WHAT DO THEY TASTE LIKE?
So far white wines are New Zealand's most successful creations. Some are still 'back-blended' into juice to produce soft, Germanic styles, but most are now made sharply defined and full of very bright, straight fruit. The reds, from a thinnish beginning, are now producing some very exciting, dry, 'northern European' flavours too.

THE GOOD YEARS
There is increasing evidence that not only do the wines taste delicious young, but that some of them demand aging too. In general, the whites are drinkable within six months to a year, and 1989 and 1988 both produced delicious wines to drink now or hold a bit. The reds do take longer, but already the 1985s are very good, and, as the vineyards mature, big, ripe years like 1986 and 1989 will produce balanced classic wines, sometimes requiring five to ten years to come round.

ENJOYING THE WINES
The superb fruit of the whites makes them very easy to drink at any time, especially since some are bottled with a very slight 'fizz' to keep them fresh. However, Sauvignons and Chardonnays have fruit allied to a refreshing sharpness which makes them good with meat and fish dishes. In the same way, a light Pinot or Pinotage could almost take the place of white in a meal.

Montana's Marlborough vineyards on the South Island are massive, modern and mechanized.

CONSUMER INFORMATION

WHAT DO I GET FOR MY MONEY?
From the top wineries like **Montana, Cooks, Villa Maria** and **Vidal** and the quality estates like **Cloudy Bay, St Helena, Martinborough** and **Matawhero,** one is getting world-class wine at half-price. As New Zealand struggles with a grape glut at home, and a sceptical export market, there is the chance to pick up great wine at knock-down prices. The wines get better every year, the prices must rise too, so rush in now while you still have some spare cash and they have some spare wine.

AVAILABILITY
Both Montana and Cooks have wide distribution in Europe, but otherwise supply is still erratic. Australia increasingly takes a proportion of good estate wines. The best way to seek them out otherwise is to contact your nearest New Zealand Trade Commission.

CONSUMER CHECKLIST		
Montana	Q:	1 2 3 4 5 6 7 **8** 9 10
Sauvignon Blanc	P:	1 2 3 4 **5** 6 7 8 9 10
1989	V:	1 2 3 4 5 6 7 8 9 **10**
Cooks	Q:	1 2 3 4 5 **6** 7 8 9 10
Cabernet	P:	1 2 3 4 **5** 6 7 8 9 10
Sauvignon 1986	V:	1 2 3 4 5 6 **7** 8 9 10

Good Years Things are moving so fast in New Zealand that the latest vintage is nearly always the best. The wines are best young, many whites being at their best in less than a year. 1989 and 1986 were particularly good.

Taste Notes The quality of New Zealand's white wines is remarkable, piercingly fresh and piled with fruit and cool-climate balance. Reds are less good, but these too are beginning to develop a sharp-edged but mouth-watering style.

SOUTH AFRICA

THE GENERAL PICTURE

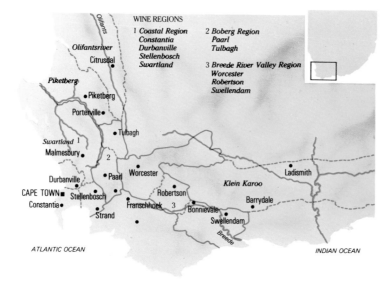

WINE REGIONS
1 *Coastal Region*
  Constantia
  Durbanville
  Stellenbosch
  Swartland
2 *Boberg Region*
  Paarl
  Tulbagh
3 *Breede River Valley Region*
  Worcester
  Robertson
  Swellendam

ATLANTIC OCEAN

INDIAN OCEAN

S outh Africa is often held up as being one of the most beautiful wine regions of the world. To visit an estate like Mont Blois in the Robertson area where the Langeberg mountains rise in contoured layers high into the sky above the neat rolling vineyards or the elegant, calm L'Ormavirs Estate in the Paarl district, is to experience a relationship between man-made beauty and nature's own brilliance, which is rare in any terms, let alone wine.

Yet this beauty is just the icing on the cake, because many experts believe that South Africa also has some of the most perfect vineyard land in the world, a mixture of soils and climate, of seasons suited to maturing grapes at the right pace, of vineyards facing north, south, east, west, all suited to different types of wine production. And, most excitingly for wine drinkers everywhere, it is only in the last ten years that we are beginning to get a hint of the astonishingly wide range of wines that she is capable of producing. Her climate runs from really very cool in the Heaven and Earth valley off Walker Bay, which boasts Africa's most southerly vineyards, to torrid sweat-shop conditions as hot as any in Europe in the Orange River district. Between these two, a wine industry which is now well over 300 years old is trying with increasing success to adapt the remarkable natural advantages of the Cape to the exciting changes the wine world is now undergoing at breakneck pace.

GRAPE VARIETIES AND WINE STYLES

It pulls one up with a start to realize that in 1982, a large vintage of high quality, over half the wine production was sent to the distillery to make brandy or industrial alcohol. South Africa's wine heritage is not in the light table wines which most wine-drinking markets crave, but in wine brandies (South Africa has the highest *per capita* brandy consumption), and in fortified wines. Port-style wines have always been produced, primarily from the Tinta Barocca and various Muscat grapes. They can be absolutely delicious, and with cask-aging of up to 30 years develop deep, memorable brown sugar and raisin flavours. South Africa is more famous, however, for her 'sherries'. They are usually a little heavier than the Spanish equivalents, but the Pale Dry can have real *flor* bite, and the old Oloroso style can have a really good nutty depth.

In table wines, although her reputation has been as the producer of fairly full chunky reds, it is the whites which are making waves just now. There has been considerable difficulty in getting authorization for the importation and planting of high-quality grape varieties ('cultivars'), so many of the most imaginative vineyard owners have literally thrown the cuttings in their suitcase after trips to Europe and hoped they would get through Customs without a search. The results have been worth it, because there are ever-increasing signs of some superb light whites being grown.

Above *Dutch influence in South African vineyards is shown in the buildings, modelled on Dutch homesteads.* **Left** *The Drakensberg mountains tower above the vines burnishing in the autumn light.*

the so-called 'workhorse whites'. Colombard, the French brandy grape, here produces a successful green apples sharp wine, while the Chenin Blanc (also known as Steen) is, in South Africa, versatility itself, producing both good basic gulping whites, and some excellent, yet cheap, quality styles, best epitomized by two commercial brands – the delicious, honeyed soft wine from **KWV** (Kooperative Wijnbouwers Vereniging) and the startling, ultra-fresh crunchy-green wine from **Fleur du Cap**.

Most red wine is sold blended from several grape varieties, and is usually surprisingly light, but often with a slightly sweet fruit-pastille fruit, and an unmistakable smoky aroma. However, single grape varieties are increasingly marketed, and the most important is Cabernet Sauvignon. At its best, and blended with the other Bordeaux grapes like Merlot and Cabernet Franc, the wines can have a delicious blackcurranty fruit. Most Cabernets also have a smoky whiff to them. The whiff becomes a positive twang with the Pinotage grape, a native South African cross between Pinot Noir and the southern French blending grape of Cinsault. Drunk young the wine is purple and bursting with rich raspberry fruit and can be so smoky it tastes as though it was grown inside a still smouldering volcano. As it ages a curious marshmallow and toffee softness creeps across it, the fruit turns to blackcurrant yet the smoke doesn't budge an inch. The finest examples are **Backsberg** and **Union Wine's Culemborg**. The Shiraz grape is fairly successful, but is usually rather soft and herby.

Chardonnay is only just being introduced, but the first results from estates like **De Wetshof**, where aging in small oak barrels is being tried, have produced lovely, honeyed dry wines with a spicy oak softness. Sauvignon Blanc is another new star, and the best are the sharp, grassy wines of **De Wetshof** and the more honeyed oaky wines of **Le Bonheur**. Riesling, here called Rhine Riesling, or Weisser Riesling, produces wines with that tart lemon steeliness which is successful in Australia and Alsace. Of the other Germanic varieties, Gewürztraminer can be quite spicy and aromatic, Sylvaner and Müller-Thurgau are a bit dull, and the Kerner can produce smoky, honeyed, soft wines. Last but not least are

THE IMPORTANT DETAILS

CLASSIFICATION

The South African 'appellation' system is the most highly organized of all the New World countries, and applies to the whole wine industry. There are three overall 'Wine of Origin' Regions, containing nine smaller Districts and a further seven wine districts outside the three main regions. The Wine and Spirit Board awards different coloured neck bands as follows: Blue – to wines certified to come from the stated region of origin; Red – given to wines containing at least 75 per cent of the vintage stated; Green – to wines con-

taining at least 75 per cent of the grape variety stated. One or more of these bands is attached to the bottle neck on a white background, or, if judged to be Superior in style, on a gold background.

ORGANIZATION/S

South African wine is highly organized; some would say over-organized. There are 75 growers' co-operatives who handle 84 per cent of the grapes. They produce some wine themselves, but primarily sell to one of the six major companies, who dominate wine pro-

SOUTH AFRICA

THE IMPORTANT DETAILS

duction and marketing. One of these, the KWV, is indeed itself a co-operative organization with control over planting and pricing nationwide and to which all growers must belong. The vineyards actually owned by these 'Big Six' only make 4 per cent of the wine total. The final 12 per cent is produced by the 70 or so private estates, who sell their wine usually with the help of one of the 'Big Six' like KWV, Oude Meester or Stellenbosch Farmers' Wineries.

READING THE LABEL
Labels are in Afrikaans and English, and several Afrikaans words are important. 'Oesjaar' means 'Vintage'. 'Oorsprong' means 'Origin'. 'Landgoedwyn' is the designation given to a single-estate wine. Increasingly, the cultivar, or grape variety, is shown, along with the origin, below the name of the producing company. Names like Premier Grand Cru, implying a French style, and Grünberger Stein, implying a German style, appear, but have no legal standing.

WHAT DO THEY TASTE LIKE?
Many South African wines taste surprisingly light and fresh. Although this is very much to the advantage of the whites, some of which are becoming very exciting, it has meant that the reds can be caught between two stools. Much of the wine is still made in an old-fashioned way from big overripe grapes, and attempts to lighten these products are not a complete success. Yet, as cooler, more temperate vineyards are developed, there should be an increase in sharply defined, soft flavoured reds and whites of individual and extremely attractive style.

THE GOOD YEARS
There is considerable vintage variation in the cooler areas of South Africa, and it is noticeable that the big companies sometimes slip a vintage on the export market. However, most of the blended wines are fairly consistent year by year, and the chief problem is getting the wines young enough. Whites are often at their best in one to two years, and reds in three to four. Even single-estate reds and whites have similar maturity scales. 1986 and 1984 are both good for reds, while 1987 and 1986 are good for whites. Ports can age well for 30 years or more.

ENJOYING THE WINES
South African whites used to be mostly Germanic in style, slightly sweet, and best for drinking by themselves. However, the new breed of whites is soft and dry, easy to drink with or without food. The reds do not usually possess great nuances but should have an attractive, direct fruit flavour, making them good wines to go with straight, sturdy food.

CONSUMER INFORMATION

WHAT DO I GET FOR MY MONEY?
The port styles are undoubtedly fine value, particularly the old **Paarl** styles, which can be fairly cheap and delicious. The best estates, like **De Wetshof, Vriesenhof, Meerlust, Le Bonheur** can be extremely good value; however, estate quality is still variable. Hamilton-Russell is world-class and expensive.

AVAILABILITY
Most outlets will have one or two table wines, almost always from one of the big companies. Estate wines are still difficult to find. Sherry styles are generally available, but the ports are mostly consumed domestically.

MEXICO & SOUTH AMERICA

With the dominance of California in modern American wine-making, it is easy to overlook the fact that wine was first grown in the Americas by Spanish missionaries in Mexico, spreading slowly up the Californian coast. However, America between California and Chile is not ideally suited to vines, and only Mexico produces any quantity or quality of wine nowadays. South America, too, is often too subtropical for successful wine-growing, but both Chile and Argentina in the south can produce fine wine, and the presence of much investment by international companies in Brazil indicates that quality production is possible there too.

MEXICO

Mexico was the first country on the American continent to cultivate vines when the original Spanish missionaries planted them in 1520. Until recently, Mexican wine production was almost entirely orientated towards brandy distillation, which still utilizes over 90 per cent of all the grapes grown, with the major Spanish and French brandy firms strongly to the fore. Paradoxically, for the country which introduced the vine to the Americas, *per capita* consumption is the second lowest of all the countries in the world who file records, with about one-sixteenth of a litre per head per annum only managing to scrape past near-teetotal Moslem Morocco by a whisper. However, government regulations requiring Mexican wine to be served in all restaurants and the efforts of companies like **Domecq** and **Santo Tomas** may have some effect. Vineyard areas have increased dramatically from 1,600 hectares (4,000 acres) in 1939 to 70,000 hectares (175,000 acres) in 1983, with the most optimistic plantings in Baja California – two hours' south of San Diego – Saltillo and Aguascalientes in the middle of the country.

ARGENTINA

Argentina is in the major league in terms of wine production and wine consumption. She has 300,000 hectares (750,000 acres) of vines, the fifth largest area in the world, and one of the reasons we see so little of her wine on the export market is that she has the fourth largest *per capita* consumption. The area of Mendoza, situated, like California, on the San Andreas Fault, is the major region of Argentina's seven areas, with half of all South America's vineyard acreage. This is basically desert land, but spreadeagled below the towering Andes, a massive irrigation system feeds what is one of the world's most efficient grape-growing regions.

Much of Argentine wine is soft, pulpy red and heavy white for immediate, indiscriminate consumption, but grapes like Cabernet, Malbec, Syrah, Semillon and Chardonnay are grown, and the reds in particular can be very good, retaining a juicy grapy taste but also packing a fair punch. **San Telmo, Bianchi, Orfila** and **Pascual Toso** all produce good Cabernet, while **Flichman** has a promising Syrah. **Peñaflor** and **Weinert** are particularly good for a dry, slightly musky Chardonnay, while **Proviar,** along with good whites, has excellent **Champaña.** So it should: the company is owned by Moët & Chandon! Argentine prices are cheap, and the quality is good, if a bit full-blooded in taste.

BRAZIL

Brazil has a similar acreage to Mexico – but is showing a more wine-orientated approach despite a *per capita* consumption which is still extremely low. Big European companies like **Moët & Chandon, Cinzano** and **Domecq** have invested in vineyards, and in the south University of California advisers have identified several areas where good strong reds can be made. At present, however, mirroring Portuguese tradition, much of the wine is still so-called **Vinho Verde,** which the real Vinho Verde producers in Portugal don't find a bit amusing, since Brazil is their most important export market!

MEXICO & SOUTH AMERICA/Chile

THE GENERAL PICTURE

Chile is not the largest wine producer in South America, but she has undeniably always produced the highest quality. However, Chile is not an easy country to get to, and, until recently, the travellers' tales of the astonishing wine to be tasted on the far side of the Andes were as close as most of us got to learning the truth. Luckily, there is now a steady trickle of wine appearing on the export markets, and there is no doubt the travellers' tales were true – Chile does have a unique style and a remarkably high standard of wine-making. This can be traced back to 1881, when a Señor Ochagavia, whose company is still making wine, decided the clean dry climate between the Pacific and the Andes would create ideal vineyards and chose to import both experts and vines from Bordeaux. His timing couldn't have been better. Hardly had the last boatload of vine cuttings left France, full of Bordeaux's best Cabernet, Merlot, Malbec, Sauvignon and Semillon – along with a little Pinot from Burgundy – than Europe was struck by the two most destructive vine scourges the world has known – Oidium, a lethal fungus disease, and Phylloxera (see p. 26). While France's vineyards were devastated, Chile was able to propagate fungus-free, Phylloxera-free vineyards which she still has to this day. The vineyard areas are so dry that fungi never develop, and the mixture of the Andes mountains, the Pacific Ocean and the shrivellingly hot deserts to the north, has meant that Phylloxera has never plucked up enough courage to even attempt an invasion. Chile is the only major wine-producing country which does not have to graft its wine vines on to American Vitis Labrusca rootstocks.

GRAPE VARIETIES AND WINE STYLES

The centre of Chile, below the capital of Santiago, is the chief wine region. Traditionally the Maipo valley has produced the best reds, but in 1978 Miguel Torres from Spain – one of Europe's great wine geniuses – bought a winery and vineyard in the cooler Maule valley further south, and his new releases of whites are Chile's best yet.

The Maipo is famous for Cabernet Sauvignon, and here it produces a wine full of intense blackcurrant fruit with a coal-fires smokiness quite unlike any other Cabernet. The quality is uniformly good, from the basic wines of **Linderos, Concha y Toro** and **Caliterra**, through to the top-line releases such as **Cousiño Macul** and Concha y Toro's **Marques de Casa Concha. Los Vascos**, further south, produces highly successful juicy structured Cabernet. Pinot Noir is grown, but so far with less success.

Traditionally, Chilean whites have been big, oily and oak-aged. The Semillon is the chief grape, and it can develop a petrolly, yet honeyed, flavour which matches Australian Semillon for shock value. Riesling, too, can produce wine with an overpowering perfume rather like some sort of grape eau de Cologne. Yet modern methods of wine-making by preserving freshness are catching on. **California** and **Santa Rita** are already making extremely attractive Chardonnay as well as light, grassy Sauvignon. Their quality could improve a great deal further if they were prepared to reduce their stupendous yields. **Torres** in the cool south has reduced yields and is producing steely Riesling, scented Gewürztraminer and remarkable barrel-aged Sauvignon.

THE IMPORTANT DETAILS

CLASSIFICATION
Although Chile has six viticultural regions, only the Central Valley Zone is important, and all the best vineyards are here, between the Aconcagua River in the north and the Maule River in the south. There is, however, no further appellation system.

ORGANIZATION/S
Organization is still confused. The pre-1973 government pursued a policy of dispossessing landowners in favour of peasant ownership. At present the large wine-making companies are back in control, and quality is consequently on the up. Some co-operatives are also important and the large co-op de Taca in the south produces good bulk wine.

READING THE LABEL
Labels can be unhelpful, since many simply sport brand names, and there is no requirement for great accuracy. One firm has both a

Pommard and a Pinot Noir made up of Semillon and Cabernet! There is, however, an age classification. Special is two years old, Reserve four years and Gran Vino a minimum of six. Ideally, look for grape names, especially Cabernet, Chardonnay and Sauvignon.

WHAT DO THEY TASTE LIKE?
The tastes are *not* conventional, but they are exciting, so don't open a bottle with too many pre-conceptions. Too much aging in wood is a problem, especially for whites, but the reds can often triumph over considerable wood-aging.

THE GOOD YEARS
With a regular climate, and irrigation in the vineyards, actual vintages are less important than the winemaker's aging policy. Most whites should be drunk as young as possible, which is difficult if they're spending two or

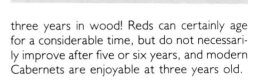

three years in wood! Reds can certainly age for a considerable time, but do not necessarily improve after five or six years, and modern Cabernets are enjoyable at three years old.

ENJOYING THE WINES
These are certainly food wines. Their strong assertive tastes are particularly well matched to grilled fish and meat, though the reds will go well with cheeses, casseroles and even some of the less fiery Oriental dishes.

CONSUMER INFORMATION

WHAT DO I GET FOR MY MONEY?
Excellent value for money. These wines are never expensive, and they have far more character than most European bottles in the same price range.

AVAILABILITY
This is rapidly improving and is no longer limited to South American markets. However, Concha y Toro, Cousiño Macul, Caliterra and Santa Rita are easily obtainable, and, as one might expect, the new Torres wines have immediately gained fairly wide distribution in Europe and the USA.

Miguel Torres, the Spanish winemaker, here working on his vines in the lee of the Andes.

WESTERN EUROPE/Switzerland

To record that Switzerland has Europe's highest vineyards at Visp, where grapes are grown on steep terraced outcrops of mountain at a chilling 1,100 m (3,600 ft) is not surprising. But to record that Switzerland nowadays regularly suffers from a grape glut, when such honours are usually only the bane of the gutless, sprawling vineyards of the Mediterranean South, cheap to cultivate, rarely asked to achieve anything but spewing out millions of litres of unwanted, undrinkable

rubbish every year, is both disturbing and puzzling. Switzerland is a mountain land. Her wines are notoriously expensive to produce, since she has a high wage economy and grape-growing is usually thought of as an occupation best suited to low overhead rural areas with no urban demands on the land; there is no such thing as a low overhead rural area in Switzerland. And to all but the Swiss themselves the wines seem excessively dear to purchase. But you would expect the Swiss

to lap up all the available produce, since they are avid and patriotic consumers of the Fendants and Dorins of the Valais and the Vaud, or the pale, smoky Pinot Noirs of Neuchâtel.

The thing is that, although logically the lesser vineyards should be going out of production, as the cost of maintaining hillside vineyards becomes increasingly uneconomical, in fact the trend for the vineyard acreage to shrink has been reversed, and between 1974 and 1984 the vineyard acreage increased by 13 per cent. Much of this is on lower, more fertile valley floor land, which until recently was thought neither suitable nor profitable to cultivate for vines.

This helps to explain why the yields of grapes in the vineyard rise inexorably year by year. Through heavy fertilization, efficient but not obsessive pruning, and irrigation – (yes!! Switzerland, particularly the Valais, actually has a need for irrigation!) – the vineyards have traditionally produced twice as much as similar French areas, but things are getting closer to the Germanic notion of enormous yields nowadays. In 1982, the average production reached 132 hectolitres to the hectare – nearly three times what one might expect from mountain vineyards – and even though 1983 saw a slight drop, the harvest was still 50 per cent bigger than the average for the previous ten years. 1984 continued this trend.

Certainly the Swiss drinkers have been doing their best to keep up with this increase in wine; in 1984, for instance, Swiss domestic wine consumption rose by 30 per cent for whites and 20 per cent for reds. They've even put more effort into exporting – up 40 per cent in the year 1984 – but that grape glut remains! Given the predominant Chasselas grape, the basis of **Fendant** and **Dorin** and all the 'café' white wines, one can push such a neutral grape variety to pretty big yields

without much changing its already semi-invisible flavour, but the Swiss authorities are obviously not happy either with the grape glut, or with the quality of some of the cheap wine now coming on to the market, and one can expect some reaction, unless growers voluntarily limit their yields and stop planting new vineyards in unsuitable areas.

FRENCH-SPEAKING CANTONS

Grapes are grown in all the regions of Switzerland, but by far the most important are the French-speaking cantons, and in particular the hot, wide valley of the Rhône centred on the town of Sion, which makes up the Valais area, and the longer arc of vineyards beginning at Martigny where the Rhône makes a very abrupt right turn northwards, continuing in a wide and spectacularly scenic arc past Montreux and Lausanne round to Geneva. Geneva itself is the centre of a rather lesser area called the Mandement.

The most exciting of these areas is the Valais, where almost all of Switzerland's decent red is made. The Swiss are the biggest purchasers of burgundy as well as having a great fondness for Beaujolais, and this shows in the Valais red wine varieties. Two-thirds of the red wine vines are Pinot Noir, the burgundy grape, and about one-third is the Beaujolais grape, Gamay. They are usually mixed together and the top quality blends are called **Dôle**. This is usually relatively light, but perfumed in a strawberryish way, and it often has some bite as well. The reds which don't pass the tasting panel to gain the Dôle appellation are called **Goron,** and are usually a rather tougher proposition.

However, two-thirds of the Valais vineyards are white, and the Chasselas, here called the Fendant, is the predominant grape; unless drunk very young it makes a rather flabby wine. Ironically for an Alpine country, many Valais vineyards are too hot for such a neutral grape. Much better are either the Sylvaner wines, here called Johannisberg, which are quite full and grapy, or the Muscat, Pinot Gris (called Malvoisie) and Riesling wines which, from companies like **Caves de Riondaz** or **Domaine du Mont d'Or,** can achieve a delicious wistful delicacy, as fragrant and as perfumed as you could hope for.

The Valais also has some remarkable old grape varieties, rarely seen, but well worth trying from a good grower like Domaine du Mont d'Or or **Vuignier**. **Petite Arvine**, **Armigne**, and **Humagne** make big, honeyed, chewy wines, rather resembling some of the whites from much further down the Rhône near Hermitage.

The Vaud makes the best Chasselas, here usually called **Dorin,** but often parading under the name of a village. The slopes of Chablais are perhaps the best, just before the Rhône river becomes Lake Geneva, and the village of Aigle makes a sharp, slightly *spritzig* Dorin which has almost enough slightly peppery lemony flavour for you to be able to remember what it tastes like!

The Lavaux slopes are Switzerland's most famous – and most photographed, clinging to the lakeshore hillsides between the major towns of Montreux and Lausanne. **Dezaley** is the best known Dorin appellation, and the wine is at its driest and stoniest here, again needing to be drunk young and slightly *spritzig* to give most pleasure. From Lausanne to Geneva the vineyards become flatter and less spectacular, and so do the wines. In the Valais and the Vaud, though many large companies make good fresh wine, to get the real personality of the area one has to go the single-domaine wines, and growers like Testuz and Pinget in Dezaley and Badoux and Isoz in Chablais are the ones to seek out. Isoz, incidentally, makes a Gewürztraminer which has unbelievable spicy perfume for a wine which is almost feather-frail in the mouth.

Around Geneva, the enormous co-op of Vin-Union-Genève controls over 80 per cent of the production. The Chasselas (Perlan this time!) really is a bit light by now, and more interesting wine is coming from the white Müller-Thurgau and the red Gamay.

Neuchâtel, north of Lake Geneva, is also predominantly Chasselas land, but the Pinot Noir is its most renowned wine, occasionally just about getting enough colour to be called red, but more likely to be a light and rather good rosé or even a tasty Blanc de Noir white. Some Pinot, and a lot of Chasselas, is made into sparkling wine at Neuchâtel.

GERMAN-SPEAKING CANTONS
The German cantons, further north, don't have the microclimates to produce regular amounts of fully ripened grapes, but several have a fair reputation. Bern has the almost waterlight wines of **Schafis** and **Twann**. The Graubünden area near the Austrian border produces some quite big, chewy-tasting **Blauburgunder** (Pinot Noir) and a most unusual big, sweet white called **Completer;** and Zurich and Schaffhausen also produce light Blauburgunders.

ITALIAN-SPEAKING CANTONS
The Italian south has a totally different wine culture, based almost entirely on the red Merlot grape. Certainly the grape ripens well in the Ticino vineyards, and the best, or at least the ripest, with more than 12° of alcohol, are designated VITI – a quality guarantee. With the Italian influence at their heels, these can suffer from being dried out by too much aging in wood, and the ordinary **Merlot,** soft, juicy and very drinkable, is the best bet. And it's cheap – not an attribute usually associated with Switzerland!

The shores of Lake Geneva are often blanketed with vines, seeking the sun in the Alps.

WESTERN EUROPE/Luxembourg

Luxembourg really doesn't do herself any favours. Nearly all the wines which appear under her national colours are simply flying a flag of convenience based on Luxembourg's position as the duty-free capital of Europe, with an endless troop of Northern Europeans stopping by en route to fill up with basement-priced bargains. And, apart from spirits, what is most profligately sold is sparkling wine.

The first few times I tasted Luxembourg sparkling wine, I gazed in disbelief, first at the sullenly fizzing sulphurous muck in my glass, and then at the pop-eyed charlatans who swore the wine was pure as driven snow. I looked on the map and found Luxembourg twined round the upper reaches of the Mosel – perfect vineyard land for delicate Rieslings and Müller-Thurgaus. What was happening was that, Luxembourg's table wine production being limited and quality-orientated, large amounts of second-rate Italian grape must were being imported and fizzed-up. Just like in Germany up the road. And, as with Germany, the real thing is so delicious it makes you despair at the way its image is debased. Not only that, but Luxembourg wine production has been strictly and effectively controlled by government decree since 1935. Wines are all tested by tasting panel and by chemical analysis, and achieve four different statuses, from Marque Nationale, through Vin Classé and Premier Cru, to Grand Cru.

The vines are usually Germanic, and are in general of very high quality in a delicate, hill-cool way. The Elbling, German Mosel's least distinguished grape, is light and appley here, while the Müller-Thurgau, here called Rivaner, is surprisingly soft in an apple and apricot way. Both Auxerrois and the related Pinot Blanc produce lightweight but creamy wines, the rather sharp, fresh fruit just tinged with enough honey to make it resemble a slightly raw Chardonnay. Pinot Gris, surprisingly, manages a good honey and nuts style, and is quite distinguished at the Grand Cru level.

The same could be said of Gewürztraminer, here in the upper reaches of the Mosel making delicious wine, gently spicy yet fresh and thirst-quenching. However, Mosel vineyards must be judged by Riesling, and Luxembourg, without achieving the heights of the German Mosel, produces a delicate, steely, green Riesling, quick to age to a petrolly austerity, but absolutely straight and unmistakable.

The prices are low for all these wines, but export efforts are only now being made to widen availability. In the 1,200 hectares (3,000 acres) of vines, there are 1,600 growers, so co-operatives are more important than merchant houses for quality. Probably the best is the **Wormeldange** co-op.

AUSTRIA

THE GENERAL PICTURE

Austria is in an unenviable position. Her greatest wines are undervalued and under-appreciated. That doesn't, on the surface of it, sound so unusual – export markets are notorious for failing to appreciate a country's finest wines. The difference here is that the Austrians don't go for them either! I'm talking of Austria's fabled dessert wines, made round the steamy Neusiedler See, where 'noble rot' comes round so regularly every year you could almost set your wristwatch by it; the Sauternais and Rheingau-growers would give their eye teeth to be in the Austrians' position, making large amounts of Beerenauslese wines *every* year! But the *Austrian* taste is for dry wine, so, up till now, trucks of Trockenbeerenauslese have simply trundled to ill-deserved obscurity.

Moves are afoot to stop this bulk trading of some of the world's greatest wines, but in the meantime the Austrian taste in wine stays resolutely dry. And this does have many plus points, because, being further south than Germany, yet with many similar grape varieties and a wine law which is regarded as an improved version of the German one, it is possible to see just how good the dry wines can be from grapes like Rhine Riesling, Müller-Thurgau, Muscat and Gewürztraminer. And it also gives ideal ripening conditions to Austria's favourite grape, the Grüner Veltliner.

GRAPE VARIETIES AND WINE STYLES
Austria has all her vineyards loaded into the eastern part of the country, and there are four basic regions comprising almost 60,600

Lenz Moser's headquarters in Rohrendorf – one of Europe's leading experimental vineyards.

hectares (151,500 acres) of vines, about 84 per cent white and 16 per cent red.

Lower Austria, in the north-east, has 35,000 hectares (87,000 acres) of vine and over 60 per cent of the national production volume. Its most exciting wines are created along the achingly beautiful Danube valley north-west of Vienna, at Wachau and Krems, with the steep, rocky terraced vineyards which perch giddily above the river producing brilliant dry but aromatic **Rhine Rieslings, Grüner Veltliners** and **Müller-Thurgaus**.

Langenlois to the north produces wonderfully spicy Rhine Rieslings, and the nearby village of Rohrendorf is the headquarters of **Lenz Moser** – the most innovative and influential of all Austrian wine concerns. To the north in Retz, some fair red is grown, and Lenz Moser is planting Merlot and Cabernet Sauvignon with encouraging results. Further east, to the north of Vienna, the Weinviertel, or 'wine quarter', is the chief supplier of good, light jug wines from the Welschriesling and Grüner Veltliner grapes. Immediately north of Vienna, **Klosterneuberg** is perhaps the most renowned wine of Austria's traditional wine producers, while just to the south of the city, Lower Austria concludes with Voslau which makes some decent jug red, and a small amount of excellent Cabernet and Merlot wines, primarily at the **Schlumberger** estate, and Baden, whose best wine is the big, blowzy and aptly named **Gumpoldskirchen.**

Burgenland is Austria's next biggest area; here the sweet dessert wines are the star performers. The greatest come from the village of Rust on the west shore of the Neusiedlersee, especially from **Weissburgunder, Muscat** and **Welsch** and **Rhine Rieslings,** and the most thirstily available come from the sandy, Phylloxera-free eastern shore, between Podersdorf and Apetlon.

Styria used to be a very important vineyard, but 90 per cent of the original vineyards are now in Yugoslavia, and of what is left, about 2,500 hectares (6,250 acres) makes light reds and some good spicy **Traminers** and **Ruländers** (Pinot Gris).

And then there's the capital, Vienna, where up in the hills above the city, yet still within the city boundaries, there are 800 hectares (2,000 acres) of vines devoted to growing the Grüner Veltliner grape, which gives a green, bitingly fresh wine, to be sold in the *Heurigen,* or 'new wine taverns'. Indeed, these wines get as close to the heart of what the simple joy of wine should be all about as anything I've

AUSTRIA

THE IMPORTANT DETAILS

ever stumbled on in the travels of a wine-drinking man.

CLASSIFICATION
The Austrian Wine Law was promulgated in 1972, and is similar to the German one, but the ripeness levels for each category are higher.

Tafelwein is 20 Oechsle degrees higher than Germany's equivalent at 65–73°. **Ordinary Qualitätswein** may be strengthened with sugar or concentrated must starts with grapes of a 73° Oechsle natural ripeness, the equivalent of a Rheingau Kabinett. **Kabinett**, in Austria may still be strengthened and needs grapes as ripe as for a Rheingau Spätlese. The very strict, 'no sugaring', Prädikat laws start with Spätlese and Auslese, both riper than German equivalents, and then Beerenauslese, Ausbruch and Trockenbeerenauslese at the same level as Germany of 150° Oechsle. **Beerenauslese** may be made from simply overripe grapes, but **Ausbruch** wines, at nearly Trockenbeerenauslese sweetness, must have been attacked by 'noble rot'. **Eiswein** need achieve a lower ripeness count than in many parts of Germany. A grower must register his intention to make Prädikat wine by 9 a.m. on the day he picks the grapes, and take a sample the same day to the local control station. Three weeks later, he has to declare the quantity, grape variety and must weight. There is a further 'Austrian Seal of Quality' on the better wines.

ORGANIZATION/S
The two most important elements in Austrian wine are the large private producers and the co-operatives. Lenz Moser is a world leader in vineyard technology and white wine vinification. The large Klosterneuberg is good, as is the Metternich Alliance of Austrian Estates, while smaller companies like Sepp Hold and Schlumberger, growers and dealers, are of a high quality. The co-ops are very important and the Wachau and Krems co-ops in Lower Austria and the St Martinus co-op in Burgenland are especially good.

READING THE LABEL
Austrian labels are mostly quite straightforward, except that some of the area names and grape varieties may not be familiar. Do look for the Wine Seal in red and white, and check the quality classification.

WHAT DO THEY TASTE LIKE?
The Grüner Veltliner should be peppery and dry, while the dessert wines are tremendously rich, but not so excitingly balanced as German equivalents. Red wines are usually light and off-dry.

THE GOOD YEARS
Good wine is produced most years, but 1989 and 1988 were particularly good. Yet there is little point in keeping many of the wines for long. Paradoxically, the sweet wines need drinking pretty quickly while the Donau and Wachau drier wines can age better.

ENJOYING THE WINES
Grüner Veltliner is such an irreverent wine you can do what you like with it. The other dry Lower Austria wines go well with the fairly heavily flavoured Austrian meat dishes and cheese. The sweet wines are better with rich desserts than by themselves.

CONSUMER INFORMATION

WHAT DO I GET FOR MY MONEY
Austrian wine is never as cheap as that of its neighbours, but the quality can be higher and worth paying the little extra for. The **Kabinett** and **Spätlese** whites are of high quality and relatively cheap. The dessert wines are some of the best bargains in Europe.

AVAILABILITY
Not good. Austria has only recently involved herself in the export market and the antifreeze scandal put the kybosh on that. Much of her best wine goes to Germany. Other markets get a small amount of the fine Danube and Burgenland wines.

CENTRAL & EASTERN EUROPE

YUGOSLAVIA

Yugoslavia is a particularly difficult country to get to grips with. Her eight different republics and autonomous regions have widely differing traditions, use a variety of grapes, both international and indigenous, and practise very different production methods. Coupled with this is a range of wine terms which look uncompromisingly obscure to anyone not reasonably familiar with some sort of Balkan dialect. It is little wonder, therefore, that the only two wines which have made any real impact on the rest of Europe are in effect brand names.

Lutomer Riesling was very shrewdly created for the British market by a single importer, Telscher Brothers. So successful was it in brand terms that no-one bothered to ask what Lutomer meant, and when I first discovered that Ljutomer is an actual vineyard area, one of the best in Slovenia, I was genuinely surprised. But Lutomer Riesling did more than that: it persuaded a whole generation of British drinkers that Riesling was a soft, dullish, slightly sweet wine, cheap and unmemorable, but not dangerous. **Yugoslav Riesling** is not real Riesling – it's made from the Welsch Riesling, or Laski Riesling, grape, which is nothing to do with the true German Riesling, and German high-quality Riesling has definitely suffered from the comparison.

However, it is Germany which has developed Yugoslavia's other brand – **Amselfeld**. Again, this brand, which sells 33 million bottles a year in Germany, is in fact a slightly sweetened Pinot Noir from – yes – Amselfeld, which is the German translation of Kosovo, the vineyard region the wine comes from. Amselfeld has now hit the British market, and can be expected to go further.

These two brands make up the majority of Yugoslavia's wine exports, and their importance can be gauged by noting that Yugoslavia is the world's tenth biggest wine producer and tenth biggest exporter. As well as Amselfeld and 'Riesling', she sends wine to Italy to make vermouth, reds and whites to Japan for blending, and solid Pinot Noirs to Switzerland and Germany to help out the rather pale local product. And by involving herself almost entirely in this bulk market, her own considerable qualities of individuality and regional variety have largely gone unnoticed. The most important wine-producing areas are as follows:

SLOVENIA

Ljutomer is the most famous wine region in this northern province, which borders both Hungary and Austria. It is the centre of Yugoslavia's best white wine area and it is a pity that it is so heavily planted with the mediocre Laski Riesling. The best wines come from the real German Riesling, Gewürztraminer, Pinot Blanc and Pinot Gris.

CROATIA

Croatia has the highest acreage – nearly 33 per cent of the national total. Much of this is yet more Laski Riesling, but down on the Dalmatian coast there are some far more exciting flavours to be found. Many of the vineyards are on the islands and peninsulas, and the Plavac Mali or 'little Plavac' grape is the basis of some real hard nuts. **Faros**, from Hvar, is a remarkable, almost dry red wine, with high acidity and at the same time a dark sweet perfumed fruit reminiscent of figs and almonds. **Dingač**, from Peljesač, is another amazing strong red, with a sturdy toughness rather resembling an Italian Nebbiolo or Refosco and a most unexpected passion-fruit finish! The Dalmatian coast is full of these surprises and is probably Yugoslavia's most fascinating, and unpronounceable, region.

SERBIA

Serbia, with Belgrade as its capital, is the large inland republic. The notorious Kosovo is in the south, but Vranje to the east is more interesting and can produce some extremely good soft, blackcurranty **Merlot**, as good as any in southern Europe. The northern region of Vojvodina, although once renowned for the red **Carlowitz**, is now producing some of the best white wines, and is slightly less subservient to the Laski Riesling than the rest of the north. There is a lot of big, spicy **Traminer**, and some ripe and powerful gooseberry-flavoured **Sauvignon**.

CENTRAL & EASTERN EUROPE

YUGOSLAVIA

BOSNIA

Bosnia, in the centre of the nation, is largely Moslem but does produce one famous wine – **Zilavka** – which is something of an acquired taste, since it has a curious flavour resembling a not entirely successful mixture of talcum powder and bruised apple skins. However, Montenegro and Macedonia to the south are somewhat more successful.

MONTENEGRO

Montenegro produces the excellent **Vranac**, a big, strong-flavoured style, but with the brute force tempered by a soft almost buttery taste which is extremely good. Of all Yugoslavia's own grape styles – this is the most cosmopolitan.

MACEDONIA

Macedonia, down by Albania, has a bewildering array of wine names – 44 at the last count – most of them big, impenetrable reds. But there are some good wines here too. **Kratosija** is a big dark earthy red, but with a chocolaty softness similar to Vranac, and **Teran** is a deep red with a most unusual 'white wine' acidity, peppery, yet citrus.

Bijelo = white. **Crno** = red. **Slatko** = sweet. **Polsuho** = medium. **Suho** = dry. **Vrhumsko** or **Čuveno** = better quality.

BULGARIA

Of all the wine-producing countries in the Eastern Bloc, only Bulgaria seems to go out of her way to satisfy anything approaching an international style. Maybe because, while Eastern Europe in general has a long and respected wine tradition, sadly left behind at present, Bulgaria has had it all to do from scratch.

Up till World War Two, Bulgaria was fairly heavily under Moslem influence, and that certainly isn't the ideal way to nurture an interest in fine wine-making. However, after the war, this virtual-blank sheet could be regarded as something of a blessing. The country needed hard currency and an inspired political decision was made to plant vineyards and begin to create a currency-earning table wine trade. With no very fierce local partisans determined to 'do things their own way', it was possible to treat the whole thing as an industry. And there was one other thing. They set out to listen to what the export market consumers wanted, not saying – 'take it or leave it' as many traditional producers still do against all advice. Consequently, Bulgarian wines, while not having an enormous range of styles, usually manage to achieve what they set out to do remarkably well. Up to 80 per cent of the wine is exported, and Bulgaria is one of the largest exporters of bottled wine in the world. This shows in the fact that in many parts of Western Europe, Bulgarian Cabernets, Merlots, Chardonnays and Rieslings are some of the cheapest wines available, as well as being regularly praised for their flavour and value for money.

The Cabernet Sauvignon is the star grape. Ideally it is quite light, and often slightly tawny red in colour, but bursting with a frank, sweet, blackcurrant fruit that is almost a parody of Cabernet's taste. A delicious parody, though, and recent heavier releases have been less enthusiastically received. Merlot, too, is grown with some success, and these two grapes account for 75 per cent of all red plantations, especially round Suhindol, Stara Zagora and Kasovo. The **Pamid** and **Gamza** are pale local reds often beefed up with Cabernet and the **Mavrud** is a rather solid traditional red.

Whites are often based on the bland Rkatsitelli, and come from the eastern side of the country. Both Laski- and Rhine-Riesling show up here, as do Sauvignon and Chardonnay. Chardonnay has been around from the start for sparkling wines. It is still just a little too powdery dry, but oak has sweetened recent releases, and it looks certain to become a partner for the Cabernet Sauvignon in providing some of the world's best table wine.

ROMANIA

Of all the countries with an illustrious past and a colourless present in wine, Romania is one of the most difficult to pin down for a moment, in the hope of catching the merest glimpse of fabled quality of old. Yet there is no doubt that the wines once were of considerable renown. In nineteenth-century Paris, Moldavian wines were sought after and *'la perle de la Moldavie'*, sounding more like a French translation of an Irish folk song than a serious wine, was a common restaurant favourite.

This wine was in fact **Cotnari**, Romania's most famous wine. Cotnari's vineyards are next to the Russian border, and one can only assume that most of this quite intense, sweetish wine heads over the frontier. Indeed, much of the rest of what does surface seems to be strong and sweet and intended to please Russian rather than Western palates. Merlots, Cabernets and Pinot Noirs are grown in the area of Moldavia, Dealul Mare and Banat, and are at last showing some signs of realizing their potential. Banat also produces **Laski Riesling**, which is usually dull. This is unfortunate, since it could be a far fresher, brighter wine than Yugoslavia's or Hungary's offerings.

Murfatlar, on the Black Sea, is producing some curiously perfumed, but quite attractive **Chardonnay**, as well as what are the best of her exported wines – **Traminer** and **Pinot Gris** – honeyed, rich flavours showing why Romania used to be a name to conjure with.

HUNGARY

For a country whose wines gave me some of my first really exciting revelations about the thrillingly different flavours which can be hiding behind a label and beneath a cork stopper, I find the present range of wines which Hungary offers uniform and depressing. And for a country whose wonderful wine names clang and thunder with the resonances of a wild and untamed wine tradition I find her modern-day whites and reds confusingly tame and limp. Just roll these names around your mouth and then imagine the spicy, fiery flavours which should by rights be punching their way through your pre-conceptions – **Debröi Hárslevelü, Kéknyelü, Tokay Szamorodni, Badacsonyi Szürkebarát** – memorable, bewitching names, and I remember when their flavours were every bit as rich and tangled as their names were tongue-twisting and tantalizing like the rhythms of a gipsy dancer.

It isn't that the Hungarians have gaily abandoned their traditional grape varieties and gone the whole hog with the fad varieties from the West like Cabernet Sauvignon and Chardonnay. Far from it. Of all the Eastern Bloc exporting nations they have shown least enthusiasm for Frenchifying their wines. No, it is the standards of wine-making, and a failure to adapt modern aids to traditional grape varieties which seems to be the problem, leaving a country with a great deal of personality inherent in her wines showing a very dull, tired face to her markets. Surely the momentous political events of 1989 and 1990 will help to change this.

Vines on the slopes of Mount Badacsonyi stretch down to Hungary's biggest lake, Balaton, where they benefit from the moist warm climate.

CENTRAL & EASTERN EUROPE

HUNGARY

There are four main areas of Hungarian viticulture. The Alföld, or 'Great Plain', to the east of the Danube, has half of the country's vineyards. These are modern plantations, mostly light red from the Kadarka and insipid white from Olasz Riesling (the same as Laski Riesling, Riesling Italico etc., i.e. *not* real Riesling). Production is heavily centralized.

The Kisalfold, or 'Small Plain', is more like the 'minuscule plain' in wine terms, overshadowed by its Big Brother, and by Austria's Burgenland just over the Neusiedler See; it is primarily the producer of light, soft **Soproni Kékfrancos** red.

Below the Small Plain, Transdanubia has many of Hungary's best vineyards, centred on the largest freshwater lake in Europe, Lake Balaton. Here there is some blending of Western varieties with Hungarian ones, and Vilányi and Pecs in the far south use Pinot Noir and Blanc, but the most important areas are Mór, west of Budapest, which makes a fair peppery red, and Lake Balaton itself. The vineyards of Mount Badacsonyi are the most famous. The Kéknyelü and Szürkebarát are capable of a tremendous spicy honeyed flavour, soft *and* fiery, and are amongst the few white wines which could cope with the highly flavoured Hungarian foods. At present, though, they are a pale shadow, silently waiting for a return to glory.

From the north-east, in the Northern Massif, come Hungary's two most famous wines and one of her most gutsy. **Debröi Hárslevelü** is the gutsy one, the most successful survivor of the old-style fiery but dry whites. Eger is the home of **Bull's Blood**, a successful export brand of red, but far better, plummy and able to age, when labelled as Egri Bikaver and bottled on the spot.

And then there's **Tokay**. This is one of the world's great wines, made in fog-bound isolated splendour on the muddy banks of the Bodrog River. Three grapes are grown, the Yellow Muscat, the Hárslevelü, and, above all the Furmint, all kept on the vines to droop and rot long into the warm humid autumn. 'Noble rot' conditions on the aptly named Bodrog River are as perfect as anywhere in the world, and by the time the slimy grapes are scraped off the vines, they are thick with luscious, scented, golden essence.

Tokay has several classifications:
Tokay Szamorodni Tokay 'as it comes'. This is the basic wine, big, raisiny, and often rather harshly oxidized.

Tokay Aszu This is where it gets exciting. *Aszu* is a paste made of overripe and 'noble rot' infected grapes. It is succulently sweet and is kept separate from the basic wines, until carefully prescribed amounts are added during fermentation. The sweetness of Tokay is gauged by how many *puttonyos* there are per 140 litres of wine. (A *puttonyo* is literally a big shovelful of about 35 litres.) So a 3-*puttonyos* Tokay will be a wine where 3×35 litres of *aszu* sweet paste were added to 140 litres of basic wine. 3-*puttonyos* Tokay is the usual sweetness, but 4, 5 or, rarely, 6 *puttonyos* are all significantly better, since after the *puttonyos* are added, the resulting mix ferments slowly for a long time, and is then aged in small, unbunged oak casks of 140 litres, where a fungus like sherry's *flor* (see p. 226) is allowed to develop on the surface of the wine. This explains why, along with a sweetness which is rich and brown and gooey, there is also a remarkable dry sherry edge like the twisted peel of fresh apple skin. And there is the calculated oxidation which makes for such terrifying intense flavour in old sherry too. Some modern 3-*puttonyos* wines seem to lack the sweetness to cope with the oxidation, but the 4- or 5- or 6-*puttonyos* wines are still a revelation.

There are two further, much rarer, classifications:
Tokay Aszu Essencia This is where the wine is made entirely from hand-selected 'noble-rotted' grapes, like a German Beerenauslese.
Tokay Essencia This is, literally, the tears of the grapes. As they stand on the table waiting to be crushed into paste, a few drops of thick golden essence ooze out and are carefully stored. Each *puttonyo* of 35 litres will lose perhaps 3 per cent of its juice this way, and it is old bottles of this 'essence' for which the queues form at modern-day auction rooms.

UNITED KINGDOM

THE GENERAL PICTURE

Harvest-time in England.

The map shows wine regions and vineyards including: Elmham Park, Norwich, Pulham, CAMBRIDGE, Chilford Hundred, Three Choirs, Gloucester, OXFORD, BRISTOL, Newbury, READING, LONDON, Shepton Mallet, Wootton, Chalk Hill, Lamberhurst, Biddenden, Chilsdown, Southampton, Carr-Taylor, EXETER, Chichester, Adgestone. WINE REGIONS ▲ VINEYARDS

The torrid summer of 1989 produced the first vintage of ripe grapes from mature vines since the Dissolution of the Monasteries in 1536. The shock here is not that the 453-year gap between high spots, but that they ever *could* produce fine wine. But English winemakers are now producing several million bottles of wine each year, taking on European competition, and giving it a thrashing on quality alone! With the 1982, 1983 and 1984 vintages, a clearly definable, sharp but thirst-quenching orchard-apple-fresh style appeared which was truly, uniquely, *English,* and even within *that* style we are beginning to see an East Anglian style, a Sussex/Kent style, a Wessex style, developing. Already one can see the partisan-ship developing which makes Frenchmen Burgundy men, Bordeaux men or Rhône men (till the daggers are drawn), and Italians Chianti men, Barolo men or Valpolicella men (to the death). And a little bit of healthy prejudice and competition is exactly what is needed if England is going to have the courage and pride to take its place amongst the wine-growing nations of Europe. After all, with only a couple of million bottles a year, often having to share premises with the sugar beet, the apple crops and the dairy herd, they'll never compete on quantity. A single appellation in the South of France could swallow the entire English national production. No, they must compete on individuality, and quality, and that, at last, is what they are beginning to do.

There are about 500 hectares (1,250 acres) of vineyard in Britain. With a couple of Welsh and Channel Island exceptions, these are all in England, with over 400 vineyards; about 80 of these are sufficiently professional to be run on a commercial basis. Forgive the 'about' but things are changing so fast in England as the wine fever catches on. Plantings are increasing by 10 per cent a year, and a whole crop of new wineries debuts each vintage, but never-theless we're still dealing in very small quan-tities; even one of Burgundy's smaller villages, Volnay, has over 360 hectares (900 acres) in-side its own 'Parish boundaries'. However, these new plantings are increasingly done by hard-headed farmers who see English wine as a good enough proposition to make them a proper return. Vineyards like Pulham St Mary in Norfolk, Chilford Hundred in Cambridge, Lamberhurst and Biddenden in Kent, and Carr-Taylor in Sussex are run as business ven-tures, with the eye clearly on the balance sheet, to provide the backbone of the new English wine industry. But luckily the bubble-eyed enthusiasm of the two be-tweeded ladies who make Berwick Glebe on a patch of field between the church and the pub, or the green-wellies-and-headscarves good humour of the elegant newcomers at Swiftsden House (both in Sussex) as well as the bluff determina-tion of the owner of Chalk Hill in Wiltshire, whose prototypes began the vineyard revival in the 1950s, still figure largely in the spectrum of English wine.

GRAPE VARIETIES AND WINE STYLES
Though there are regional styles developing, the most important influence as yet is the

UNITED KINGDOM

THE GENERAL PICTURE

winemaker. Many small vineyards employ a contract winemaker and so, while the Kent/Sussex style seems softer and riper than many areas, being furthest removed from the wet westerly weather, the influence here of Kit Lindlar, the consultant winemaker at 25 different local wineries, is at least as important. Wiltshire and Wessex in general seem to produce sharply defined, strong, greenly aromatic styles, yet that is also the style of local consultant Mark Thompson, so you could say the winemaker was moulding the area in his own image. East Anglia is less exact, but seems to favour the direct, most neutral, French style so far, while Hampshire, also keen on dry wines, makes use of the warmer maritime climate round the Solent to give a gentle perfume to the green tang of the fruit. Of overriding importance is the vineyard's decision as to whether or not to use 'sweet reserve'. This is a Germanic practice whereby unfermented grape juice is added back to the totally fermented wine before bottling, giving at least a slightly grapy fresh edge to an otherwise completely dry wine, and at most a big sweetish fruit juice perfume more like a blowzy Liebfraumilch. Few owners use none at all, but the move is now towards using less, since too much does blank out personality, and also, when possible, to using English grape 'sweet reserve' rather than the more highly flavoured, imported German 'sweet reserve'.

The chief grapes in England are Germanic cross-breeds, initially bred to produce very high sugar contents quickly in Germany, but finding in England that the long cool summers cut down on their sickly-sweet perfumes, and allow a delicious orchard-fruit scent to develop. Müller-Thurgau is the most commonly planted and often makes better wine in England than in Germany.

The Reichensteiner is another major variety and can be a little neutral, but at best gives a very straight lemon and apples fruit with just a whiff of honey. Seyval Blanc is the sort of 'Muscadet' of the wine scene, light, clean, reliable, unmemorable, while both Schönburger and Gutenborner give a much bigger, rather musky, honeyed wine. The real aromatics are Huxelrebe, Ortega, Bacchus and various others which do have a tremendous amount of fruit ranging from rather ripe perfumy grapefruit to a tangy nettly Sauvignon sharpness. What is increasingly happening is that the more neutral types are being blended with the more aromatic to produce a fragrant but milder wine. Reds are so far pretty unimpressive, with Pinot Noir doing its usual 'won't come out to play' act, but this time with due reason because the autumn heat is rarely enough to tempt it, but **Triomphe d'Alsace** provides rather a good, tart red which might yet turn out to be at least a 'qualified success de South Coast et Wessex'.

THE IMPORTANT DETAILS

Meadows and grazing are augmented by vineyards at Adgestone on the Isle of Wight.

CLASSIFICATION

Classification of English wines and vineyards is still unofficial, since the EEC decreed that ten years of officially scrutinized production records must be filed before the wines could legally be anything more than the most basic table wine. So the English Vineyards Association awards a 'Seal of Quality' for wines which pass a much stricter analytical and tasting test than is at present applied in either the French or the German quality control systems.

ORGANIZATION/S

Usually independent growers, with vineyards often forming only a part of a more diverse farming operation. A few big concerns, e.g. Ready Mixed Concrete, are also involved and

there are several big new plantings, particularly in Surrey and Sussex. Several informal groupings exist to try to publicize a region's wines, like East Anglian Wines. Some large outfits like Lamberhurst will vinify smaller vineyards' grapes on a contract basis, while others will send their grapes to the centre used by their consultant.

READING THE LABEL
The label should indicate the grape type or types, the style – dry, medium, etc. – and the name and address of the grower. Almost all wines are vintage dated. The English Vineyards Association (EVA) seal is gold and black and is a genuine quality pointer.

WHAT DO THEY TASTE LIKE?
At their best, English wines have a wonderfully limpid fragrance, as pure, as free, and as cool as the late morning in a spring-time or-chard when the sun draws the moisture off the leaves and the grass and into the air. Low in alcohol, greenly-perfumed, they are some of Europe's most refreshing wines.

THE GOOD YEARS
Many English wines will age, surprisingly, particularly those from East Anglia and Wessex, because high acidity balanced by fruit prevents oxidation. However, in general the wines should be drunk young, and 1989, 1986, 1985 and 1984 are very good years.

ENJOYING THE WINES
They are excellent outdoor wines, with enough tangy fruit to be able to cope with picnic carefreeness. With food, they are some of the few wines to go really well with Colchester oyster and Dover sole, but otherwise are best with fairly light dishes or even salads. Ideally, though, drink them by themselves for their smack of green perfumed fruit.

CONSUMER INFORMATION

WHAT DO I GET FOR MY MONEY?
They are not that cheap, but each year, while other white wine prices rise, English prices fall, as vineyards become more efficient and productive. Now that they are creating such a distinctive flavour style, they are certainly worth a try.

AVAILABILITY
Most operations are only about 1 hectare (2.5 acres) in size, so availability is frequently only local, sometimes only at the vineyard. However, an increasing number of English supermarkets and retail chains are beginning to list the wines. Elsewhere, they are almost impossible to find, though David Carr-Taylor has succeeded in selling some to the French!

CONSUMER CHECKLIST

Breaky-Bottom	Q:	1 2 3 4 5 6 7 **8** 9 10
Müller-Thurgau	P:	1 2 3 4 5 **6** 7 8 9 10
1989	V:	1 2 3 4 5 6 7 8 **9** 10
Lamberhurst	Q:	1 2 3 4 5 6 7 8 9 10
White	P:	1 2 3 4 **5** 6 7 8 9 10
	V:	1 2 3 **4** 5 6 7 8 9 10

Good Years Many English wines will age but they are ideally drunk at about 12 to 18 months old. 1989 and 1984 were particularly warm and ripe and 1986 and 1985 were two other years for southern English wines, 1984 was particularly warm and ripe.

Taste Notes English (and Welsh) wines are almost always characterized by lightness and sharp fruit.

GREECE & TURKEY

Just as, when you step off the plane at Athens airport armed with a First Class degree in Classical Greek, you find that all your knowledge of the *Iliad* and *Elegiacs* cuts no ice at all with a people who can't even understand your request to be directed to the nearest bar, and you realize with a mixture of panic and despair that things have changed language-wise in the last couple of thousand years – so it is with Greek wine.

There is no question that Greek wines, in the Golden Age of Greece, were famous, and it cannot only have been the rush of alcohol to the brain which caused their renown. Or can it? The Greeks were the first European people to get in on the wine act. If you have the proto-type of something, others – like the Italians, the French and the Spaniards – are going to attempt to improve upon your product. As their civilizations wax and yours wanes, it is just possible that the coarse, heady wines, which often needed a strong dose of resin to keep them half-drinkable, become a demoralized norm when there is little outside contact with other countries' wines to encourage improvement.

Despite entry to the EEC in 1981, and the first signs that the wine producers might be willing to change their ways (in search of an export market), both with a government-approved Appellation Contrôlée system and the earmarking of tiny sums to help overseas promotions, little has so far been achieved, with the exception of the German market, where an interest in Greece as a holiday centre has been accompanied by a considerable upsurge of interest in Greek wine – but nearly all of it is **Retsina**, the archetypal sea-shore

Greek wine. Elsewhere, since accession to the EEC, exports of wine are actually down. This is quite simply because, in a highly competitive market place for cheap wine, virtually the only place where Greek does not come off badly against the opposition is when placed next to kebabs and *kalamares* in a Greek or Cypriot restaurant. And almost the only wine which gains any positive recall is Retsina, which in any case accounts for 37.5 per cent of Greek wine production.

The domestic market is dominated by various Retsina brands, with three brands in the top five sellers. This lop-sided feel is evident in the organization of the local market too. Two companies, **Courtakis** and **Achaia Clauss**, control over 40 per cent of the sales, and over 70 per cent of the market is controlled by ten companies. The growing of grapes is less monopolistic, since 25 per cent is produced by 'individual' growers, little of which gets a label or a cork before it is drunk at home or sold in the local bars. The remaining 75 per cent of grape-growing is shared between 360 wineries and co-ops.

Of this, only 12 per cent is covered by the 'Appellation d'Origine', or VQPRD, which stands for 'Quality Wine Produced in a Delimited Region'. There are 25 such appellations in eight different regions. On the mainland, Macedonia and Thrace to the north have had a fine wine tradition since classical times, and this is best manifested today by **Naoussa** – a dark, tough wine which has fruit to match the roughness. It is made from the Xynomavro grape which means 'acid and black'. It also has Greece's best rosé from Mount Athos, and a strongly French-influenced operation at Château Carras where excellent reds are produced – but modelled on Bordelais not Greek traditions.

Central Greece is almost entirely involved with growing the heavy, rather fruitless Savatiano grape, which is then briskly turned into

Retsina for Athens and Piraeus. It is Greece's most individual wine – and it's certainly an improvement on Savatiano without resin.

The Peloponnese, across the Corinth Canal, has another of Greece's finest wines – **Nemea,** which is a full, soft, almost rich but dry red, occasionally seen outside Greece. The Peloponnese has eight other appellations, the most famous being the sweet, musky **Mavrodaphne** from Patras.

The remainder of Greece's wines are largely island wines. Crete is the original producer of Malmsey, and still produces a scented golden sweet wine at Sitia and Daphnes from the Liatiko grape – presumed to be the Malmsey's descendant. The Ionian islands are not that special, though Cephalonia is modernizing its range, but the Cyclades, with sweet wines based on the Liatiko and Aidani, and the Aegean islands, led by the **Muscats** of Samos, do have some good natural products which, with a little forward planning and more stringent wine-making, could make a splash abroad as well as in the beach-side tavernas.

Here, on Samos, the Muscat grapes produce one of Greece's best sweet wines.

CYPRUS

Claret '62 isn't claret, and it isn't from 1962. What it is, is one of Cyprus's better reds, made from the completely unclaret-like Carignan, Grenache and Syrah grapes (Châteauneuf '62 might have been a better title). Presumably 1962 was a good year locally and the habit stuck. The name 'claret' was probably chosen because claret is historically the Englishman's drink and it is the British influence which has always guided the Cypriot wine industry. Indeed, there is little tradition of everyday wine-drinking amongst the Cypriots themselves, although the intensely sweet **Commandaria** has an age-old High Days and Holy Days importance.

What brought Cyprus to a position of significance was the destruction of European vines by Phylloxera in the nineteenth century. Cyprus has never been hit by Phylloxera and consequently was strongly exploited while Europe learned how to deal with the louse. The very neutral local grapes of Mavron and Xinisteri, black and white respectively, were primarily grown for manufacture into grape concentrate or sherry-type wines at the low end of the price range, which Britain took a great deal of before her EEC membership.

Now this market is declining and, indeed, the USSR is Cyprus's biggest customer. So Cyprus is attempting to develop new, fresh table wine styles, but her vineyard practices are very old-fashioned and there is so far little sign of a common will. There is a research institute producing some good Syrah at least, and the enormous SODAP co-op is trying to motivate its growers, but the large KEO winery is the outfit which is doing most to give Cyprus a light table wine future, and is the only company to show any really promising modern wines as yet.

TURKEY

Turkey's vineyard land is the fifth largest in the world, yet her wine is almost unknown. This is simply because, as a Moslem country, she eats a lot of grapes and drinks very little wine. Even so, she does have a great wine tradition, stretching back to Sumerian and Hittite cultures at least 4,000 years ago. More recently, when Phylloxera was at its most destructive in Western Europe, a lot of Turkish wine was made and exported, but the twentieth century has seen a steady decline. However, the government is now trying to return viticulture to a position of importance, and has recently delineated wine administrative zones, with the intention of setting up proper regulations for wine in due course. As yet little Turkish wine is seen, though the large Tekel state monopoly does

THE MIDDLE EAST & NORTH AFRICA

export bulk wines to northern Europe, and the occasional bottle of wines like **Buzbag, Dikmen** or **Doluca** appears now and then, to bemuse Western palates.

MIDDLE EAST

For the area of the world which probably has the best claim of anywhere to be called 'the birthplace of wine', the Middle East is nowadays almost extinguished as an important production area, but there are signs that, despite the political and social pressures, good wine is beginning to be made once more.

LEBANON

Of all the Middle Eastern countries, Lebanon is the one which has had the most sensational impact, because of the exploits of Gaston Hochar who makes **Château Musar** in the Bekaa valley. This is no normal wine-making task, since the frontline of hostilities has usually managed to run fairly effectively between his vineyards and his winery. Normally he manages, by a mixture of heroism and cool cunning, to duck and weave through the political minefield all round him, and get his grapes to the winery, where he then makes some astonishing rich, piny and plummy reds as well as some slightly less exciting pinks and whites. In 1984 his luck ran out and the single truck of grapes he managed to deliver was rotten and useless on arrival. Lebanon has other wineries, including the large **Ksara** cellars, and the promising **Domaine de Tournelles**. Reds, from the southern French Carignan, Cabernet and other varieties, are the most exciting.

ISRAEL

Israel had a wine-growing tradition in biblical times, but her modern industry is only a century old. Baron Edmond de Rothschild founded wineries at Richon-le-Zion and Zichron-Jacob on Mount Carmel during the 1880s. These are now the basis for Israeli wine production, producing three-quarters of her volume. The Carignan and Grenache account for 75 per cent of the plantations often being vinified to produce heavy sweet styles. However, Cabernet Sauvignon is planted and producing fair wine in Galilee, and both Semillon and Sauvignon Blanc, despite a certain overripeness, are nonetheless adequate. However, all the best Israeli table wine comes from the Golan Heights, whose Cabernet Sauvignon and Sauvignon Blanc are astonishingly good.

EGYPT

Egypt, too, has a Biblical wine tradition and much archaelogical evidence shows wine to have been of some importance. Now it is only made in the Nile Delta near Alexandria. The whites have names like **Reine Cléopatre** and **Crus des Ptolémées**. The red **Omar Khayyam** is more enthusiastically received and supposed to taste like a mixture of dates and Turkish Delight.

NORTH AFRICA

It is a long time since North Africa had any great influence on the rarefied heights of the wine world. But, until the 1960s, the majority of French wine, and a good deal of other European wine was given a very welcome helping hand from the big, strong toffeeish reds of Tunisia, Algeria and Morocco. With the end of French domination, and the reaction to all things French which inevitably set in, the considerable vineyard acreage shrank, and the quality, which had always been of a reliable, robust, but basically anonymous sort, slumped too. During the 1970s, despite the establishment of Wine Offices and wine standards intended to produce an export-quality product, the reds were mostly marked by stale, sweet, oxydized fruit, the rosés by alcohol and raisins, and the whites, with the exception of some Muscats, by a dead, browning emptiness.

Given the torrid climate, skilled winemakers are probably the most important commodity one needs, but these had all returned to France with independence. It is only now that one can see some signs of improvement, and **Morocco** is very definitely to the fore. She has an Appellation Contrôlée system based on the French one, and the central organization SODEVI is returning her reds at least to the gluey, plummy standards of French times.

Algeria also has a French-style system based on VDQS, but, except for the **Maskara** wines, is finding it more difficult to adjust her wine-making to modern taste. **Tunisia** seems to have made little progress, and what has been achieved is in the big, sugared, overweight reds supposedly suited to the German market.

INDEX/1

INDEX/2

INDEX/3

INDEX/4

ACKNOWLEDGEMENTS

Cover left to right; Denis Hughes-Gilbey; CIV Bourgogne; Denis Hughes-Gilbey; Michael Newton/Dartington Glass. Prelims; Michael Newton; 13-15 Gugliemo Galvin; 16-17 Michael Newton; 18 Gugliemo Galvin.; 20 QED/Jon Wyand; 22 QED/Jon Wyand; 23 CIV Bourgogne; 24 QED; 33 QED/Jon Wyand; 35 CIVB; 37 Chateau Margaux; 39 Denis Hughes-Gilbey; 41 GIVB; 44 QED; 46 QED/Colin Maher; 52 CIVB; 55 Denis Hughes-Gilbey; 57 QED; 58 Denis Hughes-Gilbey; 61 Denis Hughes-Gilbey; 62 QED/Colin Maher; 64 CIVE; 66 Denis Hughes-Gilbey; 69 BWC Berkmans; 71 QED/Jon Wyand; 73 QED/Colin Maher; 79 QED/Jon Wyand; 80 Patrick Eager; 91 Denis Hughes-Gilbey; 92 Denis Hughes-Gilbey; 94 Denis Hughes-Gilbey; 100-1 Laurent-Perrier; 102 H. Parrot, Champagne Bureau; 103 Laurent-Perrier; 108 Laurent-Perrier, Desjeux; 110-1 Wine and Spirit Education Trust; 112 Denis Hughes-Gilbey; 113 Denis Hughes-Gilbey; 115 Desjeux; 116 Denis Hughes-Gilbey; 118-9 Desjeux; 120 Desjeux; 122 Desjeux; 123 Desjeux; 125 C.I.V.A.S.; 127 Desjeux; 129 C.I.V.A.S; 131 Denis Hughes-Gilbey; 132 Desjeux; 133 Desjeux; 135 Denis Hughes-Gilbey; 138-9 Denis Hughes-Gilbey; 141 Desjeux; 143 Denis Hughes-Gilbey; 147 Sookias and Bertaut; 148 Sookias and Bertaut; 149 C.I.V.R.B.; 152-3 Robert Harding Picture Library; 153 Fotobank; 154 Robert Harding Picture Library; 155 Zefa; 157 Zefa; 158 Zefa; 159 QED/Jon Wyand; 160 Fotobank; 160 Zefa; 161 Zefa; 163 QED/Jon Wyand; 164 Deutsche Wein Information; 166 Deutsche Wein Information; 167 Deutsche Wein Information; 169 Deutsche Wein Information; 170 Deutsche Wein Information; 172 Zefa; 172 Zefa; 173 Fotobank; 174 Zefa; 175 German Wine Information Services; 176 Counsel Ltd; 177 German Wine Information Services; 171 Zefa; 182 Fiore; 183 QED/Jon Wyand; 185 Fiore; 187 Fiore; 188 Michael Joyce PR; 189 Michael Joyce PR; 190 Michael Joyce PR; 192 Michael Joyce PR; 194 Fiore; 193 QED; 197 Alivini; 198 John Sims; 198 Patrick Eagar; 201 QED/Jon Wyand; 201 Patrick Eagar; 204 QED/Jon Wyand; 207 Italian Trade Centre; 208 Belloni; 211 Fiore; 211 Italian Trade Centre; 214 Archivo Iconografico; 217 Archivo Iconografico; 218 Archivo Iconografico; 223 Gonzalez Byass; 225 Gonzalez Byass; 226 Gonzalez Byass; 227 Gonzalez Byass; 231 Hedges and Butler; 231 Wine and Spirit Education Trust; 233 Hedges and Butler; 238 Madeira Wine Company; 243 Susan Griggs/Dick Rowan; 243 Susan Griggs/George Hall; 244 Susan Griggs/Dimitri Ilic; 244 Spectrum; 246 Susan Griggs/Dimitri Ilic; 247 Mark Savage; 251 Geoffrey Roberts; 251 Vernon East; 253 Mark Savage; 255 Mark Savage; 255 Mark Savage; 256 Taylor Vineyard; 256 Taylor Vineyard; 259; Rosemount Vintners Ltd; 259 S. Smith and Sons; 262 Patrick Eagar; 263 Patrick Eagar; 264 Patrick Eagar; 265 Patrick Eagar; 270 Patrick Eagar; 273 Vernon East; 274 Satoun; 275 Satour; 279 Miguel Torres; 281 John Sims; 283 Lawlers Charles Heidsieck Ltd; 287 Counsel Ltd; 289 Patrick Eagar; 290 Patrick Eagar; 293 Patrick Eagar.